AI Starts with Data

A Practical Blueprint for Trusted, Governed, Enterprise AI

JEFFREY HARRIS

Technics Publications
SEDONA, ARIZONA

TECHNICS PUBLICATIONS

115 Linda Vista, Sedona, AZ 86336 USA
https://www.TechnicsPub.com

Edited by Steve Hoberman

Cover design by Lorena Molinari

First Printing 2026

ISBN, print ed. 9798898161170
ISBN, Kindle ed. 9798898161187
ISBN, PDF ed. 9798898161194

Contents at a Glance

Chapter 1: AI Does Not Fail Because of Models 1
Chapter 2: Why Traditional Data Readiness Is No Longer Enough 13
Chapter 3: What AI-Ready Data Actually Means 27
Chapter 4: Traditional Data Structures: What They Were Built For 41
Chapter 5: Structured Data in the Age of AI 53
Chapter 6: Semi-Structured Data as the Missing Middle 67
Chapter 7: Unstructured Data as a First-Class Enterprise Asset 81
Chapter 8: Why Document Repositories Alone Are Not Enough 97
Chapter 9: Metadata Is the Control Plane for AI 113
Chapter 10: Business Meaning: Glossaries, Taxonomies, and Ontologies 127
Chapter 11: Knowledge Graphs, Entity Resolution, and Relationship Intelligence 141
Chapter 12: Provenance, Lineage, and Explainability from the Data Side 155
Chapter 13: The AI-Ready Data Capability Pillars 169
Chapter 14: Converged Data Patterns: Relational, Vector, Graph, and Content 183
Chapter 15: Integration Patterns for AI-Ready Data 195
Chapter 16: Retrieval and Grounding as Architecture Concerns 211
Chapter 17: Serving Data to Copilots, Assistants, and Agents 225
Chapter 18: Security, Identity, and Access-Aware Data Delivery 237
Chapter 19: Why Governance for AI Is Different from Governance for Analytics 249
Chapter 20: Governing Structured and Unstructured Data Together 259
Chapter 21: Responsible AI Starts Upstream in the Data Estate 271
Chapter 22: The Policy Layer: Retention, Legal Hold, Privacy, and Records 283
Chapter 23: Who Owns AI-Ready Data? 297
Chapter 24: AI-Ready Data Products 311
Chapter 25: Federated Delivery: Platform Teams, Domain Teams, and Centers of Excellence 325
Chapter 26: Adoption, Literacy, and Organizational Change 341
Chapter 27: Current-State Assessment 353
Chapter 28: Prioritizing Use Cases and Choosing the First Domains 365
Chapter 29: Designing the Target State 377
Chapter 30: Sequencing the Transformation 391
Chapter 31: Measuring AI-Readiness and Business Progress 405
Chapter 32: What Goes Wrong When You Layer AI on Top of Bad Data 419
Chapter 33: Anti-Patterns That Look Modern but Fail in Production 433
Chapter 34: From Dashboards to Agents 445
Chapter 35: The AI-Ready Enterprise 459

TABLE OF CONTENTS

Chapter Outlines .... **xxxv**

Chapter 1: AI Does Not Fail Because of Models **1**

Why This Matters 2

Enterprise AI Fails at the Point of Trust 2

Pilots Succeed Where Enterprises Fail 3

Core Concepts 3

Model Capability Is Rarely the First Limiting Factor 3

AI-ready Is Not the Same as Report-Ready or ML-Ready 4

Metadata Is the Control Plane 4

Semantic Context Is What Turns Data into Interpretable Evidence 5

Trust Is an Architectural Property 5

Architectural Implications 5

The Enterprise Data Estate, Not the Model, Is the System of Consequence 5

Structured, Semi-Structured, and Unstructured Data Must Be Designed Together 6

Retrieval Quality Is an Architecture Responsibility 6

Different AI Consumers Require Different Serving Contracts 7

Failure Modes and Anti-Patterns 7

Treating Repository Presence as Readiness 7

Confusing Data Quality with AI Usability 8

Ignoring Provenance Until After Deployment 8

Simplifying Permissions for the Pilot and Never Recovering 8

No Clear Owner for Trusted Business Meaning 8

Practical Application 9

Start with Diagnostic Discipline, Not Implementation Enthusiasm 9

Templates 9

Enterprise AI Failure Diagnostic 9

Case Example 10

A Manufacturing Assistant That Worked Brilliantly in the Lab and Failed in the Field 10

Closing Synthesis 12

Chapter 2: Why Traditional Data Readiness Is No Longer Enough **13**

Why This Matters 14

The Consumer Has Changed 14

The Interaction Model Has Changed 14

The Risk Surface Has Changed 15

The Meaning of "Usable" Has Changed 15

Core Concepts 15

Report-Ready Data 15

Analytics-Ready Data 16

ML-Ready Data 16

GenAI-Ready Data 16

Agent-Ready Data 17

Readiness Ladder 17

Agent-Ready 18

Architectural Implications 18

The Architecture Must Serve Machine Interpretation, Not Just Human Access 18

Unstructured Content Becomes First-Class 19

Semi-Structured Data Becomes Strategically Important 19

Retrieval Becomes an Architectural Responsibility 19

Provenance Must Be Machine-Available 19

Different AI Consumers Need Different Serving Contracts 20

Failure Modes and Anti-Patterns 21

Mistaking BI Maturity for AI-readiness 21

Treating Repositories as Knowledge Architecture 21

Over-focusing on Model Selection 21

Ignoring Provenance Because Users "Just Want Answers" 22

Building One Readiness Standard for Every AI Use Case 22

Practical Application 22

Assess Domains Against the Right Readiness Target 22

Score What Traditional Assessments Missed 22

Templates 23

Data Readiness Classification Worksheet 23

Data Readiness Scorecard 23

Case Example 23

From Twelve Dashboards to One Daily Briefing 23

Closing Synthesis ... 25
Chapter 3: What AI-Ready Data Actually Means ... 27
Why This Matters ... 27
Core Concepts ... 28
AI-Readiness Is a Composite, Not a Binary State ... 28
Quality Is Necessary, but Not Sufficient ... 30
AI-Readiness Differs by Data Class and Use Case ... 30
AI-Ready Data Is Both an Architectural Condition and an Operating Discipline ... 31
Maturity Models Matter Because Transformation Must Be Sequenced ... 31
Architectural Implications ... 32
Metadata Becomes the Control Plane ... 32
The Architecture Must Serve Both Retrieval and Reasoning ... 32
Unstructured Content Must Be Treated as Enterprise-Grade Data ... 32
Different AI Consumers Require Different Serving Contracts ... 33
Failure Modes and Anti-Patterns ... 34
Mistaking Repository Presence for Readiness ... 34
Treating Search as Governance ... 34
Assuming Structured Data Speaks for Itself ... 34
Ignoring Temporal Correctness ... 34
Bolting Governance on After Deployment ... 34
Practical Application ... 35
Start with an Enterprise Definition ... 35
Define Readiness by Consumer and Data Class ... 35
Assess Current Assets Against Dimensions ... 35
Build the Minimum Evidence Standard ... 35
Introduce a Readiness Maturity Model ... 35
Templates ... 36
AI-Ready Data Definition Canvas ... 36
Case Example ... 37
What AI-Ready Looks Like Across Different Data Domains ... 37
Closing Synthesis ... 38
Chapter 4: Traditional Data Structures: What They Were Built For ... 41
Why This Matters ... 41

AI Changes the Consumption Contract 41
Legacy Success Can Hide AI Weakness....42
Design Intent Does Not Disappear 42
Core Concepts 42
OLTP Structures: Built for Transactional Correctness 42
Star Schemas: Built for Repeatable Analytical Consumption....43
Lakes: Built for Accumulation and Flexibility....43
File Repositories: Built for Storage and Collaboration 44
AI Workloads Expose Embedded Assumptions....44
Architectural Implications 45
The Architecture Must Separate Storage from Serving 45
Every Structure Now Needs Compensating Controls....45
Consumer-Specific Data Contracts Become Essential....46
Failure Modes and Anti-Patterns 47
Treating Existing Repositories as AI-ready by Default....47
Assuming Structured Data Alone Is Sufficient....47
Mistaking Data Accumulation for Enterprise Understanding 47
Preserving Hidden Logic and Tribal Knowledge 47
Ignoring Authority and Freshness 48
Practical Application....48
Start with a Structure-By-Structure Assessment....48
Templates....49
Traditional Data Structure Suitability Assessment....49
Case Example....50
Excellent Reporting, Poor Policy Assistance....50
Closing Synthesis 51
Chapter 5: Structured Data in the Age of AI 53
Why This Matters....54
Structured Data Still Anchors Enterprise Authority 54
Query Success Is Not Interpretation Success....54
Action-Taking Systems Raise the Bar Further 54
Core Concepts 55
Structured Truth and Interpreted Truth....55

Why Columns Are Not Concepts 55
Semantic Models and Business Rules Are Safety Mechanisms 56
Structured Data Must Be Prepared for Explanation 56
Architectural Implications 58
From Data Pipelines to Data-Serving Contracts 58
Metadata Becomes the Control Surface 58
Structured Data and Unstructured Context Must Meet Deliberately 59
Failure Modes and Anti-Patterns 59
Exposing Raw Tables as AI-Ready Data 59
Treating Semantic Layers as Optional 60
Allowing Metric Plurality Without Governance 60
Optimizing Only for Query Performance 61
Using Prompt Logic to Compensate for Missing Data Design 61
Practical Application 61
A Practical Path to AI-ready Structured Data 61
Start with High-Consequence Domains 62
Identify Core Entities and Metrics 62
Define Business Meaning Explicitly 62
Attach Lineage, Policy, and Quality Signals 62
Expose an AI-Serving Contract 62
Templates 62
Structured Domain AI-Readiness Checklist 62
Case Example 63
Finance Variance Analysis Assistant 63
Closing Synthesis 65
Chapter 6: Semi-Structured Data as the Missing Middle 67
Why This Matters 68
Semi-structured Data Is Where Operational Reality Appears First 68
It Is the Bridge Between Systems of Record and AI Inference 68
AI-Ready Data Fails When the Middle Layer Is Ignored 68
Core Concepts 69
Semi-structured Does Not Mean Semantically Optional 69
Event Context Is Often More Valuable Than Static Attributes 69

Schema Drift Is Not Just a Technical Inconvenience 70
Logs and Events Are Not Merely Engineering Exhaust 70
Architectural Implications 71
The Ingestion Pattern Must Preserve Meaning, Not Just Move Payloads 71
Normalization Is Not Flattening 71
Metadata Must Mediate Semi-Structured Data 72
Event Semantics Must Be Intentional 72
Retrieval Architecture for Semi-Structured Data Is Different 73
Failure Modes and Anti-Patterns 73
Treating Payload Capture as Readiness 73
Letting Source Teams Invent Semantics Independently 74
Ignoring Schema Drift Until Breakage Becomes Visible 74
Over-relying on Logs as Explanation 75
Separating Governance from Operational Telemetry 75
Practical Application 75
Start by Profiling Semi-Structured Sources as Assets 75
Use a Profiling Worksheet Before Production Use 75
Architect for Canonical Events, Not Endless Source Exceptions 76
Build AI-serving Views Around Tasks 76
Templates 76
Semi-Structured Source Profiling Worksheet 76
Case Example 77
From Ticket Summaries to SLA Risk Intelligence 77
Closing Synthesis 78
Chapter 7: Unstructured Data as a First-Class Enterprise Asset 81
Why This Matters 81
The Business Meaning Gap 81
AI Needs More Than Availability 82
The Cost of Treating Content as Secondary 82
Core Concepts 83
Unstructured Data Is Not a Residual Category 83
Content Architecture Versus Content Storage 83
Governance Must Include Narrative Content 84

Semantic Context Is the Bridge ... 84
Architectural Implications ... 85
Treat Content Types as Managed Asset Classes ... 85
Make Metadata the Control Plane for Content ... 86
Design for Authority and Freshness ... 87
Embed Access Control Into Serving Logic ... 87
Establish Lifecycle and Criticality Treatment ... 88
Failure Modes and Anti-Patterns ... 89
Repository Presence Mistaken for Readiness ... 89
Unowned Content ... 89
Duplicate Drift ... 89
Stale But Plausible Content ... 90
Over-Indexing Low-Value Noise ... 90
Treating Chunking as the Whole Problem ... 90
Practical Application ... 90
Start With a Content Estate Inventory ... 90
What the Inventory Reveals ... 90
Prioritize by Value and Risk ... 91
Elevate Document Strategy Into Data Strategy ... 91
Templates ... 92
Content Estate Inventory Template ... 92
Case Example ... 93
Contract Intelligence That Failed for the Right Reasons ... 93
Closing Synthesis ... 95
Chapter 8: Why Document Repositories Alone Are Not Enough ... 97
Why This Matters ... 98
Repositories Create a False Sense of Readiness ... 98
The Risk Increases as the AI Consumer Becomes More Powerful ... 98
Most Enterprise Meaning Lives Outside Rows and Columns ... 98
Core Concepts ... 99
Storage Location Does Not Equal Semantic Readiness ... 99
Most Repositories Contain Noise, Duplicates, and Weak Authority Signals ... 100
Retrieval Quality Depends on More Than Search Indexing ... 100

AI-Serving Metadata Is Different from Repository Metadata 100
Document Preparation Is an Architectural Function....101
Architectural Implications 102
The Architecture Must Insert a Preparation Pipeline Between Repository and Model 102
Inventory Must Precede Ingestion 102
Enrichment Must Make Enterprise Meaning Explicit....104
Chunking Must Preserve Meaning, Access, and Evidence 104
Citations Must Be Designed, Not Appended....105
Permissions Must Remain Intact Across Transformation 105
Failure Modes and Anti-Patterns 105
"Connect Everything and Let Search Sort It Out"....105
Treating Filename Conventions as Governance....106
Assuming Repository Metadata Is Enough....106
Ignoring Freshness and Review Cycles....106
Preparing Content Without an Evidence Model 107
Practical Application....107
Build a Content Eligibility Model....107
Establish Authority Rules by Document Class 107
Treat Curation as a Funnel, Not a One-Time Cleanup....108
Design Retrieval Around User Trust, Not Just Relevance Score....108
Templates....108
Document Enrichment Checklist....108
Case Example....109
The Hidden Architecture Problem Behind Policy Assistant Failure....109
Closing Synthesis 110
Chapter 9: Metadata Is the Control Plane for AI 113
Why This Matters 113
AI Needs More Than Access 113
AI-Serving Systems Amplify Metadata Gaps 114
The Enterprise Trust Problem Is a Metadata Problem....114
Core Concepts 115
Technical Metadata Is Necessary, but Insufficient....115
Business Metadata Gives Meaning 115

Policy Metadata Governs Safe Use ... 115
Operational Metadata Determines Reliability ... 116
AI-Serving Metadata Closes the Final Gap ... 116
Architectural Implications ... 117
Metadata Must Be Modeled Across All Data Classes ... 117
Metadata Must Be Runtime-Relevant, Not Just Catalog-Deep ... 117
Metadata Must Support Access-Aware Delivery ... 118
Ranking Is a Metadata-Driven Discipline ... 118
Explainability Depends on Metadata Structure ... 118
Failure Modes and Anti-Patterns ... 119
Metadata Poverty ... 119
Technical Metadata Only ... 120
Uniform Metadata for Fundamentally Different Assets ... 120
Governance After Retrieval ... 120
Weak Lifecycle Control ... 121
Practical Application ... 121
Start with a Minimum Viable Metadata Standard ... 121
How to Use the Standard ... 121
Prioritize Enrichment Where AI Value and Risk Are Highest ... 122
Treat Trust Scoring Carefully ... 122
Templates ... 122
Enterprise Metadata Minimum Viable Standard ... 122
Case Example ... 123
How Better Metadata Turned a Knowledge Assistant into a Trusted One ... 123
Closing Synthesis ... 125
Chapter 10: Business Meaning: Glossaries, Taxonomies, and Ontologies ... 127
Why This Matters ... 127
Core Concepts ... 128
Controlled Meaning Begins with a Glossary ... 128
Taxonomies Organize for Navigation, Grouping, and Retrieval ... 129
Ontologies Model Relationships, Constraints, and Domain Logic ... 130
Semantics Can Mature in Layers ... 130
Not Every Organization Needs a Heavy Ontology Effort ... 131

Architectural Implications 132
- Meaning Must Be Treated as Shared Enterprise Infrastructure 132
- Semantics Must Connect Structured and Unstructured Data 132
- Retrieval Pipelines Should Use Semantic Enrichment, Not Only Text Similarity 132
- Ontology Use Should Be Selective and Operational 133
- Different AI Consumers Need Different Semantic Depth 133

Failure Modes and Anti-Patterns 133
- Treating Semantics as Optional Documentation 133
- Confusing Naming Conventions with Meaning 134
- Designing Taxonomies No One Will Use 134
- Pursuing Ontology for Prestige Instead of Need 134
- Ignoring Conflicting Definitions 134
- Failing to Assign Ownership 134

Practical Application 135
- Start Where Ambiguity Causes the Most Risk 135
- Build a Practical Semantic Operating Loop 135

Templates 136
- Business Meaning Design Template 136

Case Example 137
- When Shared Language Creates Unsafe AI Answers 137

Closing Synthesis 138

Chapter 11: Knowledge Graphs, Entity Resolution, and Relationship Intelligence 141

Why This Matters 141
- AI Value Often Depends on Relationship Intelligence 141
- Cross-System Trust Begins with Resolved Identity 142
- Relationship-rich Use Cases Justify the Investment 142

Core Concepts 143
- Knowledge Graphs Are a Modeling Pattern, Not a Religion 143
- Entity Resolution: Determining Sameness with Evidence 143
- Relationship Types Matter 144
- Confidence and Provenance Must Travel with the Connection 145

Architectural Implications 145
- Convergence Beats Purity 145

The Graph Should Be Selective, Not Universal ... 146
Entity Resolution Must Be Operationalized ... 147
Governance Becomes More Important, Not Less ... 147
Failure Modes and Anti-Patterns ... 148
Treating Graph as an Answer in Search of a Problem ... 148
Confusing Inferred Similarity with Trusted Identity ... 148
Building Vague, Low-Semantic Relationship Models ... 149
Ignoring Temporal Truth ... 149
Hiding Uncertainty ... 149
Practical Application ... 149
Start with the Use Case, Not the Ontology ... 149
Define Entity Classes and Match Strategies Explicitly ... 150
Keep Graph-Serving Aligned to AI Use ... 150
Templates ... 150
Entity Resolution Design Sheet ... 150
Case Example ... 151
From Retrieval to Relationship Intelligence ... 151
Closing Synthesis ... 153
Chapter 12: Provenance, Lineage, and Explainability from the Data Side ... 155
Why This Matters ... 155
AI Changes the Burden of Proof ... 155
High-Stakes Use Cases Demand Traceability ... 156
Trust Rises Sharply When Evidence Is Exposed ... 156
Regulated Environments Make This Non-Optional ... 156
Core Concepts ... 157
Provenance: Where the Evidence Came From ... 157
Lineage: How the Information Was Transformed ... 157
Explainability: Why the Answer Makes Sense in Context ... 158
Temporal Context: The Overlooked Layer ... 158
Trust Signals: The Visible Result of Invisible Architecture ... 159
Architectural Implications ... 159
Provenance Must Be Captured at Ingestion, Not Retrofitted at Response Time ... 159
Lineage Must Include Unstructured and Semi-Structured Transformations ... 159

Metadata Is the Control Plane for Traceability 160
Retrieval Architecture Must Preserve Evidence, Not Just Optimize Relevance 160
Explainability Requires a Multi-Layer Response Model 160
Trust Thresholds Vary by AI Consumer 161
Failure Modes and Anti-Patterns 162
Treating Citations as Decoration 162
Losing Source Identity During Chunking 162
Failing to Distinguish Authoritative from Supporting Sources 162
Ignoring Transformation Opacity 162
Hiding Temporal Ambiguity 162
Substituting Model Confidence for Evidentiary Confidence 162
Practical Application 163
Designing for Provenance 163
Designing for Lineage 163
Designing for Explainability 163
A Practical Trust Signal Model 164
Templates 165
Provenance and Trust Signal Template 165
Case Example 166
Executive Intelligence Briefing That Became Trustworthy After Traceability Was Exposed 166
Closing Synthesis 167
Chapter 13: The AI-Ready Data Capability Pillars 169
Why This Matters 170
AI Failures Are Usually Capability Failures Across the Architecture 170
Traditional Readiness Models Do Not Go Far Enough 170
The Pillars Must Support Multiple AI Consumers 170
Core Concepts 171
The Model Is Organized into Capability Pillars 171
Cross-cutting Controls Matter as Much as the Pillars Themselves 172
Centralize What Must Be Common; Federate What Must Remain Close to the Business 173
Architectural Implications 174
Sources Are Broader Than Databases 174
Ingestion Must Preserve Meaning, Not Just Move Bytes 174

Metadata Is the Control Plane ... 175
Semantics Reduce Ambiguity Before Retrieval ... 175
Governance Must Act Across All Pillars ... 175
Retrieval Is a Formal Architecture Domain ... 175
Serving Patterns Must Reflect the Consumer ... 176
Failure Modes and Anti-Patterns ... 176
Tool Sprawl Without Capability Design ... 176
Repository-as-readiness Thinking ... 176
Schema-only Metadata ... 177
Governance Bolted on After Deployment ... 177
Retrieval Without Evaluation ... 177
One Serving Contract for Every Use Case ... 177
Practical Application ... 177
How to Assess the Current Capability Pillars ... 177
Templates ... 178
Capability Pillars Assessment ... 178
Case Example ... 178
Mapping Two Use Cases onto One Architecture ... 178
Closing Synthesis ... 180
Chapter 14: Converged Data Patterns: Relational, Vector, Graph, and Content ... 183
Why This Matters ... 183
AI Questions Are Structurally Different from Reporting Questions ... 183
Different Structures Solve Different Enterprise Problems ... 184
The Enterprise Challenge Is Orchestration ... 184
Core Concepts ... 184
Relational Stores Anchor Truth and Metrics ... 184
Content Stores Preserve Evidence and Narrative Context ... 185
Vector Indexes Support Similarity-Based Retrieval ... 185
Graph Supports Relationship Intelligence ... 186
Content, Vector, Graph, and Relational Are Complementary ... 186
Metadata Is the Control Plane Across All Four Patterns ... 186
Architectural Implications ... 186
Design for Coordinated Serving, Not Isolated Storage ... 186

Make Semantic Alignment Explicit 187
Preserve Provenance All the Way Through the Answer 187
Treat Freshness as Multi-Speed, Not Uniform 187
Use Access-Aware Orchestration 188
Failure Modes and Anti-Patterns 189
Forcing Every Use Case into One Store 189
Treating Vector Retrieval as if It Were Truth 189
Building Graph Without Mastering Entities 189
Leaving Content Ungoverned Because It Is Messy 189
Separating Retrieval Design from Architecture 189
Ignoring Different Data-Serving Contracts 190
Practical Application 190
Start with Workload Decomposition 190
Choose a Primary Pattern, Then Add Supporting Patterns Deliberately 190
Templates 191
Converged Pattern Decision Matrix 191
Case Example 192
Contract Intelligence as a Converged Pattern 192
Closing Synthesis 194
Chapter 15: Integration Patterns for AI-Ready Data 195
Why This Matters 195
AI Operates Across Fragmented Enterprise Reality 195
Integration Determines Whether AI Is Trustworthy at Scale 196
AI-Ready Data Requires Intentional Integration Across Content as Well as Records 196
Core Concepts 197
Integration Is a Meaning-Preserving Discipline 197
Pattern Choice Is Not Arbitrary 198
Canonical Layers Are Useful but Dangerous When Overextended 199
SaaS and Collaboration Platforms Are Part of the Real Architecture 199
Architectural Implications 200
Integration Architecture Must Carry Metadata as a First-Class Payload 200
Pattern Selection Must Align to AI Consumer Type 200
When API Access Beats Replication 201

Shadow Copies Are an Architectural Liability ... 201
Source Onboarding Must Start with Governance, Not End with It ... 202
Failure Modes and Anti-Patterns ... 202
Universal Replication ... 202
Canonical Model Absolutism ... 203
Content Integration Without Content Governance ... 203
Event Streams with No Semantic Contract ... 203
SaaS Onboarding by Connector Convenience Alone ... 204
No Excluded-Use Discipline ... 204
Practical Application ... 204
A Decision Framework for Selecting Integration Patterns ... 204
Integration Pattern Guidance by Source Type ... 205
Templates ... 205
Source Onboarding Template ... 205
Case Example ... 207
Sales Enablement Assistant Across CRM, Pricing, Proposals, and Product Content ... 207
Closing Synthesis ... 209
Chapter 16: Retrieval and Grounding as Architecture Concerns ... 211
Why This Matters ... 211
Enterprise AI Fails at the Moment of Contact with Real Content ... 211
Trust Thresholds Differ by Use Case ... 212
Explainability Depends on Evidence Design ... 212
Core Concepts ... 212
Retrieval Quality Starts Long Before the Query ... 212
Chunking Must Respect Business Meaning, Not Token Size ... 213
Metadata-Aware Ranking Is Essential ... 213
Freshness and Re-Indexing Are Governance Concerns ... 214
Good Grounding Makes Answers Explainable and Safer ... 214
Architectural Implications ... 215
Treat Retrieval as a Pipeline, Not a Lookup Step ... 215
Build Document-Type-Specific Segmentation Models ... 216
Design Metadata as Retrieval Infrastructure ... 217
Make Access-Aware Filtering Mandatory ... 217

Separate Authority from Popularity 218
Failure Modes and Anti-Patterns 218
Dump the Repository into the Index 218
Optimize for Recall While Ignoring Evidence Quality 218
Chunk by Size, Then Hope Ranking Recovers Meaning 218
Ignore Temporal Correctness 219
Treat Citations as Decorative 219
Evaluate Only with Generic Benchmarks 219
Practical Application 219
Start with Content Classes, Not Tooling Features 219
Create a Retrieval Contract for Each AI Consumer 220
Make Enrichment Part of Ingestion 220
Templates 220
Retrieval Readiness Checklist 220
Case Example 222
A Policy Assistant That Improved When the Architecture Improved 222
Closing Synthesis 223
Chapter 17: Serving Data to Copilots, Assistants, and Agents 225
Why This Matters 225
The Cost of Error Is Not Uniform 225
AI Consumers Interpret Data Differently 226
Operational Scale Amplifies Weak Design 226
Core Concepts 226
Consumer Classes Determine Serving Patterns 226
Q&A Assistant 227
Analyst Copilot 227
Recommendation System 227
Bounded Agent 227
Read Paths and Action Paths Are Not the Same Architecture 228
Context Packaging Is a First-Class Architectural Concern 228
AI-Serving Contracts Define What "Good" Looks Like 229
Architectural Implications 229
Metadata Must Mediate Consumption 229

Serving Contracts Should Align to Data Classes, Not Just Systems 230
Answer Generation, Decision Support, and Execution Need Different Control Stacks 230
The Action Trust Boundary Must Be Explicit 231
Evidence Must Travel with Output 231
Failure Modes and Anti-Patterns 232
The Generic Enterprise Super-Agent 232
Repository Exposure Mistaken for Readiness 232
Conflating User Permission with Consumer Permission 232
Missing Freshness and Temporal Controls 232
No Explicit Human Review Triggers 233
Weak Audit Design 233
Practical Application 233
Designing with the AI Consumer Design Worksheet 233
Templates 233
AI Consumer Design Worksheet 233
Case Example 234
Executive Briefing Assistant Versus Remediation Agent 234
Closing Synthesis 236
Chapter 18: Security, Identity, and Access-Aware Data Delivery 237
Why This Matters 237
Discovery Becomes Easier Than Navigation 237
Inference Creates Exposure Even Without Direct Document Access 237
Security Errors Become Scalable and Repeatable 238
Core Concepts 238
Access-aware Retrieval 238
Identity Propagation 239
Permission Drift 239
Classification and Sensitivity-Aware Delivery 239
Architectural Implications 240
The AI-serving Layer Is Part of the Security Architecture 240
Metadata Must Carry Authorization Truth 241
End-to-end Enforcement Is Required 241
Classification Should Shape Architecture, Not Just Compliance Reporting 242

Revocation Latency Becomes an Architectural Metric 242
Failure Modes and Anti-Patterns 242
Broad Indexing Under a Service Account 242
Coarse Labels Replacing Real Permissions 243
Content Freshness Without Permission Freshness 243
Answer-Layer Filtering Only 243
One Assistant for Every Use Case 244
Missing Auditability 244
Practical Application 244
Design for Access-Aware Delivery from the Start 244
Templates 245
Access-Aware Retrieval Control Checklist 245
Case Example 246
When Retrieval Ignores Entitlement: Why Permission Fidelity Must Survive into AI Serving 246
Closing Synthesis 247
Chapter 19: Why Governance for AI Is Different from Governance for Analytics 249
Why This Matters 249
Core Concepts 250
Governance Must Move from Asset Control to Behavior Control 250
Metadata Becomes Operational, Not Descriptive 250
Unstructured Content Is Now in Scope 251
Evidence Is Part of the Answer 251
Consumer Type Shapes Governance Design 251
Architectural Implications 252
Govern Retrieval as an Architectural Layer 252
Design for Permission Fidelity, Not Broad Access 252
Separate Knowledge Permission from Action Permission 253
Build Provenance and Temporal Correctness into the Serving Layer 253
Failure Modes and Anti-Patterns 254
Treating AI as Just Another BI Channel 254
Governing Sources but Not Answers 254
Allowing Plausible Language to Substitute for Evidence 254
Ignoring Semantic Ambiguity 254

Overlooking Semi-Structured Operational Signals ... 255
Allowing Broad Retrieval with Weak Content Hygiene ... 255
Practical Application ... 255
Layer 1: Existing Analytics Governance ... 255
Layer 2: Content Governance ... 255
Layer 3: Runtime AI Controls ... 255
Layer 4: Consumer-specific Policy ... 255
Templates ... 256
AI Governance Gap Assessment ... 256
Case Example ... 257
Beyond Analytics Governance: Why Conversational AI Requires a New Control Model ... 257
Closing Synthesis ... 258
Chapter 20: Governing Structured and Unstructured Data Together ... 259
Why This Matters ... 259
AI Consumes Business Reality, Not Storage Categories ... 259
Structured and Unstructured Assets Describe the Same World ... 260
Governance Failure Becomes Answer Failure ... 260
Core Concepts ... 261
Cross-asset Governance ... 261
Governance Must Span Records, Documents, Relationships, and Narrative Evidence ... 261
Metadata Is the Bridge ... 262
Cross-asset Alignment of Ownership, Retention, and Classification ... 262
Architectural Implications ... 263
The Architecture Must Model Truth Chains, Not Just Data Stores ... 263
Access-aware Delivery Must Cross Asset Classes ... 263
Provenance Has to Survive Transformation ... 263
Freshness Standards Must Be Explicit ... 264
Failure Modes and Anti-Patterns ... 264
Split Stewardship ... 264
Taxonomy Without Operational Linkage ... 264
Repository-first Governance ... 265
Orphaned Narrative Evidence ... 265
Practical Application ... 266

Start with High-Risk Cross-Asset Use Cases....266
Define the Cross-Asset Operating Model....266
Make Derived AI Assets Governable....266
Design for Disagreement....267
Templates....267
Cross-Asset Governance Operating Model Canvas....267
Case Example....268
When Policy Documents Alone Could Not Define Compliance Truth....268
Closing Synthesis....269
Chapter 21: Responsible AI Starts Upstream in the Data Estate.... 271
Why This Matters....271
Harm Rarely Starts Where It Becomes Visible....271
Coverage Gaps Distort Behavior Even When Facts Are Technically Correct....272
Freshness and Authority Shape Reliability....272
Core Concepts....273
Data-Side Problems Materially Shape AI Outcomes....273
Responsible AI Is Partly a Data Stewardship Problem....273
Coverage, Imbalance, and Representational Risk....273
Freshness Is a Control, Not a Convenience....274
Authority Must Be Explicit in Metadata....274
Human Review Belongs in the Data Contract....275
Architectural Implications....275
Treat Source Readiness as a First-Class Design Concern....275
Build Authority-Aware, Freshness-Aware Retrieval....275
Make Gaps and Conflicts Visible Instead of Hiding Them....276
Use Metadata to Enforce Responsible Delivery....276
Design Review Triggers as Operating Controls....276
Failure Modes and Anti-Patterns....277
Assuming Repository Presence Equals Responsible Readiness....277
Optimizing for Answer Rate Instead of Safe Answer Rate....278
Treating Stale Content as a Minor Issue....278
Failing to Model Sensitive Population Impacts....278
Leaving Escalation to Prompt Wording....278

Practical Application ... 278
Start with a Responsible-Source Assessment for Each Use Case ... 278
Put the Checklist into the Delivery Lifecycle ... 279
Design a Review-Trigger Model ... 279
Templates ... 280
Responsible Data for AI Checklist ... 280
Case Example ... 281
Responsible Automation Means Knowing When Not to Answer ... 281
Closing Synthesis ... 282
Chapter 22: The Policy Layer: Retention, Legal Hold, Privacy, and Records ... 283
Why This Matters ... 284
AI Amplifies Policy Mistakes ... 284
Retrieval Without Lifecycle Awareness Creates False Confidence ... 284
High-stakes Use Cases Need Evidence, Not Good Intentions ... 284
Different AI Consumers Need Different Policy Envelopes ... 284
Core Concepts ... 285
Retention Is a Lifecycle Rule, Not a Storage Accident ... 285
Legal Hold Suspends Disposition, Not Judgment ... 285
Privacy Is About Purpose, Necessity, and Exposure ... 286
Records Management Defines Evidentiary and Lifecycle Obligations ... 286
Minimization Belongs Upstream ... 286
Policy Metadata Must Be First-Class Metadata ... 287
Architectural Implications ... 287
The Policy Layer Must Span the Lifecycle ... 287
Lifecycle State Must Travel with the Asset ... 287
Ordinary Retrieval and Preservation Retrieval Must Be Separated ... 288
Deletion Events Must Propagate to AI Layers ... 288
Policy Enforcement Needs Multiple Control Points ... 289
Records and Policy Need Explicit Ownership ... 289
Failure Modes and Anti-Patterns ... 289
Treating Policy as Post-Ingestion Cleanup ... 289
Assuming Retained Means Useful ... 290
Flattening Lifecycle Distinctions in the Index ... 290

Minimization Only at the User Interface 290
No Auditable Evidence Path 290
Exception-driven Governance 291
Practical Application 291
Start with Policy-Bearing Asset Classes 291
Build a Policy Eligibility Model for AI Use 291
Represent Policy as Metadata and Service Logic 291
Design for Review, Not Only Automation 292
Templates 293
Policy Control Checklist for AI-Ready Data 293
Case Example 294
Legal Review Assistant with Lifecycle-Aware Retrieval 294
Closing Synthesis 295
Chapter 23: Who Owns AI-Ready Data? 297
Why This Matters 297
AI Consumes More Than Data Quality 297
Ownership Is What Turns Repositories into Usable Assets 298
Scaling Fails Where Pilots Tolerate Ambiguity 298
Core Concepts 299
Ownership Must Exist at Multiple Layers 299
Platform Teams Cannot Own Business Meaning 299
Domain Teams Cannot Alone Own Cross-Enterprise Standards 300
Stewardship Must Be Explicit, Funded, and Measured 300
Decision Rights Matter as Much as Responsibilities 300
Freshness and Authority Are First-Class Ownership Concerns 301
Architectural Implications 301
The Architecture Must Encode Ownership, Not Merely Describe It 301
AI-Serving Introduces a New Ownership Boundary 302
Decision Rights Should Be Modeled as Part of the Control Plane 303
Architecture Should Differentiate Consumer Trust Contracts 304
Failure Modes and Anti-Patterns 304
The Platform-As-Owner Fantasy 304
Domain Autonomy Without Shared Standards 305

Stewardship as Volunteer Labor ... 305
Governance as Approval Theater ... 305
No Owner for Freshness or Source Authority ... 306
Practical Application ... 306
Establish a Layered Ownership Model ... 306
Use a Decision-Rights Model, Not Just a Role List ... 306
Fund Stewardship as an Operating Capability ... 307
Make Ownership Machine-Visible ... 307
Templates ... 307
AI-Ready Data Ownership Charter ... 307
Case Example ... 308
What Looked Like a Model Problem Was Really an Ownership Problem ... 308
Closing Synthesis ... 310
Chapter 24: AI-Ready Data Products ... 311
Why This Matters ... 311
The Enterprise AI Bottleneck Is Usually Upstream ... 311
AI Consumers Need Stronger Assurances Than Analytics Consumers ... 312
Product Thinking Reduces Bespoke AI Plumbing ... 312
Core Concepts ... 313
From Dataset to Product ... 313
The AI-Ready Product Contract ... 313
Intended Use and Restricted Use Belong in the Definition ... 314
Not Every Dataset Should Become a Product ... 315
Architectural Implications ... 315
Productization Shifts Work from Model Teams to the Data Estate ... 315
The Product Must Support Multiple AI Serving Patterns ... 315
Product Metadata Must Be Operational, Not Ceremonial ... 316
Product Lifecycle Is Part of Architecture ... 317
Failure Modes and Anti-Patterns ... 318
Calling Anything Reusable a Product ... 318
Treating Documentation as Optional ... 318
Separating Retrieval Design from Product Design ... 319
Ignoring Restricted Uses ... 319

Productizing Low-Value Assets 319
Assuming Access Control at the Repository Is Enough 319
Practical Application 319
Where to Start 319
Minimum Viable AI-Ready Product Components 320
Product Design Questions Architects Should Force Early 320
Templates 321
AI-Ready Data Product Template 321
Case Example 322
HR Policy as an AI-ready Product 322
Closing Synthesis 324
Chapter 25: Federated Delivery: Platform Teams, Domain Teams, and Centers of Excellence 325
Why This Matters 325
AI-Ready Data Requires Both Scale and Context 325
Centralization Alone Becomes a Bottleneck 326
Full Decentralization Creates Drift and Risk 326
Core Concepts 326
Federated Delivery Is a Separation-of-Responsibilities Model 326
Shared Services Should Be Centralized Where Consistency Matters 327
Meaning Must Remain Local 327
Centers of Excellence Enable, They Do Not Absorb Responsibility 328
Standards and Templates Increase Speed 328
Architectural Implications 329
The Operating Model Becomes Part of the Architecture 329
Platform Teams Should Publish a Service Catalog 329
Domain Teams Should Publish Accountable Data Products and Knowledge Assets 330
Governance Must Be Embedded as an Operating Role, Not an Approval Committee 331
Security Must Provide Reusable Control Services 331
AI Enablement Should Accelerate Adoption Without Becoming an Empire 331
Federated Accountability Should Be Explicit 332
Failure Modes and Anti-Patterns 333
The Central Hero Team 333
Every Domain Builds a Stack 333

The Center of Excellence Becomes a Shadow Owner 334
Governance Is Advisory Only 334
Security Is Bolted on at the End 334
Practical Application 335
Start with a Responsibility Inventory 335
Define the Service Boundaries 335
Standardize the Templates That Matter 335
Fund Shared Services Centrally and Stewardship Locally 336
Measure the Model with Operating KPIs 336
Templates 337
Federated Operating Model Worksheet 337
Case Example 338
Federated Delivery Turns Local Knowledge into Enterprise-Scale AI 338
Closing Synthesis 339
Chapter 26: Adoption, Literacy, and Organizational Change 341
Why This Matters 341
Adoption Determines Whether Architecture Produces Value 341
Trust Is Not Automatic, Even When Controls Exist 342
AI Changes What "Data Literacy" Must Include 342
Core Concepts 342
Trust Adoption Depends on Clarity and Evidence 342
Users Need Literacy About Source-Aware AI, Not Just Prompts 343
Stewards and Owners Need New Habits and Incentives 344
Change Management Should Be Tied to Operating Model Shifts 344
Measured Adoption Is a Design Feedback Loop 344
Architectural Implications 345
Adoption Must Be Designed into the Serving Layer 345
Workflow Fit Matters as Much as Model Quality 345
Literacy Design Should Align to Role 346
Governance Signals Should Be Made Visible 346
Failure Modes and Anti-Patterns 347
Treating Adoption as a Launch Campaign 347
Measuring Activity Instead of Trust 347

Assuming Users Understand Grounded Answers....348
Leaving Stewards Outside the Adoption Loop....348
Confusing Resistance with Irrationality....348
Practical Application....348
Designing Adoption Into Delivery....348
Templates....350
AI-Ready Data Adoption Plan....350
Case Example....351
Adoption Fails When Trust Is Not Designed Into the Workflow....351
Closing Synthesis....352
Chapter 27: Current-State Assessment....353
Why This Matters....353
Assessment Is the Difference Between Ambition and Architecture....353
Most Organizations Misdiagnose the Real Problem....354
Assessment Must Be Domain-Based....354
Use-Case Pressure Should Shape Depth....354
Core Concepts....355
Current-State Assessment Is an Architectural Inventory of AI-Readiness....355
Maturity Must Be Scored by Dimension, Not Assumed by Reputation....356
Architectural Implications....356
The Roadmap Must Follow Evidence, Not Politics....356
Domain Architecture Becomes the Unit of Change....357
AI-serving Contracts Must Be Designed from the Findings....357
Metadata and Semantics Become First-Order Investment Targets....357
Failure Modes and Anti-Patterns....357
Enterprise-Average Maturity....357
Source Inventory Without Retrieval Assessment....358
Treating Content as an Afterthought....358
Assuming Ownership Where None Exists....358
Premature Roadmap Certainty....358
Assessing Without Use-Case Pressure....358
Practical Application....359
How to Run the Assessment....359

What a Good Heatmap Reveals 360
Templates 361
AI-Ready Current-State Scorecard 361
Case Example 362
The Current-State Assessment Revealed a Knowledge Problem, Not Just a Data Problem 362
Closing Synthesis 363
Chapter 28: Prioritizing Use Cases and Choosing the First Domains 365
Why This Matters 365
Core Concepts 366
Attractive Use Cases Are Not Always Suitable Starting Points 366
Internal Enterprise Use Cases Are Usually the Best Proving Ground 366
Domain Readiness Matters as Much as Business Demand 367
Quick Wins Must Still Build Reusable Capability 368
First-Wave Choices Shape Credibility and Direction 368
Architectural Implications 368
Prioritization Must Be Tied to Data-Serving Contracts 368
Domain Choice Determines Which Architectural Muscles Are Built First 369
Prioritization Should Reward Reuse, Not Local Optimization 369
Domain Selection Should Be Sequenced, Not One-Off 370
Failure Modes and Anti-Patterns 370
Choosing the Most Visible Use Case Instead of the Most Viable One 370
Treating Domain Demand as Proof of Domain Readiness 370
Optimizing for Speed at the Expense of Control 371
Assuming Documents in Repositories Are Ready for AI 371
Ignoring Reuse Potential 371
Practical Application 371
A Disciplined Prioritization Method 371
A Domain Selection Framework 372
Templates 373
Use Case Prioritization Model 373
Case Example 374
Choose the First Use Case That Builds the Right AI Architecture 374
Closing Synthesis 375

Chapter 29: Designing the Target State 377
Why This Matters 377
The Wrong Target State Creates Expensive Motion Without Progress 377
The First Executable State Sets the Trajectory 378
AI-ready Architecture Must Show Control as Well as Capability 378
Core Concepts 378
Constrained Scope Is a Design Strength 378
A Target State Is a Set of Decisions, Not a Picture 379
The First Target State Must Enable Later Expansion 380
Principles Matter More Than Tool Names 380
Architectural Implications 380
The Target State Must Name the Major Layers 380
Metadata Standard Is Not Optional 381
Semantics Must Be Explicit Enough to Reduce Ambiguity 382
Governance Must Be Visible in the Design 382
Operating Assumptions Belong Inside the Target State 383
Failure Modes and Anti-Patterns 383
Designing the Universal Future State First 383
Equating Repositories with Readiness 384
Over-Indexing on the Retrieval Engine 384
Treating Governance as a Later Phase 384
Failing to Distinguish AI Consumer Types 384
Practical Application 384
How to Design the First Target State 384
Making the Target State Testable 386
Templates 386
Target-State Blueprint Template 386
Case Example 388
Designing the First Target State for an Enterprise Knowledge Assistant 388
Closing Synthesis 390
Chapter 30: Sequencing the Transformation 391
Why This Matters 391
AI Adoption Magnifies Architectural Mistakes 391

Rework Is More Expensive After Rollout 392
Trust Is Built Upstream 392
Core Concepts 392
Sequence Is Not Project Management Trivia 392
The Six Transformation Waves 393
Pilot Debt Usually Forms in Five Ways 393
Wave Checkpoints Matter 394
Reusable Assets Are the Real Output 394
Architectural Implications 394
Stabilize and Govern Before Scaling Retrieval 394
Metadata and Context Cannot Be Deferred 395
Ownership and Operating Model Must Appear Early 395
Different Consumers Require Different Sequencing Tolerances 395
Failure Modes and Anti-Patterns 397
Retrieval-First Transformation 397
Governance After Adoption 397
Metadata as a Documentation Project 397
Scaling Usage Before the Estate Is Ready 397
One-Off Implementation Logic 398
Practical Application 398
Use the Waves to Plan, Not Just to Describe 398
The Six Transformation Waves 398
How to Apply Wave Checkpoints 399
Transformation Wave Planning Canvas 399
What Good Sequencing Looks Like in Practice 400
Templates 400
Transformation Wave Planning Canvas 400
Case Example 401
Sequence the Foundations Before You Scale Retrieval 401
Closing Synthesis 402
Chapter 31: Measuring AI-Readiness and Business Progress 405
Why This Matters 405
Metrics Shape Architecture 405

Executive Confidence Is Earned Through Evidence....405
Leading Indicators Matter More Than Anecdotes....406
Core Concepts....406
Readiness Is Not a Single Score....406
Trust Is Measurable....407
Domain-Based Measurement Is Essential....407
Business Progress Must Be Traced Back to Readiness....408
What Trust Looks Like in Measurable Terms....408
Architectural Implications....409
Measurement Must Be Built into the Architecture....409
Metadata Is the Measurement Backbone....410
Different AI Consumers Require Different KPI Thresholds....410
Executive Dashboards Should Show Risk Reduction and Capability Growth....410
Failure Modes and Anti-Patterns....411
Reporting Activity Instead of Readiness....411
Measuring Only Lagging Incidents....412
Using Enterprise Averages to Hide Domain Weakness....412
Treating Trust as Survey Sentiment Only....412
Overloading One KPI with Too Many Meanings....412
Failing to Baseline Before Rollout....412
Practical Application....413
Build a Domain Readiness Scorecard First....413
Separate Readiness Reviews from Adoption Reviews....413
Instrument Evidence Quality Explicitly....413
Tie Every KPI to an Owner and Action....413
Templates....414
AI-Readiness KPI Catalog....414
Case Example....415
Trust Grew When the Program Measured Readiness, Not Usage....415
Closing Synthesis....416
Chapter 32: What Goes Wrong When You Layer AI on Top of Bad Data....419
Why This Matters....419
AI Failure Is Rarely Isolated....419

The Cost Is Larger Than Answer Quality ... 420

Prevention Is Cheaper Than Credibility Repair ... 420

Core Concepts ... 421

Bad Data for AI Is Not the Same as Bad Data for Reporting ... 421

Hallucination Is Only One Failure Mode ... 421

Metadata Is the Control Plane ... 422

Semantic Context Is What Prevents Contradictory Truth ... 422

Repositories Are Not Readiness ... 422

Architectural Implications ... 423

The Enterprise Must Design for Source Authority ... 423

Freshness Must Be Designed, Not Assumed ... 423

Retrieval Quality Is an Architecture Responsibility ... 423

Governance Must Span Structured and Unstructured Assets Together ... 424

Different AI Consumers Need Different Data-Serving Contracts ... 424

Failure Modes and Anti-Patterns ... 424

Contradictory Answers from Legitimate Sources ... 424

Security Exposure Through Flattened Retrieval ... 425

Obsolete Truth Presented as Current Guidance ... 425

Incorrect Action Recommendations from Context-Poor Data ... 425

Explainability Gaps That Block Adoption ... 426

"We Will Fix Governance After the Pilot" ... 426

Treating Document Ingestion as Readiness ... 426

Using One Generic Retrieval Pipeline for Every Use Case ... 426

Assuming SMEs Can Compensate for Architectural Weakness ... 426

Practical Application ... 427

Start with Failure-Oriented Architecture Reviews ... 427

Establish a Source Hierarchy ... 427

Make Freshness Visible ... 427

Build Access-Aware Retrieval End to End ... 428

Introduce a Reusable Diagnostic Template ... 428

Use the Template to Find Recurring Causes ... 428

Templates ... 429

AI Failure Mode Diagnostic ... 429

Case Example 430

An Internal Assistant Loses Credibility in Two Weeks 430

Closing Synthesis 431

Chapter 33: Anti-Patterns That Look Modern but Fail in Production 433

Why This Matters 433

Demos Can Hide Structural Weakness 433

Anti-Patterns Waste More Than Money 434

Many Failures Are Predictable in Advance 434

Core Concepts 434

Modern-Looking Architecture Can Still Be Structurally Unsound 434

Vector-First Patterns Often Skip Context 434

Chatbot-First Patterns Often Skip Service Design 435

Pilot-First Patterns Often Skip the Operating Model 435

Anti-Patterns Thrive Where Ownership Is Weak 435

Architectural Implications 436

The Retrieval Layer Is an Enterprise Control Surface 436

Semantic Context Is Not Optional Decoration 436

Governance Must Span Structured and Unstructured Data Together 436

Different Consumers Require Different Serving Contracts 437

Failure Modes and Anti-Patterns 437

The Vector-First Shortcut 437

The Chatbot-First Facade 438

The Pilot-First Escape Hatch 438

The Repository Equals Readiness Assumption 438

The Metadata-Light Stack 438

The One-Size-Fits-All Trust Model 439

The Ownership Vacuum 439

The No-Evidence Response Pattern 439

Practical Application 441

Use Architecture Review to Stop Predictable Failure 441

Templates 441

AI Architecture Review Questions 441

Case Example 442

The Demo That Everyone Loved 442
Closing Synthesis 444
Chapter 34: From Dashboards to Agents 445
Why This Matters 446
Dashboards Solved One Class of Problem 446
AI-Mediated Intelligence Changes Speed, Format, and Expectation 446
The Transition Period Is Unavoidable 447
Core Concepts 447
Reports, Dashboards, Copilots, and Agents Are Not Interchangeable 447
Agents Need Stronger Controls Than Assistants 448
Passive Insight and Active Intervention Require Different Readiness 448
Architectural Implications 449
The Serving Layer Must Become Consumer-Specific 449
Metadata Becomes Even More Important as Systems Become More Active 449
Unstructured and Semi-Structured Sources Become Operational Inputs 450
Control Boundaries Must Be Explicit 450
Governance Must Move Closer to Runtime 451
Failure Modes and Anti-Patterns 452
Treating an Agent as a More Powerful Dashboard 452
Over-Rotating to Interface Innovation While Neglecting Serving Architecture 452
Failing to Distinguish Wrong Answer Risk from Wrong Action Risk 452
Ignoring Coexistence During Transition 453
Practical Application 453
Choosing the Right Interaction Model 453
Designing for Escalation, Not Only Automation 453
Example Design Questions Architects Should Ask 454
Templates 454
Decision Framework — Dashboard, Copilot, or Agent 454
Case Example 455
From Dashboards to Copilots to Bounded Agents 455
Closing Synthesis 456
Chapter 35: The AI-Ready Enterprise 459
Why This Matters 460

AI Failure Is Usually a Data-Estate Failure 460
AI-Readiness Is Now a Competitive Operating Condition 461
The Real Target Is Governed Reuse 461
Core Concepts 461
AI-Readiness Is an Architectural State 461
The Enterprise Trust Model Must Span All Data Shapes 462
Metadata Is the Control Plane 462
Semantics Reduce Ambiguity Before the Model Sees the Data 463
Different AI Consumers Need Different Serving Contracts 463
Architectural Implications 463
The Target State Is Layered but Coherent 463
Unstructured Content Must Be Engineered, Not Merely Stored 464
Retrieval Quality Belongs in Architecture 465
Governance Must Move Upstream 465
Failure Modes and Anti-Patterns 466
Mistaking Repository Presence for Readiness 466
Treating Metadata as Optional Decoration 466
Building Isolated AI Pipelines by Use Case 466
Leaving Semantics Unresolved 466
Overexposing Data to Agents 467
Bolting Governance on After Deployment 467
Practical Application 467
Start by Defining the Enterprise Condition You Are Trying to Reach 467
Templates 469
90-Day AI-Ready Enterprise Action Agenda 469
Case Example 470
Global Enterprise in Its Third Year of AI Modernization 470
Closing Synthesis 471
Index 473

Chapter Outlines

Chapter 1: AI Does Not Fail Because of Models 1

This chapter establishes the book's central argument: enterprise AI rarely fails because the model is weak. It fails because the data estate was not designed to support trustworthy retrieval, semantic interpretation, secure access, provenance, and governed use. The chapter reframes AI failure as an architectural trust problem and sets the foundation for the rest of the book.

Chapter 2: Why Traditional Data Readiness Is No Longer Enough 13

This chapter explains why data that is report-ready, analytics-ready, or even ML-ready is not automatically fit for copilots, assistants, and agents. As AI becomes a machine-mediated consumer of enterprise information, the architecture must support grounding, interpretation, policy-aware delivery, and explainability in ways traditional readiness models never required.

Chapter 3: What AI-Ready Data Actually Means 27

This chapter defines AI-ready data as a multidimensional condition rather than a simple label. It shows that quality alone is not enough and that trustworthy AI depends on discoverability, semantics, lineage, freshness, policy, authority, and business context being designed into the data estate.

Chapter 4: Traditional Data Structures: What They Were Built For 41

This chapter revisits the design intent of transactional systems, warehouses, lakes, and repositories to show why each remains valuable yet incomplete for AI use. It argues that organizations must understand the original optimization bias of each structure, then add the controls and serving layers needed for trustworthy AI consumption.

Chapter 5: Structured Data in the Age of AI 53

This chapter shows that structured data remains the backbone of enterprise truth, but raw tables and fields are no longer sufficient. To support AI safely, structured data must be paired with semantic definitions, lineage, policy constraints, and explanation-ready serving contracts so that business facts can be interpreted and justified, not merely queried.

Chapter 6: Semi-Structured Data as the Missing Middle 67

This chapter explores the operational importance of events, logs, messages, and payloads as the connective tissue between systems of record and AI inference. It explains why semi-structured data often captures the most current business context and why enterprises must model its meaning, govern its use, and monitor its drift deliberately.

Chapter 7: Unstructured Data as a First-Class Enterprise Asset 81

This chapter argues that much of the business meaning AI depends on lives outside databases, in policies, procedures, contracts, notes, transcripts, and other narrative content. It shows why unstructured content must be treated as a governed enterprise asset with ownership, lifecycle, enrichment, and retrieval design rather than as passive storage.

Chapter 8: Why Document Repositories Alone Are Not Enough.......................................97

This chapter explains why a repository is not the same thing as an AI-ready knowledge system. Documents must be inventoried, curated, enriched, segmented, permission-preserved, and citation-ready before they can safely ground AI responses, recommendations, or actions.

Chapter 9: Metadata Is the Control Plane for AI 113

This chapter presents metadata as the operating control system of trustworthy AI. It shows how business, technical, policy, and AI-serving metadata determine what can be found, trusted, ranked, explained, governed, and safely reused across structured, semi-structured, and unstructured sources.

Chapter 10: Business Meaning: Glossaries, Taxonomies, and Ontologies 127

This chapter addresses the problem of ambiguity by showing how glossaries, taxonomies, and ontologies help enterprises establish controlled meaning. It explains why shared semantic infrastructure is essential if AI systems are to interpret business terms consistently across domains, repositories, and use cases.

Chapter 11: Knowledge Graphs, Entity Resolution, and Relationship Intelligence 141

This chapter examines how identity resolution and relationship modeling enable higher-value AI use cases that depend on connected meaning across systems. It treats knowledge graphs as a selective architectural pattern and shows that trusted relationship intelligence depends on explicit evidence, provenance, and governance.

Chapter 12: Provenance, Lineage, and Explainability from the Data Side 155

This chapter focuses on the upstream architectural foundations of explainable AI. It shows why provenance, lineage, temporal context, and evidence design must be built into the data estate so users can understand where answers came from, how they were shaped, and why they should be trusted.

Chapter 13: The AI-Ready Data Capability Pillars...169

This chapter organizes the discipline of AI-ready data into a set of core capability pillars, spanning sources, ingestion, metadata, semantics, governance, retrieval, and serving. It provides a practical way to assess readiness and shows that AI failure is usually a breakdown across capabilities, not a shortfall in any single tool.

Chapter 14: Converged Data Patterns: Relational, Vector, Graph, and Content 183

This chapter explains why enterprise AI requires orchestration across multiple data patterns rather than allegiance to one. It shows how relational, vector, graph, and content architectures each solve different problems and must be combined deliberately through shared metadata, semantics, provenance, and control.

Chapter 15: Integration Patterns for AI-Ready Data 195

This chapter explores how integration for AI differs from conventional movement and replication of data. It argues that integration must preserve meaning, carry metadata, respect governance, and align to AI consumer needs so that the enterprise can connect fragmented reality without introducing new trust failures.

Chapter 16: Retrieval and Grounding as Architecture Concerns...................................... 211

This chapter reframes retrieval as a core architectural responsibility rather than a thin model-side feature. It shows that retrieval quality depends on segmentation, enrichment, ranking, freshness, authority logic, access-aware filtering, and evaluation design, all of which determine whether AI outputs are grounded and trustworthy.

Chapter 17: Serving Data to Copilots, Assistants, and Agents 225

This chapter explains that different AI consumers require different data-serving contracts. It distinguishes between assistants, analyst copilots, recommendation systems, and agents, and shows why evidence requirements, permissions, action boundaries, and trust thresholds must be designed according to the role the AI system plays.

Chapter 18: Security, Identity, and Access-Aware Data Delivery..................................... 237

This chapter makes the case that the AI-serving layer is part of the enterprise security architecture. It shows why identity propagation, access-aware retrieval, permission fidelity, classification, and auditability are essential when AI can discover and synthesize information at scale.

Chapter 19: Why Governance for AI Is Different from Governance for Analytics............. 249

This chapter explains why the governance disciplines built for reporting and analytics do not go far enough for AI. It shows that governance must extend beyond source control into behavior control, covering evidence, retrieval, permissions, ambiguity, and runtime constraints for different AI consumers.

Chapter 20: Governing Structured and Unstructured Data Together............................... 259

This chapter argues that AI consumes business reality across asset classes, not storage categories. It shows why governance must connect records, documents, narrative evidence, ownership, retention, provenance, and access into one cross-asset model if enterprise AI is to remain coherent and trustworthy.

Chapter 21: Responsible AI Starts Upstream in the Data Estate 271

This chapter shows that responsible AI begins long before model output. It explains how authority gaps, coverage issues, stale content, imbalance, and weak review controls shape harmful outcomes, and it argues that responsible delivery depends on disciplined source readiness and explicit human oversight triggers.

Chapter 22: The Policy Layer: Retention, Legal Hold, Privacy, and Records......................283

This chapter examines how retention, legal hold, privacy, minimization, and records obligations must be represented inside the AI-ready data architecture. It shows that lifecycle state and policy metadata must travel with assets if retrieval and response generation are to remain defensible and compliant.

Chapter 23: Who Owns AI-Ready Data? 297

This chapter addresses the ownership problem at the heart of enterprise AI scale. It argues that trusted AI depends on explicit accountability across platform teams, domain teams, and stewards, with clear decision rights, funded stewardship, and machine-visible ownership built into the operating model.

Chapter 24: AI-Ready Data Products 311

This chapter applies product thinking to the data estate by defining AI-ready data products as governed, reusable serving contracts rather than reusable datasets alone. It shows why intended use, restricted use, metadata, lifecycle, access, and retrieval design must all be part of the product definition.

Chapter 25: Federated Delivery: Platform Teams, Domain Teams, and Centers of Excellence 325

This chapter explains why AI-ready data requires a federated operating model that combines scale with business context. It shows how platform teams, domain teams, and centers of excellence must divide responsibilities so shared services remain strong while local meaning and accountability stay close to the business.

Chapter 26: Adoption, Literacy, and Organizational Change 341

This chapter argues that AI adoption is not merely a launch activity but a design outcome. It shows that trust, literacy, workflow fit, stewardship, and visible governance signals all shape whether people use AI responsibly and effectively across the enterprise.

Chapter 27: Current-State Assessment 353

This chapter positions assessment as the bridge between aspiration and executable architecture. It shows why organizations must assess AI-readiness by domain and by dimension, exposing gaps in metadata, retrieval, semantics, content readiness, ownership, and governance before building a roadmap.

Chapter 28: Prioritizing Use Cases and Choosing the First Domains 365

This chapter explains how to select the first AI use cases and domains in a way that creates real value while building reusable enterprise capability. It emphasizes readiness, reuse potential, control, and sequence over visibility, novelty, or executive excitement alone.

Chapter 29: Designing the Target State 377

This chapter focuses on how to design a realistic and testable target state for AI-ready data. It shows that the target state must make explicit decisions about layers, semantics, metadata, governance, retrieval, and operating assumptions so the organization builds a foundation that can expand without rework.

Chapter 30: Sequencing The Transformation 391

This chapter explains why sequence matters as much as architecture itself. It presents transformation as a staged progression in which source stability, permissions, metadata, governance, ownership, and context must mature before the enterprise can safely scale retrieval and broader AI use.

Chapter 31: Measuring AI-readiness and Business Progress 405

This chapter argues that serious AI programs should measure readiness, trust, and business progress directly rather than relying on activity metrics alone. It shows how the right measures make architectural maturity visible and help leaders track whether AI is becoming more grounded, more reusable, and more trustworthy.

Chapter 32: What Goes Wrong When You Layer AI on Top of Bad Data 419

This chapter examines the predictable failure modes that emerge when AI is placed on top of weak, stale, or poorly governed information. It shows how contradictory truth, broken permissions, weak semantics, stale guidance, and missing provenance turn plausible output into operational and reputational risk.

Chapter 33: Anti-Patterns That Look Modern but Fail in Production 433

This chapter identifies the shortcuts that appear current and sophisticated but collapse under enterprise conditions. It explains why vector-first, chatbot-first, pilot-first, and metadata-light approaches often impress in demos while failing in production because they avoid the harder work of architecture, governance, and ownership.

Chapter 34: From Dashboards to Agents 445

This chapter describes the transition from passive business intelligence toward AI systems that interpret conditions, recommend responses, and, in bounded cases, take action. It shows why dashboards, copilots, and agents are not interchangeable and why more active systems require stronger controls, clearer trust contracts, and richer runtime context.

Chapter 35: The AI-Ready Enterprise 459

This concluding chapter brings the book together into a practical vision of what an AI-ready enterprise looks like. It argues that the real destination is not isolated AI success but a governed, contextualized, reusable data estate in which metadata is the control plane, semantics reduce ambiguity, retrieval is designed for trust, and every AI consumer operates within an explicit serving contract.

Chapter 1: AI Does Not Fail Because of Models

Most enterprise AI programs do not fail because the models are weak. They fail because the organization's data estate was never designed to support trustworthy retrieval, contextual interpretation, secure access, semantic alignment, or operational use by AI systems.

That distinction matters more than most executives, architects, and even AI teams initially realize. When a generative AI assistant produces a wrong answer, the visible failure is linguistic. The answer sounds plausible, but it is incomplete, ungrounded, stale, contradictory, or unsafe. That surface symptom tempts people toward a model-side diagnosis: upgrade the model, tune the prompt, add another orchestration layer, try a different vendor. In the enterprise, that is often the wrong diagnosis.

A model can only reason over what the enterprise makes discoverable, interpretable, permissible, current, and defensible. If the organization's contracts live in five repositories, its policies exist in multiple conflicting versions, its business terms are undefined, its access controls are inconsistently inherited, and its metadata is thin or wrong, the model is not the first problem. The model is simply the first place the problem becomes visible.

Key Insight

Common illusion – "We just need a better model."

When enterprise AI disappoints, organizations often assume the model is underpowered. In reality, many failures originate in the data estate: unclear source authority, weak metadata, missing semantic context, stale content, broken permissions, and absent provenance. A stronger model may produce smoother language, but it cannot manufacture trust where the architecture provides none.

Enterprise AI exposes architectural debt that reporting systems were able to tolerate. Dashboards can survive on carefully curated datasets and fixed definitions. Human analysts can compensate for missing context because they know which spreadsheet not to trust, which knowledge base is stale, and which operations leader to call before acting. AI systems cannot compensate in the same way. They require the enterprise to externalize context, encode trust, and operationalize governance in the data estate itself.

This book begins there because every subsequent decision depends on it. Before discussing AI-ready architecture patterns, metadata strategies, unstructured content design, or governance operating models, the first point must be made plainly: bad AI outcomes are usually downstream symptoms of data architecture failure.

WHY THIS MATTERS

Enterprise AI Fails at the Point of Trust

In enterprise settings, usefulness is not enough. The answer must also be trustworthy. That means the system must be able to retrieve the right source, interpret it in the right business context, honor the right permissions, reflect the right moment in time, and provide defensible evidence for what it says or does.

That is why enterprise AI programs rarely collapse because of raw model capability. Most contemporary models are already good enough to expose whether the surrounding information architecture is fit for purpose. The critical question is not whether a model can generate a sentence. It is whether the enterprise can support grounded, governed, explainable output at production scale.

A model can summarize a policy document. But can it tell which version is active? Can it distinguish global policy from regional exception? Can it avoid citing a draft? Can it respect legal hold? Can it explain why two sources disagree? Can it avoid surfacing a restricted HR memo to a manager who should not see it? Those are not model selection questions. They are data architecture questions.

❖ FIGURE 1 – THE FAILURE ICEBERG

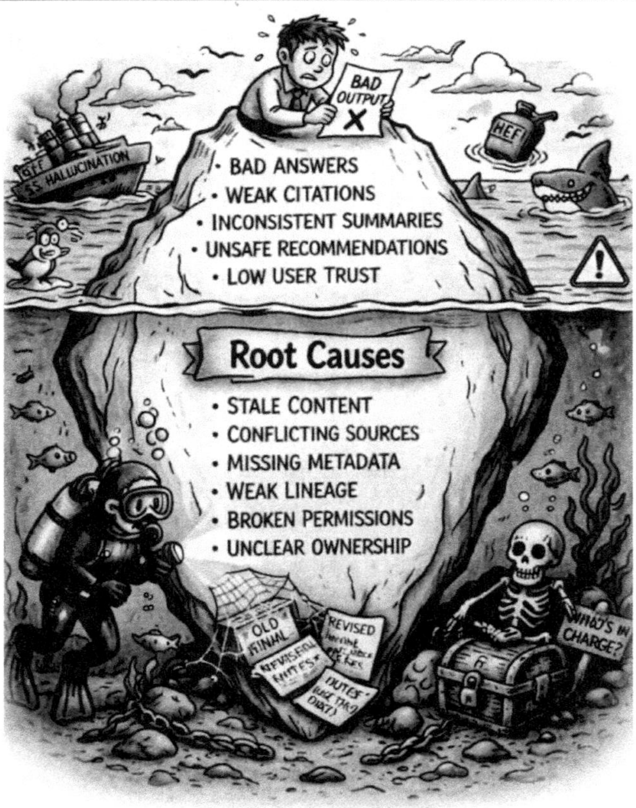

Pilots Succeed Where Enterprises Fail

This is why early pilots so often mislead leadership teams. A demo is typically built on a narrow, curated corpus. The documents are handpicked. Permissions are simplified. Duplicates are removed. Known-good content is promoted. Subject matter experts quietly fill in missing context. The retrieval space is small, stable, and forgiving. Production is the opposite. Production means contested definitions, overlapping repositories, undocumented lineage, mixed content quality, unclear ownership, retention complexity, and live permission boundaries. It means the AI system must operate inside the real enterprise rather than the clean room version of it.

A successful pilot, therefore, proves much less than organizations assume. It may show that the user interface is compelling, the use case is attractive, and the model can express value. It does not prove that the enterprise data estate can sustain trustworthy operation.

KEY INSIGHT

Pilot trap – Why demos succeed while production fails

Demos often use a curated subset of content with hidden manual controls: selected documents, simplified permissions, known-good source material, and expert oversight. Production introduces the full reality of enterprise data: duplicate documents, conflicting versions, missing metadata, inconsistent security, unclear source ownership, and constant change. Pilot success is real, but it is not evidence of architectural readiness.

WARNING SIGN

Why this is not an LLM selection problem

Executives often ask which model the company should standardize on. That is a reasonable procurement question, but it is usually not the first transformation question. The first question is whether the organization can provide AI systems with governed access to trusted, contextualized, semantically interpretable data and content.

If the answer is no, model switching becomes a distraction. The organization is arguing about the intelligence of the speaker while ignoring the quality of the evidence it is allowed to use.

CORE CONCEPTS

Model Capability Is Rarely the First Limiting Factor

In the enterprise, the first limiting factor is usually one of five things: source quality, metadata quality, semantic clarity, permission fidelity, or provenance. These determine whether the model can retrieve and interpret the right information safely. If those conditions are weak, model improvements have diminishing returns.

This does not mean models do not matter. They do. But in the order of operations for enterprise AI, the model is rarely the first bottleneck once a baseline level of capability has been achieved. The more strategic bottleneck is whether the data estate has been designed for AI consumption rather than human-only navigation.

AI-ready Is Not the Same as Report-Ready or ML-Ready

A dataset can be excellent for reporting and still be unusable for AI. Reporting systems depend on pre-modeled facts, stable metrics, and fixed semantics. Machine learning systems may work on curated training data created for a specific predictive task. Generative AI and agentic systems impose a different burden.

AI-ready data must support:

- Discovery across heterogeneous sources.
- Contextual interpretation of meaning.
- Access-aware retrieval.
- Source ranking and authority signals.
- Freshness and temporal correctness.
- Provenance and citation.
- Safe reuse across multiple AI consumers.

A finance table with perfect completeness can still be AI-unready if the field names are cryptic, the business definitions are undocumented, the transformation lineage is opaque, and the relevant policy interpretations live only in emails and meeting notes. High quality is necessary, but not sufficient.

Metadata Is the Control Plane

Metadata is not administrative decoration. In AI systems, metadata becomes operational control. It determines what can be found, what should rank, what can be trusted, what should be excluded, what is current, what is authoritative, and what can be explained.

For structured data, that means business definitions, lineage, stewardship, freshness indicators, sensitivity labels, intended use, and relationship context. For unstructured content, it means document type, authoritativeness, lifecycle state, version, classification, audience, jurisdiction, and source ownership. For semi-structured signals such as logs, events, and API payloads, it means schema meaning, event semantics, and linkage to business entities and processes.

Without metadata, retrieval becomes lexical luck. With robust metadata, retrieval becomes governed selection.

Semantic Context Is What Turns Data into Interpretable Evidence

AI systems routinely encounter ambiguity that humans resolve unconsciously. Does "customer" mean legal account holder, billing entity, household, or active subscriber? Does "policy" mean information security policy, HR policy, or insurance policy? Does "current contract" mean signed contract, amended contract, or contract currently in force?

This is why semantic context is essential. Business glossaries, taxonomies, entity models, and relationship models reduce ambiguity. They connect raw fields and raw files to business meaning. They also allow different data forms to be interpreted together. A customer record, a support transcript, a product manual, and a service event log can only be meaningfully combined if the enterprise models the concepts that connect them.

Trust Is an Architectural Property

Trustworthy enterprise AI is not achieved by instructing the model to "be accurate." Trust emerges when the architecture supports evidence-based output. That requires:

- Source authority.
- Provenance.
- Permission fidelity.
- Freshness controls.
- Temporal correctness.
- Explainability.
- Stewardship and accountability.

An answer becomes trustworthy when a user can understand where it came from, why that source was selected, whether it was current, whether the system had a right to use it, and whether the business meaning was interpreted correctly.

Architectural Implications

The Enterprise Data Estate, Not the Model, Is the System of Consequence

Once AI is placed into a real operating environment, the system that matters most is the enterprise data estate. By estate, we mean the full collection of data assets, systems, platforms, processes, controls, and governance structures through which enterprise data is created, stored, moved, secured, described, interpreted, and used. Source systems, ingestion pipelines, metadata services, classification layers, semantic models, retrieval services, access controls, and feedback loops together determine whether AI output is reliable enough to use. This reframes the architecture agenda. The goal is not merely to connect a model to data. The goal is to redesign the data estate so that AI can consume it safely and repeatedly.

Structured, Semi-Structured, and Unstructured Data Must Be Designed Together

Enterprises often over-focus on structured data because that is where traditional data management invested most heavily. But AI use cases derive meaning from all three forms.

Structured data provides state, transactions, reference entities, and measurable facts. Semi-structured data provides events, system interactions, process signals, and operational context. Unstructured data provides the language of the business: policies, contracts, design notes, procedures, exceptions, decisions, transcripts, and communications.

Most enterprise AI failures happen because these forms are managed separately. The customer master is governed, but the call transcripts are not. The product hierarchy is defined, but the service bulletins are unmanaged. The compliance taxonomy exists, but it is not linked to the documents it should govern. The result is an AI system that can retrieve pieces of reality but not assemble trusted business context.

❖ FIGURE 2 – AI FAILURE CHAIN

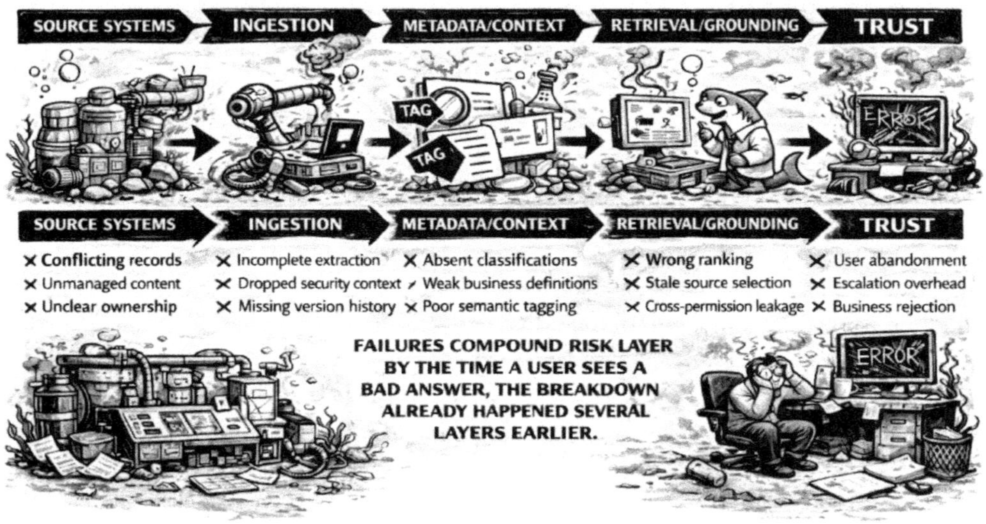

Retrieval Quality Is an Architecture Responsibility

Retrieval is not a thin middleware function. It is where information architecture either succeeds or fails under AI load. Decisions about chunking, enrichment, ranking, source authority, access filtering, duplication handling, freshness, citation design, and semantic expansion all sit squarely in the architecture domain.

When teams treat retrieval as a model-side tuning exercise, they miss the real work. Poor retrieval is often the direct result of poor content architecture, missing metadata, inconsistent source ownership, and weak classification. The fix is not only better prompts. The fix is better architecture.

Different AI Consumers Require Different Serving Contracts

Not all AI consumers need the same data-serving model.

A knowledge assistant may tolerate some uncertainty if it can cite sources clearly. An analyst copilot may need deeper provenance and traceable transformations. An executive briefing assistant needs synthesis across curated authoritative sources with strong temporal correctness. An action-taking agent requires the strictest controls of all: deterministic access boundaries, validated business rules, and explicit operational authority.

This means AI-ready data cannot be defined once at a generic level. It must be designed as a set of serving contracts aligned to the risk profile, trust threshold, and action scope of the AI consumer.

KEY INSIGHT

Architect's lens – The five data causes of enterprise AI failure

Poor source design: critical knowledge is fragmented, duplicated, or trapped in unmanaged repositories.

Weak metadata: the system cannot distinguish authoritative from stale, draft from approved, or public from restricted.

Broken permission fidelity: AI retrieval does not reliably inherit and enforce access boundaries.

Missing provenance: answers cannot be traced to defensible sources with clear lineage and time context.

Semantic ambiguity: the same business term means different things across systems, documents, and functions.

FAILURE MODES AND ANTI-PATTERNS

Treating Repository Presence as Readiness

Many organizations assume that because their content is "in SharePoint," "in the data lake," or "in the knowledge base," it is ready for AI. It is not. Repositories store material; they do not automatically provide authority, context, lifecycle control, semantic labeling, or access-aware retrieval.

A folder full of policy documents may contain drafts, superseded versions, regional variants, and local guidance mixed together. Without metadata and lifecycle discipline, retrieval systems cannot distinguish among them reliably.

Confusing Data Quality with AI Usability

Traditional data programs ask whether data is accurate, complete, and timely enough for reporting or operational processing. AI adds different requirements. The system must know what the data means, when it should be used, under what permissions, with what confidence, and in relation to which other sources.

This is why clean data alone is not enough. A table can be accurate and still be dangerous in AI if its intended use is unclear or its lineage is invisible.

Ignoring Provenance Until After Deployment

Some teams launch assistants that produce answers first and plan to add citations, lineage, or source evidence later. That sequence is backward. Provenance is not a cosmetic enhancement. It is a precondition for enterprise trust.

If a user cannot inspect the source and understand why it was selected, adoption collapses, or risky overreliance begins. Neither outcome is acceptable.

Simplifying Permissions for the Pilot and Never Recovering

A common pilot shortcut is to flatten or over-broaden access so the demo works. Later, the team tries to reintroduce enterprise permissions. That is where many deployments stall, because security inheritance across documents, data products, attachments, transcripts, and derived content is harder than expected.

Permission fidelity is not a detail to bolt on in phase two. It is a core architectural requirement.

No Clear Owner for Trusted Business Meaning

AI systems often sit at the intersection of functions. Legal owns the contracts. Procurement owns the supplier policy. IT owns the platform. Data teams own pipelines. Security owns controls. Nobody owns the semantic coherence of the whole answer. When ownership is diffuse, quality defects persist because no single team is accountable for business meaning at the point of AI consumption.

⚠ WARNING SIGN

Why this is not an LLM selection problem

If the assistant cites obsolete policy, exposes restricted content, or gives contradictory answers from two business units, changing the model will not solve the problem. The enterprise has an information architecture problem: source authority is unclear, metadata is weak, governance is fragmented, and the operating model does not assign accountability for trustworthy AI output.

PRACTICAL APPLICATION

Start with Diagnostic Discipline, Not Implementation Enthusiasm

The first task in any enterprise AI program should be diagnostic. Before adding another model, connector, or orchestration layer, the organization should identify where trust is breaking in the data estate. That requires examining the use case across source systems, metadata, semantics, permissions, freshness, governance, and ownership. The purpose is not to produce a generic maturity score. The purpose is to isolate the structural causes of unsafe or unreliable AI behavior.

TEMPLATES

Enterprise AI Failure Diagnostic

Program name	<name of the AI-enabled program, product, or initiative>
Primary AI use case	<main job the AI system is intended to perform for users>
Observed symptoms	<visible problems, failures, inconsistencies, or trust issues users are experiencing>
Source systems involved	<systems, repositories, platforms, and data sources that the AI depends on>
Structured data issues	<problems in structured data such as inconsistent codes, missing keys, mismatched hierarchies, or nonstandard statuses>
Unstructured data issues	<problems in documents, PDFs, notes, transcripts, or repositories such as duplication, outdated content, or unmanaged high-value knowledge>
Metadata gaps	<missing or unreliable metadata needed for filtering, ranking, governance, and grounding>
Semantic/context gaps	<missing shared definitions, relationships, business meaning, or conceptual models that prevent consistent interpretation>

Access control gaps

<problems with permissions, entitlement logic, role-based access, or exposure of restricted content>

Freshness/version issues

<problems with update cadence, supersession handling, temporal validity, or distinguishing current from historical content>

Ownership/stewardship issues

<unclear or fragmented accountability for maintaining trusted, governed AI-Ready content and answer composition>

Governance/policy issues

<missing rules, controls, or policies for approval, retention, evidence use, and safe AI behavior>

Trust impact

<effect on user confidence, adoption, reliance, or willingness to use the AI system>

Business impact

<effect on operations, cost, productivity, service quality, escalation rates, risk, or value realization>

Immediate stabilizing actions

<near-term actions to reduce harm, improve reliability, and stabilize performance quickly>

Structural remediation actions

<longer-term architectural, semantic, governance, and operating-model changes needed to make the system AI-Ready>

Executive summary statement

<concise diagnosis of why the AI program is struggling and what underlying enterprise data or governance problem must be addressed>

Case Example

A Manufacturing Assistant That Worked Brilliantly in the Lab and Failed in the Field

Consider a global manufacturer launching an AI assistant for field service engineers. The use case appears straightforward: technicians should be able to ask natural-language questions about equipment faults, service procedures, and warranty coverage while on site with customers.

The pilot is impressive. A small team curates several hundred technical manuals, the latest service bulletins, and a limited set of warranty rules for one product line in one region. The assistant performs well. Engineers praise the speed of issue diagnosis. Leadership sees a path to lower service costs and faster resolution times.

Then the deployment expands.

The problems begin immediately. The same product family is labeled differently in the ERP system, the service platform, and the manual repository. Regional bulletins include local exceptions that were not tagged as such. Some "latest" manuals are current only for North America; EMEA uses a different approved sequence. Engineering has published draft advisories in a collaboration site that was indexed during the pilot. Warranty policy language references service codes that do not align cleanly to operational statuses in the case system. Call transcripts contain valuable troubleshooting detail, but no one has linked them to governed product entities or filtered them for approval status.

The assistant now answers with confidence but not consistency. One technician receives a troubleshooting sequence from a superseded manual. Another sees a correct procedure but the wrong warranty interpretation. A third is shown as an engineering advisory that has not yet been approved for field use. None of these failures originates in the language model. They originate in the data estate.

What the case reveals

This case is instructive because nothing in it is unusual. The organization did not neglect AI. It neglected the architectural preconditions for trustworthy AI.

Its real problems were these:

- Source authority was not explicit.
- Metadata did not distinguish current, approved, regional, and draft content.
- Semantic mapping across systems was weak.
- Permissions were not consistently inherited.
- Provenance and temporal logic were insufficient.
- No one owned trusted answer composition across domains.

The pilot had masked those weaknesses by narrowing the problem space. Production exposed them because production always does.

The architectural lesson

The manufacturer does not need to begin by replacing the model. It needs to redesign the service knowledge estate. That means:

- Defining authoritative sources by content type and business purpose.
- Standardizing lifecycle and approval metadata.
- Linking structured product entities to bulletins, manuals, events, and transcripts.
- Enforcing access-aware retrieval and regional scoping.
- Creating freshness logic suitable for fast-changing technical guidance.
- Assigning stewardship for AI-consumable service evidence.

Only then will the model's capabilities translate into reliable enterprise value.

Closing Synthesis

The first mistake many organizations make in enterprise AI is to misdiagnose failure. They look at bad answers and conclude they have an intelligence problem. In most cases, they have an architecture problem.

The enterprise data estate was built for human navigation, application workflows, analytics pipelines, and compliance storage. It was not built to support machine-mediated discovery, retrieval, contextual interpretation, grounded reasoning, and governed action. Enterprise AI makes that gap impossible to ignore.

This is why AI-Ready data must be treated as an architectural state rather than a cleanup exercise. It requires structured data with business meaning, unstructured content with lifecycle discipline, semi-structured signals with operational context, metadata as a control plane, retrieval as an architecture function, governance embedded by design, and ownership aligned to trust.

The work is not glamorous, but it is decisive. Model choice influences performance. Data architecture determines whether performance can be trusted. And in the enterprise, trusted performance is the only kind that matters.

Key Takeaways

- Most enterprise AI failures are symptoms of weak data architecture, not weak models.
- Pilot success often hides the source, metadata, permission, and provenance problems that appear in production.
- AI-Ready Data is not simply clean data; it must be discoverable, contextualized, governed, current, and defensible.
- Retrieval quality, trust, and explainability depend on architectural choices across the data estate.
- The path to scalable enterprise AI begins with diagnosing and redesigning the data environment, not merely selecting a better model.

Chapter 2: Why Traditional Data Readiness Is No Longer Enough

For years, organizations have measured data maturity through familiar outcomes: trusted reports, reconciled metrics, governed warehouses, scalable BI platforms, and well-managed machine learning pipelines. Those were sensible goals. They still may be. But none of them, by themselves, define AI-readiness.

Traditional data readiness was built around a human consumer working inside relatively fixed interfaces. A finance analyst opens a report. An operations leader reviews a dashboard. A data scientist pulls a curated dataset and engineers features for a model. In each case, the consumer brings context, domain judgment, and an ability to notice ambiguity. The data does not need to explain itself completely because a skilled human interpreter fills in the gaps.

AI systems do not consume data this way.

A copilot, assistant, or agent is not merely displaying data. It is retrieving, interpreting, combining, prioritizing, and expressing information on behalf of a user. It may summarize a policy, compare current performance with prior periods, explain an exception, recommend an action, or initiate one. That changes the burden on the data estate. The data must now support discovery, semantic interpretation, trust scoring, provenance, access-aware retrieval, temporal correctness, and explainable outputs. The old definition of "usable" is no longer enough.

This is why organizations with strong business intelligence programs are often surprised by weak AI outcomes. They assume that because data is reconciled, governed, and available, it is, therefore, ready for AI use. In practice, AI exposes the architectural layers that BI could often tolerate as implicit: incomplete metadata, missing business definitions, disconnected unstructured content, weak provenance, inconsistent permissions, poor freshness signals, and no clear retrieval contract.

The issue is not that traditional readiness was wrong. The issue is that it was optimized for earlier consumption patterns. AI introduces a new class of consumer, and with it a new class of architectural requirements.

Why This Matters

The Consumer Has Changed

A dashboard answers questions a designer anticipated. An AI assistant is asked questions that the designer did not fully predict. A report presents metrics in a fixed structure. An AI system must assemble context dynamically. A human dashboard user knows where to drill next, what caveat to apply, and which source system is more trustworthy when numbers conflict. An assistant must be guided by architecture to do the same. That is the first reason traditional readiness is no longer enough: the consumer is no longer only human, and the delivery contract is no longer fixed.

The Interaction Model Has Changed

In traditional analytics, the user pulls information. In enterprise AI, the system increasingly pushes synthesized responses, recommendations, and exceptions. That sounds like a user experience change, but it is actually a data architecture change.

When a user pulls a dashboard, they can visually inspect the data, compare charts, scan footnotes, and bring their own skepticism. When an assistant pushes an answer, the enterprise must ensure that the answer is grounded in authoritative sources, framed with the correct time horizon, filtered by permissions, and accompanied by evidence. The tolerance for ambiguity drops sharply because the system is now packaging judgment, not just exposing records.

Key Insight

Why dashboards are different from AI answers

Dashboard	AI answer
A dashboard presents curated information inside a bounded design.	An AI answer assembles information across sources in real time or near real time.
A dashboard expects the user to interpret.	An AI answer is itself an act of interpretation.
A dashboard may tolerate undocumented assumptions because experienced users know them.	An AI answer must be guided by explicit metadata, semantics, and policy because the system is making those assumptions on the user's behalf.

The Risk Surface Has Changed

BI errors are serious. AI errors are often more dangerous because they can sound complete, confident, and actionable even when they are poorly grounded. A stale report may mislead a quarterly review. A poorly grounded AI assistant can misstate a policy, summarize the wrong contract clause, or recommend an action based on incomplete entitlement logic. An agent can do worse: it can trigger workflow, notify customers, or alter records.

Traditional readiness rarely had to treat action safety as part of the data-serving layer. Agent-Ready Data does.

The Meaning of "Usable" Has Changed

For reporting, usable often means accurate, timely, reconciled, and understandable to analysts. For AI, usable means much more:

- Discoverable at retrieval time.
- Interpretable without human tribal knowledge.
- Linked to semantic definitions.
- Constrained by policy and permissions.
- Explainable with source evidence.
- Fresh enough for the use case.
- Attributable to authoritative systems.
- Structured for safe response generation or safe action.

A dataset can be excellent for analytics and still fail nearly all of those tests.

Core Concepts

Report-Ready Data

Report-ready data is optimized for stable human consumption in predefined formats. It supports recurring business questions: monthly revenue, claims volume, inventory turns, call center performance, and budget variance. It emphasizes reconciliation, consistency, and presentability.

Its strengths are clarity, metric stability, and trust in recurring outputs. Its weaknesses, from an AI perspective, are equally important. Report-Ready Data often hides complexity behind the report design. Definitions may live in people's heads or separate documentation. Source lineage may be known to the report author but not machine-readable. Exceptions and caveats may sit outside the dataset entirely. The dashboard works because the human consumer supplies the missing context.

Analytics-Ready Data

Analytics-ready data extends beyond reporting. It supports exploration, slicing, drilling, and flexible analysis. It often involves dimensional models, semantic layers, governed marts, feature-rich curated datasets, and standardized business logic. This is a significant maturity step, and many organizations stop here because it delivers enormous value.

But analytics-ready is still not AI-ready. Why? Because it is optimized for analyst-led exploration, not for retrieval and machine-mediated explanation. An analyst can navigate ambiguity by asking follow-up questions and recognizing when a data source is incomplete. A copilot cannot safely rely on that assumption unless the architecture has encoded those guardrails.

ML-Ready Data

ML-ready data is optimized for training suitability, feature extraction, labeling, and repeatable model development. It often includes curated historical data, training sets, feature stores, evaluation baselines, and reproducible pipelines. It is built to maximize signal for prediction or classification tasks.

This is an important but different objective. ML-Ready Data can be excellent for model performance while still being poor for enterprise explanation. Feature vectors do not tell a business user why an answer should be trusted. They do not expose the relevant policy clause, business definition, source document, or operational lineage. They support model learning, not grounded interaction.

GenAI-Ready Data

GenAI-ready data is optimized for grounding, retrieval, semantic interpretation, and explainable response generation. This requires far more than storing documents or exposing tables through an API. It requires:

- Metadata that supports discovery and ranking.
- Semantic context that reduces ambiguity.
- Content segmentation designed for retrieval.
- Source authority signals.
- Provenance and citation support.
- Access-aware retrieval and response generation.
- Freshness and temporal relevance controls.
- Alignment between structured facts and unstructured business meaning.

This is where many enterprises discover that repositories are not ready. A million files in SharePoint are not an AI knowledge layer. A warehouse full of governed tables is not a grounded enterprise context layer. GenAI-ready architecture has to bind these worlds together.

Agent-Ready Data

Agent-ready data adds a further requirement: action safety. It is not enough for the data to support a plausible answer. It must support safe decisioning and controlled operational execution. That means the system needs explicit policy boundaries, reliable entitlements, unambiguous business semantics, traceable source evidence, and confidence thresholds tied to action type.

An agent that recommends reviewing an exception has a different risk threshold from one that sends a legal notice, updates a customer record, or approves a discount. Agent-Ready Data, therefore, requires serving contracts that are explicit about what the agent may know, what it may infer, and what it may do.

Readiness Ladder

Report-Ready

Optimized for fixed human consumption.

Primary value: consistency and presentation.

Primary risk: hidden assumptions remain invisible to machines.

Analytics-Ready

Optimized for exploration and metric coherence.

Primary value: flexible human analysis.

Primary risk: semantic and contextual gaps still depend on analysts.

ML-Ready

Optimized for training and predictive performance.

Primary value: model development.

Primary risk: weak explainability and limited business grounding.

GenAI-Ready

Optimized for grounding, retrieval, semantic interpretation, and explainable answers.

Primary value: trustworthy AI interaction.

Primary risk: failure if metadata, provenance, or access controls are weak.

Agent-Ready

Optimized for safe action and operational trust.

Primary value: controlled automation.

Primary risk: unsafe execution if policy and trust contracts are incomplete.

❖ FIGURE 3 – STAGES OF READINESS

ARCHITECTURAL IMPLICATIONS

The Architecture Must Serve Machine Interpretation, Not Just Human Access

Traditional data architectures were designed to centralize, integrate, transform, and present data to human users. AI-ready architectures must also serve machine interpretation. That means every major data asset should be evaluated not only for storage and quality, but also for discoverability, semantics, provenance, policy expression, and retrieval behavior.

A table with perfect referential integrity but no business definition is architecturally incomplete for AI. A document repository with accurate permissions but no content classification, chunking strategy, or source authority signals is architecturally incomplete for AI. A semantic layer that supports BI tools but is disconnected from enterprise content is architecturally incomplete for AI.

Unstructured Content Becomes First-Class

One of the clearest breaks from traditional readiness is the status of unstructured data. In many enterprises, unstructured content has been managed as a repository problem rather than a data architecture problem. Contracts live in one place. Policies in another. Meeting notes somewhere else. Knowledge articles, emails, transcripts, case summaries, engineering runbooks, and operating procedures are spread across collaboration platforms and file stores.

That was tolerable when analytics relied primarily on structured systems of record. It is not tolerable for AI. In many enterprise use cases, the meaning needed for trustworthy answers lives primarily in unstructured content. The architecture must, therefore, treat unstructured content as a governed enterprise asset with metadata, classification, provenance, freshness handling, and retrieval design.

Semi-Structured Data Becomes Strategically Important

Semi-structured data is often the connective tissue between systems of record and operational reality. Events, logs, messages, API payloads, and workflow traces capture sequence, timing, and state transitions that matter deeply to AI use cases. They often reveal what happened, in what order, and under which conditions.

Traditional readiness frequently downplayed these assets because they were noisy or difficult to model. AI-ready architecture cannot. A useful assistant often needs structured master data, unstructured policy meaning, and semi-structured event context at the same time.

Retrieval Becomes an Architectural Responsibility

Many organizations frame poor AI performance as a model problem. Often it is not. Retrieval quality is an architecture problem. It depends on how content is segmented, enriched, labeled, linked, secured, ranked, and refreshed. It depends on whether the system can distinguish authoritative policy from commentary, current guidance from archived material, and global standard from local exception.

If the retrieval design is weak, even a strong model will produce unreliable outcomes. If the retrieval design is strong, model variability becomes more manageable because the system is grounded in the right evidence.

Provenance Must Be Machine-Available

Executives and regulators increasingly expect AI outputs to be explainable. That cannot be solved by asking a model to "show its work." The architecture itself must make source evidence available. Provenance needs to be explicit, not implied. A trustworthy answer should be able to point to the governing policy, source transaction, reference table, document section, or event trace that supports it. It should also be able to indicate recency and confidence.

Different AI Consumers Need Different Serving Contracts

An executive briefing assistant, a service desk copilot, a finance exception analyzer, and a workflow agent do not require the same data contract. They differ in:

- Acceptable latency.
- Freshness expectations.
- Tolerance for ambiguity.
- Access rules.
- Source evidence requirements.
- Action permissions.
- Escalation thresholds.

This is why AI-readiness is not a single platform setting. It is an architectural discipline of defining fit-for-purpose serving contracts for different AI consumers.

❖ FIGURE 4 – TRADITIONAL DASHBOARD VS AI ASSISTANT INTERACTION

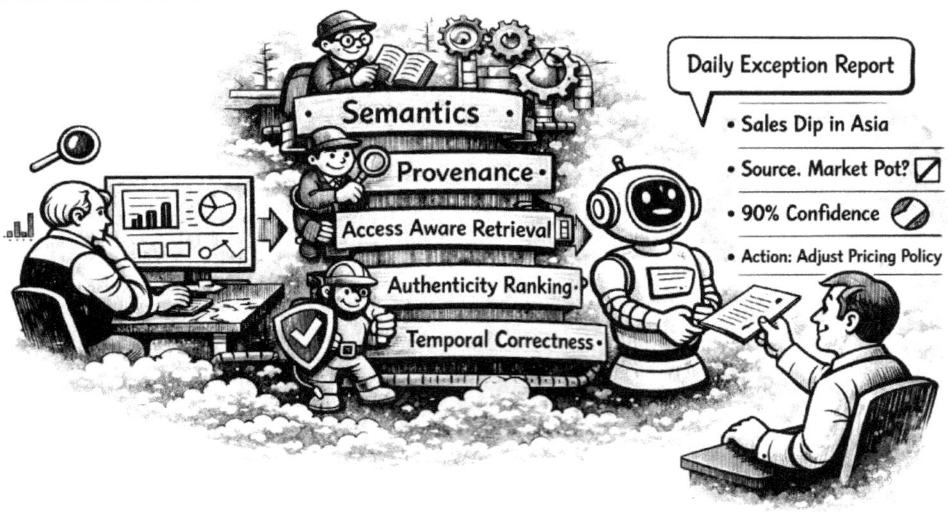

Failure Modes and Anti-Patterns

Mistaking BI Maturity for AI-readiness

This is one of the most common mistakes. An organization with polished dashboards, governed KPIs, and strong warehouse discipline assumes it is nearly AI-ready. Then the first enterprise assistant underperforms. Responses are vague. Citations are weak. Policy answers are inconsistent. Users lose trust.

The root problem is usually not poor data quality in the traditional sense. It is missing machine-usable context: unclear source authority, poor semantic alignment, disconnected unstructured content, weak lineage visibility, and inconsistent access-aware retrieval.

Treating Repositories as Knowledge Architecture

Many enterprises attempt to make content "AI-ready" by indexing whatever already exists in collaboration platforms and file shares. This usually creates a brittle retrieval layer over unmanaged sprawl. Duplicate documents compete with official versions. Outdated material surfaces beside the current policy. Local workarounds rank near enterprise standards. Permissions may be partially preserved while semantic signals remain absent.

The problem is not that the repository is bad. The problem is that the storage location is not the same as the governed knowledge architecture.

Key Insight

High BI maturity does not imply AI-readiness

If your best data assets depend on experienced analysts to interpret caveats, definitions, and exceptions, your architecture is still carrying knowledge in people rather than in machine-usable metadata and semantics.

Over-focusing on Model Selection

Another anti-pattern is to change models repeatedly while leaving retrieval and metadata weak. Organizations test one model, then another, then a larger one, then a more recent one. Some improvements appear, but trust remains inconsistent because the underlying architectural defects remain: poor content segmentation, missing source authority, inconsistent policy metadata, and no explicit freshness handling.

Ignoring Provenance Because Users "Just Want Answers"

This is a dangerous assumption. In enterprise settings, users often want fast answers, but what they actually need is defensible answers. When the answer affects a customer decision, compliance posture, audit trail, or executive judgment, provenance is not optional. If the architecture cannot expose why the answer should be trusted, adoption will stall or risk will accumulate silently.

Building One Readiness Standard for Every AI Use Case

Another failure mode is designing a single generic "AI-ready" layer and assuming every AI consumer can use it the same way. In reality, use cases vary sharply. A knowledge bot for HR policy can tolerate some ambiguity if it cites authoritative sources and routes edge cases to humans. A payment exception agent cannot. Architecture should, therefore, separate readiness by trust tier and action class. The enterprise needs a readiness taxonomy, not a slogan.

Practical Application

Assess Domains Against the Right Readiness Target

The first practical move is not to ask whether a domain is "AI-ready" in the abstract. Ask what kind of AI consumer it must support. Does the domain need to serve reporting, exploratory analytics, feature engineering, grounded question-answering, or operational action? The answer determines the next architectural step.

A procurement policy domain may need GenAI-ready retrieval and explanation but not agent-grade autonomy. A service recovery workflow may eventually require agent-ready controls. A finance close domain may need exceptionally strong provenance and temporal controls before any assistant is trusted.

Score What Traditional Assessments Missed

Traditional data readiness assessments emphasize quality, completeness, governance, and usage. Those remain important, but AI-readiness requires additional dimensions:

- Metadata maturity.
- Semantic context maturity.
- Trust and provenance visibility.
- Unstructured content readiness.
- Security and policy fidelity.
- Retrieval readiness.
- Agent safety.

These dimensions expose why otherwise mature domains still fail AI pilots.

Templates

Data Readiness Classification Worksheet

Domain name	<name of the business domain, process area, or operational capability being assessed>
Current primary consumer	<main user groups, teams, or roles that currently rely on this domain and its outputs>
Current architecture pattern	<existing data and information architecture used to support this domain, such as warehouse, lakehouse, BI layer, document repository, workflow platform, or event-stream design>
Current readiness level	<present state of readiness, such as report-ready, analytics-ready, ML-ready, GenAI-ready, or agent-ready>
Evidence for the current level	<specific reasons, observed capabilities, and current limitations that justify the readiness classification>

Data Readiness Scorecard

Metadata maturity score	?/5
Trust/provenance score	?/5
Semantic context score	?/5
Unstructured content readiness score	?/5
Security/policy score	?/5
Retrieval readiness score	?/5
Agent safety score	?/5

Case Example

From Twelve Dashboards to One Daily Briefing

Consider a regional operations manager responsible for order fulfillment, customer commitments, and service escalation. For years, she has begun every morning by opening twelve dashboards. One shows the order backlog by region. Another tracks late shipments. Another highlights returns. Others track credits, exception codes, customer complaints, service tickets, inventory shortages, and warehouse performance.

The dashboards are good. They are reconciled. Definitions are mostly stable. Her team trusts them.

But the process is inefficient. The manager spends the first hour of the day pulling together an operating narrative: Which exceptions matter most? Which customer commitments are at risk? Which cases are blocked by policy? Which late shipments are supply-related versus carrier-related? Which issues already have approved remediation paths?

A new initiative proposes replacing this routine with a daily AI exception briefing. Every morning, the manager would receive a concise summary:

- The top five issues requiring intervention.
- The customers most at risk of service failure.
- The likely causes based on recent events and case patterns.
- The governing policy or playbook for each class of exception.
- The recommended next review action.
- Direct links to supporting evidence.

At first glance, this seems like a presentation upgrade. It is not. It is a fundamentally different data requirement.

The dashboards only needed clean, structured data, stable dimensions, and governed metrics. The AI briefing needs those things plus a great deal more. It must integrate shipment events, case notes, customer communication summaries, inventory exception logs, return policies, service recovery rules, and current escalation playbooks. It must know which policy is authoritative for a given region. It must distinguish between a globally approved remediation path and a local workaround in an old slide deck. It must honor customer confidentiality and role-based access. It must indicate whether the recommendation is based on current guidance or a historical pattern. It must cite the evidence.

Without those capabilities, the assistant may still produce a fluent briefing, but it will not produce a trustworthy one.

What changed underneath

Several architectural changes are required to make the briefing real:

Structured data must be semantically anchored

Order, shipment, return, credit, and complaint data need explicit business definitions and relationship modeling. Terms like “at risk,” “committed date,” “premium customer,” and “avoidable return” must be machine-usable, not merely documented in a report catalog.

Unstructured content must be governed and linked

The relevant policy documents, escalation procedures, case-resolution playbooks, and service communications must be classified, authority-ranked, segmented for retrieval, and connected to the operational entities they govern.

Provenance must survive synthesis

When the assistant says a customer commitment is at risk because of a carrier delay combined with a stock transfer failure, it must be able to point to the shipment events, inventory signals, and policy rules behind that synthesis.

The serving contract must be explicit

The manager's assistant can recommend review priorities, but it cannot autonomously notify customers or alter commitments until the enterprise has defined stronger policy, approval, and action controls. That means the use case is GenAI-ready before it is agent-ready.

The lesson

The manager's old dashboard environment was not a failed architecture. It was a successful architecture for a different kind of consumer. The move to AI briefing exposed the hidden dependencies that dashboards could tolerate. This is exactly what enterprises should expect. AI-readiness is not a verdict on past investments. It is a recognition that the delivery contract has changed.

Closing Synthesis

Traditional data readiness remains necessary, but it is no longer sufficient. Reporting, analytics, and machine learning each created important maturity disciplines. None should be discarded. But none should be mistaken for AI-readiness.

AI changes the consumer from primarily human to increasingly machine-mediated. It changes the interaction model from fixed presentation to dynamic synthesis. It changes the risk surface from interpretive error to potentially confident and actionable misinterpretation. And it changes the architecture's obligations from exposing data to enabling trustworthy retrieval, semantic understanding, provenance, policy fidelity, and safe operational use.

This is why enterprises must stop asking whether their data is "good enough" in general and start asking what kind of readiness each domain must achieve for the AI consumer it is expected to serve. Report-ready, analytics-ready, ML-ready, GenAI-ready, and agent-ready are not interchangeable labels. They are distinct architectural states.

Once that distinction is understood, the path becomes clearer. The enterprise does not need to rebuild everything at once. It needs to classify domains honestly, identify the missing architectural layers, and raise readiness deliberately. In that work, metadata becomes the control plane, semantics become an operational necessity, unstructured content becomes first-class, retrieval becomes a design discipline, and governance becomes embedded rather than external.

That is the real shift. Traditional readiness prepared data for human consumption. AI-ready architecture prepares the enterprise data estate for trustworthy machine-mediated understanding and action.

Key Takeaways

- Data that is ready for reporting, analytics, or model training is not automatically ready for GenAI or agents.
- AI changes the data contract from human interpretation of fixed outputs to machine-mediated synthesis that must be grounded and explainable.
- Metadata, semantics, provenance, and retrieval design are central architectural requirements, not optional enhancements.
- High BI maturity can mask serious AI-readiness gaps, especially around unstructured content, authority ranking, and access-aware retrieval.
- The right question is not whether a domain is "AI-ready," but which readiness state it currently supports and what must change to reach the next one.

CHAPTER 3: WHAT AI-READY DATA ACTUALLY MEANS

Most enterprises still define data readiness using yesterday's standards. They ask whether data is clean enough for reporting, modeled enough for analytics, or labeled enough for machine learning. Those questions matter, but they are no longer sufficient. AI systems consume data differently. They do not simply query a dashboard, execute a predefined model, or read a curated metric. They discover, retrieve, combine, summarize, infer, recommend, and increasingly act. That changes the threshold for what "ready" means.

AI-Ready Data is not simply clean data. It is not merely governed data. It is not centralization for its own sake, nor is it a pile of documents stored in a collaboration platform and declared searchable. AI-Ready Data is data that can be securely discovered, interpreted, grounded, traced, and used by AI systems with enough context and control to produce trustworthy outcomes.

That definition has consequences. It means readiness is multidimensional. It means a table with perfect null handling can still be unusable for an assistant if no business definition explains what a field means. It means a policy document in a content repository may still be unfit for retrieval if it has no ownership, no effective date, no classification label, and no way to distinguish draft from approved guidance. It means a service ticket stream may be valuable to an operational copilot, but dangerous if permissions, retention obligations, and source reliability are unclear.

In other words, AI-readiness is not a cosmetic improvement to the data estate. It is an architectural condition and an operating discipline. It reflects whether the enterprise has designed its data, metadata, controls, and stewardship model for machine-mediated use, not just human interpretation.

KEY INSIGHT

Formal definition of AI-Ready Data

AI-Ready Data is data that can be securely discovered, semantically interpreted, contextually grounded, policy-governed, temporally validated, and evidentially traced for use by AI systems in ways that support trustworthy decisions, responses, and actions.

WHY THIS MATTERS

The urgency is not theoretical. Enterprises are already putting assistants, copilots, and agents in front of employees, customers, and decision-makers. These systems are expected to answer questions, summarize situations, explain issues, recommend actions, and, in some cases, initiate workflows. When they fail, the visible symptoms are familiar: bad answers, weak citations, conflicting summaries, outdated recommendations, unsafe actions, and eroding trust. The deeper cause is usually not the model. The deeper cause is that the underlying data estate does not carry enough meaning, evidence, or control to support trustworthy AI use.

Traditional readiness models were designed for human-led consumption. A report consumer tolerates a degree of implicit meaning because the dashboard is interpreted by someone who knows the business. An analyst can compensate for ambiguity through experience. A data scientist can perform feature engineering and domain interpretation by hand. An AI system has no such luxury. It consumes what the architecture makes legible. If the architecture supplies ambiguous fields, stale documents, missing lineage, broken permission inheritance, and unranked source authority, the system will produce outputs that merely sound plausible. This matters because AI compresses the distance between data and decision. In a dashboard era, poor semantics or weak metadata may slow analysis. In an AI era, they can become operational risk. A summarization assistant may collapse contradictory policy statements into a single confident answer. A sales copilot may present obsolete account guidance as a current fact. An action-taking agent may trigger a process based on content that was never approved for operational use. The speed and fluency of the interface can conceal the fragility of the underlying evidence.

The result is that data architecture now carries a new obligation. It must not only store and serve data. It must make data interpretable, governable, rankable, and defensible for machine-mediated retrieval and use.

KEY INSIGHT

Definitive Principle

Clean without context is still not AI-ready.

CORE CONCEPTS

AI-Readiness Is a Composite, Not a Binary State

Enterprises often ask whether a dataset is ready for AI as though readiness were a yes-or-no property. It is not. Readiness is composite. A source may be high on quality but low on semantics. It may be rich in business context but poor in permission fidelity. It may be current but impossible to trace. It may be authoritative but not structured for retrieval. These distinctions matter because AI use depends on the combination of readiness dimensions, not on any single one. A useful way to think about AI-Ready Data is as a set of interacting dimensions:

- **Trust.** The source has known authority, approved status where relevant, and a clear confidence profile.
- **Semantics.** Terms, entities, fields, and relationships have explicit meaning, not just technical names.
- **Discoverability.** AI systems can locate relevant data through metadata, indexing, and retrieval design.
- **Lineage.** The enterprise can trace where the data came from, how it changed, and what transformations affected it.
- **Policy.** Classification, access constraints, legal obligations, and intended-use restrictions are machine-enforceable or at least machine-aware.
- **Freshness.** Temporal correctness is visible. The system knows what is current, obsolete, superseded, or effective only for a given period.
- **Interoperability.** Data can be linked across systems, domains, and formats through identifiers, reference models, and shared semantics.
- **Grounding suitability.** The content can be chunked, enriched, ranked, cited, and retrieved in ways that support answer generation or action.
- **Business context.** The source reflects enterprise meaning, not just technical structure. It carries definitions, ownership, purpose, and relevance.
- **Quality.** The data is accurate enough, complete enough, consistent enough, and formatted well enough for the intended AI use.

❖ FIGURE 5 – AI-READY DIMENSIONS WHEEL

An enterprise does not need every source to score equally across all dimensions. It does need to know which dimensions are required for which AI consumers.

Quality Is Necessary, but Not Sufficient

This is the mistake that derails many AI programs. Teams assume that if data quality programs exist, then the data estate is ready. But data quality mostly addresses data as a record of transactions, measurements, or events. AI requires data to function as evidence, explanation, and context.

A customer master table may be complete and deduplicated, yet still be unsuitable for an assistant if "active customer," "household," or "primary relationship" mean different things in different business units. A policy PDF may be spellchecked and versioned, yet still be unsuitable if it lacks approval metadata, effective dates, and classification tags. A service ticket feed may be voluminous and timely, yet still be poor grounding material if issue categories are inconsistent and account identifiers cannot be resolved across systems.

The shift is subtle but important. For reporting, quality often means correctness of values. For AI, quality must be paired with interpretability, provenance, and use constraints.

AI-Readiness Differs by Data Class and Use Case

Not all data becomes AI-ready in the same way. Structured, semi-structured, and unstructured data each require different readiness interventions.

Structured data typically needs semantic enrichment, lineage, business definitions, and policy context layered onto tables and fields. Semi-structured data often needs normalization, schema handling, event semantics, entity extraction, and stronger temporal treatment. Unstructured data requires classification, chunking strategy, authorship and approval metadata, retrieval enrichment, and authority ranking.

Readiness also varies by consumer. A knowledge assistant answering policy questions needs authoritative text, access-aware retrieval, citations, and effective-date handling. An analyst copilot needs semantic mappings to metrics, dimensions, and business logic. An executive briefing tool needs synthesis across trusted sources with recency weighting and contradiction handling. An action-taking agent needs the highest threshold of permissions, policy checks, transaction boundaries, and evidence standards.

There is no single AI-ready state detached from purpose. There are readiness profiles aligned to data classes and serving contracts.

KEY INSIGHT

What AI-Ready Data Is Not

AI-Ready Data is not:

- Merely centralized data.
- Merely clean data.
- Merely cataloged data.
- Merely searchable content.
- Merely labeled training data.
- Merely documents stored in enterprise repositories.
- Merely governed in policy documents without technical enforcement.

None of these alone is enough.

AI-Ready Data Is Both an Architectural Condition and an Operating Discipline

Architecture creates the conditions for AI use. Operating discipline keeps those conditions trustworthy over time.

The architectural side includes metadata design, canonical identifiers, taxonomies, lineage capture, retrieval indexing, chunking strategies, source ranking, access-aware delivery, and evidence structures. The operating side includes stewardship, ownership, review cycles, approval processes, exception handling, quality controls, policy updates, and accountability for misuse or drift.

If either side is absent, readiness fails. A beautifully modeled metadata layer without stewardship decays. A strong governance committee without technical enforcement becomes advisory theater. Durable readiness requires both design and discipline.

Maturity Models Matter Because Transformation Must Be Sequenced

Enterprises rarely move from fragmented data estates to trustworthy AI-serving platforms in one step. A maturity model helps sequence the transformation. It creates a language for prioritization and investment.

A basic maturity path might progress from report-ready to analytics-ready to ML-ready to GenAI-ready to agent-ready. The jump between those stages is not cosmetic. Each step raises the requirement for semantic explicitness, provenance, policy fidelity, and operational trust.

AI-readiness, therefore, should be managed as a maturity journey, not declared through aspiration.

ARCHITECTURAL IMPLICATIONS

Metadata Becomes the Control Plane

If AI systems must discover, rank, explain, and safely use enterprise data, metadata cannot remain an afterthought. It becomes the control plane. Metadata tells the system what a source is, who owns it, how current it is, whether it is authoritative, what policies apply, how it relates to other sources, and whether it is suitable for specific forms of use.

This expands the role of metadata beyond cataloging. It becomes operational. It influences retrieval, ranking, confidence, citation, access enforcement, and auditability. In many cases, it determines whether two apparently similar sources should be treated as equivalent, conflicting, or differently authoritative.

Without robust metadata, AI systems are left to infer structure and trust from content alone. That is a brittle strategy for enterprise use.

The Architecture Must Serve Both Retrieval and Reasoning

A traditional data architecture focuses on integration, storage, reporting, and analytics performance. An AI-ready architecture adds another responsibility: it must serve retrieval and reasoning.

That means data and content must be prepared not only for storage and query, but for decomposition, enrichment, ranking, contextualization, and evidential use. Documents need chunking strategies aligned to meaning. Structured data needs business definitions and entity resolution. Source systems need freshness markers and lineage capture. Content repositories need approval states and ownership surfaced as retrievable metadata. Access control must survive the retrieval path, not disappear during indexing.

A high-level capability stack typically includes source systems, integration and ingestion, metadata and semantics, governance and policy services, retrieval and indexing services, trust and evidence services, and finally AI-serving interfaces. The point is not the layers themselves. The point is that AI-serving depends on the interaction between them.

Unstructured Content Must Be Treated as Enterprise-Grade Data

Many of the answers AI systems are asked to produce cannot be derived from tables alone. They depend on policies, procedures, knowledge articles, contracts, meeting notes, case histories, and communications. Yet most enterprises still manage these assets as content, not as data.

That distinction becomes untenable. If unstructured content carries business meaning that AI relies on, then it must be governed, classified, versioned, linked, and ranked with the same seriousness as structured assets. It needs owners. It needs lifecycle rules. It needs effective dating. It needs retrieval enrichment. It needs to be integrated into the enterprise trust model.

AI-ready architecture, therefore, collapses the artificial separation between "data platforms" and "content repositories." Both become part of the same governed evidence plane.

❖ FIGURE 6 – CAPABILITY STACK

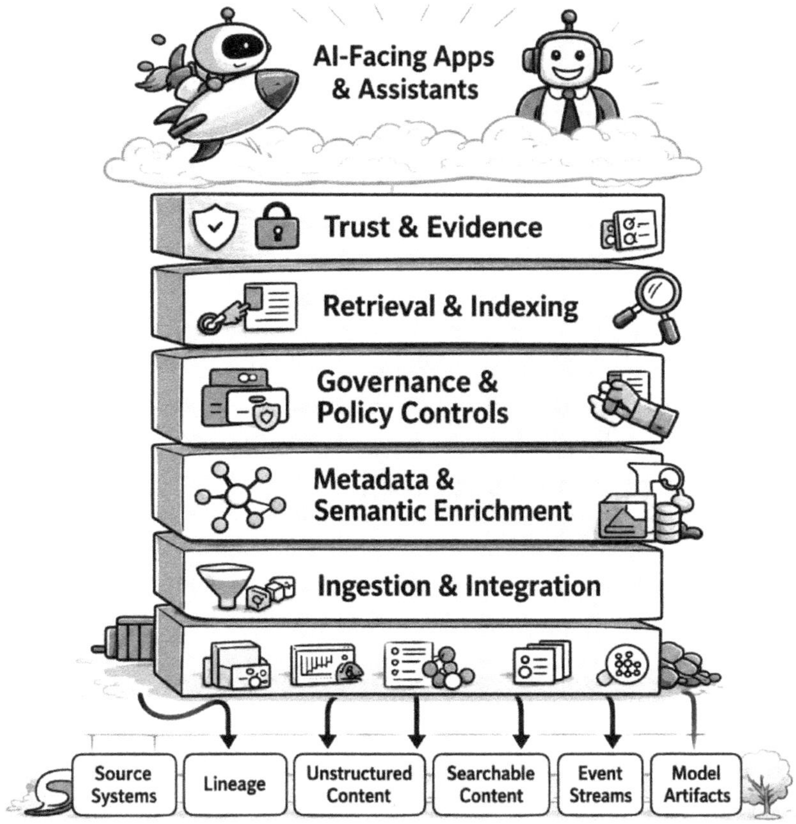

Different AI Consumers Require Different Serving Contracts

An assistant who explains policy does not need the same contract as an agent who updates a case or authorizes a transaction. The former may tolerate limited ambiguity if citations are clear and confidence is visible. The latter requires explicit authorization, stronger provenance, deterministic control checks, and often human review points.

Architecturally, this means the enterprise should not define readiness once and apply it uniformly. It should define serving contracts by consumer type. Each contract specifies what evidence, freshness, authority, permissions, explainability, and action controls are required.

This is how AI-readiness becomes practical rather than abstract. It is translated into minimum conditions for safe use.

FAILURE MODES AND ANTI-PATTERNS

Mistaking Repository Presence for Readiness

One of the most common failures is assuming that because content exists in SharePoint, a file store, or a knowledge platform, it is ready for AI retrieval. It is not. Presence is not preparedness. Repositories frequently contain duplicates, drafts, conflicting versions, stale materials, incomplete permissions, and missing ownership.

If those conditions are invisible to the retrieval architecture, the AI system will surface noise with confidence.

Treating Search as Governance

Another failure is believing that enterprise search plus a large language model constitutes readiness. Search can locate text. It does not establish authority, semantics, temporal validity, intended use, or evidential sufficiency. Without those controls, search merely broadens exposure to ambiguous content.

Assuming Structured Data Speaks for Itself

Tables do not explain themselves. Field names, codes, and reference values are often intelligible only to people close to the source system. When AI systems retrieve or summarize structured data without business definitions, relationship context, or lineage, they amplify hidden ambiguity.

Ignoring Temporal Correctness

A source may be accurate and still be wrong for the moment. Policies change. Entitlements change. Product terms change. Organizational roles change. AI systems that do not distinguish effective from obsolete content are not trustworthy, no matter how elegant their answers sound.

Bolting Governance on After Deployment

When governance is introduced after AI experiences are already live, the enterprise is forced into reactive patching. Sensitive content must be retroactively removed. Citations must be redesigned. Permissions must be reconciled. Exceptions multiply. Trust drops. Governance works best when embedded in architecture from the beginning.

Practical Application

Start with an Enterprise Definition

An organization should write down its own formal definition of AI-Ready Data. Not a slogan, but a working definition tied to consumers, data classes, risks, and minimum evidence requirements. This creates a shared standard across architecture, data management, security, legal, and business teams.

Define Readiness by Consumer and Data Class

Rather than declaring broad readiness, define the scope. Which AI consumers are in scope? Which data classes matter first? What level of trust is required? What evidence must be present in answers? What uses are explicitly excluded?

This moves the discussion from aspiration to design.

Assess Current Assets Against Dimensions

For each high-value source, assess the dimensions that matter most: semantics, authority, lineage, policy, freshness, discoverability, and grounding suitability. The goal is not to generate a theoretical scorecard. The goal is to expose what blocks trustworthy use.

A customer table might need definition harmonization and master identifiers. A policy corpus might need approval metadata, version cleanup, and effective-date handling. A ticket stream might need entity extraction, classification normalization, and sensitivity controls.

Build the Minimum Evidence Standard

Every AI-serving pattern should define what constitutes sufficient evidence. For some use cases, a single authoritative source may be enough. For others, multiple corroborating sources may be required. For action-taking systems, evidence thresholds should be especially high and explicit.

Introduce a Readiness Maturity Model

A maturity model helps sequence work and avoid grand but vague programs. It lets the enterprise say, with precision, that a domain is analytics-ready but not yet GenAI-ready, or that it is GenAI-ready for summarization but not agent-ready for autonomous action.

TEMPLATES

AI-Ready Data Definition Canvas

Organization definition of AI-Ready Data	<the organization's formal definition of what makes data and content fit for approved AI use cases>
In-scope AI consumers	<types of AI systems, assistants, copilots, tools, or agents that are intended to rely on this definition>
In-scope data classes	<categories of data and content covered by the definition, such as structured, semi-structured, and unstructured sources>
Required trust characteristics	<trust-related capabilities required for AI use, such as authority identification, ranking, duplication handling, approval visibility, contradiction handling, and confidence signaling>
Required semantic/context characteristics	<semantic and contextual capabilities required for interpretation, such as glossary alignment, entity resolution, taxonomy support, relationship modeling, and domain meaning>
Required governance characteristics	<governance controls required for AI use, such as classification, retention, privacy, policy inheritance, intended-use constraints, stewardship, and ownership>
Required security characteristics	<security capabilities required to ensure access-aware retrieval, permission fidelity, masking or exclusion of restricted content, and auditable use>
Required freshness characteristics	<temporal and currency requirements needed for AI use, such as effective dates, review dates, recency metadata, supersession handling, and refresh expectations>
Required explainability characteristics	<explainability and evidence requirements, such as citations, lineage, rationale traceability, timestamps, and disclosure of confidence or ambiguity>
Minimum evidence standard	<minimum threshold of evidence, corroboration, policy checking, and control required before answers, recommendations, or actions are allowed>
Excluded uses	<uses that are explicitly prohibited because they are unsafe, weakly governed, insufficiently evidenced, or not approved>
Readiness maturity model adopted	<readiness framework or maturity stages used by the organization to classify current and target states>

Sponsoring executive	<senior executive accountable for sponsorship, direction, and enterprise backing of the definition or program>
Architecture owner	<role or function accountable for designing and maintaining the supporting enterprise architecture>
Review date	<cadence or trigger for formal review and update of the definition, such as quarterly or upon major regulatory, architectural, or operating-model change>

Case Example

What AI-Ready Looks Like Across Different Data Domains

Consider three domains: a customer master, a policy document library, and a service ticket corpus. Each is valuable to AI. Each becomes ready through different means.

Customer master

At first glance, the customer master appears to be the strongest candidate. It is structured, governed, and central. Yet for AI use, its weaknesses emerge quickly. Customer identifiers differ across channels. "Customer" may mean individual, household, subsidiary, or billing account, depending on the process. Relationship hierarchies may be incomplete. Ownership of definitions may be fragmented between sales, service, finance, and risk.

For an analyst copilot, the customer master becomes AI-ready only when business definitions are explicit, identifiers are reconciled, hierarchies are governed, lineage is visible, and sensitive attributes are policy-tagged. Raw structure is not enough.

Policy documents

The policy library looks less disciplined. It consists of PDFs, knowledge pages, and procedural documents spread across repositories. Yet for a knowledge assistant, this may be the most important domain because it contains the business meaning that employees actually need.

Its readiness challenge is different. The enterprise must identify authoritative versions, distinguish draft from approved content, capture effective dates, classify sensitivity, map topics to business taxonomies, and implement chunking and retrieval patterns that preserve context. It must also design how citations appear so that an answer can be checked against source evidence.

For a policy assistant, document governance and retrieval architecture matter more than the existence of the files themselves.

Service tickets

The service ticket corpus is dynamic, messy, and often under-governed. It contains real operational signals: recurring problems, outage narratives, workaround language, resolution notes, and customer impact patterns. It is strategically valuable for AI, especially for service copilots and operational briefings.

But its readiness issues are acute. Language is inconsistent. Sensitive data may be embedded in free text. Issue categories drift. Resolution quality varies by team. Temporal relevance decays quickly. Entity links to products, customers, and incidents may be weak.

For a service assistant, AI-readiness requires normalization, classification controls, entity extraction, retention policy alignment, access-aware retrieval, and strong recency handling. Without those, the system will confidently summarize noise.

What the comparison shows

These three domains prove the central point of this chapter: readiness is multidimensional and context-specific. The customer master needs semantic clarity and identifier discipline. The policy library needs authority and evidence design. The ticket corpus needs normalization, recency control, and sensitivity governance. None becomes AI-ready through generic "data quality" work alone.

Closing Synthesis

AI-Ready Data is a higher standard than most enterprises have historically designed for. It is not a synonym for clean data, governed data, centralized data, or cataloged data. It is data and content that can be securely discovered, semantically interpreted, contextually grounded, evidentially traced, and used within clear policy boundaries by AI systems.

That makes AI-readiness both architectural and operational. Architecture provides the metadata, semantics, retrieval design, policy integration, lineage, and evidence structures that make trustworthy AI possible. Operating discipline keeps those structures valid through ownership, stewardship, review, and accountability.

The practical implication is clear. Enterprises should stop asking whether they "have data for AI" and start asking whether their data estate can support trustworthy AI use repeatedly and at scale. Those are not the same question. One is about possession. The other is about design.

The organizations that succeed will be the ones that define readiness precisely, differentiate it by data class and AI consumer, and treat metadata, governance, and retrieval quality as foundational architecture. The rest will continue mistaking available content for reliable evidence and fluent output for trustworthy intelligence.

Key Takeaways

- AI-Ready Data is not just clean data; it is data that can be discovered, interpreted, governed, grounded, and traced for trustworthy AI use.
- Readiness is multidimensional, combining quality with semantics, policy, lineage, freshness, authority, and business context.
- Different data classes and AI consumers require different readiness interventions and serving contracts.
- Metadata is the control plane that makes AI retrieval, ranking, explainability, and policy enforcement possible.
- AI-readiness is both an architectural state and an operating discipline that must be designed, governed, and sustained over time.

Chapter 4: Traditional Data Structures: What They Were Built For

Enterprise data architecture did not emerge by accident. Every major data structure in the modern enterprise was created to solve a specific class of problem under a specific set of constraints. Transaction systems were built to record business activity correctly and quickly. Warehouses were built to standardize reporting and analytical consistency. Lakes were built to absorb growing data variety and volume without requiring immediate modeling discipline. File repositories were built to store, share, and collaborate on documents. Each of these structures can be valuable. None of them, by design, were built to support AI-driven interpretation across mixed data classes.

That distinction matters. AI does not consume data the way a transaction processor, dashboard, or batch analytics pipeline does. An AI system must discover relevant information, interpret meaning across formats, reconcile conflicting evidence, respect permissions, rank sources by authority, and explain where an answer came from. Those requirements expose assumptions that traditional structures were never designed to handle.

The mistake many organizations make is not in having these traditional structures. The mistake is assuming that because those structures served prior generations of enterprise consumption well, they are automatically sufficient for AI. They are not. The question is no longer whether an OLTP database, warehouse, lake, or document repository is "good." The question is what each structure was optimized for, what it leaves unresolved, and what architectural work is now required to make it usable for trustworthy AI.

Why This Matters

AI Changes the Consumption Contract

Traditional enterprise data structures were shaped by human and application consumers with relatively stable access patterns. Applications needed row-level correctness, predictable latency, and strict transactional behavior. Analysts needed consistent dimensions, reconciled facts, and repeatable metrics. Knowledge workers needed document storage, search, and collaboration. Those use cases did not require a system to synthesize meaning across tables, policies, transcripts, tickets, contracts, and event streams in real time.

AI does.

A reporting stack can succeed even when business meaning is distributed across undocumented SQL logic, tribal knowledge, wiki pages, and email attachments. A monthly board pack may still be accurate enough. An AI assistant, however, cannot safely operate in that environment. It will retrieve the wrong artifact, miss the governing policy, fail to interpret a coded field correctly, or answer confidently from stale content.

Legacy Success Can Hide AI Weakness

This is why many organizations are surprised when their "mature" data estate performs poorly in AI pilots. The estate may already support financial reporting, KPI dashboards, regulatory extracts, and machine learning features. But those successes prove only that the estate is fit for its original workloads. They do not prove readiness for grounded retrieval, semantic interpretation, or governed action.

A warehouse can be excellent for month-end reporting and still be poor for answering, "What is our current travel exception policy for vice presidents visiting customer sites?" A file repository can be excellent for collaboration and still be poor for answering, "Which of these three policy versions is authoritative today?" A data lake can be excellent for retention and exploratory analysis, and still be poor for an agent that must make a policy-aware decision with evidence.

Design Intent Does Not Disappear

The central architectural lesson is simple: design intent persists. Systems continue to behave according to what they were optimized for. If you do not account for that, AI will inherit the blind spots of your existing structures at enterprise scale.

KEY INSIGHT

Design intent matters

Every data structure carries an optimization bias. Performance, consistency, flexibility, interoperability, and collaboration are all legitimate design goals. Problems begin when architects mistake prior fitness for universal fitness. AI exposes design intent with unusual brutality because it relies on context, semantics, provenance, and governed retrieval that earlier workloads could often ignore.

CORE CONCEPTS

OLTP Structures: Built for Transactional Correctness

Online transaction processing systems exist to record business events correctly, enforce application rules, and support high-volume operational throughput. Their strength is precision at the point of capture.

Orders, claims, bookings, payments, inventory movements, and case updates are all well served by normalized application schemas, indexes, constraints, and transactional semantics.

But OLTP structures are not modeled for broad interpretation. Their schemas reflect application logic, not enterprise meaning. Field names may be cryptic. Reference data may be encoded. Important business definitions may live outside the database entirely. Cross-domain relationships are often fragmented across systems. Even when the data is accurate, it is rarely self-explanatory.

For AI, that creates a predictable problem. The system can retrieve rows but not reliably understand what those rows mean in business terms unless metadata, semantic definitions, lineage, and policy context are attached.

Star Schemas: Built for Repeatable Analytical Consumption

The enterprise warehouse and its dimensional models were designed for a different purpose: stable, governed analysis. Facts and dimensions reduce ambiguity for recurring analytical use. Time series, hierarchies, conformed dimensions, and agreed metric definitions make star schemas exceptionally effective for dashboards, standard reports, and ad hoc business analysis within known analytical boundaries.

This is one of the most successful design patterns in enterprise data architecture. It remains indispensable.

But dimensional models also encode assumptions. They prioritize analytical questions that the enterprise already knows how to ask. They pre-shape the world into curated views. That is a feature for reporting and a limitation for open-ended AI inquiry. Many AI questions do not map neatly to existing facts and dimensions, especially when answers require policy documents, operational notes, exceptions, approvals, or the latest unstructured context.

A star schema can tell you the number of expense claims rejected last quarter. It often cannot tell you which version of the expense policy was in force for a specific employee class, what exception was granted by Finance, and whether that exception is still valid today.

Lakes: Built for Accumulation and Flexibility

The lake emerged as a response to rigidity and cost. It promised scalable storage, schema flexibility, and a place to accumulate raw and semi-curated data for future use. Those are real benefits. Lakes allow organizations to preserve source fidelity, ingest diverse formats, and support exploratory use without the immediate burden of full enterprise modeling.

The tradeoff is clarity.

Lakes often defer meaning. Schemas may be implied, inconsistent, or unstable. Naming conventions drift. Data quality varies by zone and producer. Lineage is partial. Business ownership is often weak. The same business entity may appear many times in different forms. Lakes are highly accommodating to data producers but often unforgiving to downstream consumers who need confidence, especially AI consumers.

This is why many lakes become excellent storage environments and mediocre interpretation environments. They accumulate data faster than they accumulate meaning.

KEY INSIGHT

Myth: "A data lake makes us AI-ready."

A lake makes it easier to collect data. It does not make that data discoverable, semantically interpretable, policy-aware, fresh, authoritative, or safe for grounded AI use. Without metadata, enrichment, ranking, and governance, a lake is more likely to expand retrieval ambiguity than resolve it.

File Repositories: Built for Storage and Collaboration

Enterprise content platforms, file shares, email systems, chat platforms, and collaboration tools hold a large portion of the business meaning AI needs most. Policies, contracts, meeting notes, architecture decisions, SOPs, ticket histories, and approval trails are often unstructured or semi-structured. This content is critical.

Yet repositories were not designed for machine grounding. They were designed for people to store, share, review, and collaborate. Folder structures substitute for weak metadata. Versioning is inconsistent. Authority is often implicit. Access control may exist, but classification, canonicality, and semantic extraction are uneven. Search may find a document, but not determine whether it is current, authoritative, or superseded.

For a human employee, those gaps are often manageable because the employee supplies context from experience. For AI, the absence of that context is dangerous.

AI Workloads Expose Embedded Assumptions

The common thread across all these structures is that they contain hidden assumptions about consumer type, query form, trust model, and interpretation burden. Earlier architectures assumed that applications would know the schema, analysts would understand curated metrics, and humans would infer meaning from documents. AI breaks that pattern. It is neither a fixed application nor a fully informed human. It is a probabilistic consumer that requires explicit context to operate safely.

That is why AI-readiness cannot be judged by data quality alone. A clean table with no business definitions is not AI-ready. A well-governed warehouse with no link to policies and source evidence is not fully AI-ready. A large document repository with weak authority signals is not AI-ready. Readiness depends on whether the architecture can support interpretation, retrieval, provenance, freshness, and governed use.

ARCHITECTURAL IMPLICATIONS

The Architecture Must Separate Storage from Serving

One of the most important shifts for AI-Ready Data is recognizing that storage architecture and serving architecture are no longer the same thing. Traditional structures remain valuable as systems of capture, record, analysis, and collaboration. But AI consumption requires an additional serving layer that resolves semantics, policy, freshness, authority, and evidence across those structures.

This means architects should stop asking which single platform will make the enterprise AI-ready. The more useful question is how to build an AI-serving architecture that can safely and coherently draw from existing stores.

That serving architecture typically requires:

- Metadata as a control plane for discoverability, trust, ranking, lineage, and policy enforcement.
- Semantic enrichment for business definitions, entity resolution, and relationship context.
- Content processing for unstructured and semi-structured assets.
- Access-aware retrieval and delivery.
- Source authority logic and temporal validity handling.
- Citation and provenance services for explainability.
- Differentiated serving contracts for assistants, copilots, and agents.

Every Structure Now Needs Compensating Controls

The practical implication is not to discard traditional structures, but to wrap them intelligently.

An OLTP source may need business glossaries, API-aware semantic mapping, and event capture to become usable for assistants or agents. A warehouse may need linkage to policy content, lineage back to operational sources, and freshness transparency. A lake may need aggressive metadata curation, product ownership, and authority ranking. A file repository may need classification, canonical source designation, chunking strategy, citation policy, and access-aware retrieval. In AI architecture, compensating controls are not optional refinements. They are what convert "stored data" into "usable evidence."

Consumer-Specific Data Contracts Become Essential

A knowledge assistant that answers policy questions, an analyst copilot that explains KPI movements, and an agent that initiates remediation actions do not need the same thing.

The knowledge assistant needs authoritative content, source citations, version awareness, and permission-safe retrieval.

The analyst copilot needs reconciled metrics, dimensional context, lineage to source facts, and business definitions.

The agent needs deterministic policy boundaries, event context, freshness guarantees, explicit confidence thresholds, and reversible action logging.

Traditional structures rarely expose those contracts directly. Architecture must now create them.

❖ FIGURE 7 – HISTORICAL ARCHITECTURE EVOLUTION

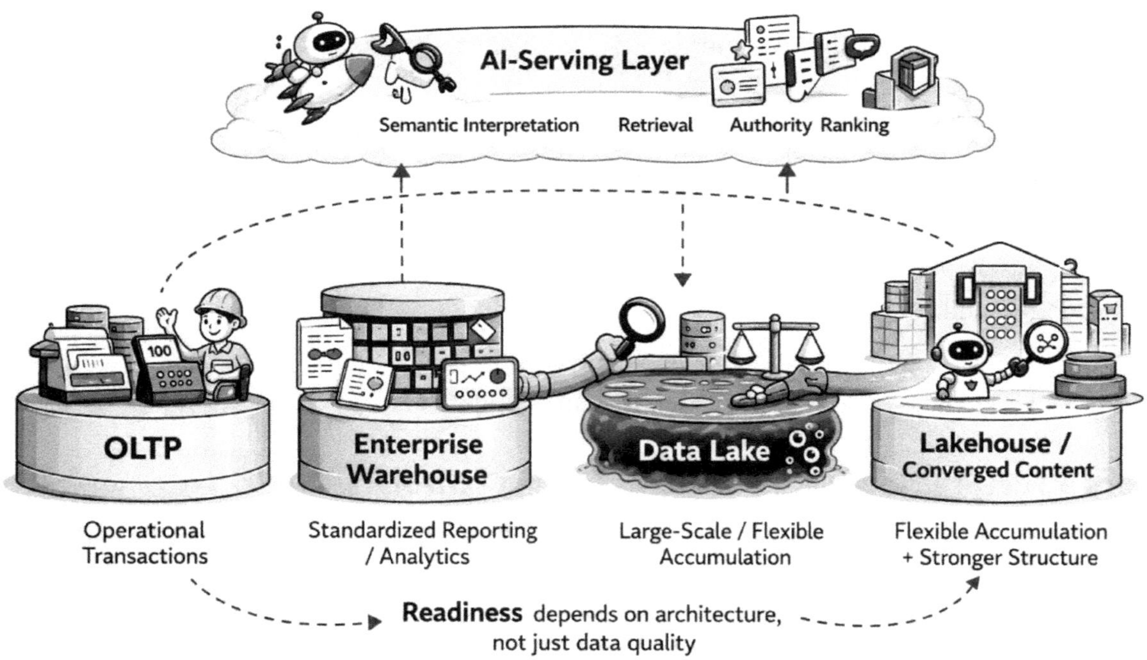

Failure Modes and Anti-Patterns

Treating Existing Repositories as AI-ready by Default

A common anti-pattern is assuming that because data already exists in enterprise platforms, it is ready for retrieval and grounding. This produces the familiar failure pattern: an assistant retrieves a plausible document, answers fluently, and cites a source that is outdated, local, or non-authoritative. The root problem is not the model. The root problem is that the repository was never architected to express canonicality, policy status, business scope, or temporal validity in a machine-usable way.

Assuming Structured Data Alone Is Sufficient

Another failure mode is over-indexing on structured assets because they feel more governable. Structured data is vital, but it does not contain all enterprise meaning. Exceptions, policies, approvals, legal language, procedural nuance, and decision rationale are often outside the warehouse. Architectures that ignore unstructured content will produce assistants that are numerically informed but operationally naïve.

Mistaking Data Accumulation for Enterprise Understanding

Lakes often create this illusion. The enterprise feels prepared because "all the data is there." But stored rawness is not operational understanding. Without enrichment, ownership, and serving discipline, a lake can increase ambiguity, duplicate evidence, and surface contradictory records that AI cannot adjudicate safely.

Preserving Hidden Logic and Tribal Knowledge

Some of the most serious AI failures occur when critical meaning lives in undocumented SQL transformations, analyst conventions, spreadsheet workarounds, or institutional memory. Human teams compensate for these gaps through experience. AI systems cannot. If the meaning required for trustworthy interpretation is implicit, the architecture is fragile.

Key Insight

Why yesterday's best practice can become today's bottleneck

Normalization, dimensional modeling, raw landing zones, and document collaboration were all rational responses to the needs of their time. The bottleneck appears when those patterns are treated as complete rather than context-specific. AI does not invalidate them. It reveals what they omit.

Ignoring Authority and Freshness

AI is especially sensitive to stale or conflicting content because it synthesizes across sources. If multiple policy versions, multiple metric definitions, or multiple operational states coexist without explicit authority and freshness signals, the system will often answer with a smooth blend of incompatible truths.

That is unacceptable in enterprise settings.

Practical Application

Start with a Structure-By-Structure Assessment

A useful first step is to assess each major data structure in the estate against the workload it was built for and the AI workloads now being introduced. This reframes the conversation from ideology to design fit.

Ask for each structure:

- What was its primary design purpose?
- What type of consumer was assumed?
- What interpretation burden was pushed onto the user?
- What metadata exists today?
- What authority, freshness, and lineage signals are missing?
- What governance controls are explicit versus implied?
- What compensating controls are needed for AI use?

This assessment is not a scorecard for declaring winners and losers. It is a decision aid. Most enterprises should keep their core structures. The real work is deciding where to modernize, where to wrap with control services, and where to replace brittle patterns that cannot safely support AI.

In practice:

- Keep OLTP systems as systems of record, but do not expose them to AI without semantic and governance mediation.
- Keep warehouses as systems of analytical trust, but connect them to evidence, definitions, and policy context.
- Modernize lakes with ownership, metadata, and canonicality, or accept that they will remain low-trust inputs.
- Wrap file repositories with content intelligence and authority logic before using them for enterprise Q&A.
- Replace unmanaged shadow structures when they become material to AI-supported decisions.

❖ FIGURE 8 – OPTIMIZATION TARGET MATRIX

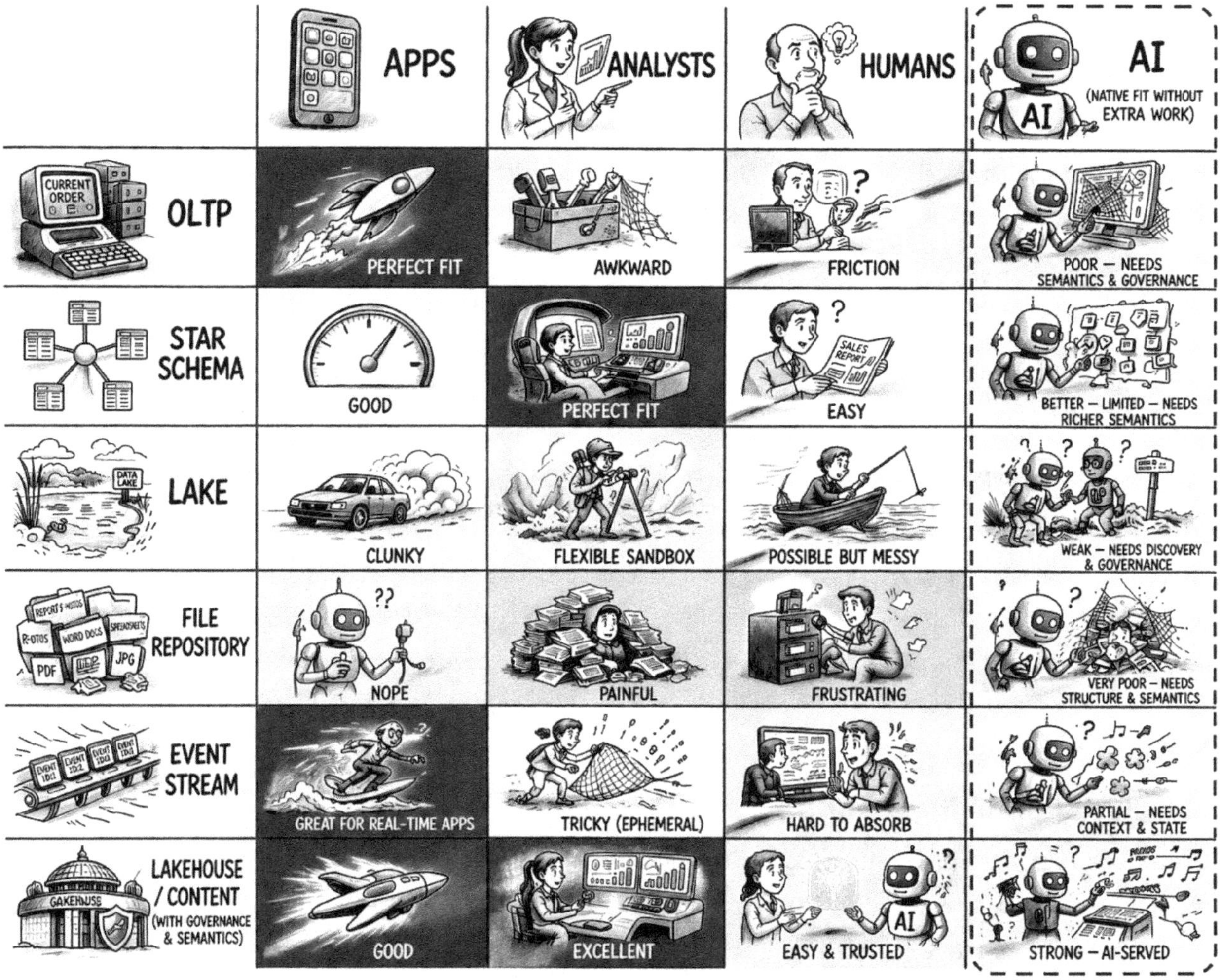

TEMPLATES

Traditional Data Structure Suitability Assessment

Structure or platform type	<name of the data structure, platform, or architectural pattern being assessed>
Primary design purpose	<main reason this structure was originally built, such as transaction processing, analytics, storage flexibility, collaboration, or event capture>
Typical strengths	<core strengths of this structure in practice, such as speed, control, historical analysis, flexibility, freshness, or business proximity>

Typical blind spots	<common weaknesses, limitations, or AI-relevant gaps, such as weak semantics, poor lineage, inconsistent metadata, hidden logic, or weak authority signals>
AI suitability	<assessment of how suitable this structure is for different AI use cases, such as question-answering, analytics copilots, and agents>
Metadata dependency level	<degree to which strong metadata is required to make this structure usable and safe for AI>
Governance risk level	<level of governance, compliance, security, or operational risk associated with using this structure for AI>
Semantic enrichment need	<degree of additional semantic modeling, glossary alignment, entity resolution, or contextual enrichment required>
Recommended compensating controls	<controls, overlays, and supporting capabilities needed to make this structure more trustworthy and usable for AI>
Recommended decision	<recommended strategic treatment of this structure, such as keep and wrap, keep and modernize, modernize aggressively, or replace where critical>

Case Example

Excellent Reporting, Poor Policy Assistance

Consider a large enterprise with a mature finance warehouse. The warehouse produces accurate monthly reporting for travel, entertainment, procurement, and cost-center performance. It has conformed dimensions for employee, department, time, expense category, and geography. Leadership trusts the dashboards because numbers reconcile, definitions are stable, and period-close processes are disciplined.

On paper, this looks like a strong foundation for an internal AI assistant.

The company then launches a policy Q&A assistant for employees and managers. One of the first questions is straightforward: "Can a regional vice president approve business-class travel for a customer escalation if the trip is booked within 24 hours?"

The assistant performs poorly.

Why it fails

The warehouse contains expense claim facts, approval hierarchies, employee attributes, and historical travel spend. It does not contain the full travel policy language in machine-groundable form. It does not capture the authoritative distinction between standard policy, emergency exception, and executive override. It does not expose whether the current policy changed two weeks ago. It does not identify which document version superseded the old one. It does not link policy clauses to the expense workflows where they are applied. It cannot distinguish a local practice note from the official global policy.

So the assistant responds with fragments. It may infer from historical approvals that exceptions are common. It may retrieve an outdated policy PDF from a file share. It may cite a manager's memo that was never authoritative. It may answer in a way that sounds sensible but is not defensible.

The architectural lesson

Nothing is "wrong" with the warehouse. It is doing what it was built to do: produce trusted analytical views of expense activity. The failure occurs because the organization mistook analytical readiness for policy-grounding readiness.

To fix the issue, the enterprise must supplement the warehouse with:

- Authoritative policy content with explicit status and effective dates.
- Metadata marking canonical documents and superseded versions.
- Semantic links between policy clauses, employee classes, approval roles, and expense categories.
- Access-aware retrieval from the content platform.
- Citations tied to current source language.
- Freshness controls to prevent the use of retired guidance.

Only then can the assistant answer in a way that is both useful and defensible.

This example is common across domains. A warehouse can explain what happened. It often cannot, by itself, explain what should happen according to current policy, legal language, operating guidance, or contractual obligation.

Closing Synthesis

Traditional data structures remain essential because the enterprise still needs transactions processed, reports reconciled, data stored, and documents shared. AI does not erase those needs. But AI does force a more disciplined understanding of what each structure was actually built for.

OLTP systems were built for correctness and operational speed. Warehouses were built for analytical consistency. Lakes were built for scalable accumulation and flexibility. File repositories were built for human storage and collaboration. None of these purposes is obsolete. But none of them, on their own, satisfy the demands of enterprise AI for semantic interpretation, grounded retrieval, provenance, authority, freshness, and policy-aware use.

That is why the path to AI-Ready Data is architectural, not rhetorical. Organizations do not become AI-ready by declaring a lakehouse strategy, indexing a file share, or pointing a model at a warehouse. They become AI-ready when they understand the design bias of their existing structures, preserve their strengths, and add the control layers, semantic enrichment, and governance mechanisms required for trustworthy AI serving.

The mature architectural posture is, therefore, neither nostalgia nor replacement frenzy. It is precision. Keep what works for its intended purpose. Modernize what can be elevated. Wrap what must be mediated. Replace what is fundamentally unsafe or opaque. Above all, stop asking traditional structures to do jobs they were never designed to do.

Key Takeaways

- Traditional enterprise data structures were designed for specific workloads, not for AI-driven interpretation across mixed data classes.
- OLTP, warehouses, lakes, and repositories remain valuable, but each carries design biases that AI exposes.
- AI-readiness requires compensating controls: metadata, semantics, lineage, authority, freshness, and governance.
- Storage architecture and AI-serving architecture are no longer the same thing.
- The right modernization strategy is usually not to replace everything, but to keep, modernize, wrap, or selectively replace based on design intent.

Chapter 5: Structured Data in the Age of AI

Structured data remains the backbone of enterprise truth. That statement is still true in the age of copilots, assistants, and agents. Core facts about customers, orders, payments, claims, products, inventory, employees, and financial results still live primarily in structured systems: ERP platforms, CRM systems, warehouse applications, industry platforms, operational databases, and curated analytical stores. When an enterprise needs to know what happened, what is true, what is billable, what is contractually binding, what is in stock, what was recognized as revenue, or what exposure exists, the answer ultimately has to rest on structured data. But the age of AI changes the burden placed on that data.

Structured data is data organized according to a predefined schema, typically in rows, columns, fields, tables, keys, and controlled relationships. Its structure is known in advance and enforced by the systems that create, store, or manage it. In the enterprise, structured data includes transaction records, master data, reference data, financial measures, operational statuses, and curated analytical models. This structure makes the data easier to query, validate, and govern, but it does not automatically make the data meaningful or safe for AI interpretation.

For decades, structured data was prepared mainly for query, reporting, and downstream application logic. A table could be considered usable if it had stable schemas, acceptable quality, and enough documentation for engineers or analysts to work out how to join and interpret it. That standard is no longer enough. AI systems do not merely query fields. They interpret them, combine them, explain them, rank them against competing evidence, and increasingly use them to justify actions. In that setting, raw fields and tables are insufficient.

AI requires structured data to be accompanied by business definitions, semantic context, lineage, policy constraints, freshness signals, and clear intended use. Without those layers, the system may retrieve correct values but still produce misleading conclusions. A model can read a column named margin_pct. It cannot know, from the column alone, whether the value is gross margin or contribution margin, whether it is booked or forecast, whether it includes intercompany eliminations, whether it is current-period only, or whether it is appropriate to expose to a regional manager.

That is the central point of this chapter: structured data remains essential, but its role in enterprise AI is no longer satisfied by storage and queryability alone. Structured data must be architected for explanation, justification, and governed operational use.

Why This Matters

Structured Data Still Anchors Enterprise Authority

In enterprise AI, unstructured content often provides rich narrative context, but structured data anchors authoritative facts. A policy manual may explain how credit exposure should be managed. A transcript may reveal why a deal is at risk. A product specification may clarify what a SKU represents. But when an AI assistant answers, "How much open receivables risk do we have with this customer?" or "What drove the unfavorable manufacturing variance last month?" the defensible answer must be tied to authoritative, structured records.

This is especially important because AI users do not consume data the way analysts traditionally did. They ask in natural language. They expect the system to synthesize across domains. They often do not see the joins, filters, assumptions, or definitional choices being made on their behalf. That means the architecture must absorb ambiguity before the answer reaches the user.

Query Success Is Not Interpretation Success

A conventional analytics stack can tolerate a surprising amount of semantic ambiguity as long as a trained analyst sits between the data and the decision. Analysts learn which tables to trust, which fields are misleading, which measures are provisional, and which numbers must be reconciled before presentation.

AI compresses that human mediation layer.

If a copilot accesses a finance model, a supply chain mart, and a sales performance dataset, it may technically retrieve all the right records and still combine them in the wrong way. It may compare booked revenue to forecast pipeline, interpret a lagging inventory snapshot as current, or cite a local definition of operating margin as though it were the enterprise definition. None of these is a model failure in the narrow sense. They are architectural failures in how structured data was exposed.

Action-Taking Systems Raise the Bar Further

The stakes rise again when AI is allowed to recommend or trigger actions. An informational assistant that summarizes last quarter's variance can cause confusion if it misinterprets a metric. An action-taking agent that adjusts thresholds, routes approvals, or triggers remediation based on that same misunderstanding can cause operational and financial damage.

This is why structured data is so important for AI-readiness. It is not just useful for answering questions. It is the substrate for justification, auditability, and safe action. Enterprises need a way to say not only, "This number is from the ERP," but also, "This is how the metric is defined, this is its lineage, these are the policy constraints on who can see it, these are the freshness expectations, and these are the approved use cases for AI."

CORE CONCEPTS

Structured Truth and Interpreted Truth

Structured data gives enterprises structured truth: records, states, transactions, amounts, timestamps, statuses, and relationships represented in stable forms. But AI works one level above that. It produces interpreted truth: a claim about what those records mean in a business context.

A row in an ERP ledger is structured truth. "North America operating performance deteriorated because freight and expedited sourcing costs rose faster than realized revenue" is interpreted as true.

The second statement can be excellent, useful, and correct. It can also be dangerously wrong even when it references valid records. The difference lies in whether the system understands the definitions, transformations, assumptions, and boundaries that govern interpretation.

KEY INSIGHT

Structured truth vs interpreted truth

Structured truth is the recorded fact: invoice posted, shipment delayed, credit memo issued, journal entry booked. Interpreted truth is the business statement built from those facts: revenue declined because product mix shifted, margins compressed because freight costs rose, customer churn risk increased because service incidents spiked. AI operates at the level of interpreted truth. That is why structured data must carry enough context to support interpretation defensibly.

Why Columns Are Not Concepts

A persistent mistake in enterprise data work is to confuse schema with meaning.

Columns are technical representations. Concepts are business meanings. The two are related, but they are not equivalent.

A column named cust_id may represent a bill-to customer in one system, a sold-to customer in another, and a legal counterparty in a third. A field called order_date may mean order creation date, requested fulfillment date, or date of commercial acceptance. A metric labeled revenue may mean gross invoiced amount in one domain, net recognized revenue in another, and forecasted revenue in a planning application.

An analyst can often work through these differences manually. An AI system cannot be expected to infer them reliably from names alone.

This is why semantic models matter. Semantic models do not just rename fields. They define entities, metrics, hierarchies, relationships, calculation logic, grain, and context in business terms. They create a layer in which "customer," "open order," "recognized revenue," and "inventory on hand" are governed concepts rather than loose collections of columns.

KEY INSIGHT

Why columns are not concepts

A column tells you how data is stored. A concept tells you what the business means by it, when it is valid, how it is calculated, who owns it, what policies apply, and what decisions it may support. AI needs concepts. Raw columns are merely ingredients.

Semantic Models and Business Rules Are Safety Mechanisms

Many teams still treat semantic models as presentation conveniences for dashboards. That view is outdated. In an AI-ready architecture, semantic models and business rules are safety mechanisms.

They are what prevent an assistant from comparing non-comparable measures. They are what allow a copilot to explain, in plain language, how "net sales" differ from "gross sales." They are what let an agent know that a risk score can inform human review, but cannot automatically trigger a customer hold without additional controls.

Business rules are equally important. Raw structured data rarely encodes decision boundaries clearly enough for trustworthy AI use. Thresholds, exclusions, override rules, exception handling, authoritative source precedence, and approval requirements all need to be made explicit. Otherwise, the model is left to infer operational meaning from storage artifacts.

Structured Data Must Be Prepared for Explanation

Historically, structured data programs were optimized for extraction, transformation, and performance. AI adds a new requirement: explanation.

An AI-serving layer for structured data should be able to answer questions such as:

- What does this metric mean?
- Which system is authoritative for it?

- At what grain is it valid?
- How fresh is it?
- What business rules shaped it?
- What upstream transformations produced it?
- Who owns it?
- Which users or agents are permitted to access it?
- What limitations or cautions apply?

That is not documentation on the side. It is part of the serving contract.

❖ FIGURE 9 – STRUCTURED DATA SERVING

In practical terms, this ladder describes architectural maturity. A raw table makes data accessible. A semantic model organizes it. A governed concept stabilizes meaning. An AI-serving contract determines how that meaning can be safely discovered, explained, cited, and used.

ARCHITECTURAL IMPLICATIONS

From Data Pipelines to Data-Serving Contracts

The traditional question for structured data architecture was, "How do we move and model data efficiently?" The AI-era question is, "How do we serve structured data safely and intelligibly to multiple AI consumers?"

That shift matters. A knowledge assistant, a finance copilot, an executive briefing tool, and an action-taking agent do not have the same tolerance for ambiguity or the same access requirements. The architecture must, therefore, expose structured data through explicit data-serving contracts.

A data-serving contract for AI should define:

- The authoritative source or ranked source hierarchy.
- The business definitions attached to exposed entities and metrics.
- Grain and aggregation rules.
- Freshness expectations.
- Lineage and transformation traceability.
- Policy and permission constraints.
- Quality indicators and confidence conditions.
- Intended AI uses and prohibited uses.
- Citation and evidence behavior.

Without that contract, teams end up exposing tables and trusting model behavior to compensate. That is not a scalable design.

Metadata Becomes the Control Surface

In conventional data estates, metadata is often fragmented across catalogs, modeling tools, pipelines, BI layers, governance repositories, and tribal knowledge. In an AI-ready architecture, that fragmentation becomes a serious liability.

Structured data needs metadata that can be used operationally, not just descriptively. The AI stack must be able to discover the right dataset, understand its meaning, assess its freshness, apply the correct access rules, retrieve lineage, and determine whether it is fit for a given AI task. This is why metadata functions as the control plane. For structured data, the most important metadata categories include:

- Business glossary terms and definitions.
- Metric logic and approved calculation methods.

- Entity definitions and relationship mappings.
- Source system authority.
- Lineage across ingestion, transformation, and semantic layers.
- Quality indicators and known limitations.
- Classification and policy tags.
- Temporal validity and freshness.
- Ownership and stewardship.
- Approved AI usage patterns.
- Governance must travel with the data.

Governance cannot remain an external review process. It must be embedded in how structured data is modeled and served.

If a finance metric is restricted to certain roles, that restriction should not depend on whether an AI product team happens to remember it. If an HR field should never be used for generative summarization outside a specific process, that should be expressed as a policy attached to the data product or concept, not buried in a policy document.

Embedding governance means that structured data products carry their constraints with them. It also means AI systems consume those constraints programmatically. The same architecture that serves data should also serve permissible use boundaries.

Structured Data and Unstructured Context Must Meet Deliberately

Structured data is rarely sufficient on its own for business interpretation. A margin variance may require a cost policy context. A delivery delay may require logistics exception notes. A compliance breach may require reference to procedure documents and prior approvals.

But combining structured and unstructured data does not reduce the need for structured discipline. It raises it. The structured layer must provide the factual anchors, controlled definitions, and traceable measures that allow narrative material to be grounded rather than merely suggestive.

Failure Modes and Anti-Patterns

Exposing Raw Tables as AI-Ready Data

This is the most common failure.

A team grants an assistant access to curated warehouse tables and assumes that because the data is structured and high-quality, it is, therefore, ready for AI. The result is often superficially credible but semantically unstable output. The assistant can retrieve values, but it lacks the definitional and policy context needed to use them reliably.

Raw table exposure works until the first ambiguous metric, conflicting source, restricted attribute, or cross-domain question. Then the illusion breaks.

Treating Semantic Layers as Optional

Some organizations continue to treat semantic modeling as a reporting convenience. That is a costly mistake. In AI contexts, the semantic layer often determines whether the system speaks with enterprise meaning or with technical ambiguity.

Where no semantic layer exists, every AI use case becomes a custom interpretation exercise. Definitions drift. Prompt logic starts carrying business rules that should be architected in data. Different assistants return different answers to the same question. Trust erodes.

Allowing Metric Plurality Without Governance

Enterprises can tolerate multiple metric definitions when those definitions are explicit and context-bound. They cannot tolerate silent plurality.

❖ FIGURE 10 – METRIC INTERPRETATION FLOW

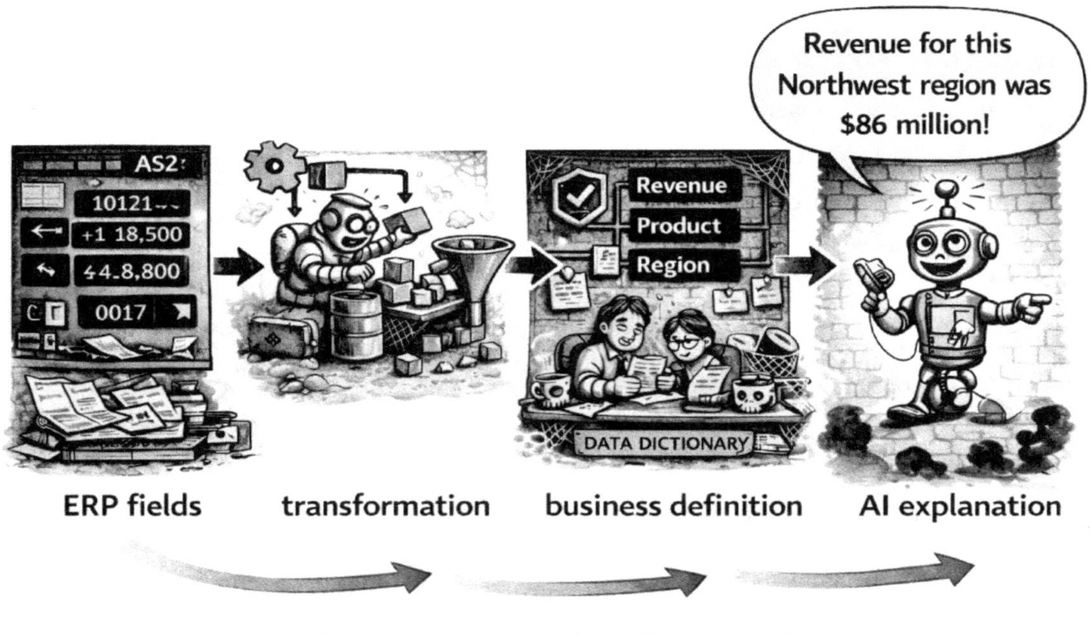

A sales organization may use gross bookings for pipeline management. Finance may use recognized revenue for reporting. Operations may use the shipped value for fulfillment planning. None of that is inherently wrong. The problem emerges when all three are casually referred to as "revenue" in AI-facing systems.

⚠ **WARNING SIGN**

When the same metric is defined differently across domains

If finance, sales, and operations all use the same business word but mean different measures, AI will eventually collapse those distinctions unless architecture prevents it. This is a warning sign, not a minor documentation issue. It indicates the need for explicit semantic separation, governed aliases, and audience-aware serving contracts.

Optimizing Only for Query Performance

A performant warehouse is not the same as an explainable serving layer. Teams that optimize solely for joins, partitioning, and dashboard latency often underinvest in interpretability metadata, lineage visibility, and policy attachment. That architecture can satisfy analysts. It will disappoint AI.

Using Prompt Logic to Compensate for Missing Data Design

When meaning is absent from the data architecture, teams often attempt to restore it in application code or prompts: "Use this field only for North America," "Treat this metric as provisional," "Prefer this table unless the quarter is not closed," and so on.

That approach does not scale. Meaning belongs in governed data and metadata layers, not in brittle downstream instructions. Prompt logic can express interaction behavior. It should not be the primary container for enterprise semantics.

PRACTICAL APPLICATION

A Practical Path to AI-ready Structured Data

Most organizations do not need to rebuild their structured data estate from scratch. They do need to identify which domains and concepts matter most for high-value AI use cases, then raise those domains up the serving ladder.

A pragmatic sequence looks like this:

Start with High-Consequence Domains

Prioritize domains where authoritative facts, policy controls, and business explanations matter most: finance, customer, product, supply chain, risk, and workforce. These are the areas where AI mistakes are most damaging and where structured data usually already anchors enterprise truth.

Identify Core Entities and Metrics

Do not start with every table. Start with the entities and measures the AI products actually need: customer, order, invoice, claim, shipment, supplier, product, account, expense, recognized revenue, on-time delivery, inventory availability, variance, and exposure.

Define Business Meaning Explicitly

For each entity and metric, establish approved definitions, grain, owner, allowable aggregations, freshness expectations, and known limitations. Synonyms and local aliases should also be documented, because users and models will use multiple phrasings.

Attach Lineage, Policy, and Quality Signals

Every exposed concept should have a traceable lineage, applicable access rules, and fit-for-use indicators. If the metric is provisional before the period close, say so. If the attribute is restricted outside a particular role, enforce it. If the source is authoritative only for one region, represent that boundary clearly.

Expose an AI-Serving Contract

Do not make the AI application reverse-engineer the data estate. Publish a serving contract that tells the AI layer what can be used, how it should be interpreted, how it should be cited, and what it must avoid.

TEMPLATES

Structured Domain AI-Readiness Checklist

Domain name	<name of the business domain or use-case area being assessed>
Authoritative source system	<system or systems designated as the trusted source of record, including any approved semantic exposure layer>
Core entities	<main business entities that define the domain, such as customers, accounts, products, periods, regions, or transactions>
Core metrics	<key business measures used in the domain, such as revenue, cost, margin, variance, volume, or forecast values>
Business definitions present? yes/no	<Yes or No>

Lineage documented? yes/no	<Yes or No>
Policy constraints documented? yes/no	<Yes or No>
Data quality signals available? yes/no	<Yes or No>
Semantic mapping completed? yes/no	<Yes or No>
Intended AI uses	<approved AI use cases for this domain, such as Q&A, explanation, summarization, briefing support, or decision support>
Restricted AI uses	<AI uses that are explicitly prohibited, restricted, or require additional control because of risk, sensitivity, or governance concerns>
Readiness blockers	<current issues preventing full AI-readiness, such as semantic inconsistencies, freshness gaps, mapping problems, or unresolved policy concerns>
Remediation owner	<role, team, or governing body accountable for resolving readiness gaps>
Target readiness date	<date by which the domain is expected or planned to reach the desired readiness state>

Case Example

Finance Variance Analysis Assistant

Consider a finance variance analysis assistant designed to support controllers and finance business partners during monthly close and forecast review.

A naïve implementation would expose ERP-derived tables, a few planning extracts, and a semantic query layer, then allow users to ask questions such as:

- Why is gross margin down in Europe?
- Which cost centers drove the unfavorable variance?
- What changed versus forecast?
- Summarize the top three drivers of operating expense growth.

At first glance, this seems straightforward. The data is structured. The questions are familiar. The model can retrieve numbers and produce fluent summaries.

The problem is that the finance interpretation is never just table access.

Gross margin may be defined differently across geographies because freight treatment differs. Forecast may refer to the last approved forecast in one dataset and a working forecast in another. Expense movements may need to exclude one-time restructuring charges. Product hierarchy mappings may differ between ERP and planning systems. Soft-close data may be available to some users but unsuitable for executive summaries. Intercompany eliminations may be included in one reporting view and excluded in another.

A trustworthy finance variance assistant, therefore, requires more than raw data access. It needs an AI-serving contract around the finance domain. In a well-architected design, the assistant does not read raw ERP fields as if they were self-explanatory. It accesses governed concepts such as recognized revenue, gross margin, operating expense, and approved forecast. Each concept carries a business definition, grain, freshness state, source authority, and policy metadata. The assistant can retrieve not only the value but also the explanation scaffolding around that value.

When a user asks, "Why is gross margin down in Europe this month?" the assistant should be able to do several things:

First, it should retrieve the approved finance definition of gross margin for that audience and reporting context.

Second, it should use lineage-aware transformations to identify the actual drivers: lower realized price in one product family, unfavorable mix in another, and higher freight allocation in two markets.

Third, it should qualify the answer with temporal correctness: for example, indicating that soft-close data is 96 percent complete and that final allocations may adjust by a defined threshold.

Fourth, it should honor access boundaries. A regional manager may receive a regional explanation without legal-entity detail. A controller may receive the detailed breakdown.

Fifth, it should cite the authoritative semantic measures and source systems used in the explanation rather than presenting a plausible narrative with no evidentiary basis.

A useful answer might read like this:

"Gross margin in Europe is down 1.8 points versus forecast, primarily due to unfavorable product mix in industrial adhesives, higher outbound freight allocation in Germany and Poland, and lower realized price on two account renewals. This explanation is based on approved month-to-date finance measures from SAP S/4HANA and the enterprise finance semantic model. Soft-close status is 96 percent complete; freight allocations may still adjust modestly before final close."

That answer is valuable because it combines structured truth with governed interpretation. It is not merely well-worded. It is architecturally grounded.

Closing Synthesis

Structured data has not become less important because AI can read text. It has become more important because enterprises now expect machines to explain and act on business facts, not just query them.

That raises the standard. Structured data must still be accurate, timely, and well-modeled. But it must also be semantically explicit, lineage-aware, policy-bound, and prepared for explanation. In other words, the enterprise must stop thinking of structured data as rows to be queried and start treating it as governed meaning to be served. This is the real architectural shift.

The question is no longer whether the data warehouse contains the necessary facts. The question is whether those facts can be exposed as governed concepts with enough context for AI to use them safely. Where that capability exists, structured data becomes the anchor for trustworthy assistants, defensible analytics copilots, and constrained action-taking systems; where it does not, even high-quality structured data will produce low-trust AI outcomes.

The organizations that succeed will not be the ones with the most tables. They will be the ones that elevate structured data from storage artifact to AI-serving contract.

Key Takeaways

- Structured data remains the authoritative backbone of enterprise truth, but raw tables and fields are not sufficient for AI use.
- AI needs structured data paired with semantic definitions, lineage, policy constraints, quality signals, and freshness context.
- Semantic models and business rules are not presentation conveniences; they are safety mechanisms for trustworthy AI.
- Structured data must be prepared for explanation, citation, and governed action, not only for querying and reporting.
- The practical goal is to expose structured domains as AI-serving contracts, not merely to grant models access to databases.

Chapter 6: Semi-Structured Data as the Missing Middle

Enterprises have spent decades learning how to govern structured data and, more recently, how to store unstructured content at scale. Yet much of the context that actually explains how the business is operating now sits somewhere in between. It lives in API payloads, event streams, ticket updates, application messages, audit records, clickstreams, device telemetry, workflow state changes, and operational logs. It is not neatly modeled like a warehouse table, and it is not fully narrative like a policy document or contract. It is semi-structured, and it is often the missing middle in AI-Ready Data architecture.

Semi-structured data is data that has recognizable organization but does not conform fully to a fixed relational schema. It may contain fields, tags, keys, nested objects, timestamps, identifiers, or event envelopes, but its structure can vary across sources, versions, or records. Common examples include JSON payloads, XML messages, API responses, event streams, application logs, audit records, telemetry, and workflow updates. Semi-structured data is therefore machine-readable, but not automatically business-readable; it still requires semantic contracts, metadata, and governance before AI systems can interpret it safely.

This matters because semi-structured data frequently contains the most operationally useful context in the enterprise. It tells you that an order changed status, that a claim entered exception handling, that a service degraded, that a customer interaction escalated, that an access grant was revoked, or that a workflow crossed a risk threshold. In other words, it carries state transitions, event timing, and system interactions. It is often the closest thing an enterprise has to a live account of what is actually happening.

And yet semi-structured data is commonly neglected. It is treated as transient plumbing, engineering exhaust, or an inconvenient byproduct of applications talking to one another. It is landed without durable semantics. It drifts without notice. It accumulates with little ownership. It is queried opportunistically, but rarely designed as part of a governed data contract. That neglect becomes dangerous when organizations try to build copilots and agents on top of it.

AI systems do not merely need data values. They need context, meaning, timing, authority, and defensible interpretation. Semi-structured data can provide those things, but only when it is architected deliberately. When it is not, the same sources that could power the best operational copilots become a source of ambiguity, false confidence, and unsafe action.

Why This Matters

Semi-structured Data Is Where Operational Reality Appears First

Systems of record usually tell you the official state of the business. Semi-structured sources often tell you how that state is changing in real time. A customer master may tell you who the customer is. An event stream may tell you that their onboarding stalled, their payment failed, their shipment was delayed, and their support case is now at risk of breach. A ticket table may record the existence of an incident. The ticket updates, service events, and API status callbacks tell you whether the incident is worsening, stabilizing, or about to violate an SLA.

For reporting, organizations can often tolerate delay. For AI systems that are expected to inform, recommend, or act; delaying changes the meaning of the answer. A copilot that explains last week's status may still be useful. An operations agent that acts on stale event semantics can do real damage.

It Is the Bridge Between Systems of Record and AI Inference

Semi-structured data forms the connective tissue of modern enterprises. APIs expose application intent. Events expose process transitions. Logs expose system behavior. Messages expose workflow coordination. These sources sit between formal transaction systems and AI-serving layers. They are often the bridge that lets an AI system move from static knowledge to situational awareness.

Without that bridge, enterprise AI becomes shallow. It can summarize policies and answer general knowledge questions, but it cannot reliably answer operational questions such as:

Which customer escalations are most likely to breach their SLA in the next two hours?

- Which orders are delayed because of dependency failures rather than inventory shortage?
- Which incidents are growing risks because the downstream service has degraded across multiple regions?
- Which approval requests should be prioritized because they block revenue, not just workflow completion?

Those answers depend on event context, state changes, and relationships across semi-structured sources.

AI-Ready Data Fails When the Middle Layer Is Ignored

Many data programs over-rotate toward the endpoints of the spectrum. They invest in curated structured data for BI and ML, and they invest in document repositories for search and retrieval. The middle layer remains underdesigned. As a result, AI systems see polished tables that lack operational nuance and large content stores that lack the current state. They miss the living context of the enterprise.

That is why semi-structured data is not a niche concern for engineers. It is an architectural concern for any organization serious about trustworthy enterprise AI.

KEY INSIGHT

The Missing Middle

Most enterprise architectures have a strong view of tables and a growing view of documents, but a weak view of events, messages, and payloads. That weak middle layer is often where timeliness, causality, and operational context live. Ignore it, and AI systems will sound informed while missing what is actually happening.

CORE CONCEPTS

Semi-structured Does Not Mean Semantically Optional

Semi-structured data has some organizing form, but not a complete or stable relational model. JSON payloads, XML messages, event envelopes, key-value telemetry, audit records, and application logs all qualify. They often have fields, arrays, nested objects, timestamps, identifiers, and status indicators. But those structures alone do not create meaning.

A field named "status" is not self-explanatory. Does it refer to order state, processing state, customer state, or transmission state? Does "closed" mean resolved, canceled, archived, or merely removed from the active queue? Does a missing field mean false, unknown, not applicable, or not yet emitted? AI systems cannot safely infer these distinctions from syntax alone.

For AI-readiness, semi-structured data needs semantic contracts: clear event or object definitions, field meaning, valid state transitions, entity references, temporal interpretation, and source authority. Event semantics must be designed, not assumed.

Event Context Is Often More Valuable Than Static Attributes

Traditional data architecture tends to privilege stable entities: customer, product, account, employee, asset. Those remain essential. But AI systems often need more than an entity description. They need to know what changed, when it changed, why it changed, and what other changes surrounded it.

That is the value of event context. A service outage event, a retry event, a ticket reassignment event, and an exception-handled event together tell a story that no single table can express well. Semi-structured data often captures that story first.

This is particularly important for operational copilots and agents. These systems are not merely retrieving facts. They are supporting judgment in time-sensitive contexts. Event-rich data gives them the sequence, causality, and recency needed to reason responsibly.

KEY INSIGHT

JSON with No Semantic Contract

JSON is not a data strategy. A payload is not self-describing because it uses readable field names. If there is no durable contract for field meaning, valid values, timing semantics, ownership, and change management, the source is not AI-ready. It is merely parseable.

Schema Drift Is Not Just a Technical Inconvenience

Schema drift occurs when the payload structure or field meaning changes over time. Sometimes the changes are obvious: a field is renamed, nested, removed, or split. More dangerous are the subtle changes: a field remains present but changes meaning, default handling, unit of measure, or business interpretation.

A log field once used for an internal processing stage may later be repurposed to represent customer-visible status. An API may keep priority but shift from numeric severity to business urgency labels. A payload may retain a timestamp while changing from event occurrence time to ingestion time. None of these changes is benign for AI.

In BI environments, such drift may cause a broken transform or a failed dashboard. In AI systems, it can cause a confident but wrong narrative. That is worse because the output may appear coherent. The issue is not only structural instability. It is semantic instability.

Logs and Events Are Not Merely Engineering Exhaust

Organizations often retain logs because engineers need them for debugging. That is too narrow a view. Many logs and events encode process state, user behavior, control execution, and system dependency signals. In aggregate, they can reveal operational risk, policy deviations, workflow bottlenecks, and emerging customer impact.

Of course, not all logs deserve equal treatment. Some are low-value noise. Some are sensitive. Some are too volatile to preserve broadly. But dismissing event and log data as exhaust is a category mistake. In many enterprises, this layer is the best available source of process truth.

KEY INSIGHT

Why Logs and Events Are Not "Just Engineering Exhaust"

Logs and events often record the first observable evidence of change: a failed handoff, repeated retries, unauthorized access attempts, a queue backlog, or an escalating ticket. These signals can be architecturally significant for AI because they provide timing, sequence, and anomaly context that curated tables usually lose.

ARCHITECTURAL IMPLICATIONS

The Ingestion Pattern Must Preserve Meaning, Not Just Move Payloads

A common failure in data platforms is to optimize for transport while neglecting interpretation. Payloads are landed, retained, and made queryable, but stripped of the information required to use them safely. The architecture must do more than ingest. It must preserve context.

That means capturing source system identity, event type, producer version, occurrence time, ingestion time, correlation identifiers, related entity keys, and access constraints. It also means distinguishing raw preservation from normalized use. The raw record should remain available for traceability, but AI-serving should not depend on raw payloads alone.

Normalization Is Not Flattening

Flattening a JSON payload into columns can make it easier to query, but it can also destroy context. Arrays, nested structures, optional fields, and envelope metadata often carry meaning. Normalization should produce usable canonical forms without erasing event semantics.

A strong pattern is to maintain three layers:

- **Raw preservation layer** for exact source fidelity and replay.
- **Semantic normalization layer** for canonical event or object interpretation.
- **AI-serving layer** for enriched, access-aware, business-meaningful delivery.

The normalized layer should map source-specific fields into business-aligned concepts while preserving the ability to trace back to source payloads. The AI-serving layer should add trust features: lineage, freshness, authority ranking, policy tags, semantic labels, and explanation-ready references.

Metadata Must Mediate Semi-Structured Data

If metadata is the control plane for AI, then semi-structured data requires especially strong metadata treatment. These sources are less self-evident than curated tables and less human-readable than documents. Without metadata, they are hard to discover, difficult to compare, and dangerous to interpret. At a minimum, semi-structured sources need metadata for:

- Source ownership and stewardship.
- Event or object type definitions.
- Business meaning of fields.
- Entity resolution rules.
- Temporal semantics.
- Sensitivity and policy classification.
- Retention obligations.
- Schema versions and change history.
- Quality and freshness indicators.
- Downstream dependencies.
- Approved AI use cases and prohibited uses.

This is not bureaucracy. It is the architecture required to make semi-structured signals usable at enterprise scale.

Event Semantics Must Be Intentional

Architects should treat core operational events as products, not incidental emissions. A meaningful event design answers questions such as:

- What business occurrence does this represent?
- What has changed, and for whom?
- Which timestamp matters?
- Which state machine governs valid transitions?
- Which entities does this affect?
- Which source is authoritative if conflicting events exist?
- What level of delay or loss is acceptable?
- Which consumers may act on this event, and under what controls?

These decisions shape whether an AI system can explain its reasoning, cite the right evidence, and avoid acting on noise.

Retrieval Architecture for Semi-Structured Data Is Different

Semi-structured data should not simply be indexed as if it were free text. AI-serving architecture needs richer retrieval logic. Some questions need event sequence retrieval. Some need entity-centric rollups. Some need state snapshots derived from recent events. Some need exception filtering, causal linking, or authority weighting.

For example, an assistant answering "Why is this order delayed?" may need to retrieve recent shipment events, warehouse exceptions, support ticket updates, and policy rules governing delay classification. A simple text search over logs will not produce a trustworthy answer. The retrieval layer needs event-aware ranking, temporal filters, semantic joins, and source-aware citation.

❖ FIGURE 11 – SEMI-STRUCTURED DATA FLOW

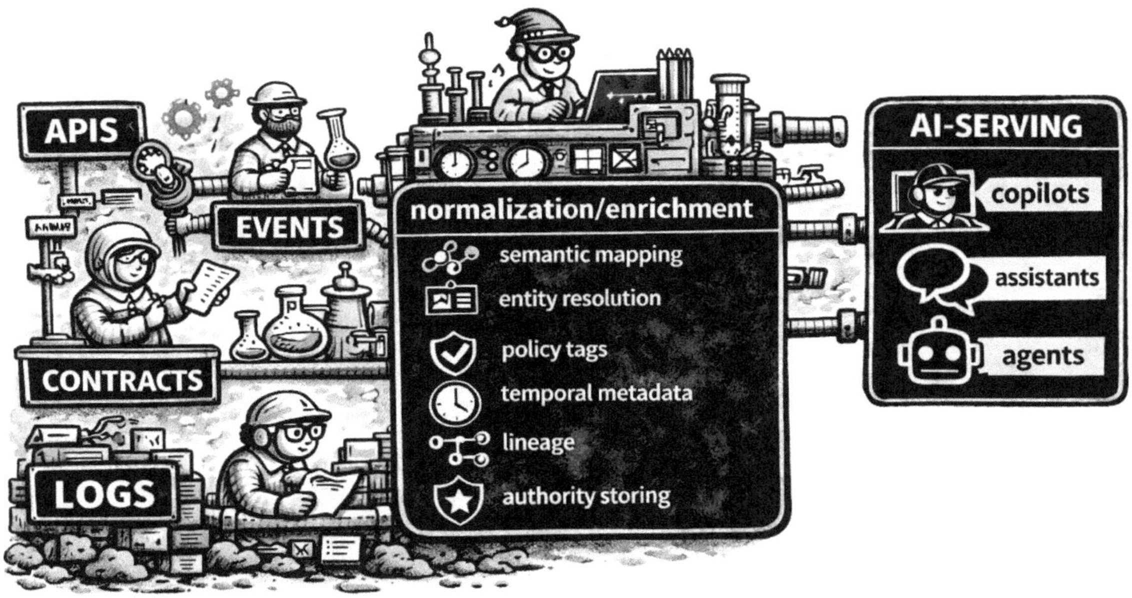

FAILURE MODES AND ANTI-PATTERNS

Treating Payload Capture as Readiness

An enterprise may proudly say it has all the logs, all the events, and all the API payloads. That says nothing about readiness. Raw capture without semantic interpretation is storage, not architecture.

The symptom appears when teams try to use these sources for AI and discover that they cannot tell which fields matter, which events supersede others, or which timestamps are trustworthy. The data exists, but the meaning does not travel with it.

Letting Source Teams Invent Semantics Independently

Different applications often emit similar concepts with incompatible meanings. One team's "resolved" may mean customer-confirmed restoration. Another team's "resolved" may mean the engineering handoff is complete. Without enterprise semantic discipline, downstream AI systems inherit ambiguity and produce inconsistent reasoning.

This does not require the centralized design of every field. But it does require common patterns for event naming, state modeling, temporal semantics, and business glossary alignment.

Ignoring Schema Drift Until Breakage Becomes Visible

Schema drift is frequently discovered only when pipelines fail. That is too late. AI systems can degrade long before transforms break. A field that still parses but now means something different may silently contaminate recommendations, summaries, and actions.

Architectures need drift monitoring at both the structure and semantics levels: field presence, cardinality, value distribution, version adoption, enum expansion, timestamp shifts, and mapping exceptions.

❖ FIGURE 12 – SCHEMA DRIFT MAP

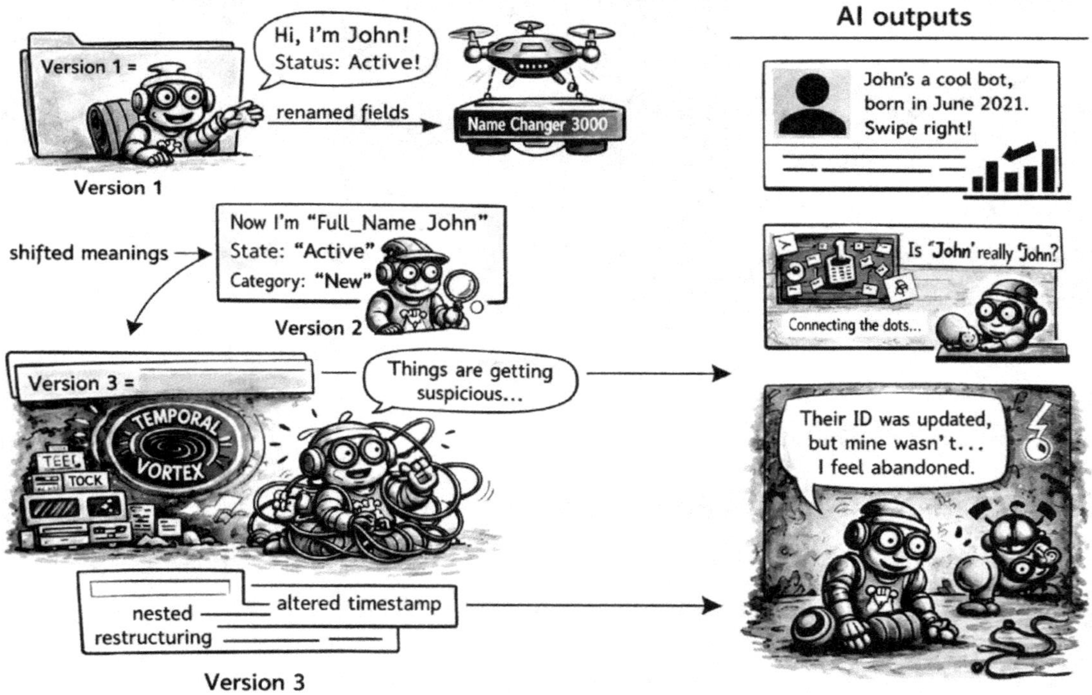

Over-relying on Logs as Explanation

Logs can provide useful evidence, but they are not always an appropriate explanation layer for business users. An AI system that cites raw stack traces or obscure internal status codes may technically ground its answer while still failing the user. Semi-structured signals often need translation into business-level meaning before they are suitable for AI explanation.

Separating Governance from Operational Telemetry

Some organizations govern customer, finance, and HR data rigorously while treating event streams and logs as outside the governance perimeter. That separation fails in AI contexts. Semi-structured sources may contain personal data, security-sensitive information, operational control signals, or regulated events. If those sources feed AI, they require classification, access controls, retention, and policy-aware delivery.

Practical Application

Start by Profiling Semi-Structured Sources as Assets

Before building AI on top of semi-structured sources, architects should identify which sources actually matter. Not every payload deserves promotion into the AI-ready estate. The priority should be sources that combine operational relevance, interpretability, and durable business value.

That usually includes:

- Event streams tied to critical workflows.
- API payloads representing customer or operational state.
- Ticket and case lifecycle updates.
- Audit trails relevant to compliance or control evidence.
- Application events tied to service delivery or exception handling.
- Select telemetry and logs that reveal risk or anomaly states.

The point is not indiscriminate ingestion. It is strategic source selection.

Use a Profiling Worksheet Before Production Use

A practical way to force rigor is to require every candidate source to be profiled before it is exposed to copilots or agents. The worksheet below is designed for that purpose.

Architect for Canonical Events, Not Endless Source Exceptions

A useful discipline is to define a small set of canonical event classes aligned to the business, such as created, updated, assigned, escalated, delayed, completed, failed, restored, approved, and rejected. Source-specific events can map into these classes while retaining source detail.

This does not eliminate source nuance. It creates a stable semantic layer that downstream AI can depend on. That stability is essential for reuse across copilots, analytics, and agents.

Build AI-serving Views Around Tasks

Semi-structured data should not be served to AI consumers as an undifferentiated stream. It should be shaped around real tasks:

- **Timeline view:** what happened, in order, with evidence.
- **Current state view:** latest trustworthy status and freshness.
- **Risk view:** signals, thresholds, confidence, and causes.
- **Action eligibility view:** what may be recommended or executed under policy.
- **Exception summary view:** what changed materially and why it matters.

Different AI consumers need different contracts. A briefing assistant may need compressed summaries and citations. An action-taking agent may need stricter freshness guarantees, explicit authority rules, and policy-enforced action boundaries.

Templates

Semi-Structured Source Profiling Worksheet

Source name	<name of the source, feed, dataset, or event-producing system>
Source type	<type of source, such as event stream, database table, document repository, API feed, or application log>
Payload examples	<representative events, records, messages, or payload types emitted by the source>
Event or object semantics	<business meaning of the events or objects, including what they represent and why they matter>
Known schema variations	<documented version changes, field renames, optional fields, structural differences, or backward-compatibility issues across source versions>
Ownership	<primary owner, technical steward, data steward, and any other accountable roles for the source>

Retention	<how long raw, normalized, and derived data from this source are retained in different forms>
Sensitivity classification	<security and privacy classification of the source, including sensitive fields and required access restrictions>
Downstream uses	<operational, analytical, reporting, or AI use cases currently supported by this source>
AI use opportunities	<approved or promising AI use cases that this source could support>
AI use risks	<key risks in using this source for AI, such as semantic confusion, exposure risk, delayed data, or overconfident conclusions>
Metadata available	<metadata fields available to support filtering, governance, provenance, access control, and interpretation>
Required semantic enrichment	<business glossary mappings, canonical models, hierarchy resolution, temporal normalization, entity linking, or other enrichment needed to make the source AI-ready>
Monitoring requirements	<controls and quality checks needed to detect schema drift, latency, duplicates, missing fields, ordering issues, or mapping failures>
Recommended handling pattern	<recommended architectural and governance approach for preserving, normalizing, enriching, securing, and serving this source for AI and analytics>

CASE EXAMPLE

From Ticket Summaries to SLA Risk Intelligence

Consider an operations agent designed to detect SLA risk for enterprise support incidents. The goal is not to generate generic summaries. The goal is to identify which open incidents are most likely to breach their response or resolution commitments and to explain why.

The naïve architecture would read a ticket table and maybe a few free-text notes. That architecture will miss the real signals. SLA risk often becomes visible first in semi-structured data:

- Ticket lifecycle events show reassignment churn, stalled ownership, and priority changes.
- API status feeds from dependent services show outages or degraded response times.
- Application events show retry storms, queue backlogs, and repeated execution failures.
- Customer communication events show whether the customer has been updated within the required window.

A robust architecture for this agent would look different.

First, raw events from the ticketing platform, integration APIs, and service status feeds are preserved. Second, they are normalized into a canonical incident risk model. Third, enrichment adds service criticality, customer tier, support policy, dependency relationships, and access classification. Fourth, an AI-serving layer produces three views: a timeline of risk-relevant events, a current state snapshot, and a risk explanation record.

Now the agent can reason on a defensible basis.

Suppose Incident A was opened 95 minutes ago. The formal ticket status still reads "In Progress." A superficial copilot might conclude there is no unusual risk. But the semi-structured layer shows the following sequence: created, reassigned twice, dependency failure event from a regional API, no customer update event within the communication window, and repeated retry failures from the automation workflow. The normalized risk model identifies these as compounding breach indicators. The agent can now produce an evidence-based recommendation:

Incident A has elevated SLA breach risk because ownership changed twice in the last 40 minutes, the downstream payment authorization service reported regional degradation at 14:12, and no customer update has been logged within the required 60-minute interval. Recommend immediate escalation to the payments reliability queue and issuance of a customer-impact update.

That is a materially different capability from summarizing ticket text. It depends on semi-structured data being treated as a first-class architectural asset.

It also depends on governance. The agent must only see incidents and service details that are permitted to access. It must distinguish internal remediation state from customer-visible restoration. It must understand the timestamp meaning. It must know which source is authoritative when a status feed conflicts with a ticket update. None of that is solved by the model alone.

This is the broader lesson. Many of the most valuable enterprise agents will be built not on documents or warehouses alone, but on the disciplined interpretation of operational events.

Closing Synthesis

Semi-structured data is the missing middle because it sits between the worlds enterprises already know how to reason about. It is not as rigid as structured data, and it is not as obviously knowledge-bearing as documents. Yet it often contains the context that matters most for AI: what changed, when it changed, how systems interacted, where risk is emerging, and which state transitions actually define the business moment.

For that reason, semi-structured data should not be treated as incidental exhaust from applications. It should be treated as an architectural layer that connects systems of record to AI inference. When designed well, it enables timelier, more grounded, more operationally useful AI. When neglected, it becomes one of the fastest ways to undermine trust.

The design principles are clear. Preserve raw fidelity, but do not serve raw payloads directly. Normalize meaning, not just structure. Use metadata as the control plane. Govern access, retention, and sensitivity at the same level of seriousness applied to other enterprise data. Monitor schema drift as a trust problem, not merely a pipeline problem. And above all, design event semantics intentionally.

Organizations that do this well will build copilots and agents that understand not only what the enterprise knows, but what the enterprise is currently experiencing. That is a decisive advantage. AI-readiness depends on more than clean tables and searchable content. It depends on whether the architecture can capture and serve the living context of the business.

Key Takeaways

- Semi-structured data often carries the most valuable operational context for enterprise AI because it records events, state changes, and system interactions.
- It is the bridge between systems of record and AI inference, especially for copilots and agents that need situational awareness.
- Schema drift in semi-structured sources is a trust problem, not just a technical nuisance, because field meaning can change without obvious failure.
- Event semantics must be designed explicitly through canonical models, metadata, governance, and AI-serving contracts.
- The most effective operational AI systems are often built on disciplined use of events, messages, logs, and API payloads rather than on tables or documents alone.

CHAPTER 7: UNSTRUCTURED DATA AS A FIRST-CLASS ENTERPRISE ASSET

In many enterprises, the most important business meaning does not live in rows and columns. It lives in policies, contracts, procedure manuals, ticket histories, meeting notes, decision logs, emails, transcripts, and knowledge articles. Databases may tell you what happened. Unstructured content often tells you why it happened, what constraints apply, who approved it, what exception was granted, what evidence supports it, and what action is permissible next.

This distinction matters because enterprise AI is not merely asked to summarize facts. It is asked to interpret obligations, explain decisions, ground recommendations, respect policy, and act with context. Those capabilities cannot be delivered from structured data alone. They depend on narrative content that has historically been treated as peripheral, messy, or outside the core data architecture.

That treatment is now untenable. If unstructured content remains unmanaged, duplicated, stale, ownerless, and disconnected from enterprise metadata, AI systems will produce answers that sound plausible but cannot be trusted. They will retrieve the wrong policy version, summarize an outdated contract clause, ignore legal status, or recommend an action without evidentiary grounding. None of that is a model failure in the narrow sense. It is an architectural failure.

The shift required is not cosmetic. Enterprises must stop treating documents and content repositories as passive storage and start treating unstructured content as a first-class enterprise asset. That means assigning ownership, lifecycle, governance, classification, semantic enrichment, and retrieval design. It also means accepting a harder truth: content architecture matters as much as content storage. A million files in a collaboration platform do not constitute an AI-ready knowledge estate. They constitute a repository. Readiness is something else.

WHY THIS MATTERS

The Business Meaning Gap

Structured systems are excellent at storing transactions, states, and measurements. They are far less effective at representing rationale, obligations, interpretation, and exceptions. A claims platform may record that a case was denied. The policy bulletin explains the rule. The underwriting memo explains the exception logic. The legal guidance clarifies which jurisdictional language governs. The ticket thread documents an operational workaround. The training article explains how frontline staff should interpret edge cases.

When AI is asked a business question, the missing layer is often not data quality in the warehouse. It is missing meaning outside the warehouse.

This is why many enterprise AI initiatives disappoint, even when the structured data platform is mature. Reporting may be strong. Dashboards may be trusted. Data quality controls may be solid. Yet the AI assistant still fails because the answer depends on unstructured evidence that has not been curated as data.

AI Needs More Than Availability

Enterprises often assume that if content exists somewhere in SharePoint, a file store, a knowledge base, or a collaboration platform, it is available for AI use. That assumption confuses access with readiness.

AI needs far more than repository presence. It needs content that can be discovered, classified, interpreted, ranked, permission-checked, temporally validated, and cited. It needs to know which version is authoritative, which owner is accountable, which policy supersedes another, which contract is executed rather than draft, which transcript is approved rather than raw, and which article is still in force rather than abandoned.

Without that layer, retrieval becomes a lottery. The system may find something relevant, but it cannot reliably determine whether it should be trusted.

The Cost of Treating Content as Secondary

When unstructured data is treated as secondary, the enterprise pays several times over. The content estate refers to the full collection of enterprise content that AI may need to interpret or retrieve from, including policies, procedures, contracts, standards, manuals, knowledge articles, presentations, emails, reports, legal language, and approved guidance. It also includes the systems, ownership models, metadata, permissions, version controls, retention rules, and governance processes that determine whether that content is current, trusted, searchable, and safe to use.

First, it pays in trust. Users quickly detect when AI cites an obsolete document, misses an exception, or ignores the current approved guidance.

Second, it pays in duplication. Teams create new notes, summaries, and local repositories because the official content estate is hard to navigate or unreliable.

Third, it pays in compliance risk. The wrong retention policy, stale legal language, or broken permission boundary is not a technical inconvenience. It is an operational and regulatory exposure.

Fourth, it pays in rework. AI teams attempt to fix retrieval problems with model tuning, prompt changes, or ad hoc indexing logic when the root issue is that the underlying content estate was never architected for governed interpretation.

KEY INSIGHT

Documents Are Not Decoration

Documents are not supporting material around the "real" data. In many enterprises, they are the only place where intent, obligation, exception logic, and evidentiary context are explicitly expressed. If they are architecturally ignored, AI will be context-poor by design.

CORE CONCEPTS

Unstructured Data Is Not a Residual Category

Many organizations still define unstructured data as "everything that is not in a database." That framing is too weak for enterprise architecture. It turns an important domain into a leftover category.

A better view is that unstructured data is a content estate with distinct asset classes. Policies, contracts, SOPs, tickets, emails, wikis, board papers, transcripts, research notes, incident reports, and knowledge articles are not interchangeable blobs. They vary by criticality, update cadence, authority, retention obligation, evidentiary value, and AI suitability.

That distinction matters because architecture decisions should differ accordingly. A regulatory policy manual should not be treated the same way as a draft team note. A customer-facing knowledge article should not be governed like an internal brainstorming transcript. A signed contract should not be indexed like an email thread.

Content Architecture Versus Content Storage

Storage answers where content lives. Architecture answers how it is understood, controlled, related, and served.

A content architecture defines:

- What types of content exist.
- How those types are classified.
- Who owns them.
- What lifecycle states they move through.

- How version authority is determined.
- What metadata is mandatory.
- How permission inheritance works.
- How duplicates are detected.
- How documents link to business entities, policies, products, customers, processes, and obligations.
- How retrieval systems rank, filter, and explain them.

This is the dividing line between repository sprawl and usable enterprise knowledge.

A collaboration platform can store millions of files. It does not, by itself, define whether an implementation guide is authoritative, whether a contract clause library is approved, or whether a regional policy memo overrides a global standard. Those are architectural questions.

Governance Must Include Narrative Content

Governance programs often focus on structured domains: customer, product, finance, supplier, orders, and transactions. The result is a blind spot. The most sensitive and interpretive enterprise content remains outside the main governance operating model.

That is a mistake. Governance for AI must address structured and unstructured assets together. Classification, retention, legal hold, privacy handling, provenance, access-aware delivery, quality review, and stewardship are just as important for documents as they are for tables.

In fact, they can be more important. A mislabeled structured field may degrade an analysis. A misgoverned policy document may lead AI to recommend a prohibited action.

Semantic Context Is the Bridge

Raw text is not enough. Enterprise AI needs semantic context to reduce ambiguity.

The same phrase can mean different things across functions and industries. "Close date," "effective date," "settlement date," and "renewal date" may all appear in documents, but they do not mean the same thing operationally. "Policy" might refer to an HR policy, an insurance policy, a network policy, or an underwriting rule. "Approved" may mean line manager approval in one workflow and legal execution in another.

This is why glossaries, taxonomies, ontologies, entity resolution, and relationship modeling matter. They help connect documents to meaning. They let the system know that a clause belongs to a contract family, that a procedure applies to a named business process, that a knowledge article concerns a specific product release, or that a transcript references a customer escalation tied to a support case.

❖ FIGURE 13 – UNSTRUCTURED DATA LANDSCAPE

KEY INSIGHT

Why Enterprise Meaning Often Lives Outside the Warehouse

Warehouses capture the measurable state of the enterprise. They rarely capture the full interpretive state. Business meaning often lives in the material that explains policy intent, contractual obligation, decision rationale, exception handling, and operational practice. AI fails when that layer is left outside the architecture.

ARCHITECTURAL IMPLICATIONS

Treat Content Types as Managed Asset Classes

The first architectural implication is classification by content type. Not all unstructured assets should be indexed, enriched, retained, or exposed in the same way.

A practical enterprise model may separate:

- Policy and regulatory content.
- Contracts and legal instruments.
- Operational procedures and SOPs.
- Support and incident records.
- Knowledge articles and FAQs.
- Communications and collaboration artifacts.
- Analytical narrative and decision papers.
- Meeting transcripts and recordings.
- Evidentiary records.

Each class should have defined ownership, metadata requirements, lifecycle states, access rules, and retrieval handling.

For example, policy content may require effective dates, supersession logic, jurisdiction, approval status, and regulatory linkage. Contracts may require party identification, clause extraction, legal status, renewal terms, governing law, and version chain. Incident records may require severity, root cause classification, remediation status, and cross-reference to system events.

Make Metadata the Control Plane for Content

If metadata is the control plane for AI, then unstructured content must be instrumented accordingly.

At a minimum, enterprises should expect metadata for:

- Content type.
- Title or identifier.
- Business owner.
- Steward.
- Creation and modification timestamps.
- Effective date and expiration date where relevant.
- Lifecycle state.
- Approval or publication status.
- Repository source.
- Access classification.
- Related business entities.
- Version lineage.
- Authority ranking.

- Jurisdiction or organizational scope.
- Retention class.
- AI suitability status.

This is not bureaucracy for its own sake. It is the basis for discovery, ranking, trust, policy enforcement, citation, and explainability. If an AI system cannot distinguish draft from approved, obsolete from current, or local note from official standard, it cannot safely answer enterprise questions.

Design for Authority and Freshness

A common mistake in retrieval architecture is to treat all retrieved text as equal once it passes relevance thresholds. Enterprise content is not equal.

Authority and freshness must be explicit ranking dimensions. A signed policy should outrank an informal summary. A current procedure should outrank an archived predecessor. An officially maintained clause library should outrank a copied excerpt in an email attachment. This implies a ranking design that incorporates:

- Source authority.
- Approval status.
- Recency or effective date.
- Supersession and version chain.
- Content type criticality.
- Owner confidence.
- Permission fidelity.
- Relationship to the user's task.

Retrieval quality is not just about semantic similarity. It is about defensible sourcing.

Embed Access Control Into Serving Logic

Unstructured content often inherits permissions from folders, teams, sites, mailboxes, case systems, or collaboration spaces. That inheritance is messy, dynamic, and frequently misunderstood. If AI delivery is not access-aware, the enterprise risks either leakage or over-restriction. Leakage is obvious and dangerous. Over-restriction is quieter but equally damaging because it causes users to mistrust the system's completeness.

Architecture must, therefore, support identity-aware retrieval, propagation of permission changes, and evidence that access rules were respected at serving time. This is especially important when content is aggregated from heterogeneous repositories with different security models.

Establish Lifecycle and Criticality Treatment

Not all content deserves the same governance intensity. But all important content needs explicit treatment.

A useful model is a content criticality pyramid.

At the base, reference material may tolerate lighter controls. Operational content requires stronger freshness and ownership. Regulatory content demands approval, version discipline, and retention rigor. Evidentiary content must preserve traceability and defensibility. Strategic content, such as board materials or merger planning documents, may require tight access segmentation and controlled reuse.

The architectural consequence is straightforward: lifecycle, validation, enrichment, and AI exposure policies should vary by criticality.

❖ FIGURE 14 – CONTENT CRITICAL PYRAMID

Failure Modes and Anti-Patterns

Repository Presence Mistaken for Readiness

The most common anti-pattern is simple: "Our files are in SharePoint, so we're good."

This statement usually means the organization has centralized some storage, not that it has architected a trustworthy content estate. Centralization may help. It does not solve ownership, quality, authority ranking, metadata completeness, duplicate detection, supersession logic, or AI suitability.

Key Insight

"Our Files Are in SharePoint, So We're Good."

A content repository is not a knowledge architecture. Storage location does not tell AI what a document means, whether it is current, who owns it, whether it is approved, or whether it should be trusted for action.

A repository can be orderly and still be unusable for AI. It can contain five versions of the same policy, inconsistent naming conventions, broken inheritance chains, and no signal of which file is authoritative.

Unowned Content

Ownerless content is one of the fastest routes to AI failure. If nobody is accountable for accuracy, currency, and lifecycle status, the system cannot reliably ground answers. The content may still be discoverable, but discoverability without accountability is dangerous.

This problem is often hidden in shared drives, collaboration spaces, and long-lived project folders. The material remains accessible long after the team disbands or the policy changes. AI systems surface it because it still looks relevant.

Duplicate Drift

Duplication is not merely a storage inefficiency. It creates semantic fragmentation.

A procedure copied into local folders, email attachments, PDFs, team wikis, and slide decks will slowly diverge. Retrieval systems may then surface near-identical but contradictory fragments. Users experience this as inconsistency. Architects should recognize it as duplicate drift.

Duplicate risk must be managed with canonical source designation, fingerprinting, version relationships, and deprecation controls.

Stale But Plausible Content

The most dangerous unstructured content is often not obviously wrong. It is stale but plausible.

An obsolete customer communication template, a superseded regulatory interpretation, or a pre-merger process guide may still read well enough to be confidently summarized by AI. That is exactly why freshness controls and effective dating matter. The problem is not that the model invents content. The problem is that the architecture serves the wrong content with insufficient temporal discipline.

Over-Indexing Low-Value Noise

Another anti-pattern is indiscriminate ingestion. Enterprises eager to expand AI coverage sometimes ingest everything they can reach: chat logs, draft notes, duplicate attachments, obsolete workspaces, raw transcripts, and unmanaged exports.

This makes the retrieval problem worse, not better. Noise competes with authority. Weak content pollutes ranking. Unreviewed material introduces privacy and compliance risk. The result is not a richer context. It is a degraded signal.

Treating Chunking as the Whole Problem

Many teams reduce unstructured readiness to a chunking strategy. Chunking matters, but it is only one layer. If the document lacks ownership, version status, criticality, and authority metadata, perfect chunk boundaries will not rescue trust.

Chunking without governance is optimization around uncertainty.

Practical Application

Start With a Content Estate Inventory

Before an enterprise can improve readiness, it needs visibility into the content estate it already has. That means inventorying repositories, content types, ownership patterns, criticality, growth, permissions, lifecycle, duplicate exposure, and AI suitability.

This is not a clerical exercise. It is the basis for prioritization. Leaders usually discover that a small portion of the content estate drives a disproportionate share of business risk and AI value. That is where the architecture effort should begin.

What the Inventory Reveals

A proper inventory usually reveals four truths.

First, the content estate is broader than leadership assumes. Important material is distributed across operational systems, collaboration platforms, archives, and local workspaces.

Second, readiness is uneven. Some domains may already have strong publication workflows and ownership. Others are effectively unmanaged.

Third, AI suitability is selective. Not every repository should be exposed to general retrieval. Some content should be excluded, heavily filtered, or limited to narrow use cases.

Fourth, enrichment demand is significant. Most high-value content needs more metadata, better lineage, and clearer status before it can serve as reliable grounding.

Prioritize by Value and Risk

Do not begin with the largest repository. Begin with the content domain where business meaning is critical, authority is knowable, and user demand is strong.

Good early domains often include:

- Approved policy libraries.
- Official knowledge articles.
- Controlled procedures.
- Executed contracts.
- Curated incident summaries.

Poor early domains often include:

- Unmanaged collaboration spaces.
- Broad email archives.
- Mixed-purpose shared drives.
- Draft-heavy project folders.
- Unreviewed transcript collections.

This is not because the latter have no value. It is because their governance and signal quality are usually too poor for broad AI grounding.

Elevate Document Strategy Into Data Strategy

Many enterprises have a document management strategy, but not a data strategy for content. The former focuses on storage, publication, retention, and access. The latter must additionally focus on discovery, semantics, evidence, ranking, explainability, and AI-serving contracts.

That is the real transition. The organization stops asking, "Where should files live?" and starts asking, "How should business-critical content be represented, governed, enriched, and served as data for trustworthy AI?"

TEMPLATES

Content Estate Inventory Template

Source or repository name	<name of the repository, platform, archive, workspace, or system>
Content type	<type of content stored or managed, such as policies, contracts, tickets, articles, emails, transcripts, project pages, or shared files>
Business owner	<business function, executive, or organizational unit accountable for the content>
Steward	<person, role, or team responsible for operational maintenance, governance, and quality oversight>
Volume	<approximate amount of content, records, pages, documents, or transcripts in the source>
Growth rate	<rate at which the content or records are increasing, such as low, moderate, high, or very high>
Business criticality	<importance of the source to operations, decisions, service delivery, risk management, or compliance>
Regulatory relevance	<degree of legal, regulatory, audit, privacy, or compliance significance associated with the source>
Typical consumers	<primary teams, functions, or user groups that use or depend on the source>
Update frequency	<how often the source changes, such as continuous, daily, weekly, monthly, or quarterly>
Permission model	<how access is controlled, such as role-based, case-based, matter-based, team-based, mailbox-based, or inherited permissions>
Version control method	<how revisions, approvals, state changes, or execution history are tracked>
Duplicate risk	<likelihood that duplicate, overlapping, or conflicting content exists within or across repositories>
AI suitability	<degree to which the source is fit for AI use cases, and for what kinds of use cases it is most appropriate>

Required enrichment	<metadata, classification, entity extraction, linking, taxonomy, status labeling, or other enhancements needed to make the source more AI-ready>
Lifecycle policy	<retention, archival, retirement, legal hold, review, or deletion rules that govern the source over time>
Readiness status	<current AI-readiness state of the source, such as not ready, emerging, partially ready, or ready>

CASE EXAMPLE

Contract Intelligence That Failed for the Right Reasons

A global enterprise launched a contract intelligence solution to help procurement, legal, and sales teams answer common questions: Which contracts contain change-of-control clauses? Which agreements auto-renew in the next 120 days? Which customer obligations differ by jurisdiction? What language governs data processing in regulated regions?

The first version of the solution seemed promising in demonstrations. It could retrieve contract text, summarize provisions, and answer natural-language questions. But production use quickly exposed a pattern of failure.

Users asked about renewal obligations and received answers drawn from draft versions rather than executed agreements. They asked about governing law and received text from an amendment that had been superseded. They asked whether a clause was standard and the system compared against copied language in email attachments rather than the approved clause library. Legal teams lost confidence almost immediately.

The root cause was not the language model. The root cause was that the enterprise had treated contracts as documents to search rather than governed assets to model.

The repository contained:

- Multiple versions of the same agreement without reliable execution status.
- Amendments not consistently linked to master contracts.
- Clause libraries stored separately from negotiated documents.
- Missing ownership for older agreements.
- Inconsistent party naming.
- No explicit legal status field distinguishing draft, signed, terminated, renewed, or expired.
- No authority logic to prefer executed terms over derivative summaries.

The system was answering questions against text, not against contract knowledge.

The Architectural Correction

The turnaround began when the enterprise stopped optimizing prompts and started redesigning the information architecture.

Contracts were re-modeled as governed assets with explicit entities and relationships:

- Contract.
- Contract family.
- Version.
- Amendment.
- Clause.
- Clause type.
- Party.
- Product or service scope.
- Jurisdiction.
- Legal status.
- Effective date.
- Expiration date.
- Renewal condition.
- Owner.
- Approval chain.

Each document was linked to its lifecycle state. Amendments were connected to master agreements. Clause instances were mapped to canonical clause types. Executed documents were ranked above drafts. Terminated agreements were excluded from standard advisory responses unless specifically requested. Entity resolution normalized party names. Legal ownership was assigned by the business domain.

Only then did retrieval become trustworthy. The system was no longer asking, "Which text looks relevant?" It was asking, "Which authoritative governed contract artifacts answer this question under the user's access rights and current legal status?"

The Result

Once clauses, versions, owners, and legal status were explicitly modeled, the solution became materially more reliable. Summaries became defensible because they were grounded in executed and current sources. Clause comparisons became meaningful because they used canonical clause types. Renewal alerts became operationally useful because they referenced effective dates, termination status, and amendment chains.

The lesson extends far beyond legal. Any AI solution built on unstructured enterprise content will fail until the content's business meaning is modeled, governed, and ranked as part of the data architecture.

Closing Synthesis

Unstructured data is not an awkward edge case in enterprise architecture. It is where much of the enterprise actually explains itself. Policies express intent. Contracts define obligation. Procedures define action. Notes capture rationale. Tickets preserve operational truth. Articles encode institutional memory. Transcripts expose real-world interaction. Emails often contain the decision path no system of record was built to capture.

If that estate is treated as secondary, enterprise AI will remain shallow and brittle. It may retrieve text, but it will not consistently retrieve authority. It may generate summaries, but it will not reliably generate trust.

The architectural mandate is, therefore, clear. Unstructured content must be governed as an asset class, not merely stored as files. It must be inventoried, classified, owned, enriched, permissioned, versioned, ranked, and lifecycle-managed. Metadata must function as the control plane. Semantics must reduce ambiguity. Retrieval design must account for authority, freshness, and evidence. Governance must extend across narrative content, not stop at structured data.

This is also an operating model question. Enterprises need stewards, decision rights, review disciplines, and accountability for content that matters. They need to know which repositories are suitable for AI, which are not, and which require targeted remediation. They need to elevate document strategy into data strategy.

The payoff is substantial. Once unstructured content is treated as a first-class enterprise asset, AI systems can do more than sound helpful. They can become grounded, explainable, policy-aware, and operationally trustworthy. That is the difference between experimentation and durable enterprise capability.

Key Takeaways

- The business meaning AI needs most often lives in documents, conversations, and narrative content rather than in structured systems alone.
- Repository presence does not equal AI-readiness; ownership, metadata, authority, lifecycle, and permissions are essential.
- Content architecture matters as much as content storage because AI must interpret, rank, and justify what it retrieves.
- Unstructured content requires differentiated governance based on criticality, regulatory relevance, evidentiary value, and intended use.
- Enterprises scale trustworthy AI only when they elevate document strategy into a governed, metadata-driven data strategy.

Chapter 8: Why Document Repositories Alone Are Not Enough

Most enterprises already have no shortage of documents. Policies live in SharePoint. Contracts sit in file shares. Knowledge articles are spread across portals. Meeting notes are buried in collaboration tools. Email threads contain critical decisions. Presentations explain strategy better than the official documentation. Teams often look at this landscape and conclude that because the content exists, the organization is ready to use it for AI. It is not.

A document repository is a storage environment, not an AI-ready knowledge system. It may be excellent at preserving files, organizing folders, applying retention labels, and supporting human search. None of that guarantees the content can be safely and reliably used by a copilot, assistant, or agent. For AI use, the problem is not whether documents exist. The problem is whether the system can discover the right content, interpret it correctly, preserve permissions, distinguish authoritative sources from noise, detect staleness, retrieve the relevant passage, and present it with enough provenance to justify trust.

That is a fundamentally different standard.

A human can often work around repository weaknesses. People know which team actually owns a policy. They know that "final_v2" is newer than "final." They know which deck is outdated even when its filename looks current. They know that an unsigned draft contract in a collaboration folder should not override the executed version in a legal system. AI systems do not possess that organizational intuition unless the architecture supplies it.

This is why document repositories alone are not enough. Storage location does not equal semantic readiness. Search indexing does not equal trustworthy retrieval. Metadata designed for records management is not the same as metadata needed for grounded AI. What matters is not whether content has been stored, but whether it has been prepared for machine use under enterprise conditions of trust, governance, and accountability.

The practical implication is decisive: document preparation is not a clerical cleanup exercise. It is an architectural function. It determines whether enterprise AI produces grounded responses or confident confusion.

Why This Matters

Repositories Create a False Sense of Readiness

Many AI initiatives begin with a seemingly reasonable assumption: "Our documents are already in one place, so we can point a model at them." This assumption fails because content repositories were usually designed for human browsing, collaboration, retention, and compliance—not for retrieval-aware machine grounding.

A repository can be well managed by traditional standards and still be unusable for AI. The files may be accessible, indexed, and retained correctly, yet still lack clear authority, version control, effective dates, semantic labeling, structural segmentation, or trustworthy citation anchors. In that condition, the repository supports storage but not reliable interpretation.

This gap matters because AI systems compress ambiguity into answers. A search engine can show ten plausible documents and let the user decide. A copilot may synthesize across those same documents and present a single response that sounds definitive. If the underlying content set contains duplicates, stale versions, contradictory drafts, or jurisdictional mismatches, the AI does not merely surface the confusion. It operationalizes it.

The Risk Increases as the AI Consumer Becomes More Powerful

The danger is not limited to chat-style assistants. As organizations move from passive Q&A to copilots and then to action-taking agents, the tolerance for content ambiguity falls dramatically.

A human employee asking, "What is the travel reimbursement limit?" can spot an odd answer and verify it. An executive briefing tool that cites the wrong policy erodes trust. An HR assistant who surfaces a superseded leave rule creates compliance risk. An agent that initiates an action based on outdated contractual language crosses from inconvenience into operational failure.

The stronger the AI system's role in decision support or action execution, the more important document readiness becomes. This is why unstructured content must be treated as a first-class enterprise asset and not as an incidental byproduct of collaboration.

Most Enterprise Meaning Lives Outside Rows and Columns

Structured data remains essential, but much of the meaning that AI needs is expressed in documents, not tables. Policies explain how rules should be interpreted. Contracts define obligations. Procedures describe exceptions. Architecture decisions are captured in memos and presentations. Regulatory nuance often appears in guidance documents, not transaction systems.

This is precisely why repositories matter—and why repository quality alone is insufficient. The most valuable enterprise knowledge is often unstructured, but unstructured does not mean unmanaged. To make it usable for AI, organizations must design for curation, enrichment, provenance, access fidelity, freshness, and retrieval quality.

KEY INSIGHT

Repository Is Not Readiness

A repository answers the question, "Where is the file stored?"

AI-readiness answers harder questions:

- Is this the authoritative version?
- Is it still current?
- Who owns it?
- What business concepts does it define?
- Which audience and jurisdiction does it apply to?
- Can the AI retrieve the right section, under the right permissions, and cite it correctly?

If those questions cannot be answered systematically, the repository is not AI-ready.

CORE CONCEPTS

Storage Location Does Not Equal Semantic Readiness

The first misconception to remove is that location carries meaning. It does not. A file stored in a "Policies" folder is not necessarily policy-grade content. A document on a legal site may be a draft. A knowledge article with a clean URL may be obsolete. Folder hierarchy and repository placement provide weak signals, not strong guarantees.

Semantic readiness requires explicit context. The system must know what the document is, what business domain it belongs to, who owns it, whether it is authoritative, when it became effective, where it applies, and what concepts it defines or governs. Without this context, retrieval becomes shallow pattern matching rather than grounded enterprise reasoning.

That distinction is critical. AI does not merely need text. It needs interpretable text with enterprise meaning attached.

Most Repositories Contain Noise, Duplicates, and Weak Authority Signals

Enterprise repositories are rarely clean. They contain meeting exports, annotated drafts, duplicate uploads, superseded versions, partial extracts, informal summaries, and copies moved between collaboration spaces. Some content is valuable for human context but inappropriate for AI grounding. Some is authoritative in one region but invalid in another. Some is obsolete but still heavily viewed. Some is technically accessible but legally restricted.

In this environment, naive ingestion creates predictable failure. The system retrieves what is easy to index, not what is safest to trust.

This is why content curation is a front-door control, not a downstream optimization. Before content is chunked and indexed, it must be filtered, classified, deduplicated, and authority-ranked. Otherwise, the system simply scales repository disorder.

Retrieval Quality Depends on More Than Search Indexing

Traditional enterprise search focused on findability. AI grounding requires much more. The relevant challenge is not whether the document can be found somewhere, but whether the right passage can be retrieved, ranked correctly, contextualized appropriately, permission-checked, and cited in a defensible way.

A keyword index may retrieve a document containing the phrase the user asked about. That does not mean the returned section is the correct one. It does not mean the document is current. It does not mean the answer should be synthesized from that document rather than from a newer policy, a regional addendum, or a system-of-record source.

Retrieval quality is, therefore, an architecture problem. It depends on chunking strategy, enrichment logic, authority signals, effective dates, source weighting, semantic mapping, access control preservation, temporal filtering, and citation design. Search indexing is one layer, not the solution.

AI-Serving Metadata Is Different from Repository Metadata

Most repositories already maintain metadata. That is useful, but it is not sufficient. Repository metadata typically supports storage, retention, records management, and navigation. AI-serving metadata must support interpretation, ranking, trust, and safe reuse.

A records manager may care that a file belongs to a retention class and has a disposition date. An AI-serving layer also needs to know whether that file is authoritative, which business concepts it governs, what audience it applies to, whether it has been superseded, how it should be chunked, how citations should be anchored, whether summarization has been approved, and what freshness service level applies.

This difference is often underestimated. Teams assume they can "reuse existing metadata" and discover too late that the fields required for trustworthy grounding were never designed into the content estate.

Document Preparation Is an Architectural Function

Because of these requirements, document preparation cannot be delegated as a low-level content task. It sits at the intersection of information architecture, metadata design, governance, retrieval engineering, and platform operations.

Someone must define which documents are eligible for AI serving. Someone must define authority rules when multiple versions exist. Someone must decide how regional applicability is represented. Someone must determine how structural sections are captured, how chunks inherit metadata, how access controls propagate, and how citations map back to source passages.

These are architectural decisions because they shape system behavior at scale. If they are left implicit, the AI layer will infer them poorly or ignore them entirely.

KEY INSIGHT

What Machine-Readiness Adds to Content Management

Traditional content management asks whether content is stored, versioned, retained, and accessible.

Machine-readiness adds new requirements:

- Explicit authority signals.
- Semantic labeling.
- Structural segmentation.
- Effective dating.
- Audience and jurisdiction scope.
- Duplicate detection.
- Access-preserving chunking.
- Citation anchors.
- Freshness controls.
- Approval for AI summarization and reuse.

This is not a replacement for content management. It is an additional architectural layer.

Architectural Implications

The Architecture Must Insert a Preparation Pipeline Between Repository and Model

❖ FIGURE 15 – REPOSITORY-TO-GROUNDING PIPELINE

The most important design principle in this chapter is simple: there must be architecture between storage and serving.

Repositories should feed an AI preparation pipeline, not the model directly. That pipeline establishes the controls needed to transform stored content into grounded content. At a minimum, it should include inventorying, curation, enrichment, chunking, indexing, retrieval controls, and citation mapping.

Inventory Must Precede Ingestion

Architecturally, the first step is not ingestion. It is inventory. The organization must know what classes of documents exist, where they live, which repositories are in scope, who owns them, and what basic metadata is available. This sounds obvious, but many programs skip it. They ingest whatever connectors make easy access possible and only later discover that key repositories are missing while low-value collaboration spaces dominate the corpus.

Inventory should identify document types, source systems, ownership domains, sensitivity levels, version patterns, regional variants, and likely authority hierarchies. It should also identify known problem zones:

abandoned team sites, uncontrolled shared folders, duplicated content libraries, and repositories with weak permission hygiene.

Without inventory, the AI corpus is shaped by convenience rather than design.

A meeting transcript may be useful for internal context, but it should not override a signed policy. A slide deck may summarize a process but should not be treated as the governing source. A draft procedure may help a subject matter expert, but it may be inappropriate for broad assistant grounding.

❖ FIGURE 16 – CONTENT CURATION FUNNEL

This is why content curation should be represented as a funnel rather than a binary include-or-exclude decision.

This funnel is a crucial design discipline. Total content represents what exists. Usable content removes obvious noise. Authoritative content identifies what the enterprise should trust as a primary source. AI-ready content further narrows the set to material that has been enriched, permission-checked, freshness-scored, and prepared for retrieval and citation.

KEY INSIGHT

Curation must separate usable content from authoritative content

Not all usable content is authoritative, and not all authoritative content is AI-ready. Architecture must distinguish these states explicitly.

Enrichment Must Make Enterprise Meaning Explicit

Once content has been curated, it must be enriched. Enrichment adds the metadata and structure that repositories often lack. This may include document type, domain, owner, effective date, version, jurisdiction, sensitivity classification, business concepts, associated entities, related policies, and authoritative status.

Enrichment also includes structural preparation. Many documents are written for human reading, not machine retrieval. They need section boundaries, heading capture, passage IDs, reference anchors, and consistent handling of appendices, tables, footnotes, and embedded exceptions.

A well-architected enrichment process ensures that when the AI retrieves a passage, it retrieves not just text but context: this section comes from the approved North America travel policy, effective January 1, reviewed by Finance, superseding the previous reimbursement memo.

Chunking Must Preserve Meaning, Access, and Evidence

Chunking is often treated as a technical implementation detail. It is not. Poor chunking destroys trust.

If chunks are too small, policy statements lose surrounding conditions and exceptions. If they are too large, retrieval becomes noisy and citations become vague. If chunks cross access boundaries, users may receive content they should not see. If chunk inheritance is weak, provenance disappears.

Architecturally, the chunking strategy must be document-type aware. A contract should not be chunked like a FAQ article. A policy should preserve section identity and applicability clauses. A procedure should maintain step order and preconditions. Tables may need special treatment so that row-level meaning is not lost.

The chunking strategy is part of the data-serving contract. It determines whether the AI system answers with evidence or with fragments.

Citations Must Be Designed, Not Appended

Trustworthy enterprise AI depends on showing where an answer came from. That requires more than displaying a file link. The system should be able to cite the exact source section, version, effective date, and repository origin in a way the user can inspect.

Citation design must account for source stability. If documents move, rename, or get replaced, citations should still resolve. This usually requires persistent document identifiers and section-level anchors rather than fragile location references.

A useful citation does three things: it lets the user verify the answer, it communicates authority, and it exposes temporal correctness. "Source: Travel Policy, section 4.2, Finance domain, effective January 1, 2026" is far more trustworthy than "Source: policy-final-v3.docx."

Permissions Must Remain Intact Across Transformation

One of the easiest ways to destroy trust is to break access control during enrichment and retrieval. It is not enough to secure the repository. Permissions must survive extraction, transformation, chunking, indexing, and serving.

This is especially important when documents contain mixed sensitivity, such as regional HR rules, customer contracts, legal correspondence, or investigation materials. If the serving layer loses permission fidelity, the AI system becomes a leakage path.

The architecture must, therefore, preserve or reapply access models at the serving layer. Eligibility for retrieval should be evaluated against the user's entitlements, not just against repository availability at ingestion time.

Failure Modes and Anti-Patterns

"Connect Everything and Let Search Sort It Out"

This is the most common failure pattern in document-grounded AI. Teams ingest vast amounts of content from collaboration platforms, shared drives, and knowledge portals without a curation model. They assume embedding, indexing, and ranking will separate the signal from the noise.

It will not.

When the corpus contains conflicting drafts, duplicate policies, obsolete manuals, training decks, and regional variants, the retrieval layer inherits ambiguity that it cannot safely resolve. Similarity search is not a substitute for authority design.

Treating Filename Conventions as Governance

Enterprises often rely on human naming habits as a pseudo-control layer: "approved," "current," "final," "published," "new," or "v2." These conventions are weak even for people and disastrous for AI. They are not persistent, not standardized, and not sufficient to establish authority.

A system that cannot distinguish between "Leave_Policy_Final" and "Leave_Policy_Final_Updated" through explicit metadata is not ready for AI grounding.

KEY INSIGHT

Multiple "final" versions of the same policy

This is not a minor hygiene issue. It is a direct indicator that authority has not been architected. If the enterprise cannot determine which document governs, an AI assistant will either choose incorrectly or merge conflicting rules into a misleading answer.

Assuming Repository Metadata Is Enough

Some teams believe that because a document has author, modified date, and folder path metadata, it is sufficiently described. Those fields help with storage management and human navigation. They do little to support grounded AI behavior.

Modified date is not the same as effective date. Author is not the same as business owner. Folder name is not the same as owning domain. A file extension is not a document type. Search tags are not semantic concepts.

If the architecture does not distinguish these categories, retrieval and ranking will remain brittle.

Ignoring Freshness and Review Cycles

Many enterprise documents do not become wrong because their text is poor. They become wrong because their context changes. Policies are revised. Regulations update. Contract clauses expire. Procedures are replaced. FAQ articles remain online long after process changes.

When freshness is not modeled, the AI system treats every retrievable document as equally live. That is how stale content becomes operational advice.

Freshness cannot be handled only at the repository level. The AI-serving layer needs review dates, effective dates, supersession signals, and refresh SLAs that determine whether content remains eligible for retrieval.

Preparing Content Without an Evidence Model

Some systems ingest and summarize documents for easier AI consumption but fail to preserve traceability back to the source. This produces polished answers with weak auditability. Users may get a clean summary but no ability to verify the exact clause, paragraph, or section from which it was derived.

That is acceptable for casual consumer use. It is not acceptable for enterprise environments where advice, policy, compliance, and action must be defensible.

Practical Application

Build a Content Eligibility Model

The first practical step is to define which content is allowed into the AI-serving estate and under what conditions. This should be explicit, not assumed. The eligibility model should answer questions such as:

- Which repositories are in scope?
- Which document types are admissible?
- Which roles can designate authoritative status?
- Which classes of content are excluded from grounding?
- What freshness thresholds apply?
- What enrichment fields are mandatory before serving?
- What access controls must be preserved?

This eligibility model becomes a governance instrument as much as a technical control.

Establish Authority Rules by Document Class

Different content types need different authority logic. Policies may require business owner approval and an effective date. Contracts may require execution status and jurisdiction. Knowledge articles may require a publication workflow and a named service owner. Process documents may require system linkage and review cadence.

These rules should not remain tribal knowledge. They should be encoded into metadata models and pipeline checks. The goal is to make authoritative status computable.

Treat Curation as a Funnel, Not a One-Time Cleanup

In practical deployment, content curation should be continuous. New documents are created every day. Existing ones are revised, copied, localized, and retired. The curation funnel, therefore, needs operating ownership, not just project funding.

A sustainable pattern is to assign domain stewards who can approve authority status, while platform teams manage the enrichment and serving pipeline. This division matters. Business domains understand meaning and ownership. Platform teams understand transformation, indexing, retrieval, and controls. AI-ready content requires both.

Design Retrieval Around User Trust, Not Just Relevance Score

In a human search experience, near matches can be useful. In an AI experience, trust often matters more than broad recall. The retrieval architecture should, therefore, rank for authority, freshness, applicability, and permission fidelity alongside semantic similarity.

The right answer is not merely the most similar chunk. It is the most defensible source for the user's context.

Templates

Document Enrichment Checklist

Document ID	<unique immutable identifier assigned to the document>
Title	<official title of the document>
Document type	<type of document, such as policy, contract, procedure, article, transcript, memo, or other>
Owning domain	<business domain or functional area responsible for the document, such as Finance, HR, Legal, Operations, IT, or Sales>
Business owner	<named accountable owner responsible for the document's business relevance and governance>
Authoritative status	<current authority state of the document, such as authoritative, supporting, draft, archived, or superseded>
Effective date	<date on which the document becomes formally in force, typically in YYYY-MM-DD format>
Review date	<date by which the document should next be reviewed, typically in YYYY-MM-DD format>

Version	<formal version number, revision label, or release designation>
Jurisdiction/region	<geographic, legal, or organizational scope to which the document applies, such as global, region, country, or state>
Audience	<intended readership or user group for the document, such as all employees, managers, HR partners, customers, legal only, or other>
Sensitivity classification	<security, confidentiality, or privilege classification assigned to the document, such as public, internal, confidential, restricted, or privileged>
Source repository	<repository, site, platform, or system in which the authoritative version of the document is stored>
Duplicate check status	<status of duplicate review, such as passed, duplicate found, or needs review>
Summarization status	<status indicating whether the document may be summarized by AI, such as approved, not approved, or approved with restrictions>
Section structure captured? yes/no	<Yes or No>
Chunking strategy	<method used to divide the document for retrieval and AI use, such as section-based, clause-based, page-based, table-aware, or custom>
Citation strategy	<method used to reference evidence from the document, such as document and section, clause and page, passage ID, URL anchor, or other>
Access model preserved? yes/no	<Yes or No>
Freshness SLA	<required review or update expectation for the document, such as 90-day review, annual review, or event-driven update>
AI-approved? yes/no	<Yes or No>
Notes	<exceptions, caveats, dependencies, special conditions, or unresolved issues related to the document>

Case Example

The Hidden Architecture Problem Behind Policy Assistant Failure

A global enterprise launched an internal policy assistant intended to answer employee questions across HR, Finance, and Operations. The technical team moved quickly. They connected the assistant to a major collaboration repository that contained thousands of policy documents, process notes, FAQs, and archived team files. Search indexing worked well. Early demonstrations looked promising.

Then, employees started asking operational questions.

A manager in Germany asked about travel reimbursement rules for client dinners. The assistant returned a clean answer with four cited sources. The problem was that the sources disagreed. One was a current regional policy. One was a global travel guide from two years earlier. One was a Finance training deck that summarized old thresholds. One was a draft FAQ created during a temporary policy exception.

From the model's perspective, the answer looked well-grounded because multiple documents mentioned the same topic. From the enterprise's perspective, it was a governance failure. The repository had never been curated for authority. Effective dates were inconsistent. Regional applicability was not modeled. Draft and training content were not separated from governing policy. Duplicate content had never been rationalized. Citations were present, but they merely exposed the confusion.

The organization initially framed this as a model quality issue. It was not. The model had done exactly what the architecture allowed: retrieve relevant-looking text from a noisy corpus and synthesize an answer. The failure originated in repository hygiene, metadata poverty, and the absence of an AI-serving control plane.

The remediation effort changed the program's trajectory. The team paused the broad rollout and implemented a content readiness process. Finance and HR identified authoritative policy sources. Regional variants were explicitly tagged. Drafts and training decks were excluded from grounding. Effective dates and supersession relationships were added. Documents were re-chunked by policy section rather than by fixed page windows. Citation anchors were redesigned to point to stable section references. The assistant's corpus became smaller, but its trustworthiness improved dramatically.

This is the key lesson. AI quality did not improve because the model became more advanced. It improved because the content estate became more governable.

Closing Synthesis

Document repositories are indispensable, but they are not enough. They solve the problem of storing content, not the problem of preparing knowledge for trustworthy machine use. That distinction is now central to enterprise architecture.

The organizations that scale AI successfully will not treat repositories as ready-made grounding layers. They will treat them as source environments feeding a broader architecture of inventory, curation, enrichment, access preservation, retrieval design, and citation control. They will recognize that the gap between "file exists" and "AI can safely use it" is not small. It is the gap between storage and trust.

This has strategic consequences. Unstructured content can no longer be managed as peripheral material surrounding the "real" data estate. In many enterprises, it contains the rules, explanations, obligations, and business meaning that AI systems need most. If that content is not governed, enriched, and operationalized, the AI layer will remain brittle no matter how advanced the models become.

The right architectural response is, therefore, clear. Treat document preparation as a first-class discipline. Define authority. Model freshness. Preserve permissions. Enrich semantics. Design chunking and citation intentionally. Build a serving layer that understands not just where content is stored, but what it means, whether it applies, and why it should be trusted.

That is how repositories become part of an AI-Ready Data estate.

Key Takeaways

- A document repository is a storage system, not an AI-ready knowledge system.
- Repository content must be curated, enriched, permission-aware, and freshness-controlled before it is suitable for AI grounding.
- Retrieval quality depends on authority, structure, chunking, metadata, and citation design—not just search indexing.
- AI-serving metadata is different from repository metadata and must be architected explicitly.
- Document preparation is an architectural responsibility because it determines whether enterprise AI is trustworthy at scale.

CHAPTER 9: METADATA IS THE CONTROL PLANE FOR AI

Metadata is not an administrative afterthought. In the AI era, metadata becomes the control plane that determines whether information can be found, interpreted, trusted, ranked, governed, and safely used. That is the architectural shift. The enterprise that still treats metadata as a sidecar to storage, integration, or compliance will struggle to scale trustworthy AI, no matter how much it invests in models, vector indexes, or copilots.

For years, many organizations treated metadata as useful but secondary. It helped populate catalogs, support impact analysis, and satisfy audit questions. Those are still valid uses, but they are no longer sufficient. AI systems consume information differently than dashboards, reports, and many traditional applications. They do not merely query named tables or display predefined fields. They retrieve, rank, summarize, compare, infer, and act across heterogeneous assets. To do that well, they need context: what a source means, who owns it, whether it is authoritative, how current it is, what policies apply, whether it is safe for a given use case, and how it should be cited back to a user.

That context is metadata.

Without metadata, AI systems do not operate on an enterprise knowledge estate. They operate on a pile of text, tables, files, and events with weak signals about meaning and trust. The result is predictable: poor retrieval, weak explanations, policy leakage, stale answers, and low user confidence. With strong metadata, the same information estate can become navigable, rankable, governable, and explainable.

The central argument of this chapter is straightforward: if data is the asset, metadata is the operating system. It is the mechanism through which enterprise AI can discover the right sources, enforce constraints, determine trust, and produce grounded outputs that can survive operational and regulatory scrutiny.

WHY THIS MATTERS

AI Needs More Than Access

Most analytics systems can tolerate a surprising amount of metadata weakness. A reporting stack can still function if a table name is cryptic, an owner is missing, or a document has no lifecycle marker. Skilled analysts compensate through institutional knowledge, tribal familiarity, and repeated exposure. AI systems do not have that luxury.

An AI assistant retrieving policy content must know which version is current, whether the policy applies in a given jurisdiction, whether a procedure document overrides a knowledge article, and whether the user is authorized to see the underlying content. An agent proposing an action based on operational data must know whether a feed is delayed, whether a value is estimated or final, and whether the source is authoritative for that decision. A briefing assistant summarizing contract risk must understand sensitivity, retention constraints, and citation requirements before it ever generates prose.

These are metadata questions, not model questions.

AI-Serving Systems Amplify Metadata Gaps

The more an organization moves from human-only consumption toward copilots, assistants, and agents, the more metadata gaps become operational risks. Weak metadata may remain invisible in a dashboard environment because humans manually compensate. In an AI-serving environment, those same gaps surface as automation defects.

A missing business owner means nobody can validate whether a source is still fit for use. A missing authoritative status means retrieval may rank a draft above a signed policy. A missing freshness indicator means stale data can be summarized as a current fact. Missing sensitivity classification means private content may leak into an answer. Missing semantic tags mean retrieval may find text with lexical overlap but no business relevance. Missing lineage means nobody can explain where an answer came from.

Metadata poverty is, therefore, not a documentation issue. It is a scale limiter.

The Enterprise Trust Problem Is a Metadata Problem

When business users say they do not trust AI, they are often describing metadata failures in practical language. They mean:

- "It cited the wrong document."
- "It used an outdated policy."
- "It mixed internal guidance with customer-facing content."
- "It could not explain where the number came from."
- "It gave a plausible answer, but I cannot tell whether it is allowed."
- "It found something relevant, but not the authoritative source."

Each complaint traces back to missing or weak metadata. Trustworthy AI is not produced by eloquence. It is produced by disciplined control over source meaning, source status, policy, lineage, freshness, and evidence.

CORE CONCEPTS

Technical Metadata Is Necessary, but Insufficient

Technical metadata includes schemas, field names, data types, pipeline dependencies, repository paths, timestamps, and system lineage. It remains essential. Without it, the enterprise cannot inventory its estate or understand how systems connect. But technical metadata alone cannot support enterprise AI-readiness.

A column name does not explain the business meaning. A file path does not indicate authoritative status. A timestamp does not reveal whether a source is valid for decision-making. A repository identifier does not express policy restrictions. A parser-generated chunk ID does not tell an assistant how to cite a source back to a user.

AI-serving systems require technical metadata, but they also require business, policy, operational, and AI-serving metadata.

Business Metadata Gives Meaning

Business metadata explains what an asset is for, what it means, and where it belongs in the enterprise context. Typical elements include business title, business description, business owner, domain, steward, intended audience, and semantic tags. This is what allows AI systems to retrieve content based on conceptual relevance rather than mere keyword overlap.

Consider the difference between two documents titled "Leave Policy Update" and "Manager Guidance on Time Off Exceptions." A purely lexical retrieval layer may treat them as peers. Business metadata distinguishes its role. One may be the authoritative employee policy; the other may be supporting guidance for supervisors. That difference is decisive for grounding.

Policy Metadata Governs Safe Use

Policy metadata expresses what is allowed, restricted, retained, classified, or jurisdictionally bounded. It includes sensitivity classification, retention category, legal hold status, privacy applicability, region, use constraints, and allowed or restricted AI uses. This metadata does not just support governance after the fact. It must shape retrieval and delivery at runtime.

An enterprise cannot safely deploy AI if policy is evaluated only after content has already been retrieved and summarized. The control plane has to constrain what can be discovered, ranked, passed to models, cached, cited, or actioned.

Operational Metadata Determines Reliability

Operational metadata describes freshness, validation status, review cadence, update frequency, lifecycle state, and source health. It tells the AI-serving layer whether an asset is active, stale, provisional, deprecated, or pending review. This is essential because many enterprise sources are not continuously trustworthy. They drift.

A knowledge article last reviewed three years ago is not equivalent to one reviewed last month. A policy with a future effective date is not equivalent to one already in force. An event feed delayed by six hours should not be treated as real-time operational truth.

AI-Serving Metadata Closes the Final Gap

AI-serving metadata is the class most organizations lack. It includes attributes such as citation method, grounding priority, trust score, chunking strategy, ranking features, answerability scope, evidence requirements, and allowed AI uses. This is the metadata specifically required to support assistants and agents.

Analytics systems rarely need to know how a source should be cited back to a user. AI systems do. Traditional catalogs rarely include explicit restrictions such as "may be used for summarization but not for prescriptive recommendations." AI-serving architectures need exactly that. Without this layer, the enterprise may have an excellent catalog and still remain unready for trustworthy AI.

❖ FIGURE 17 – METADATA CONTROL PLANE

KEY INSIGHT

If data is the asset, metadata is the operating system

Data stores content. Metadata makes that content usable. It tells enterprise systems what the asset is, who owns it, whether it is current, whether it is sensitive, how it should be interpreted, how it should be ranked, and whether it can be used for a given AI purpose. Without that operating layer, the estate may be large, but it is not governable.

ARCHITECTURAL IMPLICATIONS

Metadata Must Be Modeled Across All Data Classes

A common failure is to invest heavily in metadata for structured data while leaving documents, messages, transcripts, and collaborative content comparatively unmanaged. That split is no longer viable. AI systems often derive the most critical business meaning from unstructured and semi-structured assets. If those assets lack owner, lifecycle, authority, and policy metadata, they become retrieval liabilities.

The architecture must, therefore, support metadata enrichment across:

- Structured assets such as tables, fields, metrics, and master data.
- Semi-structured assets such as events, payloads, logs, and messages.
- Unstructured assets such as policies, contracts, procedures, transcripts, notes, and articles.

This is not a matter of cataloging everything identically. Different asset classes require different metadata shapes. But they must participate in a shared control plane.

Metadata Must Be Runtime-Relevant, Not Just Catalog-Deep

Many metadata programs are designed for offline discovery and governance workflows. That is useful, but AI requires runtime use. Metadata must be available to retrieval pipelines, orchestration layers, ranking models, security controls, and answer-generation components.

That means architecture teams should ask new questions:

- Can the retrieval layer use authoritative status as a ranking feature?
- Can the serving layer filter by allowed AI use before content is passed to a model?
- Can freshness metadata down-rank stale assets automatically?
- Can citation metadata determine how evidence is rendered to the user?
- Can lineage pointers be surfaced in explanations and audit trails?
- Can semantic tags and business definitions shape chunk enrichment?

If the answer is no, the metadata estate is still operating as documentation, not as control.

Metadata Must Support Access-Aware Delivery

Permissions alone are not metadata, but permission fidelity depends on metadata-adjacent structures: identity mappings, asset classification, inheritance behavior, audience designation, and repository context. The AI-serving architecture must know not just whether a user can technically access a file, but whether the asset is suitable for the specific interaction.

An employee may have repository access to broad internal content. That does not mean every asset is appropriate for summarization into a broad audience briefing, or for use by an action-taking agent. Allowed AI uses and audience metadata help close that gap.

Ranking Is a Metadata-Driven Discipline

Retrieval quality is often described as a search or embedding problem. In practice, enterprise ranking depends heavily on metadata. Relevance is necessary but not sufficient. A highly relevant document may still be the wrong source if it is deprecated, local, draft, or non-authoritative.

Mature ranking strategies use metadata such as:

- Authoritative status.
- Business owner presence.
- Last validation date.
- Effective date.
- Lifecycle status.
- Source system authority.
- Sensitivity and access fit.
- Semantic tag match.
- Citation readiness.
- Trust score.

This is why metadata is the control plane. It tells the system not only what might answer the question, but what should answer it.

Explainability Depends on Metadata Structure

Enterprise explainability is not achieved by simply showing users snippets. Users need context about why a source was used and whether it should be trusted. That requires metadata that can be surfaced in the answer experience: title, owner, effective date, status, source system, validation date, and citation method.

A source without enough metadata may still be technically retrievable, but it is weak evidence. In a serious enterprise setting, evidence must be interpretable by both humans and control functions.

❖ FIGURE 18 - METADATA-TO-TRUST MAP

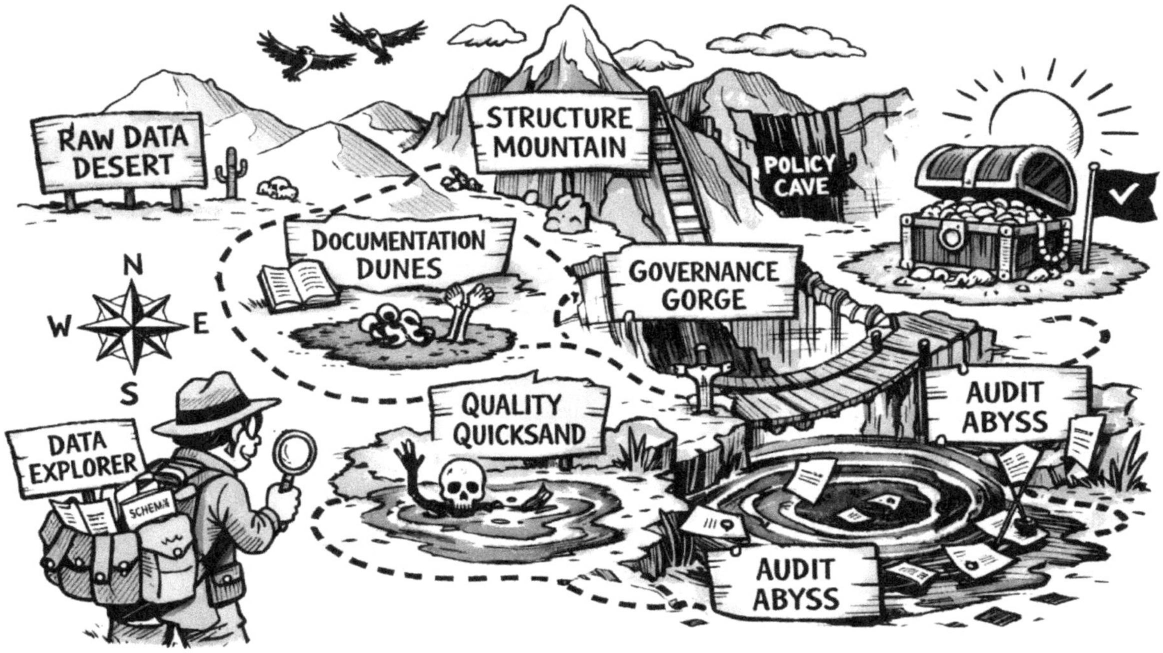

FAILURE MODES AND ANTI-PATTERNS

Metadata Poverty

Metadata poverty describes an estate where assets technically exist, but meaningful context is missing or too thin to support reliable AI use. The sources may have titles, authors, timestamps, and storage locations, but little else. The organization may claim to have a catalog, yet still lack the metadata needed for grounded retrieval and policy-aware serving.

KEY INSIGHT

Metadata poverty: what it looks like

- Assets with only title, author, and create date.
- No business owner or steward.
- No clear authoritative status.
- No review cadence or validation date.
- No sensitivity or retention category.
- No indication of allowed or restricted AI use.
- No semantic tags or business description.
- No lineage pointer.
- No citation method.
- No way to distinguish current from obsolete content.

In this state, the enterprise can search, but it cannot reliably trust, govern, or scale AI use.

Technical Metadata Only

Another anti-pattern is equating metadata maturity with data lineage tooling alone. Lineage is valuable, but lineage without a business and policy context does not solve AI-readiness. Knowing that Table B depends on Table A does not explain whether either table is authoritative for a particular decision, whether the result is suitable for external communication, or whether the source can be used in a conversational assistant.

Uniform Metadata for Fundamentally Different Assets

Some organizations attempt to solve the problem by forcing one generic metadata template onto every source. The result is shallow compliance and low usefulness. Contracts, policies, tables, transcripts, and event streams do not require identical enrichment. They require a shared control framework with asset-specific extensions.

The goal is not rigid sameness. The goal is interoperable richness.

Governance After Retrieval

A dangerous anti-pattern is allowing AI systems to retrieve broadly, then attempting to mask or filter sensitive content later in the pipeline. By that stage, risk has already materialized. Policy metadata must participate earlier, shaping discovery and ranking before content reaches the model.

Weak Lifecycle Control

Many organizations underestimate the damage caused by stale yet discoverable content. In a search-driven AI environment, obsolete material competes with current material unless lifecycle metadata clearly differentiates them. An old regional procedure can outrank a current enterprise standard if metadata does not signal authority and validity.

⚠ **WARNING SIGN**

Content with title and author only

A document that contains only a title, author, and modified date may be perfectly acceptable in a file repository. It is not acceptable as an enterprise AI asset. If the system cannot tell what the document is for, who stands behind it, whether it is current, whether it is sensitive, and whether it is allowed for a particular AI use, then it is not ready to ground trustworthy output.

PRACTICAL APPLICATION

Start with a Minimum Viable Metadata Standard

Organizations do not need to solve all metadata problems at once. They do need a minimum viable standard that reflects AI-serving realities. This standard should define the non-negotiable fields required for an asset to participate in enterprise AI scenarios.

The standard should apply first to high-value domains and high-risk use cases, not to every asset in the company on day one. The key is to make metadata useful enough to influence runtime behavior.

How to Use the Standard

This artifact should not live only in a policy document. It should be implemented into cataloging workflows, ingestion pipelines, repository enrichment, and retrieval logic. Each field should have a reason to exist in the serving architecture. For example:

- **Authoritative status** influences ranking.
- **Sensitivity classification** influences access-aware filtering.
- **Allowed AI uses** influence orchestration and prompt routing.
- **Citation method** influences answer formatting.
- **Last validation date** influences freshness confidence.
- **Semantic tags** influence retrieval and disambiguation.
- **Business owner** supports escalation and stewardship.

This is the critical design principle: metadata fields should not be collected merely because they seem administratively sensible. They should be collected because they affect real control decisions.

Prioritize Enrichment Where AI Value and Risk Are Highest

The best starting point is not "all metadata for all assets." It is high-value, high-consequence domains: policy libraries, customer support knowledge, financial definitions, HR procedures, legal templates, product specifications, operational runbooks, and executive briefing sources.

These sources are frequently used by assistants and often carry material risk if misinterpreted. They deserve metadata enrichment first.

Treat Trust Scoring Carefully

A trust score can be useful, but only if it is transparent and decomposable. It should never function as a magic number. Users and systems should be able to understand what drives it: ownership completeness, validation recency, authority, policy status, lifecycle health, and lineage completeness. Trust is not a branding badge. It is a managed signal.

TEMPLATES

Enterprise Metadata Minimum Viable Standard

Asset ID	<globally unique, immutable identifier assigned to the asset>
Asset type	<governed class of asset, such as table, metric, report, policy, procedure, contract, article, transcript, event stream, API payload, knowledge page, email, or other>
Business title	<human-readable title that reflects the asset's business meaning rather than repository or system naming conventions>
Business description	<plain-language description of what the asset contains, what it is for, and when it should be used>
Domain	<business domain, function, or capability area to which the asset belongs, such as Finance, HR, Legal, Procurement, Sales, Operations, or Risk>
Business owner	<named accountable owner responsible for the asset's business fitness, relevance, and authoritative use>
Steward	<named steward responsible for metadata quality, lifecycle maintenance, and coordination of issues or changes>
Authoritative status	<current authority state of the asset, such as authoritative, supporting, draft, deprecated, archived, superseded, or local-only>

Source system/repository	<system of record, repository, or governed platform in which the asset is mastered, maintained, or controlled>
Sensitivity classification	<security, confidentiality, privacy, or regulatory classification assigned to the asset, using the enterprise classification scheme>
Policy/retention category	<applicable retention class, legal basis, records category, or policy grouping governing the asset>
Effective date	<date from which the asset is considered valid and approved for use>
Refresh/update frequency	<expected frequency with which the asset is updated, such as real-time, hourly, daily, weekly, monthly, event-driven, ad hoc, or not expected to refresh>
Review cadence	<expected interval or trigger for formal review, such as monthly, quarterly, semiannual, annual, trigger-based, or exception-based>
Lineage pointer	<reference, link, or identifier for upstream and downstream lineage, provenance records, or source chain documentation>
Allowed AI uses	<approved AI usage patterns for the asset, such as search, retrieval, summarization, grounded question answering, classification, recommendation support, or agent input>
Restricted AI uses	<prohibited or tightly controlled AI uses, such as external summarization, prescriptive recommendations, autonomous action, model training, or cross-border transfer>
Audience	<intended user groups, roles, or stakeholder communities for the asset, such as all employees, managers, analysts, reviewers, support teams, or executives>
Semantic tags	<controlled vocabulary terms, taxonomy tags, entities, business terms, and related concepts used to improve discovery and interpretation>
Trust score	<composite confidence indicator based on factors such as ownership, validation, freshness, authority, completeness, and policy status>
Citation method	<required pattern for citing the asset in AI outputs, such as section citation, clause citation, page citation, record link, or no direct citation permitted>
Last validation date	<date on which content fitness, policy status, and metadata completeness were last confirmed>

CASE EXAMPLE

How Better Metadata Turned a Knowledge Assistant into a Trusted One

A global enterprise deployed an internal knowledge assistant intended to answer employee questions across HR, procurement, IT support, and policy content. The first release disappointed users. The assistant often returned relevant-looking answers, but the answers were inconsistent. Sometimes, it surfaced a local procedure instead of the enterprise standard. Sometimes it cited a document that had not been reviewed in years. Sometimes it mixed guidance content with formal policy language. User feedback was blunt: "helpful sometimes, but not reliable."

The model was not the main problem. The retrieval estate was metadata-poor.

Most documents had a title, repository location, and modified timestamp. Few had a clearly identified business owner. Almost none had authoritative status. Sensitivity labels were inconsistently applied. There was no lifecycle field to distinguish active from deprecated material. Source authority was implicit rather than modeled. The system retrieved content based mainly on lexical and embedding similarity.

The remediation effort focused on four metadata additions.

First, the team added business-owner metadata. This made it possible to distinguish governed content from orphaned content and created an accountability path for validation.

Second, it added lifecycle metadata: active, draft, deprecated, superseded, and archived. Retrieval pipelines began down-ranking stale content and excluding archived content from default grounding.

Third, it added sensitivity metadata and aligned it with access-aware filtering. This reduced the risk of inappropriate retrieval and narrowed the candidate set to content suitable for the user and scenario.

Fourth, it added source-authority metadata. Formal policies, signed procedures, and designated standards were marked as authoritative; FAQs and local guidance were marked as supporting unless explicitly designated otherwise.

The result was immediate and material. The assistant did not suddenly become more eloquent. It became more dependable. Authoritative sources began to outrank informal guidance. Stale content no longer dominates long-tail queries. Sensitive documents stopped leaking into broad answers. Citations became more meaningful because users could see which source represented formal policy and which source represented supplemental guidance.

Most importantly, user trust improved because the system's answers became easier to verify. The enterprise had not primarily improved generation. It had improved control.

That is the lesson. In many enterprise AI scenarios, the decisive step forward is not a better model. It is better metadata, attached to the same underlying content.

CLOSING SYNTHESIS

Metadata is the control plane for AI because it determines how information behaves in an AI-serving architecture. It governs discovery, relevance, authority, freshness, policy, explainability, and safe use. Without it, the enterprise data estate remains a collection of disconnected assets. With it, the estate becomes operable. This is why AI-readiness requires richer metadata than analytics systems typically demand. Technical metadata remains necessary, but it is not enough. Business metadata gives meaning. Policy metadata enables safe use. Operational metadata supports reliability. AI-serving metadata makes grounded responses and explainable automation possible.

Architecturally, this means metadata cannot remain a back-office function. It must be embedded into ingestion, enrichment, retrieval, ranking, serving, citation, and governance. It must span structured, semi-structured, and unstructured assets. It must shape runtime behavior, not just support audits and catalogs.

The fastest way to cap AI scale is metadata poverty. An organization may have excellent repositories, large volumes of content, and advanced models, yet still fail to produce trustworthy outcomes because its assets lack owner, status, lifecycle, policy, semantics, and evidence structure.

Enterprises that understand this will stop asking whether they have enough data for AI. They will start asking whether their metadata is strong enough to control AI. That is the better question, and it leads to better architecture.

KEY TAKEAWAYS

- Metadata is not support information; it is the control layer that makes enterprise AI governable and trustworthy.
- Technical metadata alone is insufficient for AI-readiness; business, policy, operational, and AI-serving metadata must be modeled together.
- Retrieval quality, ranking, freshness, and explainability are all heavily metadata-dependent.
- Metadata poverty is one of the quickest ways to undermine AI scale, trust, and safety.
- A minimum viable metadata standard is one of the most practical starting points for building an AI-ready enterprise architecture.

Chapter 10: Business Meaning: Glossaries, Taxonomies, and Ontologies

> ***AI cannot reason reliably over enterprise data unless the enterprise has made meaning explicit. That statement sounds obvious until one watches how most organizations actually operate. The term customer appears in dozens of systems. A field called status means one thing in underwriting, another in claims, and something else in customer support. A policy document uses the phrase active member, while a CRM platform tracks account holder, and a finance system recognizes only bill-to party. To a human insider, these differences are manageable because people carry institutional context in their heads. To an AI system, they are not manageable at all. They are ambiguity masquerading as familiarity.***

This is why glossaries, taxonomies, and ontologies matter. They are not academic extras. They are architectural mechanisms for reducing ambiguity, preserving context, and making enterprise meaning explicit enough for machines to use safely. If metadata is the control plane for AI, semantics is one of its most important control signals. It tells the system what a thing is, what it is not, how it relates to other things, where the boundaries are, and which interpretation is valid in which context.

Many enterprises still treat semantic work as optional because earlier generations of analytics could tolerate loose definitions. Reports could survive a degree of inconsistency because humans performed the final interpretation. AI changes that contract. A copilot, assistant, or agent cannot be expected to infer business meaning from contradictory labels, undocumented assumptions, and accidental naming conventions. If the enterprise does not define meaning deliberately, the model will approximate it. And approximation is not acceptable when the result drives decisions, recommendations, or actions.

The real question, then, is not whether semantics matters. The real question is how much semantic structure an organization needs, where it delivers value first, and how to introduce it without turning the effort into a detached modeling exercise. The answer is practical: start with controlled language, organize it for use, model deeper relationships where they matter, and align semantic ambition to business value and operational maturity.

Why This Matters

The enterprise data estate was not built for AI-native interpretation. It was built for transaction processing, reporting, integration, and analytics. Those environments often assume a human analyst, report author, or system integrator will reconcile meaning. AI systems do not work that way. They operate across sources, infer links, compress context, and generate responses. That makes semantic ambiguity a first-order architectural risk.

When business meaning is not explicit, several predictable failures follow.

First, retrieval becomes noisy. Search and retrieval systems cannot rank correctly when the same term refers to multiple concepts or multiple terms refer to the same concept. A user asks for "customer eligibility rules," and the system retrieves documents about policyholders, members, applicants, or account holders interchangeably, even though only one of those concepts is appropriate in the specific business context.

Second, grounding weakens. Even if the system retrieves relevant content, it may connect the wrong records, summarize the wrong policy, or merge concepts that should remain distinct. A model may answer fluently, but the answer is semantically wrong.

Third, governance becomes brittle. Access control, policy enforcement, retention, classification, and lineage all depend on the enterprise knowing what something is. If semantics is inconsistent, governance rules cannot be applied consistently either.

Fourth, explainability degrades. One of the most important questions in enterprise AI is, "Why did the system say that?" A defensible answer requires more than a source citation. It requires a chain of meaning: what business concept was recognized, under which definition, in which domain, with which relationships and constraints.

This is especially important because AI consumers are not all the same. A knowledge assistant answering a general policy question may tolerate broader semantic grouping than an underwriting copilot recommending next actions. An executive briefing tool may need concept rollups across domains, while an agent initiating a workflow may require strict ontology-backed constraints. The data-serving contract changes with the use case, and semantic precision must change with it.

In practice, this means that semantics is not a documentation exercise sitting beside the architecture. It is part of the architecture. It affects search, retrieval, ranking, access-aware delivery, evidence presentation, and operational trust.

Core Concepts

Controlled Meaning Begins with a Glossary

A glossary establishes controlled business language. It answers the most basic but most important question: What does this term mean here?

A strong business glossary does not merely provide a dictionary entry. It captures the approved term, its plain-language definition, synonyms, context, ownership, and boundaries. It helps distinguish between terms that are truly equivalent and terms that are only superficially similar. It also creates a durable reference point for data models, APIs, content repositories, documentation, and AI retrieval pipelines.

For example, a financial services firm may define:

- "Customer" as the person or organization receiving products or services.
- "Account holder" as the legal party associated with a financial account.
- "Authorized user" as an individual permitted to access an account without being the legal holder.

Those are related concepts, but they are not interchangeable. A glossary makes that distinction explicit.

Without a controlled glossary, enterprise systems accumulate local language. Teams invent labels that fit their workflow. Over time, different systems use different words for the same concept, and the same word for different concepts. That is survivable in a human-mediated environment. It is dangerous in AI.

Taxonomies Organize for Navigation, Grouping, and Retrieval

A taxonomy organizes assets into categories so that information can be grouped, navigated, filtered, and retrieved consistently.

Where a glossary defines terms, a taxonomy structures them. It provides hierarchy and classification. It tells the organization how concepts, documents, records, and content types should be grouped for discovery and use.

In an enterprise policy library, for instance, a taxonomy may classify content by domain, policy type, jurisdiction, audience, and lifecycle state. In a product knowledge environment, it may classify content by business function, product family, channel, region, and regulatory relevance. In a retrieval architecture, this classification becomes operational. It supports scoped search, relevance ranking, authorization filtering, and consumer-specific presentation.

Taxonomies are particularly important for AI because many enterprise repositories were never designed for precision retrieval. Documents exist, but are poorly categorized. Pages are searchable, but not grouped according to meaningful business structure. Chat transcripts, procedures, policies, and knowledge articles live in different systems with inconsistent labels. A taxonomy gives the architecture a way to organize this estate so that retrieval is not based solely on keywords and embeddings.

A good taxonomy is designed for use, not for theoretical elegance. It should reflect how the enterprise actually navigates meaning and how AI systems need to filter and rank content.

Ontologies Model Relationships, Constraints, and Domain Logic

An ontology goes further. It models entities, relationships, constraints, and domain logic in a machine-interpretable way.

A glossary says what a term means. A taxonomy says where it belongs. An ontology says how it behaves in relation to other concepts.

For example, an ontology may specify that:

- A "policyholder" owns one or more policies.
- A "policy" covers one or more insured assets.
- A "claim" is submitted against a policy.
- A "member" may be enrolled in a plan but is not necessarily the same as the subscriber.
- An "account holder" can authorize another party to transact on the account, but authorization does not confer ownership.

Those are not just definitions. They are domain relationships and constraints. They allow systems to reason more precisely, resolve ambiguity, and enforce valid interpretations. This matters when AI moves beyond question answering into more structured tasks. An assistant who summarizes a document may need only glossary and taxonomy support. An agent that reconciles identity, interprets eligibility rules, and initiates actions may require ontology-backed relationships and constraints.

KEY INSIGHT

Glossary vs taxonomy vs ontology

Glossary: Defines approved business terms and their meanings.

Taxonomy: Organizes concepts and assets into categories for grouping, navigation, and retrieval.

Ontology: Models entities, relationships, constraints, and logic so systems can interpret meaning more precisely.

A glossary tells you what a term means. A taxonomy tells you where it fits. An ontology tells you how it relates and what rules govern its use.

Semantics Can Mature in Layers

Most organizations do not need to begin with a full ontology program. In fact, many should not. The mistake is not starting too small; the mistake is starting without intention.

Semantic maturity works best as a layered progression. First, establish a controlled vocabulary for critical business terms. Then classify content and data assets with a usable taxonomy. Then introduce ontology modeling in domains where relationship logic, ambiguity reduction, and machine interpretation produce clear business value.

❖ FIGURE 19 – SEMANTIC STACK

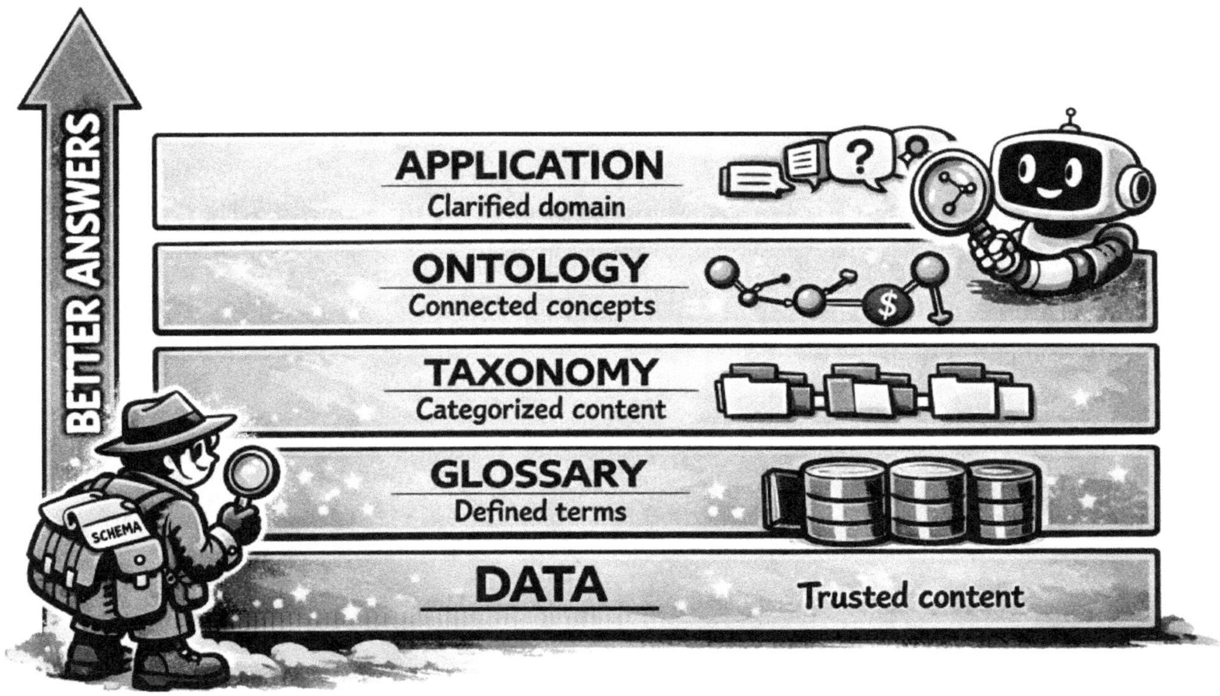

Not Every Organization Needs a Heavy Ontology Effort

This point matters because semantic work often fails when it is framed as an all-or-nothing exercise. Some organizations hear "ontology" and immediately imagine years of modeling detached from delivery. Others avoid the topic entirely and remain stuck with unresolved ambiguity.

Both reactions are mistakes.

A heavy ontology effort is justified only where the business needs it. High-value candidates include regulated domains, customer and party resolution, product and contract relationships, entitlement and eligibility logic, cross-domain reasoning, and action-taking AI systems. In lower-risk environments, a well-governed glossary plus a disciplined taxonomy may deliver most of the value.

Semantic ambition should match the enterprise's operational maturity. An organization that cannot yet govern its basic terms will not succeed by jumping directly into complex knowledge representation. But an organization deploying multi-step agents across ambiguous domains will eventually outgrow shallow semantics. Architecture has to meet the use case honestly.

ARCHITECTURAL IMPLICATIONS

Meaning Must Be Treated as Shared Enterprise Infrastructure

One of the most common semantic failures is leaving definition ownership entirely to local systems. Each application team names fields, labels records, and defines terms independently. The result is semantic fragmentation.

Architecturally, meaning must be managed as a shared enterprise infrastructure. That does not mean every term is centrally authored without domain input. It means the enterprise needs a mechanism for publishing approved definitions, mapping synonyms, tracking conflicts, assigning ownership, and exposing meaning to consuming platforms.

This mechanism may sit in a metadata platform, catalog, semantic layer, knowledge graph, governance repository, or another architecture pattern. The implementation can vary. The principle does not: business meaning must be durable, discoverable, versioned, and connected to the assets that use it.

Semantics Must Connect Structured and Unstructured Data

Enterprises often treat semantic work as a structured-data concern. That is too narrow. Much of the business meaning AI needs lives in unstructured content: policies, contracts, procedural guides, knowledge articles, decision memos, emails, and transcripts.

A term like member in good standing may appear in a policy document, a training manual, a case management note, and a data element in an operational system. If those are not semantically connected, AI systems will retrieve fragments without shared meaning. The retrieval layer may find the words, but it will not know which usage is authoritative, which is outdated, or which applies in the current domain.

The architectural implication is clear: semantic definitions cannot sit apart from the content estate. They must enrich both data assets and content assets.

Retrieval Pipelines Should Use Semantic Enrichment, Not Only Text Similarity

Keyword search alone is insufficient. Embedding similarity alone is also insufficient. Retrieval quality improves materially when pipelines incorporate semantic enrichment.

That includes approved terms, synonyms, acronyms, domain context, taxonomy categories, related concepts, owner signals, authority status, lifecycle state, and disallowed usages. These enrichments help rank better, filter better, and explain better.

For example, if a user asks, "Can an inactive member appeal a denial?" the system should recognize that the member belongs to a benefits context, inactive may carry domain-specific eligibility meaning, and appeal should prioritize policy and procedure sources over general knowledge articles. That is not prompt cleverness. It is architecture supported by semantics.

Ontology Use Should Be Selective and Operational

Where ontologies are used, they should be tied to operational problems. Common candidates include entity resolution, contract interpretation, entitlement logic, product hierarchy, supplier relationships, incident dependencies, and regulatory obligation mapping.

The value appears when the ontology is not merely documented but used: to disambiguate retrieval, validate action prerequisites, constrain agent workflows, enrich lineage, and improve evidence chains. An ontology that is never connected to operational paths is just a model. An ontology that improves interpretation and control becomes architectural infrastructure.

Different AI Consumers Need Different Semantic Depth

The same semantic assets will not be used in the same way by every AI consumer.

A general knowledge assistant may primarily rely on glossary definitions and taxonomy filters. A domain copilot may require concept relationships, allowed usage contexts, and conflict mappings. An autonomous agent may require explicit constraints and ontology-backed validation before it takes action.

The architectural design should, therefore, separate semantic assets from individual applications while allowing different serving patterns. The point is not one monolithic semantic layer for everything. The point is reusable semantic infrastructure with consumer-specific contracts.

Failure Modes and Anti-Patterns

Treating Semantics as Optional Documentation

When glossaries live in slide decks, taxonomies live in outdated spreadsheets, and ontology diagrams live in workshop artifacts, semantics never becomes operational. The enterprise may claim to have definitions, but the systems that matter do not use them. If a definition is not connected to data products, content repositories, retrieval services, or governance processes, it is not architecture. It is reference material.

Confusing Naming Conventions with Meaning

Another anti-pattern is assuming that consistent field names solve the problem. They do not. A hundred systems can use the label "customer_id" and still refer to different concepts. Naming consistency is helpful, but it is not semantic alignment.

Designing Taxonomies No One Will Use

Taxonomies often fail because they are designed as administrative schemes rather than operating structures. They become too deep, too abstract, too rigid, or too detached from how users search and how systems retrieve. A taxonomy should improve findability and control. If no one can classify content consistently, the structure is too complex.

Pursuing Ontology for Prestige Instead of Need

Some organizations adopt ontology language because it sounds advanced. They initiate large-scale semantic modeling efforts without a clear use case, operating model, or integration path. The result is predictable: high effort, low adoption, and skepticism about semantic architecture as a whole.

Ontology is powerful when it solves specific problems. It is wasteful when pursued as an intellectual signal.

Ignoring Conflicting Definitions

This is one of the most damaging failures because it is usually tolerated for too long. Different domains define the same term differently, yet no one records the conflict explicitly. Humans cope through tribal knowledge. AI systems cannot.

Key Insight

The same business term means different things in different systems

When that condition exists and remains undocumented, AI confusion is not a future possibility. It is a current architectural defect.

Failing to Assign Ownership

Semantic work without ownership decays quickly. Definitions drift. New synonyms appear. Taxonomy branches proliferate. Exceptions are added informally. Review dates are missed. In enterprise environments, every critical semantic asset needs an accountable owner and a stewardship process.

PRACTICAL APPLICATION

Start Where Ambiguity Causes the Most Risk

The right starting point is not "model the whole enterprise." The right starting point is "find the places where ambiguity is already creating cost, risk, or friction."

Useful entry points include:

- High-volume business terms used across multiple systems.
- Policy-heavy domains where definitions affect compliance.
- Customer and party concepts that vary across functions.
- Product and contract concepts used in retrieval and decision support.
- Terms that repeatedly surface in failed searches, poor summaries, or disputed outputs.

Start by identifying the terms that matter operationally. Then define them clearly, assign ownership, record synonyms, capture allowed contexts, document ambiguous usages, and connect them to source systems and content.

KEY INSIGHT

Start simple, but start deliberately

- Do not wait for perfect semantic architecture.
- Do not begin with an enterprise-wide ontology by default.
- Start with high-value terms, high-risk ambiguity, and a governance process that can endure.

Simple is acceptable. Accidental is not.

Build a Practical Semantic Operating Loop

A durable approach usually includes six repeating steps:

- Identify critical terms and conflicting meanings.
- Define approved business language in plain terms.
- Organize concepts and content into a usable taxonomy.
- Introduce ontology modeling only where relationships and constraints justify it.
- Embed semantics into metadata, retrieval, and governance workflows.
- Review definitions regularly as business processes and policies change.

This is not a one-time modeling effort. It is an operating discipline.

TEMPLATES

Business Meaning Design Template

Term/concept	<name of the business term, concept, or entity being defined>
Plain-language definition	<clear business-friendly definition of what the term means in the organization>
Alternate labels/synonyms	<other labels, synonyms, or commonly used variations of the term>
Domain owner	<business leader or function accountable for the definition and approved usage of the term>
Related domains	<other business domains or functions in which the term is relevant or commonly used>
Allowed usage contexts	<approved business, operational, analytical, reporting, or AI contexts in which the term may be used>
Disallowed/ambiguous usages	<usages that are prohibited, misleading, or require explicit clarification to avoid semantic confusion>
Parent taxonomy category	<broader taxonomy, classification, or conceptual category under which this term belongs>
Related concepts	<adjacent, overlapping, narrower, broader, or commonly confused concepts that should be linked to this term>
Key constraints or rules	<important business rules, scope conditions, qualification criteria, or interpretation constraints governing the term>
Source systems using this term	<systems, platforms, repositories, or data products in which this term appears or is operationalized>
Conflicting definitions known? yes/no	<Yes or No>
Ontology modeling needed? yes/no	<Yes or No>
AI implications	<impact of this term on retrieval, summarization, classification, grounding, or other AI behaviors, including ambiguity or control requirements>
Review owner	<role or steward responsible for reviewing and maintaining the definition over time>
Review date	<date by which the definition should next be reviewed>

Case Example

When Shared Language Creates Unsafe AI Answers

Consider a financial services and benefits enterprise that uses the terms customer, member, and account holder across multiple domains.

In the retail banking division, an account holder is the legally recognized owner of a deposit account. In the insurance division, the policyholder is the legally recognized owner of a policy. In the health benefits division, member refers to an enrolled individual covered under a plan, while subscriber refers to the person who holds the primary enrollment relationship. In marketing and service channels, all of these people may be referred to broadly as customers.

❖ Figure 20 – Ambiguity Resolution

Now introduce AI.

A user asks a knowledge assistant: "Can a customer update beneficiary information online?"

The system retrieves a benefits article about members changing dependent information, a banking procedure for account holders updating payable-on-death beneficiaries, and a life insurance FAQ for policyholders updating designated beneficiaries. All three appear relevant at the surface level because the word customer was used loosely in the query and loosely across the corpus.

Without semantic alignment, the assistant may collapse the three into a blended answer that sounds plausible and is operationally unsafe.

Now introduce explicit semantics.

The enterprise glossary defines the terms separately and records that customer is a broad external relationship term, not a legal-role synonym. The taxonomy classifies content by line of business, legal relationship type, product family, and transaction type. The ontology models that an account holder owns a deposit account, a policyholder owns a policy, a member is enrolled in a plan, and a subscriber is the primary coverage holder. Beneficiary changes are constrained by product type and relationship type.

When the same query arrives, the system can respond more carefully. It can ask a clarifying question, or it can scope retrieval to the relevant domain based on the user's context. If the user is in the banking portal, the system prioritizes account holder rules. If the user is in the insurance servicing application, it prioritizes policyholder guidance. If context remains insufficient, it explains the ambiguity rather than hiding it.

That is the real value of semantics in AI architecture. It is not more terminology. It is a safer interpretation.

This case also illustrates a broader lesson: semantic alignment does not require every term in the enterprise to be modeled with equal depth. It requires the enterprise to identify where ambiguity materially affects retrieval, interpretation, action, and trust. In those places, semantics is not optional.

Closing Synthesis

Business meaning is one of the most neglected dependencies in enterprise AI, largely because earlier data environments allowed organizations to operate with implicit understanding. Humans bridged the gaps. AI exposes them.

Glossaries, taxonomies, and ontologies are best understood as a progression of semantic control. A glossary establishes approved language. A taxonomy makes that language navigable and operational for classification and retrieval. An ontology adds relationship logic and constraints where the business requires deeper machine interpretation. Used together, they reduce ambiguity, improve retrieval quality, strengthen governance, and make explanations more defensible.

The strategic mistake is to frame this as a choice between doing nothing and launching a vast semantic modeling program. Most enterprises should do neither. They should begin deliberately, focus on business-critical ambiguity, connect semantics to metadata and retrieval architecture, and deepen modeling only where value and risk justify it.

AI-Ready Data is not just data with better pipelines and cleaner storage. It is data whose meaning is explicit enough to be discovered, interpreted, governed, and used safely. That requires more than fields and files. It requires the enterprise to decide what its words mean, where they apply, and how they relate.

An AI system cannot compensate indefinitely for semantic disorder. At best, it will guess. At worst, it will guess confidently. The architectural responsibility is, therefore, straightforward: make meaning explicit before you ask AI to act on it.

Key Takeaways

- AI fails quickly when enterprises leave business meaning implicit and tolerate ambiguous terms across systems and content.
- Glossaries define controlled language, taxonomies organize assets for retrieval and navigation, and ontologies model relationships and constraints.
- Not every organization needs heavy ontology work, but every organization needs deliberate semantic control for critical concepts.
- Semantic assets must be operationalized through metadata, retrieval pipelines, governance processes, and consumer-specific serving patterns.
- The right starting point is not enterprise-wide semantic perfection; it is the highest-value, highest-risk ambiguity already harming trust, retrieval, or decision quality.

Chapter 11: Knowledge Graphs, Entity Resolution, and Relationship Intelligence

Enterprise AI becomes materially more useful when it can do more than retrieve isolated facts. It must be able to follow relationships, reconcile identities, and connect evidence across systems that were never designed to work together. In real enterprises, business meaning rarely resides in a single table, a single document, or a single application. It lives in the connections between records, policies, people, products, obligations, transactions, decisions, and events.

A model can summarize a document. It can answer a question against a database. It can even produce a plausible recommendation from retrieved content. But enterprise value rises sharply when the system can determine that the "application owner" in a CMDB is the same person referenced in an access review, that a control exception applies to a specific business application, that the application supports a regulated process, and that the relevant policy was revised after the exception was approved. That is not merely retrieval. It is relationship intelligence.

This is where knowledge graphs and entity resolution enter the architecture. They are not fashionable add-ons. They are design patterns for capturing and serving connected meaning. Entity resolution establishes whether two or more records refer to the same real-world thing. Graph structures express how those things relate. Together, they help AI systems move from loosely informed generation to evidence-backed interpretation.

That does not mean every enterprise needs a sprawling enterprise graph program or a graph database at the center of everything. It does mean that any serious AI-ready architecture must decide how identities will be reconciled, how relationships will be represented, how confidence will be measured, and how downstream AI systems will consume that intelligence safely.

Why This Matters

AI Value Often Depends on Relationship Intelligence

Many enterprise questions are not document questions or SQL questions. They are relationship questions.

- Which suppliers support critical products affected by this new policy change?
- Which employees approved exceptions on systems that process customer financial data?
- Which contracts reference this product line, and which obligations remain open?

Which incidents are likely related because they involve the same customer, device, and service region?

These questions depend on the connected context. The answer requires the system to traverse multiple sources, align identities, rank evidence, and preserve provenance. Without that connective layer, the AI may retrieve fragments that look relevant but fail to assemble a coherent, trustworthy answer.

A reporting stack can answer a fixed question if the joins are known in advance and the semantics are stable. Enterprise AI faces a different problem. Users ask open-ended questions. Agents may need to determine the next step. Copilots must explain why a recommendation applies. In these settings, relationships are not incidental. They are the substance of the answer.

Cross-System Trust Begins with Resolved Identity

Most large organizations have more duplication than they admit and more ambiguity than they can see. One customer may appear in CRM, billing, support, claims, e-commerce, and legal systems under different identifiers and slightly different names. One employee may have separate identities in HR, identity management, learning systems, ticketing tools, and collaboration platforms. One application may be represented differently in the architecture repository, CMDB, vulnerability platform, and spreadsheet inventories maintained by control owners.

AI cannot be trusted to reason across systems if the architecture cannot determine when records represent the same entity and when they do not. Entity resolution is, therefore, not an optional enrichment. It is a trust foundation.

Without it, the enterprise gets brittle joins, duplicate retrieval, contradictory context, inflated counts, false associations, and mistaken recommendations. With it, the enterprise gets evidence-backed linkage, confidence-scored matching, auditable decisions, and the ability to explain why a connection was made.

Relationship-rich Use Cases Justify the Investment

Graph techniques and entity resolution are most valuable when the enterprise problem is inherently interconnected. Fraud, compliance, third-party risk, product impact analysis, customer 360, cyber exposure mapping, policy-to-control alignment, and root-cause analysis are classic examples. These are not cases where a single authoritative system exists and the answer can be lifted from one record. They are cases where the value comes from discovering paths across people, assets, obligations, events, and evidence.

Where the use case is simple, stable, and already well served by relational modeling, a graph may add little. But where the enterprise needs to connect evidence across fragmented systems, relationship intelligence earns its keep quickly.

CORE CONCEPTS

Knowledge Graphs Are a Modeling Pattern, Not a Religion

A knowledge graph represents entities and the relationships between them in a form that supports flexible traversal and semantic interpretation. The important point is architectural, not ideological. A graph is useful when the structure of the question is path-oriented, many-to-many, and semantically rich.

- A customer owns an account.
- An account is serviced by an application.
- That application is subject to a control.
- That control maps to a policy requirement.
- That policy has an exception.
- That exception has an approver and an expiration date.

This chain is awkward to reconstruct repeatedly from disconnected systems. It is natural to express as connected knowledge.

But a graph does not replace relational data. Relational systems remain the right foundation for transactional integrity, governed master data, and many analytical workloads. Nor does graph replace vector retrieval. Vector search is useful for semantic similarity, unstructured content retrieval, and recall across language-rich sources. Graph complements both.

Relational stores answer "What is the record?"

Vector stores help answer "What content is semantically relevant?"

Graph structures help answer "How are these things connected, and why does that connection matter?"

The strongest architectures use all three where appropriate.

Entity Resolution: Determining Sameness with Evidence

Entity resolution is the process of determining whether multiple records refer to the same real-world entity. That sounds simple until it is attempted at enterprise scale.

Exact identifiers are helpful but often absent, stale, inconsistent, or misused. Names change. Addresses vary. Source systems apply different validation rules. Some systems treat subsidiaries separately, while others collapse them. People change roles, departments, surnames, and locations. Products are rebranded. Applications are retired and reborn.

Effective entity resolution, therefore, combines:

- Matching identifiers, such as employee ID, tax ID, contract number, device serial number, or application code.
- Secondary attributes, such as legal name, address, date of birth, manager, department, email, vendor domain, or business unit.
- Business rules, such as "do not auto-merge individuals across jurisdictions without an approved identifier match."
- Confidence scoring, so matches are evidence-backed rather than asserted.
- Manual review paths for ambiguous or high-risk cases.
- Survivorship rules determine which source values become preferred values in the resolved record.

Entity resolution is not merely a deduplication job. It is a governed decision process that affects downstream analytics, risk decisions, customer communications, regulatory reporting, and AI behavior.

Relationship Types Matter

Not all relationships are equal. Enterprises often collapse too much meaning into vague "linked to" relationships. That makes the graph look connected while reducing its usefulness.

Good relationship modeling distinguishes between examples such as:

- Owns.
- Manages.
- Approved.
- Implements.
- Governs.
- Depends on.
- Processes.
- Stores.
- Violates.
- Compensates for.
- Supersedes.
- References.
- Is exception to.
- Is evidence for.

These distinctions matter for AI. A compliance assistant should not treat "references" and "governs" as equivalent. A cyber assistant should not confuse "depends on" with "communicates with." Relationship type carries business semantics, and business semantics determine whether an answer is defensible.

Confidence and Provenance Must Travel with the Connection

In an AI-ready architecture, it is not enough to say that two entities are linked. The system must know how the link was established, when it was last evaluated, which evidence supported it, and how confident the system is in the result.

A resolved supplier identity with 0.98 confidence based on tax ID, legal name, and registered address is different from a probable match with 0.67 confidence based on fuzzy name similarity and domain pattern. A policy-to-control link established through approved mapping is different from one inferred from document similarity. These distinctions must be explicit and machine-readable.

KEY INSIGHT

Entity resolution is not optional in complex enterprises

If a use case spans multiple systems, business units, or content repositories, identity ambiguity is already present whether the architecture acknowledges it or not. Refusing to design for entity resolution does not avoid complexity. It only pushes that complexity into inaccurate joins, duplicate retrieval, misleading counts, and unsafe AI conclusions.

ARCHITECTURAL IMPLICATIONS

Convergence Beats Purity

The mature pattern is not "choose graph instead of relational" or "replace graph with vectors." It is architectural convergence. In practice, this means:

- Authoritative source data remains in source-aligned or mastered relational platforms.
- Documents, policies, procedures, tickets, and transcripts are enriched and indexed for vector retrieval.
- Resolved entities and high-value relationships are represented in a graph-capable structure, whether via a dedicated graph database, a graph layer over existing stores, or a semantic relationship service.
- Metadata ties the whole system together: authority, freshness, lineage, access constraints, jurisdiction, confidence, and intended use.

❖ FIGURE 21 – CONVERGED RELATIONAL / VECTOR / GRAPH PATTERN

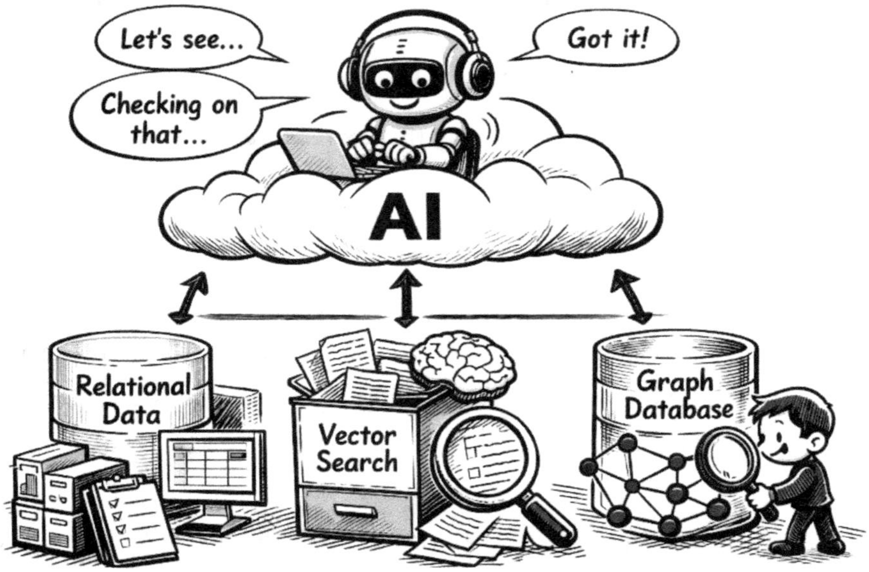

The AI-serving layer then chooses the right path. A customer address lookup should hit an authoritative mastered source. A search for policy language should hit enriched content retrieval. A question about which applications, controls, and exceptions affect a regulated process should traverse connected relationships.

The Graph Should Be Selective, Not Universal

A common mistake is trying to graph everything. That creates vast modeling programs, expensive ontology debates, and fragile pipelines with unclear value. Most enterprises do not need a universal enterprise graph before they can benefit from graph patterns.

Start with a bounded set of entities and relationships that drive high-value use cases. For example:

- Policies.
- Controls.
- Applications.
- Business processes.
- Owners.
- Exceptions.
- Incidents.
- Vendors.

Model the relationships that matter to decision-making and AI grounding. Leave the rest alone until a use case justifies expansion.

Entity Resolution Must Be Operationalized

Entity resolution is not a one-time data quality project. It is an operational capability. Records change, new systems appear, identifiers are retired, mergers happen, and source quality drifts.

Architecturally, this means the enterprise needs:

- Repeatable ingestion from participating source systems.
- Matching pipelines with versioned rules and features.
- Confidence thresholds by entity type and use case.
- Review workflows for ambiguous or high-risk matches.
- Survivorship logic.
- Audit trails for merge and unmerge decisions.
- Publishing patterns so downstream AI and analytics consume resolved identities consistently.

❖ FIGURE 22 – ENTITY RESOLUTION PIPELINE

Governance Becomes More Important, Not Less

Graphs feel intuitive because they mirror connected reality. That can mislead teams into underestimating governance needs. In fact, relationship-rich architectures intensify governance requirements.

The enterprise must define:

- Who is allowed to assert or approve a relationship.
- Which relationships are inferred versus authoritative.
- How access controls apply when traversing across sources.
- Whether a user may see the path, the conclusion, both, or neither.
- Which jurisdictions restrict identity matching.
- How long links may persist before reevaluation.
- How contested or low-confidence relationships are surfaced.

The more connected the system becomes, the more important it is to distinguish fact, inference, and confidence.

Failure Modes and Anti-Patterns

Treating Graph as an Answer in Search of a Problem

Some organizations adopt graph technologies because the concept sounds advanced. They build broad semantic models without tying them to concrete AI or business outcomes. The result is impressive diagrams, heavy complexity, and weak adoption.

Graph earns its keep where relationship traversal materially improves decisions, retrieval quality, explainability, or operational response. It is not a badge of maturity by itself.

Key Insight

When graph earns its keep

Graph is worth the investment when the value of the answer depends on traversing multiple entity types, reconciling ambiguous identities, and preserving explainable paths across disconnected systems. If a simple relational model answers the question reliably, use that instead.

Confusing Inferred Similarity with Trusted Identity

Another failure mode is using semantic similarity or fuzzy matching as a substitute for governed entity resolution. Similarity is useful. It is not the same as identity.

Two vendor names may look alike but be distinct legal entities. Two policies may be semantically similar but apply in different jurisdictions. Two applications may share naming conventions but support different regulated processes. AI systems that collapse these distinctions create quiet but serious risk.

Building Vague, Low-Semantic Relationship Models

If every connection becomes "related to," the architecture loses meaning. AI systems then retrieve paths that look rich but do not support justified conclusions. Relationship labels must carry business intent.

Ignoring Temporal Truth

Relationships change over time. An owner changes. A policy is superseded. A control is retired. An exception expires. A vendor is acquired. An application is decommissioned.

If the graph captures only current-state relationships without temporal context, the AI may produce historically false explanations or operationally unsafe recommendations. Relationship intelligence must support temporal correctness, not just connectivity.

Hiding Uncertainty

Architectures often expose the resolved entity but suppress the uncertainty behind it. That is dangerous. Downstream systems need to know whether a relationship is authoritative, inferred, reviewed, disputed, or low confidence.

> ⚠ **WARNING SIGN**
>
> **One customer, six identities**
>
> If six systems each contain a different "customer truth," and no one can explain how they should reconcile for a decision, AI will not fix the problem. It will amplify it. Multiple unresolved identities are not just a data hygiene issue. They are a governance and trust failure.

PRACTICAL APPLICATION

Start with the Use Case, Not the Ontology

The right starting point is a bounded problem with a clear decision value. Ask:

- What question cannot be answered well today because the evidence is fragmented?
- Which entities must be reconciled?
- Which relationships determine the answer?
- What confidence and explanation threshold does the AI consumer require?
- Which errors are tolerable, and which are unacceptable?

For a compliance assistant, policy-to-control-to-application-to-owner relationships matter. For fraud detection, customer-to-device-to-account-to-transaction relationships matter. For contract intelligence, party-to-obligation-to-product-to-region relationships matter.

Define Entity Classes and Match Strategies Explicitly

Each entity type needs its own design logic. Customer, employee, supplier, application, control, contract, and policy do not resolve the same way. Match attributes, business rules, risk tolerance, and review procedures differ.

This is why the architecture should use a formal design artifact rather than ad hoc rules scattered across pipelines.

Keep Graph-Serving Aligned to AI Use

The AI-serving layer should not expose raw graph traversal indiscriminately. It should apply the same discipline discussed throughout this book:

- Honor permissions at source and relationship levels.
- Rank authoritative links above inferred ones.
- Include citations or evidence traces.
- Surface confidence where it affects interpretation.
- Respect temporal context.
- Limit agent actions when relationships are inferred rather than approved

The graph is not the product. Trusted decisions and explainable AI are the product.

Templates

Entity Resolution Design Sheet

Entity type	<name of the entity class being resolved, such as application, customer, product, supplier, or asset>
Source systems involved	<systems, repositories, platforms, or inventories that contain records for this entity type>
Matching identifiers	<authoritative or high-confidence identifiers used to match records across systems>
Secondary attributes	<supporting descriptive attributes used to strengthen matching, review, and interpretation>

Business rules	<rules governing when records may be matched, merged, separated, preserved, or escalated for review>
Confidence thresholds	<score thresholds that determine whether records are auto-resolved, routed for steward review, or retained as separate candidates>
Manual review triggers	<conditions that require human review because of conflict, ambiguity, regulatory sensitivity, or insufficient match confidence>
Survivorship rules	<rules that determine which source supplies the canonical value for each attribute after entity resolution>
Relationship types to model	<business relationships that should be captured between this entity and other entities, controls, systems, or processes>
Downstream AI use cases	<AI assistants, copilots, analyses, or decisions that depend on resolved and governed entity identity>
Sensitivity/privacy concerns	<security, privacy, regulatory, or risk concerns associated with resolving and exposing this entity and its relationships>
Audit requirements	<evidence, traceability, retention, and review records that must be preserved for compliance and accountability>
Success metrics	<measures used to determine whether entity resolution is improving quality, coverage, trust, and downstream AI performance>
Owner	<role or steward accountable for the entity resolution approach and ongoing data quality>
Review cadence	<required interval or trigger for reviewing rules, matches, survivorship logic, and governance controls>

Case Example

From Retrieval to Relationship Intelligence: Architecting a Compliance Assistant That Can Reason

Consider a compliance assistant designed to answer questions such as:

Which applications are currently operating under control exceptions related to encryption, who owns them, what policies are implicated, and which exceptions expire within the next 60 days?

At first glance, this sounds like a retrieval problem. It is not. It is a relationship problem.

The relevant data is spread across a policy library, a control catalog, a GRC platform, an application inventory, an architecture repository, and spreadsheets maintained by local risk coordinators. Policies are versioned documents. Controls are structured records. Applications appear under multiple identifiers. Owners may be sourced from HR, the CMDB, or manual attestations. Exceptions may reference applications by free text.

Without entity resolution and relationship modeling, the assistant will retrieve fragments:

a policy paragraph on encryption, a few exception records, several application names that may or may not be duplicates, and owner fields that disagree. The output may sound plausible while being operationally useless.

A better architecture does the following:

First, it resolves core entities: policy, control, application, owner, exception, and business process.

Second, it models critical relationships:

policy governs control; control applies to application; application owned by person; exception granted against control for application; exception approved by person; exception expires on date; application supports business process.

Third, it distinguishes authoritative from inferred links. A policy-to-control mapping approved by compliance is authoritative. An exception-to-application link inferred from free-text matching is provisional until reviewed.

Fourth, it carries evidence and time. The assistant can show that Application A is linked to Exception E-104 through a reviewed mapping, that the current owner is Jane Lee based on the approved quarterly inventory, and that the governing encryption policy was updated after the exception approval date.

Now the assistant can produce a grounded answer:

Three applications currently operate under encryption-related control exceptions expiring within 60 days. Two support regulated payment processes. One owner record is under review because CMDB and local inventory disagree. One exception references a superseded policy version and should be reassessed.

That answer is valuable because it is connected, qualified, and explainable. It does not merely retrieve text. It assembles governed meaning across systems.

Closing Synthesis

Knowledge graphs and entity resolution matter because enterprise AI must operate on connected reality, not isolated fragments. Business meaning frequently lives in the link between things: the policy and the control, the control and the application, the application and the owner, the owner and the approval, the approval and the exception, the exception and the deadline. This does not justify graph everywhere. Overusing graph patterns increases complexity without proportional value. Many enterprise questions remain well served by relational models, strong metadata, and disciplined content retrieval. The point is not to replace existing patterns with graph purity. The point is to add relationship intelligence where it materially improves trust, explanation, and decision quality.

Entity resolution is the harder and more foundational discipline. If the enterprise cannot determine when two records refer to the same thing, relationship intelligence will remain unstable. Once resolved identity is in place, graph patterns become powerful because they can represent and serve connected evidence with clarity.

For AI-Ready Data architecture, the lesson is direct: semantic context is not complete until the enterprise can reconcile identities and model consequential relationships. Graph, relational, and vector patterns each have a role. The architect's task is to combine them deliberately, govern them rigorously, and expose them to AI systems in a way that preserves evidence, confidence, permissions, and time.

That is how connected data becomes trustworthy intelligence rather than just better-looking ambiguity.

Key Takeaways

- Enterprise AI often creates value by following relationships, not just retrieving facts.
- Entity resolution is foundational because cross-system trust starts with reliable identity reconciliation.
- Graph complements relational and vector approaches; it should not be treated as a universal replacement.
- Relationship-rich use cases such as compliance, fraud, and risk analysis justify graph investment most clearly.
- The goal is not maximum connectivity, but governed, evidence-backed, explainable relationship intelligence.

CHAPTER 12: PROVENANCE, LINEAGE, AND EXPLAINABILITY FROM THE DATA SIDE

> ***In enterprise AI, a correct-sounding answer is not enough. The answer must be traceable to a source, explainable in business terms, and defensible under review.***

That standard is higher than many organizations first expect. In reporting, users often accept an output because it came from a familiar dashboard. In analytics, they may trust a number because it was produced by an approved pipeline. In AI, neither shortcut holds. A response may sound fluent, confident, and precise while still being unsupported, outdated, misapplied, or based on an unauthorized source. Fluency creates risk when evidence is weak.

This is why provenance, lineage, and explainability are not peripheral concerns. They are part of the data contract for enterprise AI. Provenance tells us where evidence came from. Lineage tells us how information was transformed from source to serving layer. Explainability tells us why the answer is appropriate in context, including what business meaning, policy constraints, and time boundaries shaped it. These are different concepts, but they work together. Provenance without lineage can show the source but hide the transformation. Lineage without explainability can document the mechanics but fail to make the answer understandable to the business. Explainability without provenance becomes rhetoric. In high-stakes environments, that is not good enough.

Enterprise trust is not won by elegance of wording. It is won by visible evidence, defensible transformations, and clear contextual explanation. When those are absent, users may still admire the interface, but they will not trust the output when it matters.

WHY THIS MATTERS

AI Changes the Burden of Proof

Traditional systems often hide complexity behind interfaces. A report presents a number. A workflow shows a status. A search engine returns documents. Users may not see the underlying chain because the system was not designed to narrate it.

Enterprise AI changes that burden. The system is no longer only displaying stored facts. It is retrieving, assembling, ranking, summarizing, inferring, and presenting conclusions in natural language. That means the path from source to answer becomes longer and more opaque unless architects design it to be visible.

In practice, this changes the trust question from "Did the system return an answer?" to "Can the system show me why this answer should be trusted?"

For low-stakes internal convenience tasks, weak evidence may be tolerated. For policy interpretation, regulatory reporting, executive briefing, financial analysis, customer commitments, or automated action-taking, it cannot be.

High-Stakes Use Cases Demand Traceability

The more consequential the use case, the less acceptable the unsupported output becomes.

A knowledge assistant that helps employees find the correct travel policy must show the source policy, its effective date, and whether a regional override applies. An analyst copilot that explains a revenue decline must point to the authoritative data sources, the calculation logic, and the period under review. An executive briefing tool that summarizes supply chain risk must reveal which incidents, reports, and operational systems informed the conclusion, and when those inputs were last updated. An action-taking agent that recommends customer remediation must demonstrate that it used current contractual terms, not a superseded clause.

In each case, the requirement is the same: evidence, transformation visibility, and contextual explanation.

Trust Rises Sharply When Evidence Is Exposed

One of the clearest patterns in enterprise AI adoption is that trust increases dramatically when users can inspect the underlying evidence. Even when users do not open every citation, the mere availability of evidence changes behavior. The system no longer appears to be making claims from nowhere. It appears to be working from governed sources.

This is not only a user interface issue. It is a data architecture issue. Evidence display is only possible when the upstream architecture preserves identifiers, source references, timestamps, transformation history, policy context, and retrieval metadata. A beautiful explanation layer cannot invent traceability after the fact.

Regulated Environments Make This Non-Optional

In regulated or legally exposed environments, provenance and lineage are not merely useful. They are mandatory design requirements.

An answer about eligibility, risk classification, pricing justification, policy interpretation, or retention obligation may need to survive audit, legal discovery, regulator inquiry, executive review, or customer challenge. "The AI said so" is not a defensible position. Neither is "the answer looked reasonable." The enterprise must be able to show what source assets were used, what transformations occurred, what business rules applied, what time period the answer reflects, and what restrictions governed its use.

That is the difference between an impressive demo and an enterprise system.

KEY INSIGHT

Evidence beats elegance

Elegant output may improve adoption, but evidence determines trust. In enterprise AI, a plain answer with strong traceability is more valuable than a polished answer with no defensible source chain.

CORE CONCEPTS

Provenance: Where the Evidence Came From

Provenance is the documented origin of the information used in an answer. It answers questions such as:

- What source asset supplied this claim?
- Is that source authoritative or merely supporting?
- Who owns it?
- When was it published, approved, or made effective?
- When was it retrieved by the AI system?
- Was it accessed under the user's permissions?

In enterprise settings, provenance is not satisfied by a generic link or repository name. "From SharePoint" is not provenance. "From Policy-TRV-104, Global Travel Policy, version 3.2, effective 2026-01-01, owned by Corporate Finance" is provenance.

Provenance is essential because enterprise repositories contain duplicates, drafts, archived materials, regional variants, and conflicting versions. Without clear source identity and authoritative status, retrieval systems can easily surface plausible but wrong content.

Lineage: How the Information Was Transformed

Lineage captures the path from origin to output. It explains what happened to the data or content after it left the source.

For structured data, lineage may include ingestion, standardization, joins, calculations, aggregation, and semantic mapping. For unstructured content, lineage may include extraction, OCR if applicable, section parsing, chunking, metadata enrichment, classification, entity tagging, summarization, indexing, and retrieval ranking. For hybrid pipelines, lineage may also include cross-source fusion, business rule application, and answer composition.

Lineage matters because answers are rarely produced directly from raw source material. They are the result of multiple transformations, each of which can introduce distortion, loss of context, stale interpretation, or policy violations.

When lineage is absent, teams can neither diagnose failures nor defend outcomes. When lineage is strong, they can inspect where meaning changed, where evidence weakened, or where a wrong transformation introduced error.

Explainability: Why the Answer Makes Sense in Context

Explainability is often reduced to a citation list. That is too narrow. A citation can show where a statement came from, but it does not by itself explain why the statement is the right answer in the present business context. Enterprise explainability requires multiple layers:

- The source evidence itself.
- The transformation logic applied to it.
- The business meaning of the terms involved.
- The temporal context.
- The policy context governing use.

For example, an assistant may answer that a customer is eligible for expedited remediation. A citation to a service manual helps, but true explainability also requires showing which definition of "priority customer" was applied, whether the cited policy was current on the date of the case, whether a regional exception changed the rule, and whether the answer was limited because of the user's access rights. That is an explanation in enterprise terms. It is not a model explanation. It is a decision-context explanation.

Temporal Context: The Overlooked Layer

Many AI failures are not failures of relevance. They are failures of time. The system finds a real source, but not the right version. It cites a genuine policy, but one that has been superseded. It summarizes a quarterly report without indicating that newer operational data changed the picture. It answers as though all facts are timeless.

Provenance and lineage must, therefore, include temporal markers: publication date, effective date, retrieval date, processing date, and freshness window. Explainability must expose those markers when they matter. A correct statement from last year can be an incorrect answer today.

Trust Signals: The Visible Result of Invisible Architecture

Users do not inspect raw metadata models. They experience trust through signals: source links, effective dates, ownership labels, confidence cues, policy notices, and explanation panes.

These signals may look like interface details, but they are expressions of architectural maturity. A system cannot display "authoritative source," "effective as of," "derived from two reconciled systems," or "summary excludes restricted regional annexes" unless the data architecture has preserved that information upstream.

Trust signals are, therefore, not cosmetic. They are the user-facing output of provenance, lineage, and explainability disciplines.

KEY INSIGHT

Why citation is necessary but not sufficient

Citation answers "where did this come from?" It does not answer "why is this the right interpretation, for this user, at this time, under this policy context?" Enterprise explainability requires all four.

ARCHITECTURAL IMPLICATIONS

Provenance Must Be Captured at Ingestion, Not Retrofitted at Response Time

One of the most common mistakes in enterprise AI programs is to treat provenance as something the application can reconstruct later. That rarely works. By the time content has been copied, chunked, enriched, indexed, and retrieved, critical source context is often already lost.

Provenance must begin at ingestion. Every ingested asset should carry a persistent source identifier, title, owner, authoritative status, repository location, version or effective date where available, security classification, and access controls. If the source is derived from another asset, that relationship should also be captured.

This applies across data types. A row in a transactional system, an API event, a PDF policy, a contract clause, and a knowledge article all need source identity that survives downstream handling.

Lineage Must Include Unstructured and Semi-Structured Transformations

Many organizations have acceptable lineage for structured pipelines and almost none for unstructured processing. That is no longer viable.

If a policy PDF is split into chunks, classified, annotated with entities, and ranked into an answer, those are material transformations. If an incident transcript is summarized into an executive note, that summary step must be known. If an event stream is normalized into a business status object used by an AI assistant, that mapping belongs in lineage.

AI-ready architecture expands lineage scope beyond ETL. It includes enrichment logic, chunking logic, retrieval logic, summarization logic, and composition logic.

Not every system needs to expose every internal step to every user. But the enterprise must be able to inspect those steps when needed.

Metadata Is the Control Plane for Traceability

Provenance and lineage are operationally impossible without a strong metadata layer.

Metadata carries the source identifiers, timestamps, owners, classifications, definitions, transformation records, access context, ranking features, and policy tags that make traceability possible. This is why metadata is not auxiliary. It is the control plane through which AI systems discover, rank, filter, explain, and justify answers.

When metadata is weak, provenance becomes ambiguous, lineage becomes incomplete, and explainability becomes superficial. When metadata is strong, the system can make evidence visible, enforce policy-aware retrieval, and distinguish authoritative sources from convenience copies.

Retrieval Architecture Must Preserve Evidence, Not Just Optimize Relevance

Many retrieval designs over-optimize for semantic similarity and under-design for evidence integrity.

A chunk may be relevant yet detached from the document's authoritative status. A highly ranked excerpt may lose the date or clause context that determines its true meaning. A summary may flatten important distinctions between a global rule and a regional exception. A fused answer may merge evidence from sources with different trust levels without saying so.

Architects should, therefore, design retrieval systems to preserve the evidence structure. That includes document hierarchy, section relationships, version markers, effective dates, source authority, and policy labels. Retrieval should not only return text fragments. It should return evidence-bearing objects.

Explainability Requires a Multi-Layer Response Model

A good enterprise answer should be able to support at least three levels of inspection.

The first level is the concise answer. This is what the user asked for.

The second level is evidence display. This includes citations, source titles, owners, dates, and relevant excerpts.

The third level is explanatory context. This includes business definitions, transformation notes, confidence or uncertainty cues, policy restrictions, and temporal qualifiers.

Different users may need different layers, but the architecture should support all three. Without that layered design, systems tend to swing between two bad extremes: opaque brevity or overwhelming detail.

Trust Thresholds Vary by AI Consumer

A conversational assistant for internal knowledge navigation can tolerate a lighter explanation burden than an executive intelligence tool. An analyst copilot can tolerate more complexity than a frontline workflow assistant. An action-taking agent requires the strictest evidence and policy validation of all.

This means provenance and explainability are not one-size-fits-all. The architecture must support variable trust contracts by use case.

A practical design question is not simply, "Do we have citations?" It is, "What level of evidence, lineage visibility, temporal precision, and policy disclosure is required for this class of AI consumer?"

❖ FIGURE 23 – SOURCE-TO-ANSWER TRACEABILITY

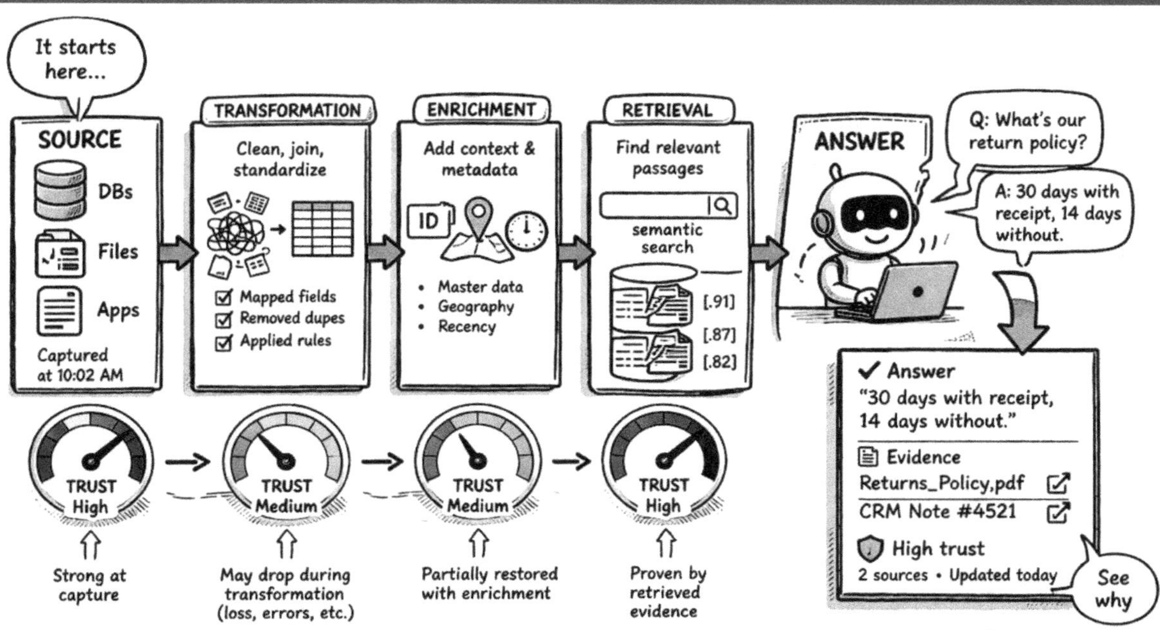

Failure Modes and Anti-Patterns

Treating Citations as Decoration

Some teams add citations late in the process to create the appearance of trust. The citations may point to generic documents, broad repositories, or loosely related pages rather than the actual evidence used. This is not provenance. It is decoration. Users notice quickly when citations do not materially support the claim. Once that happens, trust collapses fast.

Losing Source Identity During Chunking

Chunking is useful, but it often strips away exactly the context that makes evidence defensible. Teams create small text fragments for retrieval efficiency, then discover that the fragment no longer retains the policy version, section heading, effective date, jurisdiction, or authoritative status. A context-free chunk is easy to retrieve and hard to trust.

Failing to Distinguish Authoritative from Supporting Sources

Enterprise content ecosystems contain drafts, references, notes, and derived summaries alongside authoritative documents. If retrieval architecture treats them equally, AI systems will often choose the most readable source rather than the most authoritative one. That is a serious design flaw. Readability and authority are not the same thing.

Ignoring Transformation Opacity

When pipelines extract, summarize, normalize, or merge content without recording those steps, the organization loses its ability to explain why the final answer looks the way it does. This is especially dangerous when derived summaries are later treated as primary evidence. Derived content can be useful, but it must remain visibly derived.

Hiding Temporal Ambiguity

Another common anti-pattern is the timeless answer. The system presents a statement with no indication of when the source was effective, when the data was last refreshed, or whether the answer may have changed since retrieval.

This is one of the fastest ways to create executive distrust. Senior decision-makers are often less concerned with whether a statement is theoretically true than whether it is true now.

Substituting Model Confidence for Evidentiary Confidence

A fluent answer can sound certain even when its source basis is weak. Some systems then amplify the problem by presenting a confidence score that reflects internal scoring rather than evidence quality.

Enterprise trust signals should be grounded in evidence conditions: source authority, recency, consistency across sources, completeness of supporting context, and policy fit. Confidence should not become a false precision mechanism.

⚠ WARNING SIGN

"The AI said so."

The moment an organization accepts "the AI said so" as a sufficient justification, it has abandoned enterprise control. Every consequential answer should be backed by evidence, context, and a reviewable source chain.

PRACTICAL APPLICATION

Designing for Provenance

A practical provenance design starts with a source registration discipline. Every source asset that may be used by AI should have, at a minimum, a stable identifier, title, owner, authoritative status, security classification, effective or publication date, repository reference, and usage constraints.

For unstructured content, this should extend down to the segment level where needed. If a document is chunked, each chunk should retain a segment ID tied back to the source asset and section context. This is what makes precise evidence display possible.

For structured data, provenance should connect fields and records to system-of-record lineage and business meaning. A metric used in an AI answer should not be merely "from the warehouse." It should be traceable to its source domain, calculation logic, and refresh point.

Designing for Lineage

Lineage design should cover both data movement and meaning-changing transformations. Capture ingestion events, parsing steps, normalization rules, joins, calculations, enrichment routines, summary generation, indexing runs, and retrieval-time composition steps. Not all of this must be shown to end users, but it should be auditable by platform, governance, and risk teams. A useful principle is this: record every transformation that could materially affect interpretation, trust, compliance, or reproducibility.

Designing for Explainability

Explainability should be designed as a response pattern, not improvised as an afterthought.

For each answer, the system should be capable of showing:

- What evidence was used.
- What business definition shaped interpretation.
- What time context applies.
- What policy context or restrictions apply.
- What uncertainty remains.

This does not mean every answer must be long. It means every answer should be inspectable.

A Practical Trust Signal Model

A trust signal is a concise user-facing expression of provenance and context. For example:

- "Based on the authoritative Global Travel Policy, effective January 1, 2026."
- "Derived from Finance ERP and approved revenue recognition rules; refreshed at 6:00 AM ET."
- "Summary excludes restricted legal annexes not available under your access rights."
- "Two authoritative sources agree; one supporting note conflicts and was excluded."

These signals help users calibrate trust quickly. They also train the organization to expect evidence-bearing AI rather than purely fluent AI.

❖ FIGURE 24 – EXPLAINABILITY STACK

TEMPLATES

Provenance and Trust Signal Template

Source asset ID
<Unique immutable identifier for the source asset or system object>

Source title
<Official document title, dataset name, report title, event stream name, or record class>

Authoritative source? yes/no
<Yes / No>

Owner
<Named business owner or owning domain>

Date published/effective
<YYYY-MM-DD or timestamp; include effective date if policy or contractual source>

Date retrieved
<YYYY-MM-DD hh:mm:ss with timezone>

Transformation steps
<List the material steps applied before use in the answer, such as extraction, parsing, normalization, join logic, calculation, summarization, or reconciliation>

Enrichment steps
<List metadata enrichment applied, such as classification, taxonomy tagging, entity extraction, glossary mapping, jurisdiction tagging, policy labeling, or confidence scoring>

Chunk/segment ID
<Unique identifier for the exact segment, clause, row group, record set, or excerpt used>

Citation format
<User-facing citation pattern, for example: Source title, section/clause, effective date, retrieved date>

Business meaning reference
<Glossary term ID, semantic model reference, ontology node, policy definition, or metric definition used to interpret the source>

Confidence indicator
<High / Medium / Low, with rule basis such as source authority, recency, corroboration, completeness, or conflict status>

Applicable policies
<List relevant governance, legal, compliance, retention, privacy, usage, or review policies>

Restrictions
<List access limits, geographic restrictions, legal privilege, sensitivity labels, non-authoritative status, or "not for external use" constraints>

User-facing trust signal text
<Short explanation shown to the user, such as "Based on the authoritative North America Returns Policy, effective 2026-02-01, reviewed by Operations, retrieved today at 09: 15 ET.">

Audit log pointer
<Reference to the audit trail, lineage record, run ID, retrieval session ID, or observability log>

CASE EXAMPLE

Executive Intelligence Briefing That Became Trustworthy Only After Traceability Was Exposed

Consider an executive intelligence briefing tool used by a regional COO. Each morning, it produces a short summary of operational risk: supply disruption, major customer escalations, policy-sensitive incidents, and emerging financial exposure.

The first version of the tool appeared successful. The summaries were coherent. The language was polished. The topics were relevant. But adoption stalled. Executives asked the same questions in every meeting:

- Where did this come from?
- Is this based on current information?
- Did this use the official incident classification or someone's local notes?
- Why is this issue marked as high risk?
- What changed since yesterday?

The system could not answer well. It was drawing from incident logs, email summaries, regional operating notes, and weekly risk reports, but it exposed little of that chain. Citations were sparse. Dates were inconsistent. Supporting notes and authoritative reports were mixed together. The output sounded informed but was difficult to defend.

The redesign focused on provenance, lineage, and explainability from the data side.

First, every source used in the briefing was registered with authoritative status, owner, refresh profile, and sensitivity label. Incident records were tied to system-of-record identifiers. Regional notes were marked as supporting, not authoritative. Weekly risk reports carried publication timestamps and owner metadata.

Second, the transformation path was made visible. The system recorded which incidents had been normalized into common categories, which notes had been summarized, which rules mapped operational events to executive risk themes, and which retrieval session generated the briefing.

Third, the answer format changed. Every major claim in the briefing now showed:

- The underlying source or sources.
- The timestamp of the most recent supporting evidence.
- The owning domain.

- The reason the claim was classified the way it was.
- Whether the conclusion was drawn from authoritative sources alone or included supporting material.

A claim such as "Distribution risk increased in the Northeast region" no longer stood alone. It appeared with evidence such as:

- Three warehouse incident records from the operations platform, updated within the last six hours.
- One approved logistics disruption bulletin issued by the regional operations team.
- One supporting note from the daily planning call, clearly labeled as supporting rather than authoritative.

The trust effect was immediate. Executives did not review every source every day, but they no longer felt that the system was making ungrounded assertions. The briefing became defensible because every claim could be traced to a source, timestamp, and owning domain.

This is the key lesson. Trust was not won by better phrasing. It was won by making the answer reviewable.

Closing Synthesis

Enterprise AI does not earn trust by sounding right. It earns trust by showing its work in business terms.

Provenance establishes where the evidence came from. Lineage reveals how that evidence was transformed. Explainability makes the answer intelligible within the business, temporal, and policy context in which it will be used. Together, they create the conditions for defensible AI.

This is not an academic requirement. It is an architectural one. Systems that cannot preserve source identity, transformation history, and contextual meaning will eventually fail under scrutiny. They may survive as demos. They will struggle with enterprise capabilities.

The data-side responsibility is clear. Architects must design source registration, metadata capture, transformation observability, retrieval integrity, evidence display, and trust signals into the serving layer itself. They must treat explainability as a delivery property of the data estate, not as a cosmetic add-on in the user interface.

When this is done well, the enterprise gains more than compliance or audit readiness. It gains something more valuable: the ability to scale AI in environments where people must rely on the answer, act on it, and defend it later.

That is the true threshold. Not whether the system can answer, but whether the organization can stand behind the answer after it is given.

Key Takeaways

- Provenance shows where evidence came from; lineage shows how it was transformed; explainability shows why the answer is appropriate in context.
- Citation is necessary, but enterprise trust also requires business meaning, temporal correctness, and policy context.
- Provenance and lineage must be captured upstream through metadata and processing design, not improvised at response time.
- High-stakes AI use cases require visible evidence, trust signals, and audit-ready traceability as core design features.
- Enterprise AI becomes scalable only when answers are not merely fluent, but reviewable, defensible, and grounded.

CHAPTER 13: THE AI-READY DATA CAPABILITY PILLARS

Enterprise AI does not become trustworthy because a model is powerful. It becomes trustworthy because the enterprise has built the data capabilities required to supply that model, agent, or copilot with secure access, business meaning, policy context, provenance, freshness, and defensible evidence. That is why AI-Ready Data must be understood as a set of capability pillars.

An AI-ready enterprise needs a coherent set of capability pillars that connect source systems, content assets, metadata, semantics, governance, retrieval, and serving patterns into one integrated architecture. This is not a single platform purchase. It is not a search appliance, a vector database, a catalog, or a lakehouse. It is the coordinated set of capability pillars that allows AI systems to find the right information, interpret it correctly, respect policy, explain their answers, and improve over time.

This framing matters because enterprises often approach AI through tools rather than architecture. They acquire one product for indexing documents, another for metadata, another for governance, another for semantic search, and another for orchestration. They then discover that the hard problem was never the existence of tools. The hard problem was the absence of an architectural model that defines what capabilities are required, where they belong, which ones should be centralized, which ones should remain domain-owned, and how they work together.

This chapter establishes that model. It defines the AI-Ready Data capability pillars as the organizing architecture for the rest of the book. It clarifies the pillars that every enterprise needs, the cross-cutting controls that must span them, and the design choices that determine whether AI use cases can scale beyond isolated experiments.

KEY INSIGHT

Capability, Not Tool

Do not confuse the existence of products with the existence of capability. A capability is an architectural function with defined outcomes, ownership, controls, interfaces, and measures. A tool is only one possible implementation choice.

Why This Matters

AI Failures Are Usually Capability Failures Across the Architecture

When an enterprise AI system produces a wrong answer, the visible failure appears at the point of interaction. The real failure usually occurred earlier in the architecture.

A policy assistant answers from an outdated PDF because freshness was not managed. An executive briefing tool blends results from incompatible business units because terms such as "customer," "claim," or "exposure" were never semantically resolved. An agent recommends an action based on content that the requesting user should not have seen because access controls were stripped during ingestion. None of these is a fundamental model failure. They are architecture failures.

The capability pillars make those failures diagnosable. They give architects a way to separate source problems from ingestion problems, metadata problems from semantic problems, governance problems from retrieval problems, and serving problems from operational problems.

Traditional Readiness Models Do Not Go Far Enough

Most enterprises already know how to make data report-ready. Many know how to make it analytics-ready. Some have advanced to ML-ready pipelines. But none of those states automatically produce AI-Ready Data.

A reporting dataset can be accurate and still be unusable for a knowledge assistant if it lacks business definitions, access-aware delivery, traceable lineage, and the surrounding policy documents needed to explain a number in context. A document repository can be searchable and still be unfit for grounding if it lacks document status, owner, version history, classification, or chunk-level provenance. A transactional record can be pristine in a source application and still be dangerous in an agentic workflow if the allowed actions, temporal validity, and exception rules are not machine-readable.

AI-Ready Data, therefore, requires a broader architectural surface area than legacy readiness models assumed.

The Pillars Must Support Multiple AI Consumers

The same enterprise data estate must serve very different AI consumers. A policy Q&A assistant needs authoritative documents, granular citations, and strong permission fidelity. An analyst copilot needs curated business metrics, semantic definitions, and query-time contextualization. An executive briefing tool needs trusted aggregation across domains, temporal consistency, and explicit signals about uncertainty. An action-taking agent needs all of that plus tightly governed write permissions and policy-constrained execution.

The capability pillars matter because these consumers do not need identical serving contracts. They do, however, depend on the same foundational capabilities.

Core Concepts

The Model Is Organized into Capability Pillars

The AI-ready enterprise is built on a set of connected capability pillars. These pillars do not operate in isolation. They work together as one architectural model that turns raw enterprise data and content into trusted AI-ready assets.

The ten core capability pillars are:

Sources - Systems of record, content repositories, event streams, external feeds, and collaboration platforms.

Ingest - Extraction, capture, synchronization, parsing, transcription, document processing, and change detection.

Integrate - Harmonization, mastering, entity resolution, relationship mapping, and business-rule alignment across sources.

Store - Durable persistence for structured, semi-structured, and unstructured content, including version-aware and access-aware storage patterns.

Describe - Technical metadata, business metadata, operational metadata, policy metadata, and AI-serving metadata.

Contextualize - Glossaries, taxonomies, ontologies, semantic enrichment, business rules, and temporal interpretation.

Govern - Classification, privacy, retention, provenance, stewardship, approval, access control, and usage policy enforcement.

Retrieve - Indexing, chunking, enrichment, ranking, hybrid search, authority weighting, freshness handling, and evidence selection.

Serve - Data-serving contracts for different AI consumers, including APIs, retrieval services, semantic layers, grounding endpoints, and answer-evidence patterns.

Operate - Monitoring, evaluation, feedback loops, issue management, drift detection, and continuous improvement.

These pillars are not arbitrary. They correspond to the actual path by which enterprise information becomes usable by AI.

❖ FIGURE 25 - MASTER CAPABILITY

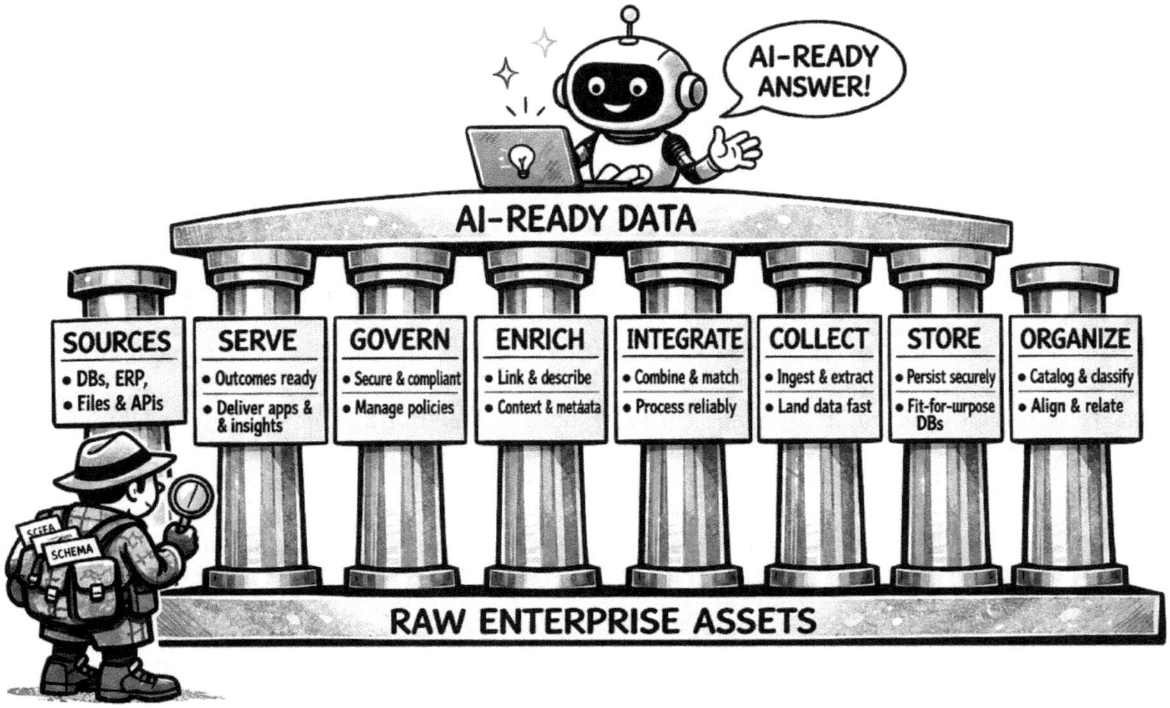

Cross-cutting Controls Matter as Much as the Pillars Themselves

The architecture cannot be secured or trusted by adding controls at the end. Identity, policy, lineage, monitoring, and stewardship must span the entire model.

Identity determines what sources can be accessed, what content can be indexed, and what evidence can be returned. Policy determines not only who may read data, but which uses are permitted, which jurisdictions matter, what retention rules apply, and what transformations are allowed. Lineage determines whether an answer can be traced back to its sources and intermediate processing steps. Monitoring determines whether the system is fresh, reliable, and behaving within tolerances. Stewardship determines who is accountable when terms conflict, ownership is unclear, or exceptions are required.

❖ FIGURE 26 - CROSS-CUTTING OVERLAY

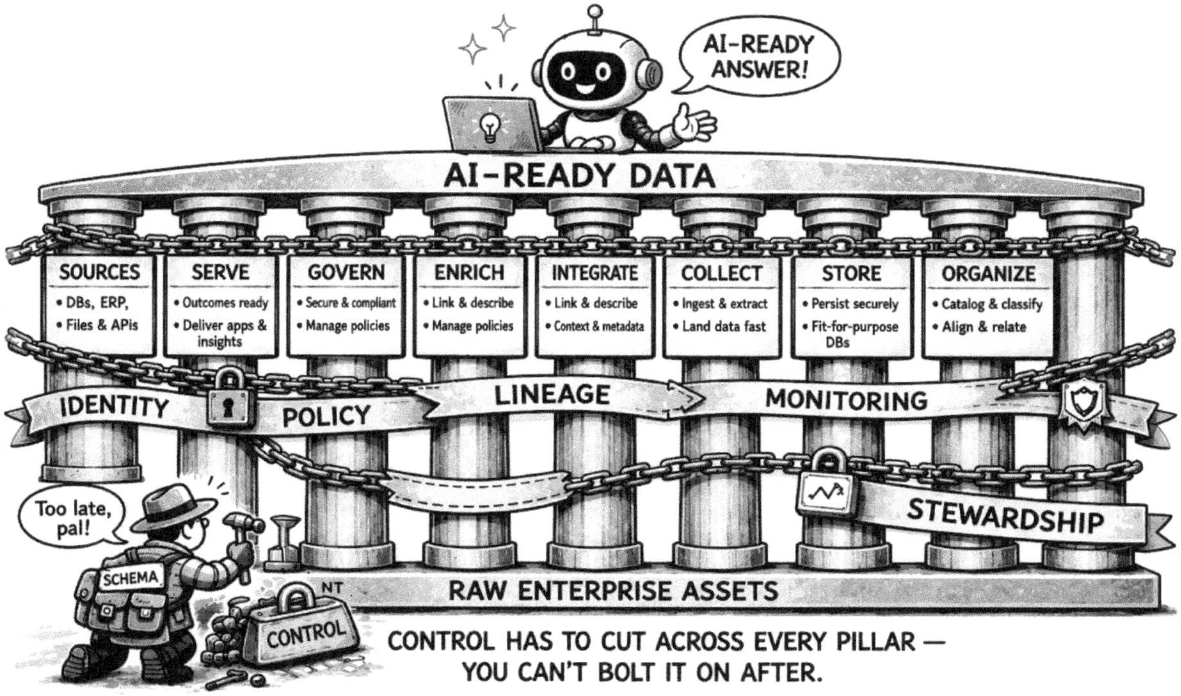

Centralize What Must Be Common; Federate What Must Remain Close to the Business

The capability pillars also clarify a core design question: what should be centralized and what should be federated?

Typically, enterprises should centralize shared control-plane capabilities such as enterprise identity integration, common policy services, lineage standards, core metadata infrastructure, retrieval evaluation frameworks, and platform observability. They should federate domain-owned content, business definitions, stewardship decisions, local quality rules, and use-case-specific serving logic where domain context matters.

This is one of the model's most practical uses. It prevents the false choice between full centralization and uncontrolled domain autonomy.

KEY INSIGHT

What Every Enterprise Capability Model Must Include

Every enterprise AI-ready capability model must include:

- Access-aware ingestion and delivery.
- Metadata beyond the technical schema alone.
- Semantic context for core business terms.
- Provenance and version awareness.
- Governance for both structured and unstructured data.
- Retrieval engineering as a formal architectural function.
- Consumer-specific serving patterns.
- Operational monitoring and accountability.

If any of these are missing, the enterprise does not have an AI-ready capability model. It has a collection of partial components.

ARCHITECTURAL IMPLICATIONS

Sources Are Broader Than Databases

For AI, the sources pillar must include more than enterprise applications and warehouses. Contracts, policies, knowledge articles, call transcripts, procedure manuals, email-driven approvals, ticket histories, and team-authored guidance often contain the business meaning that structured records alone cannot provide.

Architecturally, this means unstructured content cannot be treated as a peripheral ingestion problem. It must be managed as a first-class enterprise asset with ownership, classification, versioning, lifecycle controls, and clear inclusion criteria.

Ingestion Must Preserve Meaning, Not Just Move Bytes

Legacy ingestion pipelines were often designed for replication or reporting. AI-oriented ingestion must preserve document structure, authorship, timestamps, security context, source status, version history, and relationships to other assets.

For example, ingesting a policy document into a retrieval system without effective date, superseded date, approval status, and document owner creates a dangerous illusion of readiness. The text is present, but the meaning of the text in operational context is missing.

Metadata Is the Control Plane

The describe pillar is where AI-readiness becomes manageable. Metadata is what allows systems to decide which content is authoritative, which version is current, which domain owns a term, which policy applies, which access rules must be enforced, and which evidence should be shown to a user.

For that reason, metadata must extend beyond schema and technical lineage. It must include business definitions, classifications, sensitivity, jurisdiction, freshness expectations, ownership, document status, semantic tags, usage constraints, and AI-serving hints such as chunk boundaries, summary eligibility, and confidence signals.

Semantics Reduce Ambiguity Before Retrieval

The contextualize pillar exists because enterprise language is rarely clean. A "customer" in banking, insurance, healthcare, and marketing may not mean the same thing. A "policy" may refer to an insurance contract, an HR directive, or a security rule. A "case" may mean a legal matter, a service ticket, or a clinical encounter.

Without semantic context, retrieval systems often return plausible mixtures of these meanings. That is why glossaries, taxonomies, ontologies, and entity resolution are not academic extras. They are mechanisms for disambiguation and trust.

Governance Must Act Across All Pillars

Governance in an AI-ready enterprise is not confined to data quality councils or document retention rules. It must actively shape what is ingestible, how it is described, what transformations are acceptable, how evidence is exposed, what actions agents may take, and what monitoring triggers intervention.

The design implication is clear: governance services must be embedded into pipelines, metadata services, retrieval services, and serving endpoints. A separate governance office without technical enforcement points will not keep pace.

Retrieval Is a Formal Architecture Domain

Many organizations still treat retrieval as an application-side configuration problem. That is inadequate. Retrieval quality depends on architecture choices: chunking strategy, structure-aware parsing, authority scoring, hybrid ranking, freshness logic, duplication handling, access trimming, metadata enrichment, and evidence formatting.

A weak retrieval pillar can undermine excellent source systems and excellent models alike. A strong retrieval pillar can make modest models behave reliably because it supplies them with grounded, relevant, policy-compliant evidence.

Serving Patterns Must Reflect the Consumer

The serve pillar is where the architecture meets actual AI interaction. Different consumers need different contracts.

A policy assistant may require source excerpts, paragraph-level citations, policy-effective dates, and refusal when authoritative evidence is missing. An executive briefing tool may need domain-aggregated metrics, narrative synthesis across approved sources, and uncertainty flags where data freshness is uneven. An operational agent may need executable APIs, decision constraints, human-approval thresholds, and immutable logs of actions taken.

A single generic serving layer will not satisfy all three well.

Failure Modes and Anti-Patterns

Tool Sprawl Without Capability Design

The most common failure mode is acquiring products without defining the target capability model. The result is overlapping indexes, duplicated metadata stores, inconsistent security handling, competing glossaries, and no shared evaluation model.

⚠ Warning Sign

Tool Sprawl Without a Capability Model

You are in trouble when the architecture sounds like a shopping list. If teams describe the environment as "our catalog, our vector store, our lakehouse, our graph, our search engine, our governance tool, our assistant framework," but cannot explain the capability boundaries, control points, and ownership model, the capability model is not designed. It is accumulated.

Repository-as-readiness Thinking

Another anti-pattern is assuming that content becomes AI-ready because it is stored in SharePoint, a content platform, a data lake, or a knowledge base. Repositories store. They do not automatically classify, disambiguate, rank, govern, or explain.

Schema-only Metadata

Enterprises often overestimate the readiness value of technical metadata. Table names, column names, and pipeline lineage are useful, but insufficient. AI requires business meaning, usage constraints, source authority, temporal interpretation, and document status.

Governance Bolted on After Deployment

Organizations that launch copilots and then attempt to retrofit access rules, retention controls, or citation standards usually discover that the index, pipeline, and serving logic were never built to support them. Late governance is expensive governance.

Retrieval Without Evaluation

A retrieval capability with no relevance measurement, no freshness testing, no access-fidelity testing, and no grounded-answer review process will quietly degrade. Teams often notice only when user trust has already fallen.

One Serving Contract for Every Use Case

Trying to use the same source set, ranking logic, citation style, and response behavior for every consumer leads to brittle outcomes. The architecture should share common capabilities, but the serving contract must reflect the use case.

Practical Application

How to Assess the Current Capability Pillars

Most enterprises already possess fragments of these capability pillars. The task is not to start from zero. It is to identify which capabilities exist, how mature they are, where ownership sits, and which weaknesses directly affect priority AI use cases.

A practical assessment should answer five questions for each capability area:

- What business outcome is this capability supposed to support?
- What controls or metadata are currently missing?
- Who owns the decisions and who operates the capability?
- Which AI use cases are currently blocked or degraded by weakness here?
- Is this capability best centralized, federated, or hybrid?

TEMPLATES

Capability Pillars Assessment

Capability area	<name of the capability being assessed, such as source and content inventory, ingestion and capture, integration and entity resolution, or storage and versioned persistence>
Current state description	<summary of the current operating state, including what is in place today and where material limitations remain>
Current owner	<function, team, or role currently accountable for this capability area>
Existing tools/platforms	<tools, platforms, systems, or utilities currently supporting the capability>
Maturity score	<current maturity rating for the capability, such as 1/5 through 5/5>
Key weaknesses	<main gaps, failure points, inconsistencies, or constraints limiting the capability today>
AI use cases affected	<AI use cases, assistants, copilots, workflows, or decision processes impacted by the current maturity level>
Dependencies	<other capabilities, controls, or foundational elements that this capability depends on>
Target state	<desired future-state condition describing what this capability should look like when it is fit for AI-ready operations>
Priority level	<relative implementation priority, such as low, medium, medium-high, or high>
Recommended investment	<primary investments, design changes, standards, tooling, or operating-model improvements needed to strengthen the capability>
Timeline	<expected implementation horizon or target timeframe for improvement, such as 3-6 months, 6-12 months, or 12-18 months>
Success metric	<measure used to determine whether the capability has improved in a meaningful and operationally useful way>

CASE EXAMPLE

Mapping Two Use Cases onto One Architecture

Consider two common enterprise use cases:

- **Policy Q&A assistant** for employees asking questions about HR, security, finance, and travel policy.
- **Executive-intelligence briefing tool** that synthesizes business performance, risk signals, and strategic developments for leadership.

At first glance, these seem different enough to justify separate architectures. In reality, they should share the same capability pillars while using different serving contracts.

Use case 1: Policy Q&A Assistant

The policy assistant depends heavily on unstructured content. Its authoritative sources include policy manuals, approved procedure documents, knowledge articles, exception guidance, and official communications. The ingest pillar must preserve effective dates, supersession status, document owner, approval state, and access rules. The describe pillar must distinguish draft from approved content and identify authoritative versus advisory sources. The contextualize pillar must resolve ambiguous terms such as "policy," "exception," "manager approval," and "covered expense" in their correct enterprise context. The govern pillar must ensure that restricted HR or legal documents are not surfaced to unauthorized users. The retrieve pillar must favor current, approved policy content and return precise citations. The serve pillar must refuse to speculate when authoritative evidence is weak and must present answer-plus-evidence, not answer alone.

In this use case, trust depends on source authority, freshness, permission fidelity, and explainability.

Use case 2: Executive-Intelligence Briefing Tool

The executive briefing tool depends on both structured and unstructured assets. Structured sources include financial metrics, pipeline data, operational KPIs, risk indicators, and customer trends. Unstructured sources include board-ready narratives, analyst summaries, market research, major incident reports, and strategic memos. The integrate pillar becomes more prominent because multiple domains must be reconciled. The contextualize pillar must align terms such as "customer," "revenue," "region," "risk exposure," and "active account" across business units. The govern pillar must manage sensitivity and ensure that narrative summaries do not blend incompatible definitions. The retrieve pillar must rank authoritative internal metrics above informal commentary, while still using contextual documents to explain movement or risk. The serve pillar must expose confidence, date boundaries, and domain provenance so that leaders can see what the briefing is based on.

In this use case, trust depends on cross-domain semantic alignment, temporal consistency, authoritative aggregation, and transparent evidence provenance.

Same pillars, different emphasis

These two use cases share the same architectural model, but they stress different pillars.

- The **policy Q&A assistant** puts heavier pressure on unstructured content quality, document status metadata, access-aware retrieval, and citation behavior.

- The **executive-intelligence briefing tool** puts heavier pressure on integration, semantic reconciliation, metric provenance, temporal coherence, and synthesis controls.

This is exactly why the capability pillars are a better organizing model than a tool-centric view. They allow architects to build once at the capability level while varying serving contracts, controls, and optimization priorities by use case.

A Microsoft-oriented enterprise might implement portions of these pillars across products such as content repositories, Purview-style metadata and governance services, Microsoft 365 sources, and AI application layers. But the architectural point remains unchanged: the model is defined by capability, not by vendor boundary. A different vendor mix can support the same design if the capability coverage and control integration are sound.

❖ FIGURE 27 – MODULAR DATA ARCHITECTURE

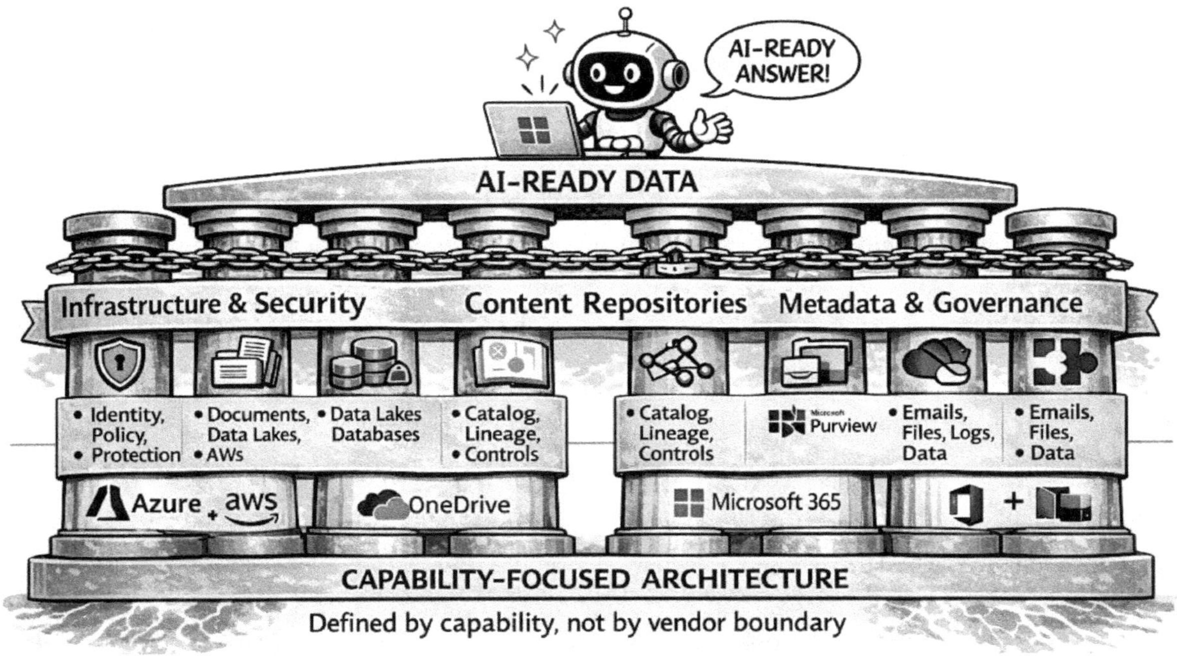

CLOSING SYNTHESIS

The AI-Ready Data capability pillars form the architectural backbone of trustworthy enterprise AI. They turn a vague aspiration, "make our data ready for AI," into a concrete design model with clear capabilities, controls, ownership, and measurable outcomes.

Its first lesson is that readiness is not a product. It is the coordinated performance of the enterprise's capability pillars: source management, ingestion, integration, storage, metadata, semantics, governance, retrieval, serving, and operations.

Its second lesson is that cross-cutting controls are not optional. Identity, policy, lineage, monitoring, and stewardship are not governance decorations around the architecture. They are structural requirements inside it.

Its third lesson is that not all AI consumers need the same contract. Enterprises should build shared capabilities, but they must serve assistants, copilots, briefing tools, and agents differently according to trust thresholds and the consequences of error.

Its fourth lesson is organizational. The capability pillars clarify what should be centralized, what should remain federated, and where accountability belongs. This is how architecture becomes an operating model rather than a diagram.

Most importantly, the capability pillars provide a durable way to design for repeatability. Enterprises do not win with one successful assistant. They win when they can support many AI use cases on a governed, contextualized, explainable, reusable data estate. That is the real meaning of AI-Ready Data.

Key Takeaways

- AI-Ready Data depends on a connected set of capability pillars, not a single platform or tool category.
- Metadata, semantics, governance, and retrieval must be treated as core architectural pillars, not add-ons.
- Cross-cutting controls such as identity, policy, lineage, monitoring, and stewardship must span every pillar.
- Different AI consumers require different serving contracts, even when they rely on the same foundational pillars.
- The capability pillars provide a practical model for deciding what to centralize, what to federate, and where to invest next.

CHAPTER 14: CONVERGED DATA PATTERNS: RELATIONAL, VECTOR, GRAPH, AND CONTENT

Enterprise AI exposes a fact that many platform teams try to avoid: no single data pattern is sufficient for all AI workloads. Relational platforms remain essential for truth, metrics, controls, and operational consistency. Content repositories hold policy, narrative, evidence, and institutional memory. Vector indexes make similarity-based retrieval practical at scale. Graph structures reveal relationships, dependencies, and paths that neither tables nor documents express well. The winning architecture is rarely a winner-take-all platform. It is a converged pattern in which each data form plays a distinct role under shared governance, metadata, semantics, and access control.

This matters because enterprise AI does not consume data the way dashboards or batch reporting do. A reporting stack can succeed with curated tables, fixed transformations, and stable definitions. An AI system must often answer questions that cut across metrics, contracts, policies, communications, entities, and relationships. It must discover relevant evidence, interpret meaning, preserve provenance, and do so within policy. That is not a storage problem alone. It is an architectural orchestration problem.

The mature question, then, is not whether relational, vector, graph, or content is the right answer. The mature question is which of them should be primary for a given workload, which should support it, and how the enterprise will keep them semantically aligned and govern them as one serving estate.

WHY THIS MATTERS

AI Questions Are Structurally Different from Reporting Questions

A report asks for an agreed metric over governed data. An AI assistant may ask for the metric, the policy behind it, the contract clause that limits its use, the recent exception logged in a ticket, and the third party connected to the issue. That is a different class of demand. It crosses structured and unstructured boundaries, and it requires the system to preserve evidence rather than merely compute output.

This is why many AI pilots appear promising in a demo and fail in production. The team proves that a model can generate fluent answers, then discovers that the answer cannot be trusted because the supporting data lives in disconnected forms with inconsistent governance. The relational warehouse knows the revenue number. The document repository contains the governing policy. A collaboration system holds the escalation history. An entity registry knows the counterparty relationship. The AI can only be as trustworthy as the architecture that coordinates those elements.

Different Structures Solve Different Enterprise Problems

Relational systems are still the best home for authoritative facts, repeatable calculations, state transitions, and auditable business logic. They are the anchor for financial metrics, customer records, order status, inventory balances, and compliance thresholds.

Content stores preserve the evidence that explains enterprise decisions. Policies, contracts, manuals, transcripts, emails, and knowledge articles often contain the business meaning AI needs most. These are not peripheral assets. In many domains, they are the source material from which operational interpretation is derived.

Vector retrieval supports semantic matching across language variation. It helps when a user asks about "termination for convenience" and the source text says "rights of early unilateral cancellation." That is an access advantage, not a replacement for source truth.

Graph adds value when the answer depends on relationships: subsidiaries, counterparties, dependencies, product hierarchies, account networks, regulatory obligations, lineage chains, and approval paths.

The Enterprise Challenge Is Orchestration

Most enterprises do not fail because they lack one of these patterns. They fail because each pattern is managed as a separate island. They implement document search without tying it to business entities. They build embeddings without preserving permissions or freshness. They deploy graphs without authoritative mastered entities. They ask the warehouse to serve narrative answers it was never designed to hold. The problem is not the absence of technology. It is the absence of convergence.

Core Concepts

Relational Stores Anchor Truth and Metrics

Relational architecture remains the backbone of enterprise trust. It is where organizations formalize business rules, enforce referential integrity, manage transactional correctness, and publish certified metrics. For AI, relational data provides the structured anchor that keeps answers from drifting into plausibility without proof. An analyst copilot asking, "What was the contract value at renewal?" should resolve that amount from governed relational records, not infer it from contract prose. A service assistant asking, "Is this customer eligible for premium support?" should read the entitlements table, not guess from a knowledge article.

But relational data alone is incomplete for AI-readiness. A table may show a status code or risk score without explaining the underlying policy, exception, or rationale. Structured truth needs semantic context, lineage, and business definitions to become AI-usable rather than merely machine-readable.

Content Stores Preserve Evidence and Narrative Context

Content stores hold the artifacts that explain enterprise meaning. Contracts establish obligations. Policies define acceptable action. Manuals describe procedures. Emails and transcripts capture exceptions and interpretation. Knowledge articles preserve institutional memory.

For AI, this evidence layer matters because users do not only ask for facts. They ask for why, according to what source, under which conditions, and with what limitations. A content-aware architecture can ground answers in cited evidence rather than in model fluency.

Yet repositories are not the same as readiness. A file system or collaboration platform does not automatically provide chunking strategy, business metadata, authoritative ranking, permission inheritance, citation design, or freshness management. Raw content availability is not the same as trustworthy retrieval.

Vector Indexes Support Similarity-Based Retrieval

Vector indexes help AI retrieve semantically related content when exact keyword matching is not enough. They are useful for natural-language questions, concept expansion, paraphrase tolerance, and discovery of relevant passages across large document sets.

This is especially valuable in enterprise language, where vocabulary differs by business unit, region, acquisition history, and regulation. Users rarely ask questions in the same terms used by source documents. Vector retrieval narrows that gap.

But the vector should be understood correctly. It is not a universal store. It is an access pattern that improves retrieval over content or structured representations. The source of truth remains elsewhere. Embeddings are derivative artifacts. They must be regenerated when content changes, constrained by permission boundaries, and tied back to authoritative sources.

KEY INSIGHT

Vector is an access pattern, not a universal answer

Vector search is powerful because it improves discovery. It is dangerous when treated as a replacement for source systems, semantic definitions, or governance. Use it to find relevant evidence, not to redefine truth.

Graph Supports Relationship Intelligence

Graph becomes essential when the meaning depends on traversal. Which legal entities are related to this supplier? Which policies apply through a control framework? Which contracts are associated with a counterparty and its subsidiaries? Which data products feed the answer and what approvals govern their use?

Relational systems can model relationships, but graph excels when those relationships become multi-hop, dynamic, and analytically important. It allows the enterprise to explore not just what exists, but how things connect.

For AI, graph helps reduce ambiguity. A user asking about "Acme" may mean a parent company, a subsidiary, an account, or a contract counterparty. Graph-supported entity resolution and relationship context allow the system to interpret requests with more precision and defend the result.

Content, Vector, Graph, and Relational Are Complementary

The central architectural idea is simple:

- Relational asks "What is the certified fact?"
- Content asks "What is the evidence or narrative context?"
- Vector asks "What is likely relevant to this question?"
- Graph asks "How are the entities, obligations, or events connected?"

A converged architecture does not blur these roles. It coordinates them.

Metadata Is the Control Plane Across All Four Patterns

Convergence fails without metadata. Metadata identifies source authority, business definition, steward, classification, freshness expectation, access policy, lineage, and intended use. It connects a document passage to a policy domain, an entity in a graph to a mastered record, a vector entry to its source chunk, and a relational metric to its certified definition.

Without metadata, convergence becomes a brittle federation of tools. With metadata, it becomes an architectural system.

Architectural Implications

Design for Coordinated Serving, Not Isolated Storage

The serving architecture for enterprise AI should begin with workload intent. Is the system answering policy questions, summarizing customer situations, supporting investigations, generating executive briefings, or enabling action-taking agents? The answer determines which pattern is primary and which patterns must support it.

A policy assistant may be content-first with vector support and relational validation. A fraud investigator may require graph-first exploration with content evidence and relational scoring. A finance copilot may be relational-first with supporting policy content and limited graph context for ownership structures.

Make Semantic Alignment Explicit

Convergence requires common identifiers, glossaries, entity resolution, and relationship models. "Customer," "supplier," "contract," "site," and "product" must mean something stable across patterns. A clause in a contract should be linkable to the counterparty, product family, jurisdiction, and policy domain it affects. Otherwise, retrieval may succeed technically while failing semantically.

This is where taxonomies and ontologies move from academic nice-to-have to enterprise necessity. They reduce ambiguity across structured and unstructured assets and make cross-pattern orchestration possible.

Preserve Provenance All the Way Through the Answer

A trustworthy AI answer should be able to show:

- Which relational record supplied the metric.
- Which content passages supplied the evidence.
- Which graph path established the relationship.
- Which retrieval logic selected the material.
- Whether the user was entitled to see all of it.

That provenance chain must survive enrichment, indexing, and serving. If the architecture cannot preserve it, explainability will collapse at the moment it matters most.

Treat Freshness as Multi-Speed, Not Uniform

Different patterns refresh at different rates. Transactional data may update in seconds. Content ingestion may be hourly. Embedding refresh may be event-driven or scheduled. Graph projections may be near-real-time for some domains and nightly for others. The architecture must make these timings visible and govern them intentionally.

An AI answer about a live order status cannot rely on a vectorized summary from yesterday. A contract clause may remain stable for months, while the counterparty risk rating changes daily. Convergence requires temporal discipline.

Use Access-Aware Orchestration

Permissions cannot be bolted on after retrieval. They must constrain ingestion, enrichment, indexing, and serving. If a document is access-restricted, its chunks, embeddings, and derivative graph assertions must inherit or respect that restriction. Otherwise, the architecture leaks through secondary forms even when the source repository is secure.

❖ FIGURE 28 - CONVERGED SERVING MODEL

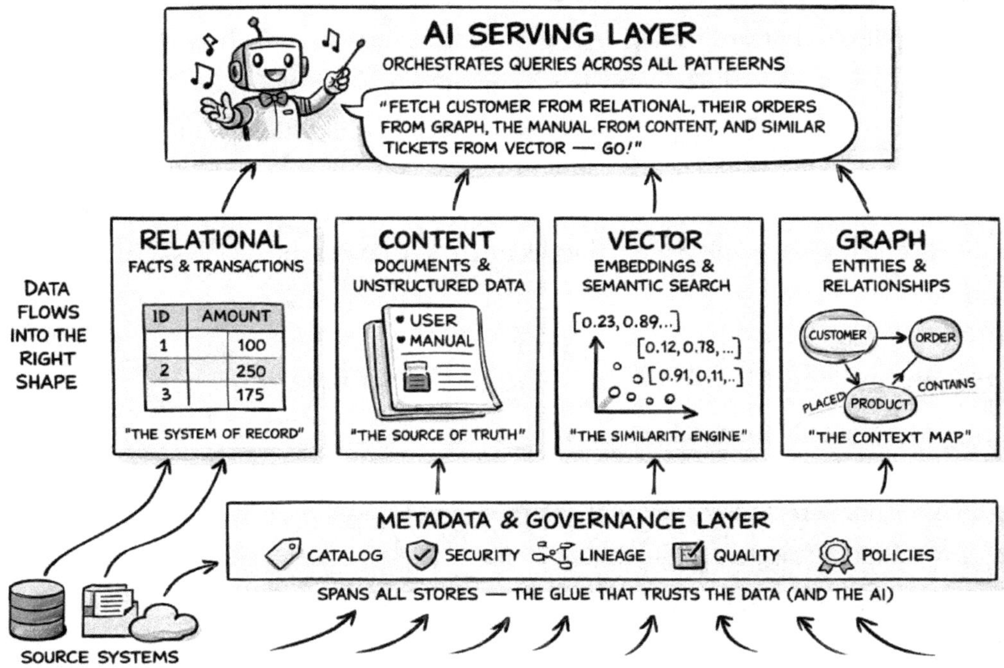

💡 KEY INSIGHT

Purity loses to pragmatism

Architects often want one elegant platform standard. Enterprise AI rewards a different instinct: use the simplest converged pattern that meets the workload's trust, evidence, and governance needs. Architectural purity is less important than defensible outcomes.

FAILURE MODES AND ANTI-PATTERNS

Forcing Every Use Case into One Store

This is the most common and most damaging anti-pattern. One team wants every question answered from the warehouse. Another wants to vectorize everything and call the problem solved. Another tries to impose graph on workloads that are basically document retrieval with a few filters.

Each of these moves mistakes a strong capability for a universal one. Enterprise workloads differ too much for that.

> ⚠ **WARNING SIGN**
>
> **A platform team trying to force every problem into one store**
>
> When the platform conversation becomes ideological, the architecture is already drifting. The right question is not "Which store wins?" It is "Which combination best serves the workload under enterprise controls?"

Treating Vector Retrieval as if It Were Truth

Embeddings compress semantics for retrieval. They do not preserve exact meaning, authority, or policy by themselves. If the answer path ends at "the vector search found this," the architecture is incomplete. Retrieval must resolve back to governed sources and, where needed, certified structured facts.

Building Graph Without Mastering Entities

Graph initiatives often fail because the edges are sophisticated but the nodes are weak. If the enterprise has not resolved entity identity, normalized core concepts, and defined relationship semantics, graph becomes an attractive visualization of underlying ambiguity.

Leaving Content Ungoverned Because It Is Messy

Many organizations govern structured data rigorously while treating documents as an operational residue. That is unsustainable for AI. Unstructured content now drives recommendations, answers, summaries, and agent actions. If it lacks classification, retention logic, owner assignment, provenance, and access-aware delivery, AI will amplify that disorder.

Separating Retrieval Design from Architecture

Chunking, enrichment, ranking, and citation are sometimes treated as implementation details for an AI application team. That is a mistake. These choices determine evidence quality, precision, explainability, and policy compliance. Retrieval quality is an architectural responsibility, not merely an application tuning exercise.

Ignoring Different Data-Serving Contracts

A general knowledge assistant can tolerate broader retrieval and softer confidence boundaries than an action-taking agent that initiates changes in a customer account. Architecture must reflect these differences. The same converged estate may support both, but not through the same serving contract.

PRACTICAL APPLICATION

Start with Workload Decomposition

Before selecting a pattern, decompose the use case into answer components:

- Authoritative fact.
- Supporting evidence.
- Semantic discovery need.
- Relationship traversal need.
- Sensitivity.
- Freshness.
- Explainability requirement.
- Actionability.

This prevents teams from defaulting to whichever platform is already funded.

Choose a Primary Pattern, Then Add Supporting Patterns Deliberately

Every workload should have a primary pattern, not because one store does everything, but because one mode of access usually dominates.

A metric-heavy executive briefing tool is relational-first.

A policy Q&A assistant is content-first.

A contract clause comparison tool is vector-supported content-first.

A fraud investigation assistant is graph-first with relational and content support.

The supporting patterns should be explicit, justified, and governed. That keeps the architecture understandable and keeps costs under control.

TEMPLATES

Converged Pattern Decision Matrix

Use case	<name of the AI use case, assistant, copilot, or decision-support scenario being assessed>
Need for authoritative metrics	<degree to which the use case depends on certified, trusted, and governed numeric measures, such as low, moderate, high, or very high>
Need for document evidence	<degree to which the use case depends on source documents, written policies, contracts, procedures, case notes, or other textual evidence>
Need for semantic similarity retrieval	<degree to which the use case depends on semantic search, embedding-based retrieval, or meaning-based matching across content>
Need for relationship traversal	<degree to which the use case depends on navigating relationships across entities, events, controls, products, parties, or dependencies>
Sensitivity level	<level of security, confidentiality, legal, regulatory, or operational sensitivity associated with the use case>
Freshness requirement	<required data and content recency for the use case, such as daily, intraday, hourly, near-real-time, or mixed by source type>
Explainability requirement	<degree to which answers, recommendations, or outputs must be transparent, traceable, and evidence-backed>
Recommended primary pattern	<primary data architecture pattern best suited to the use case, such as relational, content, graph, converged relational-content, or another approved pattern>
Supporting patterns	<secondary patterns that complement the primary pattern, such as vector retrieval, graph context, relational validation, or content evidence support>
Governance implications	<key governance, security, policy, lineage, access, evidence, or control requirements that must be addressed for this use case>
Complexity rating	<overall implementation and operating complexity of the use case, such as low, medium, medium-high, or high>
Owner	<role, team, or function accountable for delivery, governance, and ongoing performance of the use case>
Approval notes	<specific conditions, constraints, or rules that must be met before the use case may be approved or operated>

❖ FIGURE 29 - PATTERN DECISION MAP

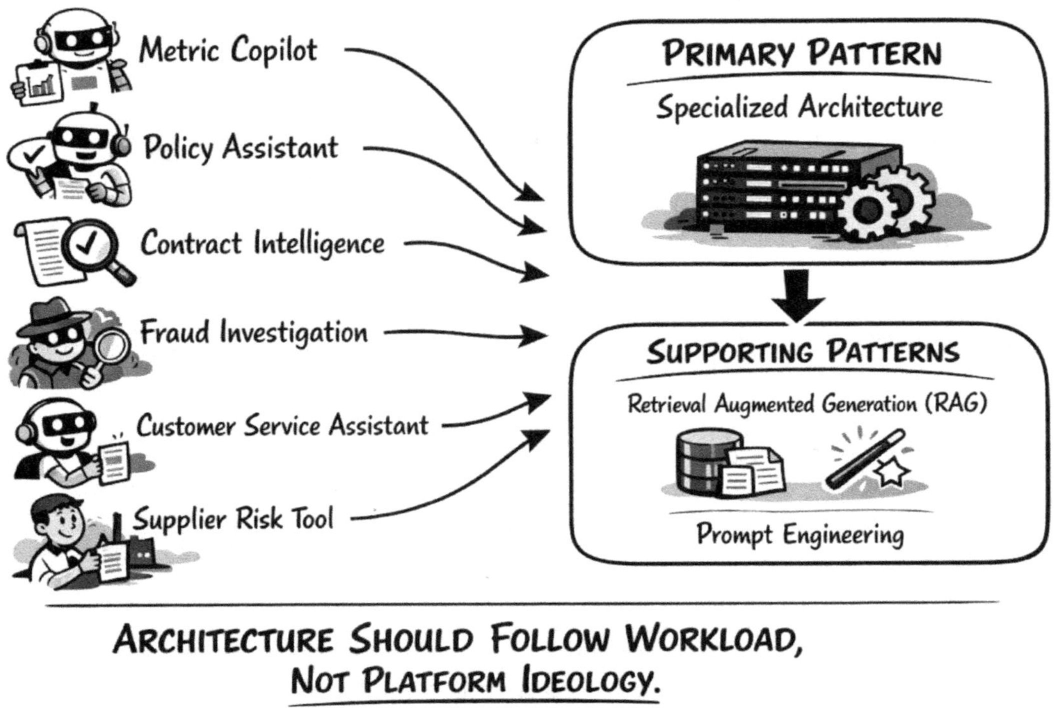

CASE EXAMPLE

Contract Intelligence as a Converged Pattern

Consider a contract intelligence solution for a global enterprise. Users ask questions such as:

- Which active contracts allow termination for convenience within 30 days?
- Which counterparties have non-standard indemnity language?
- Which agreements reference the same pricing exception language as this contract?
- Which obligations are linked to subsidiaries in high-risk jurisdictions?
- What is the annual contract value and renewal date for the affected agreements?

No single pattern can answer all of that well.

What each pattern contributes

Relational layer:

The relational layer holds contract identifiers, counterparties, contract value, renewal dates, approval status, jurisdiction codes, product associations, and obligation tracking fields. It is the source for authoritative metrics and operational status.

Content layer:

The content layer stores the contract text, schedules, amendments, email attachments, redlines, approval memos, and playbook guidance. It is the evidence base.

Vector layer:

The vector layer indexes clause-level chunks, amendment language, negotiation notes, and approved fallback language. It enables semantic retrieval for clause comparison and natural-language questioning.

Graph layer:

The graph layer maps counterparties to parent and subsidiary entities, links obligations to clauses and business units, relates contracts to products and jurisdictions, and captures approval chains or dependency structures.

How the answer flow works

A user asks: "Show me high-value active agreements with a 30-day termination for convenience clause involving counterparties connected to our Latin America distribution network."

A mature architecture does not send that question to one repository and hope for the best.

- The system resolves "high-value active agreements" against relational contract records and business thresholds.
- It retrieves candidate clause passages through vector search over contract text.
- It validates the clause language against the underlying content and cites the exact passage.
- It traverses graph relationships to identify counterparties connected to the Latin America distribution network through subsidiaries, distributors, or parent entities.
- It filters results according to user permissions, legal hold status, and jurisdictional restrictions.
- It returns the contracts, the certified values, the cited clauses, and the relationship path showing why each counterparty was included.

That is converged architecture in practice. Each pattern performs the task it is best suited to perform. The answer is both useful and defensible.

Why governance determines success

Without unified governance, this use case fails quickly. Legal may prohibit the use of draft redlines. Some contracts may be under hold. Certain clauses may be visible only to specific regions or legal teams. Embeddings must be regenerated when contracts change. Relationship mappings must be sourced from mastered legal entity records, not guessed from text. Citations must distinguish final executed language from superseded amendments.

The value of the solution comes not from combining four technologies, but from combining them under one control model.

Closing Synthesis

Converged data patterns are not an advanced embellishment for a few sophisticated use cases. They are the normal architectural conditions for enterprise AI. Relational, content, vector, and graph each solve a distinct class of problems. None should be abandoned. None should be inflated into a universal answer.

Relational stores anchor enterprise truth. Content stores preserve evidence and narrative meaning. Vector indexes make semantic retrieval practical. Graph structures expose relationship intelligence. The architectural responsibility is to orchestrate them under shared metadata, semantics, governance, lineage, and access control.

This is where enterprise AI-readiness becomes visible. Not in the existence of a warehouse, a repository, a graph database, or an embedding service, but in the enterprise's ability to make them work together coherently. The organizations that scale trustworthy AI will not be those that picked the trendiest store. They will be the ones who designed converged serving patterns around workload needs and governed them as a single, explainable system.

Key Takeaways

- No single data pattern can satisfy enterprise AI; convergence is usually the correct architectural answer.
- Relational handles certified facts, content preserves evidence, vector improves discovery, and graph reveals relationships.
- Vector is a retrieval mechanism, not a replacement for source truth, semantics, or governance.
- The hard problem is orchestration under shared metadata, permissions, provenance, and freshness controls.
- Architecture should follow workload and evidence requirements, not platform ideology.

Chapter 15: Integration Patterns for AI-Ready Data

AI-Ready Data does not emerge from integration by accident. It depends on integration patterns that preserve meaning, ownership, and policy as data moves across structured systems, event streams, SaaS applications, and content estates. That is the architectural center of this chapter: integration design determines whether enterprise context survives the journey from source to AI consumption, or is stripped away along the way.

In many enterprises, integration is still treated as a technical plumbing exercise. Data is extracted, transformed, replicated, denormalized, and pushed into warehouses, lakes, vector stores, indexes, and APIs with great mechanical efficiency. Yet the enterprise often discovers that what arrived is not what the AI system actually needed. The rows may be present, but the business meaning is not. The documents may be copied, but the permissions are wrong. The event stream may be live, but the consumer cannot interpret what a status change actually means in operational terms. The content may be searchable, but there is no authority ranking, no freshness logic, and no defensible lineage.

That is why integration patterns matter so much in an AI-ready architecture. AI systems rarely consume a single, neatly modeled database. They operate across systems of record, operational applications, content repositories, policy stores, communications platforms, and externally sourced information. The integration pattern used for each source influences freshness, explainability, duplication risk, access enforcement, semantic preservation, and operational cost. A design that works for reporting may be unsuitable for a knowledge assistant. A design that works for dashboard latency may be dangerous for an autonomous agent. A design that works for one department may create uncontrolled shadow copies across five others.

The central architectural question is, therefore, not simply, "How do we connect the systems?" It is, "How do we connect them in a way that preserves trust?"

Why This Matters

AI Operates Across Fragmented Enterprise Reality

Enterprise AI consumes a reality that is distributed by design. Customer truth may sit in CRM. Pricing guidance may live in a pricing platform or spreadsheet-controlled business process. Product entitlements may be defined in ERP. Proposal templates may reside in a document repository. Legal language may be governed in contract systems. Product launch decisions may be captured in collaboration tools. Support escalations may appear first in ticketing systems and chat threads. No single repository contains the full operating truth.

Traditional integration programs tolerated that fragmentation because the downstream use cases were narrower. Monthly reporting could accept a delay. A data science model could tolerate aggressive feature engineering and selective snapshots. Even many operational dashboards could work from curated copies updated on a schedule. But AI systems that answer questions, ground recommendations, generate content, or take actions require something more demanding: they must retrieve the right information, with the right context, under the right policy, at the right time.

If integration destroys that context, AI failure follows quickly. The failure may appear as a hallucination, but the underlying defect is often architectural. The assistant cites outdated pricing because the index was built from a replicated copy refreshed weekly. The copilot exposes contract language to an unauthorized user because permissions were flattened during ingestion. The agent misinterprets an account status because an event field was technically integrated but semantically opaque. The retrieval layer ranks the wrong policy because five near-identical copies exist and none are tagged as authoritative.

Integration Determines Whether AI Is Trustworthy at Scale

Trustworthy AI requires more than accessible data. It requires defensible sourcing, provenance, temporal correctness, permission fidelity, and business interpretability. Integration patterns directly influence each of those.

A batch pipeline can provide stable, cost-efficient delivery for slowly changing reference data, but may be unsuitable for high-stakes operational decisions that require the current state. An API-based access pattern can preserve source-of-truth semantics and access enforcement, but may introduce latency or throughput constraints. Event streams can provide timeliness and operational awareness, but often require stronger semantic contracts than organizations actually maintain. SaaS synchronization tools can expand coverage quickly, but also create unmanaged copies that fragment governance and ownership.

In other words, integration is not neutral. Every pattern makes an architectural choice about freshness, duplication, coupling, control, and trust.

AI-Ready Data Requires Intentional Integration Across Content as Well as Records

This is especially important for unstructured and semi-structured assets. Many enterprises have invested heavily in integrating structured transactional data while leaving content integration informal. Yet for enterprise AI, policies, proposals, knowledge articles, product documentation, transcripts, emails, and collaborative content often contain the business meaning the model needs most. If those assets are integrated without classification, metadata enrichment, authority rules, and access-aware delivery, the enterprise creates a retrieval estate that is broad but unreliable.

That is why AI-ready integration cannot stop at tables and APIs. It must encompass documents, messages, events, and application state in a single architectural discipline.

CORE CONCEPTS

Integration Is a Meaning-Preserving Discipline

The first principle is simple: integration for AI must preserve meaning, not merely move payloads.

Meaning is lost when the source context is stripped away. That happens when business labels are replaced with cryptic field names, when relationship context is flattened, when timestamps lose temporal significance, when document versions are merged without clear authority, or when business definitions are not carried into the downstream contract. The destination may contain "data," but not enough context for trustworthy use.

A mature integration design, therefore, preserves at least six things:

- **Source identity**: what system or repository produced the data or content.
- **Ownership**: who is accountable for its meaning, quality, and permitted use.
- **Policy context**: what access, retention, privacy, and usage rules apply.
- **Temporal context**: when it was created, changed, ingested, and valid for use.
- **Semantic context**: what the fields, events, entities, and documents mean in business terms.
- **Lineage context**: how the integrated representation was derived.

Without those, AI systems are forced to infer what the architecture should have made explicit.

KEY INSIGHT

Integration is where meaning is often destroyed

Most enterprises do not lose meaning at the source. They lose it in transit–during extraction, flattening, denormalization, synchronization, and indexing. AI exposes that loss faster than reporting ever did.

Pattern Choice Is Not Arbitrary

We identify five recurring patterns: batch, event, API, product, and sync. Each has a valid role. None is universally superior.

Batch integration

Batch remains useful for stable, moderately changing data where cost efficiency, repeatability, and large-volume processing matter more than immediacy. Reference hierarchies, curated dimensional structures, historical snapshots, and quality-controlled extracts often fit here.

For AI, batch is appropriate when the use case can tolerate bounded staleness and benefits from strong curation. It is less appropriate where the current state, entitlement fidelity, or rapidly changing content are central.

Event-driven integration

Events are powerful when the AI system must respond to business change as it happens or near it: order status changes, support escalations, inventory updates, payment failures, workflow approvals, and similar operational signals.

But events are only as useful as their semantic clarity. A field called status_code=7 may be technically real-time and architecturally useless. Event-driven AI demands well-defined event meaning, versioning, ownership, and downstream interpretation.

API-based access

APIs are often the best choice when the consumer must retrieve the current, governed state directly from the authoritative system. This is particularly valuable when permissions, business rules, or transaction consistency matter more than local replication.

API access is frequently superior for high-trust questions such as "What price guidance is valid for this deal right now?" or "Is this customer eligible for this renewal offer today?" In those cases, copying data into downstream stores may introduce unnecessary drift.

Data product delivery

A data product pattern treats an integrated dataset, service, or content collection as a governed, documented, reusable contract owned by a team. This is especially effective for enterprise-scale reuse because it clarifies accountability, semantics, service levels, policy, and intended use.

For AI-ready architecture, the data product idea is powerful because it forces the enterprise to define not only what is delivered, but also what quality, freshness, metadata, access, and explanatory guarantees accompany it.

Synchronization and connector-based replication

Sync patterns are common with SaaS applications, collaboration tools, and cloud platforms. They are fast to deploy and often necessary to broaden enterprise coverage. But they are also where uncontrolled duplication begins. Sync patterns should, therefore, be used deliberately, with clear authority rules, duplication controls, and lifecycle policies.

Canonical Layers Are Useful but Dangerous When Overextended

Canonical models promise simplification. In moderation, they are valuable. A shared representation of core business entities can reduce repetitive translation and support reuse across domains. But many enterprises overreach. They attempt to design a universal enterprise schema that mediates every integration flow. The result is delay, abstraction, semantic compromise, and political conflict over whose meaning is "standard."

For AI-Ready Data, the better discipline is selective canonicalization. Canonical definitions should be created where the enterprise truly needs common understanding—customer, product, contract, policy, order, account, entitlement—but not forced across every operational nuance. Integration must preserve local meaning where local meaning matters.

SaaS and Collaboration Platforms Are Part of the Real Architecture

SaaS applications and collaboration platforms are not peripheral to AI-readiness. They often contain the current operating truth of the enterprise: pricing exceptions, launch decisions, process notes, account strategy, product narratives, and practical interpretations of policy. Ignoring them creates blind spots. Integrating them carelessly creates chaos.

The correct stance is intentional inclusion. These platforms should be onboarded with the same seriousness applied to traditional systems of record: classification, ownership, access mapping, metadata capture, semantic enrichment, duplication analysis, and lifecycle control.

❖ FIGURE 30 – INTEGRATION PATTERN COMPARISON

ARCHITECTURAL IMPLICATIONS

Integration Architecture Must Carry Metadata as a First-Class Payload

If metadata is the control plane for AI, then integration cannot treat metadata as an optional sidecar. It must travel with the asset. That includes technical metadata, business metadata, security labels, retention tags, provenance markers, authority indicators, freshness signals, and lineage references.

A copied document without access metadata is not AI-ready content. A customer record without a business definition, owner, and valid-time context is not AI-Ready Data. An event without semantic description and contractual meaning is not AI-ready telemetry.

This has practical implications for architecture. Pipelines and connectors must support metadata propagation. Indexes must preserve source identifiers and version references. APIs must return enough context to enable interpretation. Data products must publish their metadata contract. Retrieval systems must rank with authority, recency, and policy awareness, not only vector similarity.

Pattern Selection Must Align to AI Consumer Type

Different AI consumers require different serving contracts.

A knowledge assistant can often combine indexed content, curated metadata, and selected APIs. An analyst copilot may rely more heavily on documented data products and governed semantic layers. An executive briefing tool may require curated summaries sourced from authoritative products and approved content collections. An action-taking agent requires the highest threshold: explicit permissions, current state, strong policy enforcement, and transaction-safe access patterns.

This means integration should not be standardized only by source. It should also be selected by consumer risk profile. The same pricing system may feed a batch-curated analytics product for planning, an API-based retrieval layer for in-flight deal guidance, and an event stream for monitoring approval threshold changes. That is not architectural inconsistency. It is fit-for-purpose design.

When API Access Beats Replication

Replication feels attractive because it centralizes data and simplifies downstream access. But centralization is not always the right answer. Where source rules, permissions, and current state are decisive, APIs are often superior.

This is especially relevant for sensitive operational systems, entitlement checks, dynamic pricing, contract status, approval workflows, and action-oriented AI use cases. In such cases, replicated data may be good enough for analysis and still unsafe for grounded action.

KEY INSIGHT

When APIs beat replication

Use APIs when the current state matters more than local copy performance, when source permissions must be preserved exactly, when business rules live in the source application, or when the duplication cost would create governance drift. Replication is valuable, but not as a reflex.

Shadow Copies Are an Architectural Liability

One of the most common integration mistakes is uncontrolled proliferation of copies. A document is synchronized into a search index, replicated to a data lake, transformed into a RAG corpus, embedded into a vector store, and exported to a departmental workspace. Soon, the organization no longer knows which instance is current, which is authoritative, or which permissions apply.

This is not just a storage problem. It is a trust problem. AI systems built on shadow copies are prone to stale answers, conflicting evidence, broken entitlements, and poor explainability.

Architecturally, this requires explicit duplication discipline:

- Define the authoritative source.
- Document why any copy exists.
- Assign freshness and retirement rules.
- Preserve linkage back to source version and owner.
- Prevent uncontrolled downstream re-copying.
- Audit where sensitive content has been materialized.

Source Onboarding Must Start with Governance, Not End with It

Many integration programs still treat governance as a post-ingestion activity. For AI-Ready Data, that order is wrong. Governance begins at onboarding.

❖ FIGURE 31 – SOURCE ONBOARDING FLOW

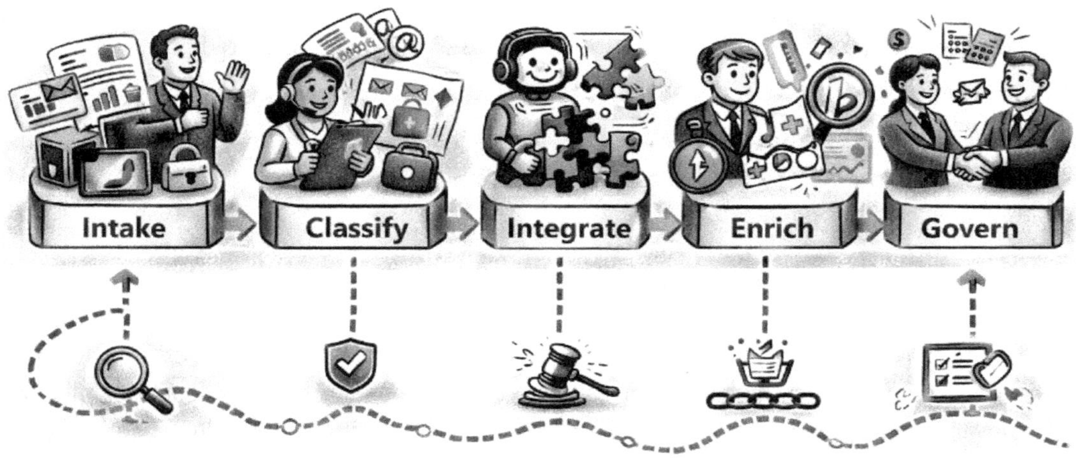

Before a source is integrated, the enterprise should know what classes of data or content it contains, who owns it, what sensitivity categories apply, what AI uses are allowed, what uses are excluded, what metadata already exists, what enrichment is required, what duplication risks are foreseeable, and how lineage will be maintained.

FAILURE MODES AND ANTI-PATTERNS

Universal Replication

The enterprise decides that every source should be copied into a central platform "for AI." This creates surface-level convenience but deep architectural fragility. Freshness varies, permissions drift, content versions multiply, and source ownership becomes blurred. Centralization becomes a substitute for design.

The corrective principle is selective integration. Not everything should be replicated. Some assets should be indexed. Some should remain accessible only by API. Some should be exposed as governed products. Some should be streamed as events. Some should not be onboarded at all for certain AI uses.

Canonical Model Absolutism

A team attempts to normalize all source variation into one enterprise representation before any AI use can proceed. This slows delivery and often erases nuance that the AI consumer actually needs. Important local semantics are treated as defects rather than context.

The corrective principle is targeted canonicalization. Standardize where shared meaning is essential. Preserve source-specific semantics where they matter for interpretation, action, or compliance.

Content Integration Without Content Governance

Documents and collaboration artifacts are ingested because they appear valuable, but with no clear source authority, no version discipline, no sensitivity handling, and no access-aware delivery. The result is a richly searchable but legally risky estate. This is especially common with policy content, sales decks, meeting notes, and product documentation. The AI assistant can retrieve something, but not necessarily the right thing.

⚠ **WARNING SIGN**

Five copies of the same policy content in five pipelines

When the same business policy exists in a document repository, a SharePoint sync, a lakehouse extract, a search index, and a vector store—without one authority rule and one lineage chain—you do not have resilience. You have architectural drift.

Event Streams with No Semantic Contract

Teams celebrate real-time integration but cannot explain what the events mean, who owns them, what version applies, or how downstream systems should interpret state transitions. AI systems then consume technically fresh but semantically unstable signals.

The corrective principle is event semantics as architecture. Every meaningful event should have a business definition, producer accountability, schema versioning, and interpretation guidance.

SaaS Onboarding by Connector Convenience Alone

A connector makes it possible to ingest a SaaS platform, so the enterprise turns it on. But the team has not defined the business purpose, retention rules, excluded uses, duplication boundaries, or owner approvals. This is not integration architecture. It is ingestion opportunism.

No Excluded-Use Discipline

Some sources are valuable for assistance but unsuitable for action, automation, or broad retrieval. Internal chat notes may support analyst investigation but be inappropriate for customer-facing response generation. Draft proposal language may support internal composition assistance but not external contractual commitments. If excluded uses are not defined, AI systems will eventually operate beyond the trust boundary that the source can support.

Practical Application

A Decision Framework for Selecting Integration Patterns

A practical enterprise approach starts with five questions.

What is the authoritative source?

Before designing the pattern, determine where the enterprise considers truth to reside for this use. Not merely where data exists, but where accountability lives. An authoritative source is as much a governance decision as a technical one.

What freshness does the AI use case actually require?

Many integration mistakes come from vague freshness demands. "Real time" is often declared when hourly would do. Weekly extracts are accepted when same-day changes are actually business-critical. Freshness should be explicit and tied to consequence. A knowledge assistant answering product overview questions may tolerate nightly content enrichment. A sales copilot giving price guardrails during deal negotiation may not.

What policy must be preserved at the point of use?

If source entitlements, privacy rules, regional restrictions, legal holds, or workflow states materially affect whether the AI may use the information, those controls must shape the pattern. This often pushes design toward API access, entitlement-aware indexing, or policy-tag propagation.

What semantic enrichment is required?

Raw payloads are rarely enough. The enterprise must decide whether glossaries, taxonomies, document classification, authority labels, entity resolution, relationship mapping, or event interpretation rules are required before the source becomes AI-ready.

What duplication is acceptable?

Every copy should have a reason. That reason may be performance, resiliency, searchability, analytics optimization, or isolation of a governed product. But it should be explicit. If the team cannot explain why a copy exists, it probably should not.

Integration Pattern Guidance by Source Type

Systems of record

ERP, CRM, HCM, contract platforms, and core operational systems usually require a mix of patterns. Use batch for curated history and broad analytics, APIs for current state and governed actions, and data products for well-documented reusable views. Use replication cautiously when permissions or workflow status matter.

Event-producing operational platforms

Use event patterns for time-sensitive state changes, but accompany them with semantic contracts and reference lookups. Do not expect event streams alone to carry all the business meaning required for AI interpretation.

SaaS applications

SaaS sources often need sync or connector-based onboarding, but only with clear ownership, classification, and duplication controls. Where the SaaS platform itself enforces important permissions or workflow logic, combine indexed content access with source API checks rather than unrestricted full replication.

Collaboration and content repositories

Treat these as governed content domains, not miscellaneous file piles. Use classification, authority tagging, metadata enrichment, and version-aware indexing. Ensure retrieval surfaces the approved or most authoritative asset first, not merely the most textually similar one.

TEMPLATES

Source Onboarding Template

Source name	<name of the source, repository, platform, or content collection being onboarded>
Source owner	<business leader or function accountable for the source and its approved use>
Data/content classes	<types of data, documents, records, or content contained in the source>

Business purpose	<business reason the source exists and the role it is intended to play in operations, decision-making, or AI use cases>
Integration pattern selected	<chosen integration approach for the source, such as batch sync, API access, event-driven ingestion, hybrid retrieval, or another governed pattern>
Freshness requirement	<required timeliness for updates, refreshes, or retrieval-time verification, including any higher standard for sensitive content>
Access model	<how access is controlled and enforced, including inherited permissions, restricted collections, and retrieval-time entitlement checks>
Sensitivity classification	<security, confidentiality, privacy, or commercial sensitivity classification assigned to the source and its contents>
Metadata available	<metadata fields currently available from the source to support discovery, governance, filtering, and retrieval>
Semantic enrichment required	<taxonomy mappings, relationship tagging, authority indicators, or other enrichment needed to make the source AI-ready>
Duplication risks	<known or likely risks of duplicate, uncontrolled, superseded, or conflicting copies across repositories, tools, or indexes>
Governance controls needed	<governance, security, compliance, retention, audit, and policy controls required before the source can be safely used by AI systems>
Lineage approach	<method for preserving source identity, version traceability, transformation history, ingestion details, and citation links back to the origin>
AI use cases enabled	<approved assistants, copilots, workflows, or AI scenarios that this source is intended to support>
Excluded uses	<uses that are prohibited, restricted, or require additional review because of risk, authority, or policy concerns>
Acceptance checklist	<required onboarding, validation, governance, technical, and operational checks that must be completed before the source is approved for AI use>
Sign-off fields	<required approvers, reviewer roles, and approval date fields needed to formally authorize the source for governed AI use>

CASE EXAMPLE

Sales Enablement Assistant Across CRM, Pricing, Proposals, and Product Content

Consider a sales enablement assistant designed to help account executives prepare for customer meetings, draft proposals, and answer questions about offers, solution positioning, and approved pricing guidance. The assistant draws from four major source families:

- CRM for account, opportunity, stage, and contact context.
- Pricing guidance systems for approved discount thresholds and escalation rules.
- Proposal repositories for reusable narratives and prior-approved content.
- Product content libraries for current positioning, capabilities, and packaging.

At first glance, the problem appears to be one of aggregation. Connect the sources, index the content, and let the model answer questions. In practice, this is where integration quality decides whether the assistant becomes trusted or sidelined.

The wrong architecture

A common design would replicate all four sources into a central platform on a nightly basis, chunk the documents, build embeddings, and expose a single search layer. That might work for a demo. It fails in live enterprise use.

Why? Because pricing guidance may change during an active quarter. Proposal repositories contain draft, approved, superseded, and deal-specific content. CRM permissions are role-sensitive. Product narratives may differ by region and release stage. If all of that is flattened into one central copy without authority logic, the assistant will eventually cite obsolete pricing, retrieve draft proposal language, expose restricted content, or blend regionally invalid product statements into a single answer.

The better architecture

A better design uses multiple patterns intentionally.

CRM context via governed product or curated batch plus entitlement logic

Opportunity and account context can be provided through a curated internal data product or a tightly governed extract with clear freshness targets. The goal is not to expose every CRM field, but to provide well-defined context entities with business meaning and access control alignment.

Pricing guidance via API-first access

Pricing thresholds and approval rules should be retrieved from the authoritative pricing source through API access, especially when in-flight deal validity matters. The assistant may cache low-risk reference data, but final guidance should reflect *the* current, governed state.

Proposal documents via indexed content with authority ranking and version control

Approved proposal documents can be synchronized into an indexed retrieval layer, but only after classification and enrichment. The system should suppress superseded versions, prefer approved templates over local derivatives, preserve citations back to the original source, and verify user access before presenting content.

Product content via governed content product

Product documentation can be delivered as a governed content product with explicit metadata for product line, release status, region, intended audience, and review date. This allows the assistant to rank official product messaging above ad hoc collateral.

What the user experience looks like

An account executive asks: "Prepare talking points and a proposal draft outline for the Acme renewal in healthcare. Include approved language for analytics add-ons and tell me what pricing flexibility exists."

A trustworthy assistant should do four things:

- Pull the current CRM opportunity context and account attributes that the user is entitled to see.
- Retrieve approved healthcare-relevant product positioning and proposal language from authoritative content collections.
- Call the pricing API for current flexibility thresholds and escalation requirements.
- Produce an answer with citations and clear separation between approved content, source facts, and generated synthesis.

The assistant should not guess. It should not rely on a week-old pricing extract. It should not pull language from an obsolete proposal. It should not blur product marketing claims with contractual commitments.

The architectural lesson

The assistant succeeds not because the model is clever, but because the integration architecture preserved meaning, ownership, policy, freshness, and authority across heterogeneous sources. That is the standard for AI-ready integration.

Closing Synthesis

Integration patterns are a decisive part of AI-ready architecture because AI systems do not consume isolated datasets. They consume the connected enterprise. The way those connections are designed determines whether context is preserved or erased, whether policies remain enforceable or drift across copies, whether freshness is appropriate to the use case, and whether answers can be traced back to authoritative sources. This is why integration for AI cannot be reduced to ingestion throughput or connector count. The architectural objective is not to connect everything to everything else. It is to connect sources in ways that preserve business meaning, ownership, provenance, and governed usability.

Batch, event, API, product, and sync patterns all have a place. The discipline lies in using each pattern where it fits, not where it is merely convenient. Canonical models should be selective, not ideological. SaaS and collaboration platforms should be onboarded intentionally, not casually. Shadow copies should be minimized and justified. Metadata must travel with the asset. Governance must begin at intake. And every integrated source should be evaluated not only for what it contains, but for what AI uses it can safely support.

The enterprise that masters this will build more than pipelines. It will build a trustworthy data estate capable of serving copilots, assistants, and agents repeatedly and at scale. That is the real purpose of integration in an AI-ready world.

Key Takeaways

- Integration for AI must preserve meaning, ownership, policy, lineage, and freshness, not just move data.
- Batch, event, API, data product, and sync patterns each solve different architectural problems; none should be used as a universal default.
- APIs often beat replication when the current state, source rules, and permission fidelity matter.
- SaaS and collaboration platforms must be onboarded with the same governance discipline as traditional systems of record.
- Shadow copies, uncontrolled content duplication, and semantically weak integrations are major causes of untrustworthy AI.

CHAPTER 16: RETRIEVAL AND GROUNDING AS ARCHITECTURE CONCERNS

Retrieval and grounding quality are too often treated as downstream tuning problems. Teams blame the model, the prompt, or the vector database when answers are vague, stale, or wrong. In enterprise settings, that diagnosis is usually incomplete. Poor retrieval is more often the consequence of upstream architectural choices: content that was never curated for reuse, metadata that does not express authority or effective date, segmentation that breaks business meaning, indexes that ignore access boundaries, and citation patterns that cannot support explanation.

This matters because enterprise AI is rarely judged on eloquence. It is judged on whether it can be trusted in consequential settings. A policy assistant who cites the wrong version of a travel policy is not slightly inconvenient. It is operationally unsafe. A sales copilot that retrieves the wrong contract clause can distort negotiation. An analyst assistant who summarizes obsolete procedures can create compliance exposure. In each case, the failure begins before the query is ever issued.

Retrieval, then, is not a feature bolted onto content repositories. It is a designed pipeline. Grounding is not simply the act of attaching a source to an answer. It is the disciplined use of evidence, provenance, temporal context, and authority so that an answer can be inspected, challenged, and defended.

In an AI-ready enterprise, retrieval and grounding are architectural concerns. They belong to the design of content models, metadata schemas, governance controls, semantic layers, indexing policies, and service contracts for different AI consumers. They are not model-side afterthoughts.

WHY THIS MATTERS

Enterprise AI Fails at the Moment of Contact with Real Content

Many organizations already have vast content estates: policies in SharePoint, knowledge articles in service platforms, contracts in document repositories, meeting notes in collaboration tools, transcripts in storage accounts, and reference data in warehouses and operational systems. The common mistake is to assume that because this information exists, it is retrievable in a form that AI can use safely.

It is not.

Repositories store files. AI systems require interpretable evidence. Those are different architectural states.

A human can often navigate a poorly organized repository because the human already understands the organization. The human knows that "HR Policy Final v3 revised" is probably the current travel policy and that the appendix can be ignored. An AI system does not possess that institutional intuition unless the architecture makes it explicit. It needs signals for document type, owner, jurisdiction, effective date, audience, sensitivity, confidence, related concepts, and source authority. Without those signals, retrieval becomes guesswork wrapped in computation.

Trust Thresholds Differ by Use Case

A casual knowledge assistant can tolerate some ambiguity. An executive briefing tool needs stronger ranking and stronger recency controls. An action-taking agent needs the strictest grounding contract of all. It must know not only what content says, but whether that content is authoritative, current, and permitted for the user and the action.

This is why retrieval design cannot be generic. Different AI consumers require different serving contracts:

- A knowledge assistant may retrieve broadly and summarize.
- An analyst copilot may need evidence from multiple sources with clear lineage.
- An executive tool may privilege authoritative summaries over raw source volume.
- An agent may require only policy-approved, current, access-filtered sources with deterministic citation rules.

When teams use a single retrieval pattern for all four, they usually degrade all four.

Explainability Depends on Evidence Design

Grounded answers are safer because they can be interrogated. A useful enterprise answer should be traceable to source material, constrained by time, and explainable in terms of why certain evidence was selected over other evidence. This is not only a model behavior issue. It is a design property of the retrieval system.

If the architecture cannot preserve section boundaries, track effective dates, rank authoritative content higher than drafts, and carry forward citations in a user-readable way, the system cannot explain itself well. It may still generate fluent answers. It cannot generate defensible ones.

Core Concepts

Retrieval Quality Starts Long Before the Query

The query is only the visible tip of the pipeline. Long before a user asks a question, the enterprise has already made decisions that determine whether the answer can be trusted:

- Which content assets are admitted into the retrieval estate.
- How documents are classified and enriched.
- Whether business metadata exists and is reliable.
- How sections are identified.
- Which relationships connect documents to policies, products, customers, controls, or jurisdictions.
- How indexes are refreshed.
- How permissions are enforced.
- How citations are rendered.

A retrieval layer cannot recover meaning that was never preserved.

Chunking Must Respect Business Meaning, Not Token Size

Segmentation is one of the most underestimated design choices in enterprise AI. Many implementations split content into uniform chunks based on character count, token count, or sentence windows. That may be adequate for generic web text. It is often disastrous for enterprise material.

Business documents are not merely streams of language. They contain structures that matter: policy clauses, definitions, control statements, exceptions, approval conditions, appendices, tables, legal disclaimers, jurisdiction-specific addenda, and audience-specific variants. If chunking slices through these boundaries, it destroys meaning.

A reimbursement policy that states a rule in one paragraph and its exception in the next should not be separated merely because a token limit is reached. A contract clause should not be detached from the section heading that defines its scope. A procedure step should not be retrieved without its prerequisite condition.

Key Insight

Bad chunking destroys good content

A well-written document can become unusable for AI when segmentation ignores its business structure. The failure is not in the source content. The failure is in the architectural decision to break meaning apart for indexing convenience.

Metadata-Aware Ranking Is Essential

In consumer search, lexical similarity and semantic proximity may be enough. In the enterprise, they are not.

A good enterprise retrieval system ranks not only on topical relevance but on metadata such as:

- Authority status.
- Effective date.
- Owner.
- Document type.
- Business domain.
- Sensitivity classification.
- User audience.
- Jurisdiction.
- Approval status.
- Source system trust level.
- Freshness score.
- Relationship to the question context.

Consider three candidate passages that all mention "leave policy." The semantically closest one may be a local manager guide from two years ago. The most trustworthy one may be the current HR global policy approved last month. Without metadata-aware ranking, the system may prefer linguistic resemblance over organizational truth.

Freshness and Re-Indexing Are Governance Concerns

Freshness is not merely a technical issue of how often an index runs. It is a governance issue of when content should no longer be treated as valid evidence.

Policies change. Product terms change. Organizational structures change. Legal obligations change. A retrieval system must, therefore, know:

- What freshness means for each content class.
- Which events trigger re-indexing.
- How stale content is demoted, flagged, or removed.
- How historical versions are preserved without being mistaken for current truth.
- How temporal correctness is exposed to the end user.

This is a control problem as much as an engineering problem.

Good Grounding Makes Answers Explainable and Safer

Grounding is not just attaching links at the bottom of an answer. It is the controlled use of evidence so that an answer remains bounded by source material. Strong grounding includes:

- Source selection based on authority and relevance.
- Explicit citation of the specific section or excerpt used.
- Preservation of effective date and version context.
- Indication of uncertainty when sources conflict.
- Isolation of unsupported model inference from sourced statements.
- Access-aware delivery of evidence to the user.

A grounded answer does not claim omniscience. It shows its work.

ARCHITECTURAL IMPLICATIONS

Treat Retrieval as a Pipeline, Not a Lookup Step

The architecture should be designed as a sequence of responsibilities, each of which affects trust.

❖ FIGURE 32 – RETRIEVAL AND GROUNDING PIPELINE

This pipeline deserves explicit ownership. Curate determines what enters the system. Enrich adds business metadata, classification, and semantic context. Segment preserves meaningful retrieval units. Index makes those units searchable. Retrieve pulls candidates. Rank orders them using relevance and enterprise trust signals. Ground constrains generation to evidence. Cite makes the result inspectable.

Organizations that collapse all of this into "load documents into retrieval" usually produce systems that are fast to demo and hard to trust.

Build Document-Type-Specific Segmentation Models

Different content types require different segmentation logic.

A policy document may be segmented by section, subsection, applicability statement, exception, and effective date block. A contract may require clause-level segmentation with party, obligation, jurisdiction, and term metadata. A knowledge article may segment by problem, cause, resolution, and product version. A meeting transcript may need speaker turns, topic shifts, and action items. A tabular procedure may need row-aware parsing so that conditions and actions remain linked.

❖ FIGURE 33 – DOCUMENT SEGMENTATION MODEL

A one-size segmentation rule is attractive because it is easy to operationalize. It is also one of the clearest signals that retrieval has not been architected for enterprise use.

⚠ WARNING SIGN

One chunking strategy for every document type

If your platform uses the same chunk size and overlap rule for policies, contracts, knowledge articles, meeting notes, and procedures, your retrieval design is driven by tooling convenience rather than business meaning.

Design Metadata as Retrieval Infrastructure

Metadata is not ornamental. It is an operational infrastructure for AI.

The retrieval architecture should define a minimum metadata contract for every indexed asset and retrieval unit. At a minimum, that often includes:

- Source identifier.
- Document title.
- Document type.
- Owner.
- Authority status.
- Effective date.
- Last reviewed date.
- Jurisdiction.
- Intended audience.
- Sensitivity classification.
- Retention category.
- Language.
- Semantic tags.
- Related entities.
- Lineage to source repository and ingestion run.
- Access control attributes.

This metadata should not exist only at the file level. Many use cases require section-level or chunk-level metadata inheritance and augmentation.

Make Access-Aware Filtering Mandatory

Enterprise retrieval that ignores permissions is not retrieval. It is leakage.

Access-aware filtering should happen before evidence is delivered and ideally before ranking is finalized for the user's retrieval context. It must account for identity, entitlements, group membership, content classification, legal boundaries, and need-to-know constraints. It must also handle derived content. A chunk copied from a restricted source remains restricted.

This means the retrieval layer must integrate with identity, policy, and content governance services rather than operating as an isolated search appliance.

Separate Authority from Popularity

Many ranking systems drift toward interaction signals such as click rates, recent use, or embedding similarity. Those can be helpful secondary features. They are poor substitutes for authority. In an enterprise, the most used document is not necessarily the right one. Teams often reuse drafts, old templates, and locally saved workarounds precisely because the official content is harder to find.

The architecture should, therefore, represent authority explicitly. A current, approved policy should outrank an older, more frequently accessed draft. A certified product definition should outrank a slide deck. A published control standard should outrank an email thread summarizing it.

KEY INSIGHT

Retrieval is architecture

When retrieval quality depends on content curation, metadata design, segmentation logic, authority modeling, freshness controls, and permission fidelity, retrieval is no longer a search feature. It is architecture.

FAILURE MODES AND ANTI-PATTERNS

Dump the Repository into the Index

This is the most common mistake. Teams ingest everything available because more content appears to promise better answers. In practice, indiscriminate ingestion dilutes signal, increases conflict, and makes grounding harder. Drafts, duplicates, obsolete versions, local notes, and unofficial interpretations crowd out authoritative sources.

The fix is curation. Not all content belongs in the same retrieval estate, and not all use cases should query the same corpus.

Optimize for Recall While Ignoring Evidence Quality

Teams often celebrate when retrieval returns many relevant passages. That metric is incomplete. Enterprise systems need evidence quality, not just topical recall. A slightly narrower set of authoritative, current, explainable sources is often superior to a larger set of loosely related fragments.

Chunk by Size, Then Hope Ranking Recovers Meaning

Ranking cannot fully repair a chunk that has lost its context. If a clause is detached from its heading, its jurisdiction, or its effective period, the retriever may surface it correctly and still mislead the user.

Ignore Temporal Correctness

A retrieval system that does not distinguish current from historical truth invites silent failure. Users often ask present-tense questions. The system must understand whether the answer should privilege the latest approved version, compare versions, or explicitly state that rules changed over time.

Treat Citations as Decorative

A citation that points only to a document title is weak. Users need enough granularity to verify the answer without rereading a fifty-page file. A good citation strategy points to the relevant section, clause, or excerpt and preserves the version context.

Evaluate Only with Generic Benchmarks

Generic retrieval benchmarks rarely reflect enterprise failure. Real enterprise evaluation should test:

- Authority selection.
- Temporal correctness.
- Permission fidelity.
- Section-boundary integrity.
- Citation usefulness.
- Conflict handling.
- Hallucination under sparse evidence.
- Performance for different user roles.

If you do not evaluate these, you do not know whether the system is safe for enterprise use.

Practical Application

Start with Content Classes, Not Tooling Features

A strong program begins by categorizing the content estate into classes such as policies, procedures, standards, contracts, knowledge articles, manuals, transcripts, reference records, and structured business objects. For each class, define:

- Business purpose.
- Authority model.
- Segmentation logic.
- Metadata requirements.
- Freshness expectation.
- Allowed AI use cases.

- Citation pattern.
- Evaluation owner.

This gives retrieval design a business shape rather than a purely technical one.

Create a Retrieval Contract for Each AI Consumer

Do not let every assistant use the same retrieval settings. Define service contracts.

A policy assistant may retrieve only approved policy content, require effective dates in citations, and suppress unofficial commentary. A technical support copilot may combine knowledge articles with product telemetry and case patterns, but only after classifying source authority. An agent that takes actions may be prohibited from acting unless the evidence set meets a minimum confidence and grounding threshold.

Make Enrichment Part of Ingestion

Enrichment should add business value at ingest time, not as an optional later enhancement. For example:

- Infer document type.
- Extract section hierarchy.
- Identify owner and approval markers.
- Detect effective dates and review dates.
- Tag jurisdiction and audience.
- Map business terms to glossary concepts.
- Attach source-system trust score.
- Assign sensitivity classification.
- Connect related structured entities.

This enrichment turns content into retrievable evidence rather than inert text.

TEMPLATES

Retrieval Readiness Checklist

Purpose statement	<brief statement explaining why this checklist or assessment exists and what explicit decisions it is intended to force, such as authority, metadata, chunking, ranking, freshness, citations, and grounding quality>

Content asset type

<type of content being assessed for retrieval readiness, such as corporate policy documents, addenda, manuals, contracts, or knowledge articles>

Business use case

<business scenario, assistant, or AI use case that depends on this content being retrieval-ready>

Authority status

<status indicating whether the source is approved, authoritative, restricted, draft, or otherwise governed for use in AI retrieval>

Metadata completeness

<degree to which required metadata is present across the content set, including percentage completeness and key fields available>

Section structure known? yes/no

<Yes or No>

Chunking strategy

<method used to segment the content for retrieval, including how sections, subsections, exceptions, tables, headings, and long passages are handled>

Ranking features

<features used to rank retrieval results, such as semantic relevance, keyword match, authority, recency, jurisdiction match, audience match, owner confidence, or type weighting>

Access-aware filtering enabled? yes/no

<Yes or No>

Freshness SLA

<required time within which source changes must be reflected in the retrieval layer, including any faster handling for urgent updates>

Re-index trigger

<events that should trigger re-indexing, such as publication, version changes, approval updates, metadata correction, jurisdiction change, or access-control change>

Citation strategy

<required citation pattern for retrieved answers, including which source attributes, anchors, links, dates, or section references must be exposed>

Grounding quality score

<measured quality score for grounding performance, including scale or evaluation basis where applicable>

Known failure cases

<known weaknesses, edge cases, tagging problems, extraction issues, or conflict scenarios that reduce retrieval quality or answer reliability>

Evaluation owner	<role, team, or individuals accountable for evaluating and improving retrieval readiness>
Improvement actions	<specific remediation steps needed to improve retrieval quality, metadata quality, structure capture, conflict handling, or policy-safe grounding>

Case Example

A Policy Assistant That Improved When the Architecture Improved

Consider an enterprise policy assistant designed to answer employee questions about travel, leave, and remote work. The first version was built quickly. The team ingested policy PDFs from a collaboration repository, applied a generic chunking rule of 800 tokens with overlap, and ranked results mostly by semantic similarity. The demo looked promising. The production behavior did not.

Employees asked, "Can I expense airport parking for a three-day domestic trip?" The assistant often returned a reimbursement paragraph from the correct policy family, but not always from the correct section. Sometimes, it surfaced an outdated regional addendum because the language happened to match the question more closely. In other cases, it cited the policy title but not the relevant clause, forcing users to open a long document and search manually. When the answer was challenged, the support team could not easily explain why one chunk had been chosen over another.

The problem was not that the policies were poorly written. The problem was that retrieval had not been architected.

The team redesigned the pipeline.

First, they curated the corpus so only approved policy publications and approved jurisdictional addenda were indexed. Drafts, email commentary, and superseded PDFs were removed from the production retrieval estate.

Second, they enriched each document with metadata: policy owner, approval status, effective date, jurisdiction, intended audience, policy family, and source repository lineage.

Third, they replaced fixed-size chunking with section-aware segmentation. Each retrieval unit preserved the section heading, subsection, applicability statement, exceptions, and approval metadata. Travel policies and leave policies were segmented differently because their structures differed.

Fourth, they changed ranking. Semantic relevance remained, but authority status, effective date, jurisdiction alignment, and audience match became first-class ranking features.

Fifth, they improved grounding. Answers had to cite the exact policy section and show the effective date. When jurisdiction-specific rules differed from global policy, the answer explicitly stated the difference and surfaced both sources with a precedence explanation.

The result was not just higher answer quality. It was a safer system. Employees could verify the answer. HR could explain the evidence path. Governance could confirm that only approved content was used. Retrieval quality improved because the architecture improved.

That is the central lesson of this chapter.

Closing Synthesis

Retrieval and grounding are not peripheral concerns in enterprise AI. They are part of the data architecture itself. The quality of an answer depends on whether the enterprise has designed content for evidence, metadata for trust, segmentation for meaning, ranking for authority, indexing for freshness, and citations for explainability.

This is why retrieval cannot be delegated entirely to model teams. The work spans content management, information architecture, metadata design, governance, identity, semantics, platform engineering, and product ownership. It requires decisions about what content belongs in scope, how it should be structured, how it should be governed, and how different AI consumers should be allowed to use it.

Organizations that understand this move beyond the illusion that AI can simply "search everything." They design retrieval systems that know what matters, what is current, what is official, what is permitted, and what can be defended. They treat grounding as an evidence discipline rather than a presentation flourish. They understand that trustworthy enterprise AI is built as much in the retrieval pipeline as in the model layer.

In that sense, retrieval is not the last mile of AI-Ready Data. It is one of the clearest tests of whether the architecture is truly ready at all.

Key Takeaways

- Retrieval quality starts before the query, in curation, metadata, segmentation, governance, and access design.
- Chunking must preserve business meaning; fixed-size segmentation is often a destructive shortcut.
- Enterprise retrieval must rank by authority, freshness, audience, and policy context, not relevance alone.
- Grounding is stronger when citations are specific, the temporal context is preserved, and evidence remains explainable.
- Retrieval is not a search feature layered onto repositories; it is an architectural capability that determines whether enterprise AI can be trusted.

Chapter 17: Serving Data to Copilots, Assistants, and Agents

The governing principle for this chapter is straightforward: different AI consumers require different data-serving contracts, and a read-only assistant, an analytics copilot, and an action-taking agent cannot safely consume enterprise data in the same way.

Too many enterprise AI programs treat every consumer as if it were simply another chat interface on top of a common retrieval layer. That is an architectural mistake. A knowledge assistant answering policy questions, a copilot helping an analyst investigate variance, and an agent proposing or executing remediation steps are not merely different user experiences. They are different trust classes. They have different error tolerances, different evidence requirements, different freshness expectations, different permission needs, and different consequences when they are wrong. This distinction matters because the enterprise data estate is not being served to a single, passive consumer. It is being served to systems that may summarize, infer, recommend, or act. Once AI moves beyond retrieval into decision support or operational execution, the architectural burden changes. The issue is no longer whether the system can generate a plausible answer. The issue is whether the enterprise can defend the answer, verify the evidence, enforce the policy boundary, and control the consequences of use.

Serving data to AI, therefore, requires more than exposing repositories, APIs, and search indexes. It requires explicit serving contracts. Those contracts must define what a given AI consumer is allowed to access, what form the context must take, what evidence must accompany output, what actions are permitted, where policy is enforced, when humans must intervene, and how the entire interaction is logged and audited.

The architecture must distinguish between answer generation, decision support, and execution. If those three modes are collapsed into one generic pattern, enterprise AI becomes simultaneously overpowered and undergoverned.

Why This Matters

The Cost of Error Is Not Uniform

In traditional analytics, an incorrect report is serious but often detected through review cycles, reconciliation, or delayed operational impact. In AI-enabled interaction, the cadence is faster and the interface is more persuasive. Users often experience the output as authoritative, especially when it is fluent, concise, and contextually relevant. That raises the cost of architectural shortcuts.

A Q&A assistant who misstates a travel policy may create inconvenience. An executive briefing assistant that summarizes stale or non-authoritative figures may distort management discussion. An operational agent that misclassifies a regulatory exception and initiates the wrong remediation step may create financial, compliance, or safety exposure. These are not variations of the same problem. They are different risk categories.

AI Consumers Interpret Data Differently

AI consumers do not merely read records. They assemble context across sources, rank evidence, compress meaning, and present conclusions. That means the architecture must serve more than raw data. It must serve a governed context. For a human analyst, a dataset may be usable because the analyst already understands the business vocabulary, reporting calendar, source hierarchy, and known defects. For a copilot, that same dataset may be unusable unless it is paired with definitions, lineage, freshness metadata, permission fidelity, and instructions about valid interpretation. Data that is suitable for reporting is not automatically suitable for AI consumption.

Operational Scale Amplifies Weak Design

A poorly governed dashboard may confuse dozens of users. A poorly governed assistant may confuse thousands. A poorly governed agent may take action repeatedly and at machine speed. That is why enterprise architecture must stop treating AI consumption as a presentation-layer concern.

The question is not, "Can the model answer from this source?" The real question is, "Under what contract is this source being served, with what semantics, for what consumer, with what evidence, and under what control?"

KEY INSIGHT

Not every AI consumer deserves the same access

A common failure pattern is to grant a broad retrieval layer to every AI use case and then rely on prompts, UI wording, or post hoc filtering to contain risk. That is backward. Access must be earned through consumer design. The more a system moves from answering toward recommending or acting, the narrower and more explicit its contract should become.

CORE CONCEPTS

Consumer Classes Determine Serving Patterns

A useful way to design AI-serving architecture is to classify consumers by purpose and consequence.

Q&A Assistant

This is a read-only consumer optimized for grounded answer generation. Its purpose is to help users find and understand information. It should retrieve from approved sources, provide citations, respect access controls, and avoid taking action. Its trust model depends on source authority, relevance ranking, provenance, and temporal correctness.

Analyst Copilot

This consumer supports exploration, comparison, and synthesis. It may combine structured metrics, business definitions, event streams, and narrative documents to help a user investigate a problem or prepare a decision. It requires broader contextual packaging than a simple assistant, because it must preserve analytical meaning across sources. It should not be treated as an autonomous decision-maker.

Recommendation System

This consumer goes a step further. It suggests next-best actions, prioritizations, or interventions. It still does not execute, but its output influences operational choices. Evidence thresholds are higher, policy boundaries are tighter, and explanation becomes more important. The architecture must make the basis of the recommendation inspectable.

Bounded Agent

This consumer may trigger or orchestrate actions inside defined limits. It is not a general actor. It must be constrained by scope, authority, policy checks, and escalation logic. A bounded agent should only operate where the enterprise can define acceptable inputs, acceptable actions, acceptable exception paths, and complete auditability.

❖ FIGURE 34 – AI CONSUMER TAXONOMY

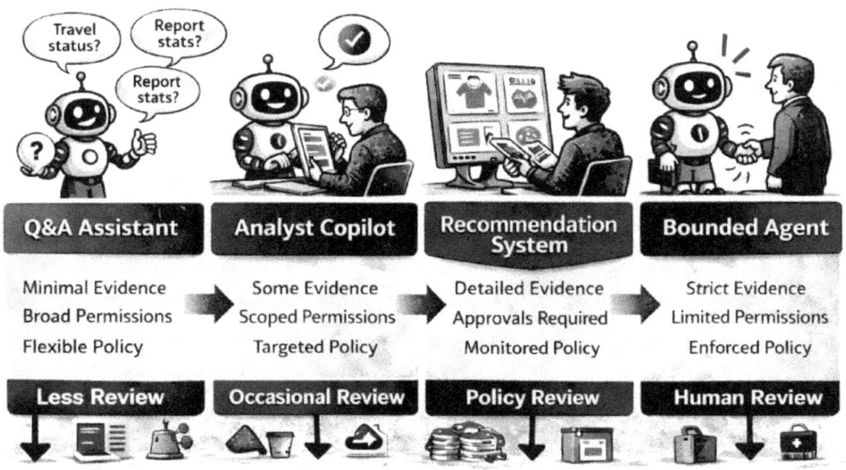

Read Paths and Action Paths Are Not the Same Architecture

A read path exists to discover, retrieve, contextualize, and present information. An action path exists to propose, validate, approve, and execute a change in an operational system. These must be separated by design.

A read path can tolerate some ambiguity, provided the system cites evidence and the human remains the final interpreter. An action path cannot tolerate the same ambiguity because it changes the state of the enterprise. Once an AI consumer can trigger workflows, create tickets, update records, send notices, or close exceptions, the architecture must move from retrieval discipline to operational control discipline. This is why a strong enterprise design often allows broad read capabilities for tightly governed assistants, but very narrow action capabilities for agents. Data access breadth and action authority should not increase together.

KEY INSIGHT

Read paths vs action paths

Read paths answer questions. Action paths change reality.

Read paths require relevance, context, provenance, and permission fidelity.

Action paths require all of those, plus authorization, policy validation, exception handling, reversibility where possible, and auditable accountability.

Treating these as the same path is one of the fastest ways to create unsafe enterprise AI.

Context Packaging Is a First-Class Architectural Concern

Raw access to data is not enough. AI systems consume packages of meaning, whether the architecture recognizes that or not. A useful context package may include:

- The source content or record.
- Source type and authority level.
- Business definitions for critical terms.
- Lineage to system of record.
- Timestamps for creation, effective date, and last refresh.
- Classification and handling restrictions.
- Entity mappings and relationship context.

- Confidence or quality indicators.
- Evidence excerpts and citation anchors.
- Allowed-use instructions for the consumer.

Without this packaging, the system is left to infer too much. That increases ambiguity, hallucination risk, improper generalization, and unsafe action proposals.

AI-Serving Contracts Define What "Good" Looks Like

An AI-serving contract is the architectural agreement between the data estate and a specific AI consumer. It should define, at a minimum, the following:

- Purpose of the consumer.
- User population served.
- Approved data classes and sources.
- Evidence requirements for output.
- Freshness requirements.
- Allowed actions, if any.
- Prohibited actions.
- Policy enforcement points.
- Human review triggers.
- Escalation path.
- Logging and audit obligations.
- Owner and approval authority.

This contract is how the enterprise turns general AI capability into governed operational design.

Architectural Implications

Metadata Must Mediate Consumption

Metadata remains the control plane for AI-serving architecture. It determines what can be discovered, how it is ranked, whether it is current enough, whether it is authoritative enough, whether the user has rights to see it, and whether the consumer is allowed to use it for its specific purpose. For AI consumers, metadata must do more than support catalog search. It must actively shape runtime behavior. That includes:

- Permission-aware retrieval.
- Policy-aware filtering.
- Source authority scoring.

- Freshness gating.
- Lineage display.
- Citation generation.
- Business-term disambiguation.
- Consumer-specific eligibility rules.

A well-architected serving layer is, therefore, not a neutral pipeline. It is a controlled mediation layer informed by metadata, semantics, and governance.

Serving Contracts Should Align to Data Classes, Not Just Systems

Many organizations define access at the application or repository level and stop there. That is insufficient for AI. A single system may contain data appropriate for read-only question answering, data appropriate only for regulated analysts, and data that must never be exposed to a generative interface. Architects should think in terms of data classes such as:

- Public or broadly internal knowledge.
- Operational reference data.
- Financial and management reporting data.
- Customer or employee personal data.
- Regulated records.
- Legal or privileged content.
- Exception and incident data.
- Action-triggering signals and commands.

Different consumer types should receive different combinations of these classes. The serving contract should make those combinations explicit.

Answer Generation, Decision Support, and Execution Need Different Control Stacks

A useful enterprise pattern is to treat these as three architectural layers:

- **Layer 1, Answer generation**: This layer supports retrieval, summarization, explanation, and citation. Its controls emphasize permission fidelity, relevance, provenance, and user-visible evidence.
- **Layer 2, Decision support**: This layer adds comparative analysis, recommendations, prioritization logic, scenario framing, and stronger explanation requirements. Its controls emphasize semantic consistency, metric integrity, freshness, and confidence boundaries.

- **Layer 3, Execution**: This layer introduces action proposals, policy checks, approval routing, transaction controls, operational APIs, and post-action auditability. Its controls emphasize authority, bounded scope, segregation of duties, and recoverability.

The mistake is to let a consumer drift upward across these layers without a corresponding redesign of its data-serving contract.

The Action Trust Boundary Must Be Explicit

Any consumer *who* can influence or trigger action should cross a formal trust boundary.

❖ FIGURE 35 – ACTION TRUST BOUNDARY

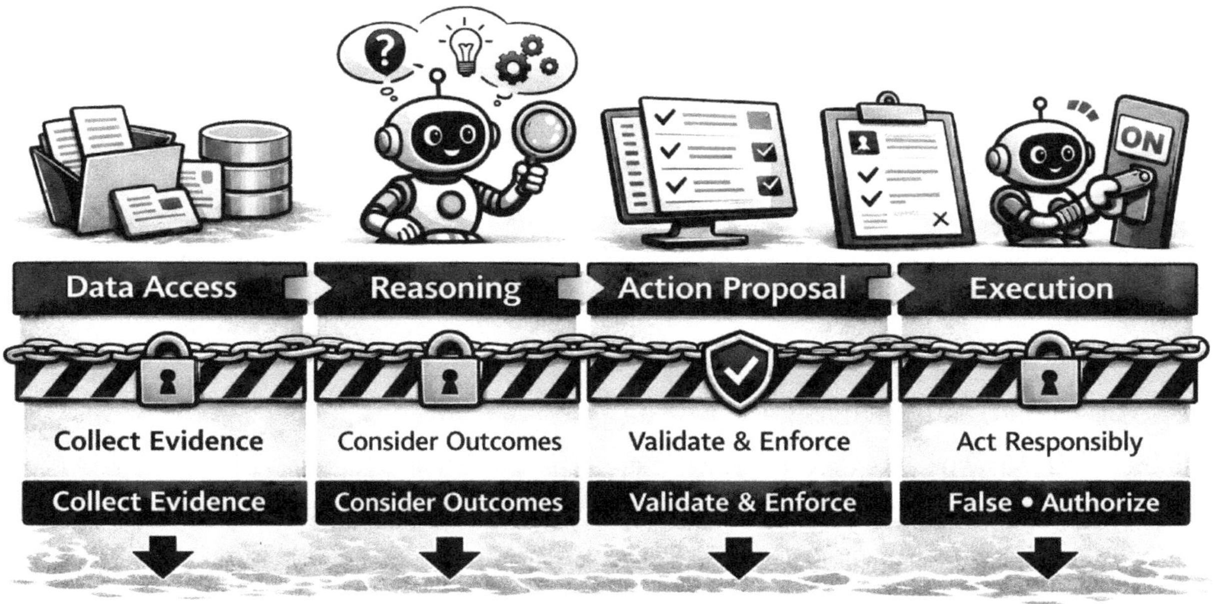

Action needs stronger controls.

This boundary matters because good retrieval does not justify action authority. A system may retrieve the right evidence and still be unauthorized to change a record, close an exception, or contact a customer. The architecture must require an explicit transition from "I found relevant information" to "I am permitted to initiate a governed action."

Evidence Must Travel with Output

Trustworthy enterprise AI does not merely answer. It shows its basis. That means the serving layer must package evidence in a way appropriate to the consumer:

- Assistants should cite source passages and timestamps.

- Analyst copilots should provide metric provenance, calculation context, and source coverage.
- Recommendation systems should expose factors, thresholds, and counterevidence.
- Agents should attach the evidence packet that justified the proposed action.

In mature architectures, evidence is not an optional UI feature. It is part of the serving contract.

Failure Modes and Anti-Patterns

The Generic Enterprise Super-Agent

This is the most dangerous anti-pattern: one agent with broad access across repositories, business systems, and operational APIs, but with vague instructions about when it may act. The architecture assumes that intelligence will compensate for weak boundaries. It will not.

⚠ **Warning Sign**

An agent with broad data access and unclear authority

If an agent can see many things, infer many things, and do many things, but no one can precisely state what it is authorized to do without human review, the design is already unsound. Capability without explicit authority is not flexibility. It is a governance failure.

Repository Exposure Mistaken for Readiness

Another common failure is to expose document stores, data warehouses, and APIs directly to an AI layer and assume the job is done. But repositories do not contain enough context on their own. They rarely encode business meaning, source hierarchy, policy usage rules, or decision fitness. The result is brittle retrieval, misleading synthesis, and weak explainability.

Conflating User Permission with Consumer Permission

A human may be authorized to view a set of records. That does not automatically mean an AI consumer acting on behalf of that human may use those records for summarization, recommendation, or action. Consumer permission must be separately defined. Otherwise, the system inherits human breadth without respecting machine-scale consequences.

Missing Freshness and Temporal Controls

Stale data is especially dangerous in executive briefings and operational remediation. If the system cannot distinguish snapshot date, effective date, event time, and last refresh time, it will confidently mix incompatible facts. Freshness requirements should be part of the serving contract, not an afterthought.

No Explicit Human Review Triggers

A system without review triggers forces one of two bad outcomes: humans approve everything because they do not trust it, or humans approve too little because the system appears confident. Mature designs specify when review is required, such as low-confidence evidence, threshold breaches, cross-domain actions, high-value transactions, or policy exceptions.

Weak Audit Design

If the enterprise cannot reconstruct what sources were used, what context package was assembled, what policy checks fired, what recommendation was made, who approved it, and what action was executed, then the system is not enterprise-ready. It is a prototype wearing production clothes.

Practical Application

Designing with the AI Consumer Design Worksheet

A practical way to prevent overgeneralized AI-serving architecture is to require a design worksheet for every consumer. This forces the team to define the contract before the build begins. It also creates a review artifact for architecture, security, governance, legal, and operational owners. The worksheet should be completed per consumer, not per platform. A single platform may host many consumers, but each one should have its own contract.

Templates

AI Consumer Design Worksheet

Consumer type	<type of AI consumer or operating model, such as bounded agent, copilot, assistant, or autonomous agent>
Business purpose	<business objective the consumer is intended to achieve, including the kinds of decisions, recommendations, or actions it supports>
User group	<primary user groups, teams, or roles that interact with or oversee the consumer>
Data classes required	<types of structured, semi-structured, and unstructured data required for the consumer to operate safely and effectively>
Allowed actions	<actions the consumer is permitted to take, including recommendations, drafting, routing, workflow initiation, or other approved interventions>
Prohibited actions	<actions the consumer is explicitly forbidden from taking because of financial, legal, control, communications, or policy risk>

Evidence requirement	<minimum evidence package required for each recommendation or action, including cited records, policy support, current state, confidence rationale, and freshness indicators>
Human review trigger	<conditions under which human review or approval is required before a recommendation or action may proceed>
Policy enforcement points	<points in the workflow where policy controls must be applied, such as retrieval, evidence assembly, recommendation generation, action proposal, approval, or downstream execution>
Logging/audit requirements	<events, decisions, evidence, prompts, policy checks, approvals, actions, and outcomes that must be captured for auditability and traceability>
Freshness requirement	<required recency standards for the different data classes the consumer depends on, such as transaction status, policy content, and entitlement data>
Trust threshold	<conditions under which the consumer may act automatically versus when it must defer to human authorization, based on risk, reversibility, confidence, policy conformance, and preapproval>
Escalation path	<defined chain of escalation for exceptions, conflicts, materiality concerns, or policy issues that require higher levels of review>
Owner	<role, team, or function accountable for the consumer's operation, governance, and performance>
Approval status	<current approval state of the consumer, including pilot scope, limitations, and conditions required for expansion>

Case Example

Executive Briefing Assistant Versus Remediation Agent

Consider two enterprise AI consumers built on top of the same underlying data estate. The first is an executive briefing assistant. Its purpose is to prepare a morning summary for senior leaders covering revenue movement, major incidents, supply chain disruptions, customer escalations, and strategic project status. It reads across management reporting data, operational KPIs, incident summaries, curated documents, and approved narrative commentary. The second is a remediation agent for operational exceptions in a finance process. Its purpose is to identify recurring exceptions, recommend corrective steps, and initiate predefined workflows where policy allows. At first glance, both seem to need *a* broad enterprise context. In practice, they require very different serving contracts.

The executive briefing assistant

This consumer is read-oriented. It synthesizes across multiple trusted sources, but it should not alter records or initiate operational changes. Its architectural priorities are:

- Source authority and ranking.
- Semantic alignment across finance, operations, and incident domains.
- Freshness controls for daily briefing windows.
- Clear citations and timestamps.
- Suppression of speculative claims when evidence conflicts.

The assistant may need broad read access to curated and approved sources, but it should have no action authority. It should surface uncertainty rather than resolve it silently. If revenue numbers conflict between preliminary operations views and official finance views, the contract should require the assistant to privilege the authoritative source and explain the distinction.

The remediation agent

This consumer is action-oriented, even if it begins by recommending. Its architectural priorities are different:

- Narrow, high-quality operational scope.
- Explicit policy thresholds.
- Validated entity resolution across transactions, exceptions, and owners.
- Evidence packets attached to every recommendation.
- Strong approval and audit controls.
- Bounded workflow execution only in approved scenarios.

Here, broad read access is not an advantage. It is a risk. The agent should see only the sources needed for the exception categories it is authorized to handle. It should not roam across unrelated repositories just because more context might be useful.

Same estate, different contract

This comparison shows why "one enterprise AI layer" is not enough as a design principle. Both consumers may use the same metadata services, identity infrastructure, governance layer, and retrieval services. But they should not share the same access profile, evidence threshold, or control flow.

The executive briefing assistant should optimize for breadth of trusted understanding with no operational authority. The remediation agent should optimize for narrow precision, explicit policy gating, and accountable execution. Confusing these two patterns leads either to a weak assistant that cannot answer useful questions or to an unsafe agent with unjustified reach.

A mature enterprise architecture supports this by standardizing the control plane while differentiating the serving contract.

Closing Synthesis

Serving data to copilots, assistants, and agents is not a matter of exposing more sources to a model. It is the discipline of defining what each AI consumer is for, what it may know, how that knowledge must be packaged, what evidence must accompany output, and whether it may influence or initiate action.

That discipline becomes more important, not less, as AI capability advances. Better models do not remove the need for contract design. They increase the urgency of it because more capable consumers can produce more convincing output and potentially more consequential actions.

The enterprise, therefore, needs a serving architecture that is differentiated by consumer type, controlled by metadata, enriched by semantics, bounded by governance, and explicit about trust. Read paths and action paths must be separated. Answer generation, decision support, and execution must be treated as distinct modes. Context packaging must be designed, not improvised. Evidence must travel with output. Policy checks must sit in the path of action, not at the end of an incident review.

The organizations that scale trustworthy AI will not be the ones that build the broadest generic agent. They will be the ones who design the clearest contracts between data, context, authority, and action.

Key Takeaways

- Different AI consumers require different data-serving contracts; one retrieval pattern is not enough.
- Read paths and action paths must be separated by design, not merely by interface wording.
- Context packaging, including semantics, provenance, freshness, and policy metadata, is as important as raw data access.
- Evidence requirements, human review triggers, and policy enforcement points must be explicit for every AI consumer.
- The most scalable enterprise pattern is a shared control plane with consumer-specific trust boundaries and action limits.

Chapter 18: Security, Identity, and Access-Aware Data Delivery

AI amplifies security flaws. That statement is not rhetorical. In a traditional application, a permissions mistake may expose one screen, one record, or one report. In an AI system, the same mistake can be operationalized into a conversational interface that makes hidden information discoverable at scale. A user no longer needs to know where sensitive content lives, what repository contains it, or which folder name to search. They can simply ask. If identity, permissions, and classification do not travel with the data into the AI-serving layer, the organization will expose information it never intended to expose.

This is why security in enterprise AI cannot be treated as a perimeter issue or a final review step. It is a data architecture issue. The serving layer for copilots, assistants, and agents must inherit and enforce the same authorization truths that govern source systems. If the AI layer becomes a simplified copy of enterprise knowledge without its permission model, the architecture is already broken.

The central principle of this chapter is straightforward: access-aware retrieval is mandatory. Retrieval must not only find relevant information. It must find only the information *that* the current identity is allowed to discover, retrieve, assemble, summarize, and act on. That requirement extends across structured data, documents, messages, transcripts, policies, logs, and every enrichment and indexing layer in between.

Why This Matters

Enterprise AI changes the risk surface in three important ways.

Discovery Becomes Easier Than Navigation

Historically, many security controls relied partly on friction. Sensitive documents were technically accessible only through specific applications, paths, or team sites. Users needed to know where to look. AI removes that friction. A conversational layer can unify search across repositories and return material from systems the user never directly opened. That is beneficial only if the system preserves permission fidelity. If it does not, it becomes a breach multiplier.

Inference Creates Exposure Even Without Direct Document Access

An AI assistant can expose information in more ways than simply returning a file. It can summarize, compare, explain, rank, or answer a question whose answer can only be derived from restricted material.

A model response such as "three directors are under formal performance review" may reveal restricted HR facts even if the underlying documents are never shown. Access-aware delivery, therefore, applies to retrieval, citations, answer synthesis, and action execution.

Security Errors Become Scalable and Repeatable

A manual mistake in a report can harm dozens of people. A permissions flaw in an enterprise assistant can harm thousands. The same flawed retrieval pattern can be triggered repeatedly by any authorized user of the assistant, often with more natural language variation than traditional controls were built to anticipate.

KEY INSIGHT

AI makes permission mistakes visible at scale

A weak permission model in a legacy repository may remain hidden for years because few people know where to look. An AI assistant removes that obscurity. Security flaws that were once dormant become searchable, conversational, and repeatable. This is why organizations that take governance seriously must treat access-aware delivery as a first-order architectural capability, not an enhancement to be added after the pilot succeeds.

CORE CONCEPTS

Access-aware Retrieval

Access-aware retrieval means the retrieval pipeline evaluates relevance within the boundaries of the requester's effective permissions. The assistant does not retrieve broadly and then hope the model behaves. It retrieves only from content, records, passages, and actions that the identity is allowed to access.

That sounds obvious, but many architectures fail here. They extract data into an AI index, enrich it, chunk it, and rank it without preserving the source authorization model. Once that happens, the index becomes its own uncontrolled content store. In enterprise environments, access-aware retrieval usually requires five controls:

- An authenticated identity for the user, service, or agent.
- A reliable mapping from that identity to groups, roles, entitlements, and contextual attributes.
- A retrievable representation of permissions at the content or record level.
- Retrieval filters that use those permissions before answer assembly.
- Auditability showing what was requested, what was eligible, what was returned, and why.

Identity Propagation

Identity propagation is the discipline of carrying identity and authorization context end to end. In practice, this means the same user context must survive across the interaction channel, orchestration layer, retrieval service, knowledge index, and source system.

If the identity is stripped away and replaced with a generic service account, the system may still function technically, but it is no longer enforcing user-specific access. At that point, the assistant is not acting on behalf of the user. It is acting on behalf of the broadest identity in the chain.

Identity propagation is often hardest at integration boundaries: content ingestion jobs, index builders, enrichment pipelines, vector stores, caching tiers, and orchestration middleware. Those layers are where enterprises unintentionally collapse individualized permissions into simplified tags such as "public," "internal," or "restricted." That simplification is often inadequate.

Permission Drift

Permission drift occurs when access rights in the AI-serving layer stop matching access rights in the source system. A document changes owner, a group membership is revoked, a site is restricted, or a legal hold changes visibility, but the index is not updated quickly enough. The AI layer continues to believe yesterday's permissions are still true.

This is a hidden AI risk because the underlying content may appear static while the authorization state changes constantly. In many enterprises, access metadata changes more often than the content itself. If index synchronization is optimized only for content freshness and not for authorization freshness, the architecture is insecure even when the content is current.

Classification and Sensitivity-Aware Delivery

Sensitivity labels and classification tags are not decorative metadata. They should shape retrieval behavior.

A document marked confidential, highly confidential, export-controlled, attorney-client privileged, or HR restricted should not simply receive a label for reporting purposes. That classification should influence whether the content is indexed, how it is chunked, whether it can be summarized, whether excerpts can be shown, whether citations can be displayed, and which identities are allowed to use it for answer generation. In mature architectures, sensitivity affects retrieval policy in at least four ways:

- Eligibility for indexing.
- Eligibility for summarization.
- Eligibility for passage display or citation.

- Eligibility for downstream actions by agents.
- Least privilege with usable delivery.

Least privilege is often misinterpreted as maximal restriction. In reality, enterprise AI must preserve least privilege without destroying usability. A security model that prevents any helpful answer will be bypassed. The goal is not to make assistants powerless. The goal is to make them precise.

That usually means designing multiple serving contracts rather than one universal assistant. A general employee knowledge assistant, a finance analyst copilot, an HR operations assistant, and an action-taking procurement agent should not share the same retrieval scope, answer behavior, or action rights. Each should operate within a clearly defined trust boundary.

KEY INSIGHT

Access-aware retrieval is not optional

In enterprise AI, retrieval quality without permission fidelity is not a quality achievement. It is a control failure. A system that returns the most relevant answer from unauthorized data is not intelligent. It is unsafe.

ARCHITECTURAL IMPLICATIONS

The AI-serving Layer Is Part of the Security Architecture

Many organizations still review the source repository for security and treat the AI layer as a neutral consumer. That is a mistake. The AI-serving layer is itself a high-risk access surface. It must be reviewed as part of enterprise security architecture, with the same rigor applied to applications that expose regulated or sensitive data. This includes:

- Authentication patterns.
- Group and role resolution.
- Token propagation.
- Row-, object-, or document-level authorization.
- Sensitivity label handling.
- Audit logging.
- Revocation behavior.
- Cache invalidation.
- Exception paths.
- Fallback behavior when policy evaluation fails.

⚠ **WARNING SIGN**

Security reviewed the source system but not the AI index

If security approved SharePoint, the data warehouse, or the document management platform, but never reviewed the retrieval index, chunk store, vector store, or answer assembly service, the control boundary has been misunderstood.

Metadata Must Carry Authorization Truth

The book's central argument that metadata is the control plane for AI applies directly here. Permission fidelity depends on metadata that is accurate, current, and enforceable. For access-aware delivery, critical metadata includes:

- Identity and group mappings.
- Object ownership.
- Access control lists.
- Inherited permissions.
- Sensitivity classifications.
- Business domain tags.
- Source-of-truth system identifiers.
- Effective timestamps for policy changes.
- Lineage from source object to chunk or embedding.
- Revocation and synchronization status.

Without this metadata, the AI layer is blind to the actual security posture of the content it serves.

End-to-end Enforcement Is Required

Security cannot be attached only at one point in the flow. It must be enforced from source authorization to the final answer assembly.

❖ **FIGURE 36 – IDENTITY PROPAGATION MODEL**

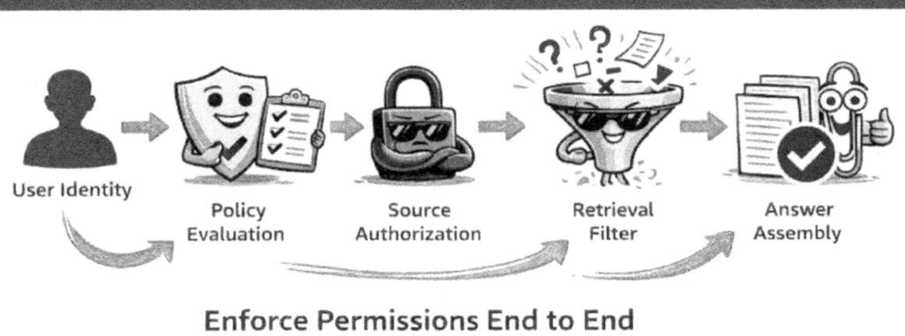

In an implementation, that means:

- The user identity is authenticated in the interface layer.
- Policy evaluation resolves effective permissions using the identity provider and authorization source.
- Source authorization metadata is attached to content or retrievable by reference.
- Retrieval filters exclude unauthorized chunks, documents, rows, or entities before ranking and assembly.
- Answer assembly prevents summaries or citations from drawing on excluded material.

If any step is skipped, the system may look secure while still leaking information.

Classification Should Shape Architecture, Not Just Compliance Reporting

Sensitive content should not necessarily follow the same indexing and serving path as general content. For example:

- Public or broadly internal policy content may be fully indexed for semantic retrieval.
- Confidential operating documents may require group-scoped indexing.
- HR or legal documents may require metadata-only discovery with source-link access checks.
- Highly restricted material may be excluded from general assistant retrieval entirely.

This is not overengineering. It is segmentation. Enterprises already segment networks, applications, and data zones. AI-serving paths should be segmented too.

Revocation Latency Becomes an Architectural Metric

In traditional systems, access revocation may tolerate modest delay. In AI systems, long delays are dangerous. If a user loses access to a repository at 9:00 a.m. but the assistant's index honors the change only after the overnight batch, the organization has created a breach window. Architects should define and monitor revocation latency targets. The right target depends on the use case, but the principle is the same: authorization freshness must be treated as a service-level objective, not an operational detail.

Failure Modes and Anti-Patterns

Broad Indexing Under a Service Account

This is one of the most common failures. Content is crawled using a powerful service identity, indexed centrally, and then served back to users through simplified filtering. The index knows what exists, but not who should see it with full fidelity.

This pattern often begins as a pilot shortcut. It later becomes a structural risk.

Coarse Labels Replacing Real Permissions

A team may decide that all content can be tagged as public, internal, confidential, or restricted. That may help ranking or reporting, but it rarely captures the nuances of enterprise authorization. Real access decisions often depend on group membership, geography, business unit, legal matter, project team, employment status, or time-bound assignment. Flattening these into coarse labels creates false confidence.

Content Freshness Without Permission Freshness

Teams often focus on getting the newest document version into the index while ignoring changes to ACLs, group memberships, or folder inheritance. This produces permission drift.

❖ FIGURE 37 – PERMISSION DRIFT FAILURE

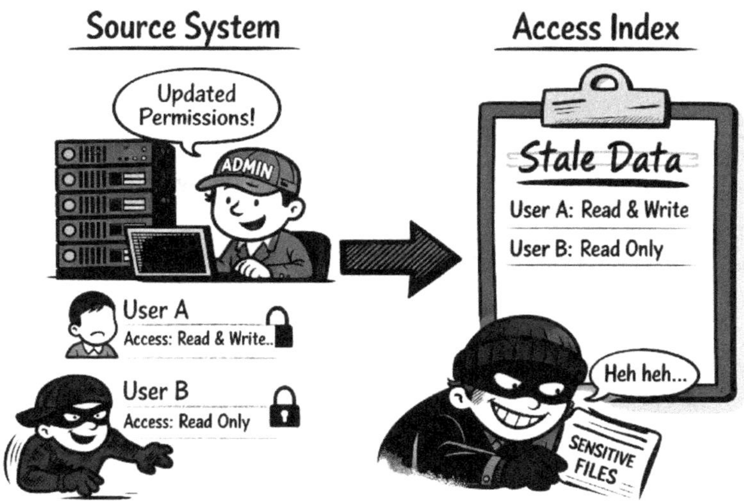

A useful illustration would show a document whose content is unchanged but whose access scope has narrowed after a reorganization or investigation. The source system blocks the former viewers, but the AI index still allows retrieval because the authorization metadata was not refreshed.

Answer-Layer Filtering Only

Some teams attempt to retrieve broadly, then suppress sensitive language in the final answer. This is fragile. If unauthorized content participates in ranking, grounding, or synthesis, the model may still leak it through paraphrase, implication, or comparative reasoning. Filtering only at the end is too late.

One Assistant for Every Use Case

A universal enterprise assistant is attractive in theory and risky in practice. Different user groups have different trust thresholds, entitlements, and needs. Collapsing all use cases into one interface usually leads to one of two bad outcomes: overexposure or overrestriction.

Missing Auditability

If the organization cannot answer the questions, "What did the user ask?", "Which sources were eligible?", "Which policy filters were applied?", and "Why was this answer returned?", it cannot investigate incidents or defend the system.

Practical Application

Design for Access-Aware Delivery from the Start

A practical design sequence looks like this:

Define the serving contract

Start by specifying who the assistant serves, what content classes it may use, what actions it may take, and what evidence it must provide. A knowledge assistant for all employees may be allowed to answer from published policy, approved knowledge articles, and team-scoped documents. An HR assistant may operate on a narrower set of sources with stronger evidence and approval requirements.

Identify the authorization source of truth

Do not assume the index is the source of truth for permissions. Identify where authorization is actually defined: application ACLs, document repositories, group memberships, row-level policies, data platform entitlements, or case-level access controls. The serving architecture must either evaluate those controls directly or synchronize them with provable fidelity.

Model permission inheritance explicitly

Inheritance is where many enterprises lose precision. Folder inheritance, workspace membership, role-based grants, and exception overrides must be modeled deliberately. If the inheritance model cannot be represented in the serving layer, the architecture should be redesigned rather than approximated.

Decide how sensitivity labels affect behavior

For each classification level, define:

- Whether content can be indexed.
- Whether full text or only metadata can be stored.
- Whether chunks can be embedded.

- Whether excerpts can be shown.
- Whether summaries can be generated.
- Whether citations are mandatory.
- Whether agents may act on the information.
- Engineer for revocation and synchronization.

Define how permission changes flow to the index. Options include event-driven updates, change-data capture, repository webhooks, scheduled reconciliation, or hybrid patterns. The method matters less than the result: permission drift must be measurable and minimized.

Log for evidence, not just debugging

Audit events should capture the acting identity, prompt, resolved entitlements, policy evaluation outcome, sources considered, sources returned, answer citations, action requests, and exceptions. This is essential for investigations, compliance reviews, and continuous improvement.

Balance security and usability

Least privilege should be paired with experience design. For example, when content is restricted, the assistant can still be helpful by saying:

- That relevant material exists but is not accessible.
- Which business function owns the information.
- How the user may request access.
- What approved public alternative exists.
- Whether a source system workflow should be used instead.

That approach preserves usability without fabricating answers or disclosing restricted information.

Templates

Access-Aware Retrieval Control Checklist

Purpose	<reason this checklist is used and the stages at which it should be applied, such as design review, pre-production approval, or major change control for assistants, copilots, or agents that retrieve enterprise data>
Use case	<specific assistant, copilot, or agent scenario being reviewed>
User groups	<intended user populations, roles, or teams permitted to use the system>
Identity provider	<enterprise identity system used for authentication, group membership, multifactor authentication, and conditional access enforcement>

Authorization source	<systems of record that define and govern user entitlements and access rights for the content or data being retrieved>
Permission inheritance model	<how permissions flow from source systems to retrieved assets, including inheritance from repository, workspace, folder, document, record, or item-level controls and any exception handling>
Sensitivity labels used	<classification labels used to distinguish content sensitivity levels and enforce retrieval restrictions>
Retrieval filter logic	<rules used to determine which chunks, records, or assets are eligible for retrieval based on requester entitlements, sensitivity thresholds, and synthesis restrictions>
Index synchronization method	<method used to keep retrieval-layer permissions aligned with source-system entitlements, such as event-driven updates, scheduled reconciliation, or drift detection processes>
Revocation latency target	<maximum acceptable time for access revocations or entitlement changes to be reflected in the retrieval and serving layers>
Exception handling	<default behavior and control steps taken when policy evaluation fails, such as deny-by-default, logging, and user-facing access guidance>
Audit events captured	<security, retrieval, policy, and outcome events that must be logged for traceability, monitoring, and investigation>
Red-team test completed? yes/no	<Yes or No>
Exposure scenarios	<known or tested scenarios in which restricted, privileged, revoked, or otherwise sensitive content could be exposed inappropriately>
Mitigations	<controls, architectural protections, operational processes, and testing measures used to reduce exposure risk and maintain access fidelity>
Security owner	<role or leader accountable for security review, approval, and control design>
Approval date	<date on which the review or approval was formally completed>

Case Example

When Retrieval Ignores Entitlement: Why Permission Fidelity Must Survive into AI Serving

A global enterprise launched an internal knowledge assistant intended to answer employee questions from policy documents, benefits materials, and shared operational content. The pilot was considered successful because retrieval relevance was strong and users praised the natural language interface.

Then a regional manager asked a seemingly ordinary question: "What are the current guidelines for role reductions and manager notification timelines?" The assistant returned a synthesized answer that referenced restricted HR planning materials, including draft severance guidance and internal escalation procedures not meant for general managers.

The breach did not occur because the source repository was openly accessible. The HR documents lived in a restricted location. The problem was architectural. During ingestion, the AI pipeline crawled documents using a privileged service account and stored enriched chunks in a central index. The team preserved content freshness and source links, but not the original permission model. At serving time, the assistant filtered by broad document category rather than effective user entitlement. The model did exactly what the architecture allowed it to do: it assembled the most relevant answer from content it should never have been allowed to retrieve.

The incident revealed four failures:

- Identity was not propagated from the user to the retrieval layer with sufficient fidelity.
- Source permissions were not preserved at the chunk and index level.
- Hr sensitivity labels did not restrict summarization behavior.
- Security had reviewed the source HR repository but not the AI index and answer assembly service.

The remediation required more than deleting the affected index. The organization redesigned the serving architecture. HR content was moved to a separate retrieval domain. Group-based entitlements were synchronized into the serving layer with event-driven updates. High-sensitivity HR documents were switched to metadata-only discovery for most users, with direct source-system access checks before display. The answer assembly was changed so that restricted content could not participate in synthesis for ineligible identities. Audit events were expanded to capture policy evaluation and source eligibility decisions.

The most important lesson was not technical elegance. It was architectural accountability. The organization learned that preserving permission fidelity is not a repository concern alone. It is a serving concern.

Closing Synthesis

Enterprise AI does not create new principles of security so much as it punishes architectural shortcuts that older systems sometimes tolerated. If the AI-serving layer strips away identity, simplifies authorization, ignores classification, or lags on permission updates, it turns enterprise knowledge into an exposure surface.

That is why access-aware retrieval is mandatory. Identity must propagate from the user through policy evaluation, retrieval, and answer assembly. Permission drift must be treated as an active breach vector. Sensitivity labels must shape what can be indexed, retrieved, summarized, and acted on. Least privilege must remain intact even as the user experience becomes easier and more conversational.

This chapter sits squarely within the broader thesis of AI-Ready Data. Trustworthy enterprise AI depends on more than clean data and strong models. It depends on metadata that carries business meaning, governance intent, provenance, freshness, and permission truth into the serving layer. Security is, therefore, not adjacent to AI-Ready Data architecture. It is one of its defining tests.

When an enterprise assistant answers a question, the architecture should be able to prove three things at once: the answer is relevant, the answer is grounded, and the answer was assembled only from information the requester was allowed to use. If it cannot prove all three, it is not ready.

Key Takeaways

- Access-aware retrieval is a mandatory control, not an optional enhancement.
- Identity and authorization must propagate from source to answer assembly without simplification that breaks permission fidelity.
- Permission drift is a real breach vector, especially when authorization changes faster than content.
- Sensitivity labels must govern indexing, retrieval, summarization, citation, and agent action behavior.
- An AI system is not enterprise-ready unless it can prove relevance, grounding, and authorized use at the same time.

CHAPTER 19: WHY GOVERNANCE FOR AI IS DIFFERENT FROM GOVERNANCE FOR ANALYTICS

Governance for analytics was built for a world in which data moved toward reports, dashboards, models, and controlled business decisions. The central questions were familiar: Is the data correct, consistent, timely enough, and approved for use in reporting? That governance model remains essential, but it is no longer sufficient.

AI changes the problem. An AI system does not simply read data and render it in a chart. It interprets, summarizes, retrieves, ranks, combines, explains, and increasingly acts. It answers in natural language. It may pull from structured records, policies, contracts, emails, transcripts, knowledge articles, and semi-structured events in the same interaction. It may present a confident answer even when the underlying evidence is thin, stale, or contextually wrong. That changes governance fundamentally.

Governance for AI must, therefore, extend beyond consistency, quality, and controlled reporting. It must govern interpretation, evidence, recency, permission fidelity, interaction risk, and action safety. It must address not only what data is allowed to exist, but how that data is discovered, retrieved, ranked, cited, explained, and used in context. In an analytics environment, a bad number is a governance issue. In an AI environment, a plausible but unverifiable answer is also a governance issue. This is the core distinction. Analytics governance governs data products. AI governance must govern data products, content products, retrieval behavior, answer evidence, and the operating boundaries of AI consumers. Existing governance programs are useful, but incomplete. They were not designed for systems that speak, infer, compose, and act.

WHY THIS MATTERS

The enterprise consequences are immediate.

A board reporting dataset may be accurate, reconciled, and fully approved for analytic use, yet still be unsafe for conversational retrieval. Why? Because a conversational assistant can expose sensitive fragments out of context, collapse exceptions into general rules, merge old and current policy language, or reveal information to a user whose access rights are valid for one system but not another. The problem is not only whether the source data is governed. The problem is whether AI behavior over that data is governed.

Analytics consumers typically know they are looking at a curated artifact. They understand there is a model, a metric definition, a refresh cycle, and a controlled interface. AI users often experience something different. They ask a question in plain language and receive an answer that feels direct, immediate, and authoritative. The interface creates a false sense of certainty. That is why AI introduces new trust and misuse vectors. The output feels more human, but the enterprise still bears the burden of proof. This matters most in environments where ambiguity is expensive: healthcare coverage explanations, financial eligibility decisions, legal policy interpretation, procurement recommendations, operational triage, security response, and employee guidance. In those settings, a wrong answer is not just an accuracy problem. It may be a privacy breach, a policy breach, a legal exposure, or an unsafe action.

Traditional analytics governance protects the integrity of reported facts. AI governance must also protect the integrity of interpretation.

KEY INSIGHT

AI governance begins upstream

AI failures often appear at the point of interaction, but their causes usually start earlier: poor metadata, weak classification, missing provenance, unresolved semantics, stale content, and broken permission inheritance. If governance begins only at the model or prompt layer, it begins too late.

CORE CONCEPTS

Governance Must Move from Asset Control to Behavior Control

In analytics, governance often centers on certifying datasets, controlling metric definitions, managing lineage, and approving report usage. In AI, those controls still matter, but they govern only part of the control surface. The organization must also govern retrieval pathways, ranking logic, source authority, evidence display, answer boundaries, and action permissions. That is because AI answers are not static artifacts. They are runtime compositions. The answer a user sees depends on what was retrieved, what was excluded, how the system ranked sources, whether freshness rules were applied, whether conflicting evidence was detected, and whether the system was allowed to answer at all.

A governed source does not guarantee governed output.

Metadata Becomes Operational, Not Descriptive

In analytics programs, metadata is often treated as support material: definitions, owners, quality rules, refresh schedules, and lineage maps. In an AI-ready architecture, metadata becomes operational control. It drives discoverability, ranking, filtering, access-aware retrieval, citation, trust signaling, and explainability.

If a contract clause has no effective date, jurisdiction, owner, sensitivity label, retention state, or business meaning attached to it, an assistant cannot safely use it. If a policy document lacks an authoritative status and a supersession relationship, an AI system may quote an outdated version. If a customer term is not semantically distinguished from subscriber, member, policyholder, or account holder, AI will collapse meanings that governance should keep separate. This is why governance for AI is inseparable from semantic architecture.

Unstructured Content Is Now in Scope

Analytics governance matured around structured data: tables, fields, metrics, dimensions, master data, and pipelines. AI requires much more. Policies, procedures, contracts, manuals, knowledge articles, meeting notes, transcripts, emails, and collaborative documents frequently contain the business meaning AI needs most.

But unstructured content has historically been governed unevenly. It may sit in repositories with inconsistent naming, weak classification, uncertain ownership, duplicate versions, and unclear retention. That is tolerable for human browsing. It is dangerous for machine retrieval at scale.

Treating unstructured content as a first-class enterprise asset is not optional for AI governance. It is foundational.

Evidence Is Part of the Answer

Analytics tools usually separate calculation from explanation. AI systems blend them. An enterprise answer without evidence is not trustworthy merely because it sounds coherent. Governance for AI must require defensible sourcing: citations, provenance, time validity, authority indicators, and traceability back to governed assets.

An answer that cannot show where it came from should not be treated as enterprise-grade.

Consumer Type Shapes Governance Design

Not every AI consumer should be governed the same way.

A human analyst copilot can tolerate more ambiguity than an executive briefing assistant. A knowledge assistant can operate with broader retrieval permissions than a workflow agent that initiates actions. A read-only assistant and an action-taking agent do not need the same controls because they do not create the same consequences.

Governance must, therefore, be matched to consequence. Trust thresholds, evidence requirements, fallback rules, and action boundaries should vary by consumer type.

❖ FIGURE 38 – ANALYTICS VS AI GOVERNANCE

ARCHITECTURAL IMPLICATIONS

Govern Retrieval as an Architectural Layer

Retrieval quality is not merely a model concern. It is an architectural responsibility. The enterprise decides how content is chunked, enriched, classified, permissioned, ranked, refreshed, and cited. Those decisions determine whether the AI system behaves safely and usefully. A strong architecture will define:

- Authoritative sources by domain.
- Freshness and supersession rules.
- Access-aware retrieval enforcement.
- Semantic enrichment requirements.
- Citation and evidence expectations.
- Confidence and abstention behaviors.
- Answer scopes by user and use case.

Without these controls, governance remains theoretical.

Design for Permission Fidelity, Not Broad Access

Analytics environments often solve access through dataset- or workspace-level permissions. AI systems need finer fidelity. They may retrieve sentence-level or paragraph-level content from documents with mixed sensitivity. They may combine content across repositories with inconsistent identity models. They may expose fragments that were never intended to be surfaced outside the original interface. AI governance must, therefore, work with identity-aware delivery. Access should be enforced as close to retrieval as possible, not only at the storage layer. Entitlements, group membership, policy labels, legal holds, jurisdictional constraints, and usage purpose may all need to shape what is retrieved and shown.

Separate Knowledge Permission from Action Permission

An assistant may be allowed to explain a policy without being allowed to apply it. It may summarize the account context without being allowed to change the account. It may draft a remediation plan without being allowed to trigger one. One of the most dangerous errors in AI architecture is collapsing retrieval permission and action permission into a single trust decision. Governance for AI must separate these explicitly. Read scope, recommendation scope, and action scope should be independently controlled.

Build Provenance and Temporal Correctness into the Serving Layer

AI answers must be temporally correct, not just generally correct. A benefit rule that was valid last quarter may be invalid today. A pricing policy may differ by effective date, region, channel, or customer segment. An assistant who answers from stale but once-authoritative material is still wrong.

❖ FIGURE 39 – GOVERNANCE BY CONSUMER TYPE

Architecturally, this means the serving layer needs more than content access. It needs effective dates, source authority, supersession logic, lineage to the approved artifact, and the ability to present that evidence to the user.

Key Insight

Why analytics controls do not fully translate

A certified dataset, a named owner, and a lineage diagram are necessary controls. They are not sufficient controls for AI. AI also needs governed interpretation, governed retrieval, governed evidence, governed abstention, and governed action boundaries.

Failure Modes and Anti-Patterns

Treating AI as Just Another BI Channel

This is the most common mistake. The organization assumes that because a dataset is approved for reporting, it is automatically safe for conversational access. It is not. Reports constrain navigation, aggregation, and wording. AI expands them.

Governing Sources but Not Answers

Some organizations invest heavily in source governance and then stop. They can explain where the data came from, but not why the assistant answered the way it did. That leaves a dangerous gap between governed inputs and ungoverned behavior.

Warning Sign

Governance team signs off on source data but not AI behavior

If the governance program can certify a dataset but cannot specify who the assistant may answer, which sources it may use, how fresh evidence must be, when it must abstain, and whether it may trigger actions, the governance program is not yet AI-ready.

Allowing Plausible Language to Substitute for Evidence

Natural-language fluency hides weakness. Users often trust an articulate answer more than a cautious one. That makes unverifiable output particularly risky in the enterprise. Coherence is not proof.

Ignoring Semantic Ambiguity

Terms that are manageable in reporting become dangerous in AI. "Customer," "member," "subscriber," "account holder," and "party" may each be distinct in policy, operations, and regulation. If governance does not encode those distinctions in metadata and semantics, AI will flatten them.

Overlooking Semi-Structured Operational Signals

Events, logs, messages, API payloads, and workflow states are often the bridge between enterprise systems and AI-driven operations. When those assets are left outside governance, assistants lack the contextual signals needed to distinguish *the* current state from static reference content.

Allowing Broad Retrieval with Weak Content Hygiene

Duplicated files, unowned documents, obsolete procedures, regional exceptions buried in appendices, and unlabeled drafts are survivable in human search. They are destructive in enterprise AI. Repositories are not readiness.

Practical Application

The practical question is not whether an organization already has governance. Most do. The question is whether that governance covers the full AI control surface. A useful approach is to assess the four layers together.

Layer 1: Existing Analytics Governance

Document what is already strong: data ownership, lineage, metric certification, quality rules, access controls, stewardship, and controlled reporting. This is the foundation, not the endpoint.

Layer 2: Content Governance

Assess unstructured and semi-structured assets. Are there authoritative versions? Sensitivity labels? Retention rules? Document status? Supersession metadata? Ownership? Access inheritance? Are knowledge articles, procedures, and contracts governed as retrievable enterprise assets rather than just stored files?

Layer 3: Runtime AI Controls

Examine what governs the interaction itself. What sources may each AI consumer use? What evidence must be shown? How is freshness applied? When must the system abstain? How are prompts, policies, and action boundaries controlled? How are logs reviewed?

Layer 4: Consumer-specific Policy

Define data-serving contracts by consumer type. What may a knowledge assistant answer? What must an executive briefing tool cite? What may a workflow agent recommend but not execute? What approvals are required for action-taking AI?

The goal is not a perfect universal policy. The goal is a governed operating model that matches the consequences of the AI use case.

TEMPLATES

AI Governance Gap Assessment

Existing analytics governance controls

<current governance controls already in place for analytics data, such as certified datasets, glossary coverage, data quality rules, lineage, access controls, and owner or steward assignments>

Existing content governance controls

<current governance controls already in place for documents and unstructured content, such as retention rules, repository permissions, sensitivity labels, legal hold processes, versioning, and ownership metadata>

Existing policy controls

<enterprise policies, standards, and formal control documents currently in force that shape data, content, security, privacy, records, and usage behavior>

Existing AI controls

<current controls governing AI use, such as approved use-case registries, human review rules, model-access restrictions, logging, pilot guardrails, and limits on autonomous action>

Gaps in provenance

<current weaknesses in source authority, supersession tracking, ownership, approval status, traceability, or passage-level evidence linkage>

Gaps in freshness

<current weaknesses in staleness rules, effective-date handling, review cadence, update propagation, temporal ranking, or expiry controls>

Gaps in permission enforcement

<current weaknesses in carrying source permissions into retrieval and serving layers, including segmentation, entitlement synchronization, context-aware filtering, and separation of read versus action rights>

Gaps in semantic control

<current weaknesses in glossary coverage, synonym control, ontology support, domain meaning, exception encoding, and distinction between similar business terms>

Gaps in answer evidence

<current weaknesses in citation display, source authority visibility, effective-date exposure, answer templates, confidence signaling, and abstention behavior when evidence is weak or conflicting>

Gaps in action safety

<current weaknesses in defining recommendation boundaries, approval thresholds, rollback patterns, tool-use permissions, and escalation rules for AI-supported or agentic actions>

Priority remediation items	<highest-priority actions required to strengthen governance, metadata, permission enforcement, evidence standards, semantic modeling, freshness controls, and consumer-specific AI safeguards>
Owners	<roles, leaders, and functions accountable for sponsorship, architecture, metadata, security, legal interpretation, content lifecycle, platform controls, and domain-specific stewardship>
Timeline	<phased implementation sequence showing what should be addressed over time, including immediate, near-term, mid-term, and longer-term governance and control actions>

CASE EXAMPLE

Beyond Analytics Governance: Why Conversational AI Requires a New Control Model

A global insurer has a mature analytics governance program. Financial reporting datasets are certified. Claims metrics are reconciled. Business glossaries exist. Access to dashboards is controlled by role. On paper, governance looks strong.

The company then launches an internal assistant for service representatives. The assistant can answer questions about claims handling, policy exceptions, and customer communication guidance. The project team assumes that because the source material is already approved for reporting and internal use, it can be indexed for conversational retrieval.

Problems appear quickly. First, some claims guidance documents include regional legal variations buried in appendices. The assistant retrieves the general rule but not the exception, and representatives begin giving incomplete guidance. Second, several policy interpretation documents exist in multiple versions across collaboration sites. Humans usually know which one is current because they work in the process every day. The assistant does not. It retrieves an obsolete interpretation note because it contains highly similar language and better keyword density. Third, reporting data approved for analytical aggregation includes fields that are acceptable in a dashboard context but too revealing in conversational form when combined with case notes and customer correspondence.

None of these failures came from a lack of analytics governance. They came from the difference between reporting approval and conversational approval.

The remediation required architectural and governance changes, not better prompting. The insurer established authoritative source sets for service guidance, added effective-date and supersession metadata, enforced paragraph-level sensitivity filtering, separated guidance retrieval from case action permissions, and required source citations for policy answers. It also limited the assistant to explanation and draft generation, while reserving final policy exceptions for human review.

That is governance for AI in practice. It is not a rejection of analytics governance. It is an expansion beyond it.

Closing Synthesis

Governance for analytics remains necessary because the enterprise still needs trustworthy data, reconciled metrics, clear ownership, and controlled reporting. But AI changes what must be governed.

It is no longer enough to govern datasets while leaving interpretation unmanaged. It is no longer enough to approve content for storage while leaving retrieval behavior implicit. It is no longer enough to certify source data while ignoring whether the assistant can provide evidence, apply freshness rules, honor permissions, or decline unsafe actions.

AI governance is different because AI changes both the interface and the consequence. It turns governed assets into runtime answers, and sometimes runtime actions. That means the enterprise must govern not just what data is, but how AI systems discover it, interpret it, justify it, and use it.

The organizations that scale trustworthy AI will not be the ones with the loudest AI strategy. They will be the ones that redesign governance to match this new control surface: structured and unstructured data together, metadata as control plane, semantics as disambiguation, retrieval as architecture, evidence as requirement, and action boundaries as non-negotiable design. That is the shift. Analytics governance protects reported truth. AI governance must protect interpreted truth.

Key Takeaways

- Analytics governance governs trusted data; AI governance must also govern trusted interpretation.
- A plausible answer without verifiable evidence is a governance failure.
- Content approval for reporting does not equal approval for conversational retrieval.
- Governance for AI must include retrieval, permissions, semantics, freshness, and action boundaries.
- The right governance model depends on the consequence of the AI consumer, not just the source data.

CHAPTER 20: GOVERNING STRUCTURED AND UNSTRUCTURED DATA TOGETHER

Enterprise AI collapses an illusion that many organizations have been able to preserve for years: the illusion that structured data and unstructured content can be governed separately without consequence.

That separation was always imperfect. A customer record was never only a row in a CRM table. It was also the contract they signed, the service transcript that explained their issue, the email that documented an exception, the policy that governed their eligibility, the workflow event that recorded a decision, and the control evidence that proved the decision was valid. Traditional operating models tolerated fragmented governance because reporting, analytics, and line-of-business applications often consumed only one slice of that reality at a time.

AI does not.

A retrieval pipeline, a copilot, or an agent can traverse records, documents, messages, events, and policies in one interaction. It may summarize a case, explain a decision, recommend a next action, or answer a compliance question by combining multiple asset classes in one chain of reasoning. The moment that happens, split governance regimes become visible as a structural defect. Definitions drift. Permissions conflict. Retention rules diverge. Ownership is ambiguous. Lineage breaks at the boundary between systems of record and document repositories. The result is not merely inconvenience. It is a conflicting truth, incomplete answers, and unsafe behavior.

The enterprise, therefore, has to govern structured and unstructured data as one connected estate. This is not a philosophical preference. It is an architectural requirement for trustworthy AI.

WHY THIS MATTERS

AI Consumes Business Reality, Not Storage Categories

Humans understand that a document, a database record, and an event log may all refer to the same underlying business fact. Most enterprise architectures, however, still govern those assets in separate domains, with different metadata standards, control owners, and policy enforcement paths.

AI systems expose the weakness of that arrangement because they do not naturally respect repository boundaries. They retrieve what is available, rank what appears relevant, and generate answers from what they can access. If a control record says one thing, a policy PDF says another, and a recent email explains the exception but is governed elsewhere, the system will surface an inconsistency that the organization itself failed to reconcile. That is why governance for AI cannot be organized around storage type alone. It must be organized around business meaning, evidence chains, and intended use.

Structured and Unstructured Assets Describe the Same World

In nearly every enterprise process, structured and unstructured assets co-describe the same reality:

- A supplier master record is linked to contracts, onboarding forms, risk assessments, and approval emails.
- A patient episode is linked to orders, clinician notes, discharge summaries, and audit events.
- A financial control is linked to policy documents, exception logs, attestation records, and issue remediation narratives.
- A customer complaint is linked to case fields, chat transcripts, call recordings, knowledge articles, and escalation notes.

When governance is split, these connected assets are classified differently, retained differently, and trusted differently, even though AI will use them together. That is how ambiguity enters the system.

Governance Failure Becomes Answer Failure

In traditional BI, a governance failure might show up as a disputed metric, a broken dashboard, or a compliance finding after the fact. In AI, the same failure appears directly in the answer, the recommendation, or the automated action.

A knowledge assistant might cite a superseded procedure because retention and freshness controls were not aligned across repositories. An analyst copilot might misinterpret a business term because the glossary covered tables but not policy language. An agent might escalate the wrong case because narrative evidence in notes was excluded from the authoritative truth chain.

AI compresses the latency between governance failure and operational consequence.

KEY INSIGHT

One enterprise, one trust problem

When structured and unstructured data are governed separately, the enterprise does not have two governance problems. It has one trust problem showing up in different places.

Core Concepts

Cross-asset Governance

Cross-asset governance means that policies, ownership, classification, retention, lineage, and access rules are designed to operate across records, documents, events, messages, and narrative evidence. It does not require all assets to be stored in one platform. It requires them to be governed through a coherent model.

The objective is not uniformity for its own sake. The objective is consistency of meaning and control where assets participate in the same business process, regulatory obligation, or AI use case.

A customer eligibility decision, for example, may involve a structured policy rules table, a PDF policy statement, a case note documenting an exception, and workflow events showing who approved the outcome. Cross-asset governance ensures that these assets can be interpreted together with aligned semantics, permissions, provenance, and retention expectations.

Governance Must Span Records, Documents, Relationships, and Narrative Evidence

Many organizations still define governance too narrowly. They focus on structured data elements and treat documents as a records management issue, or they govern repositories and leave relationship modeling to application teams. AI requires a broader scope.

Governance now has to encompass four things together:

- **Records.** The structured entities, attributes, and reference data that represent core business objects.
- **Documents**. Policies, contracts, procedures, manuals, forms, and supporting evidence that provide context and instruction.
- **Relationships**. The links among customers, cases, contracts, products, controls, incidents, and decisions that allow AI to reason about connected business meaning.
- **Narrative evidence**. Notes, transcripts, emails, tickets, and explanations that often contain the "why" behind a decision.

This is especially important because structured data often captures the final state, while unstructured material captures the rationale, exception path, or governing rule. AI needs both.

Metadata Is the Bridge

If governance must span multiple asset classes, metadata becomes the binding layer. Metadata is what allows the enterprise to declare that a field called customer_status, a policy paragraph about eligibility, a case note describing a waiver, and an approval event all relate to the same governed concept.

That metadata has to include more than the technical schema. It needs business definitions, asset classifications, ownership, source authority, provenance, effective dates, applicable policies, sensitivity levels, lineage, and relationship context. Without this layer, structured and unstructured content remain merely co-located, not governable together.

Cross-asset Alignment of Ownership, Retention, and Classification

Ownership cannot stop at the boundary of the application database. If a business domain owns a process, it must own the governing meaning of the records, documents, and evidence that define that process.

The same applies to retention and classification. An enterprise cannot credibly govern a control library as confidential, retain the associated exception tickets for one year, archive the policy PDFs indefinitely in a separate repository, and then expect an AI system to produce coherent compliance answers. The asset classes may differ, but the governance intent must align.

❖ FIGURE 40 – UNIFIED GOVERNANCE MODEL

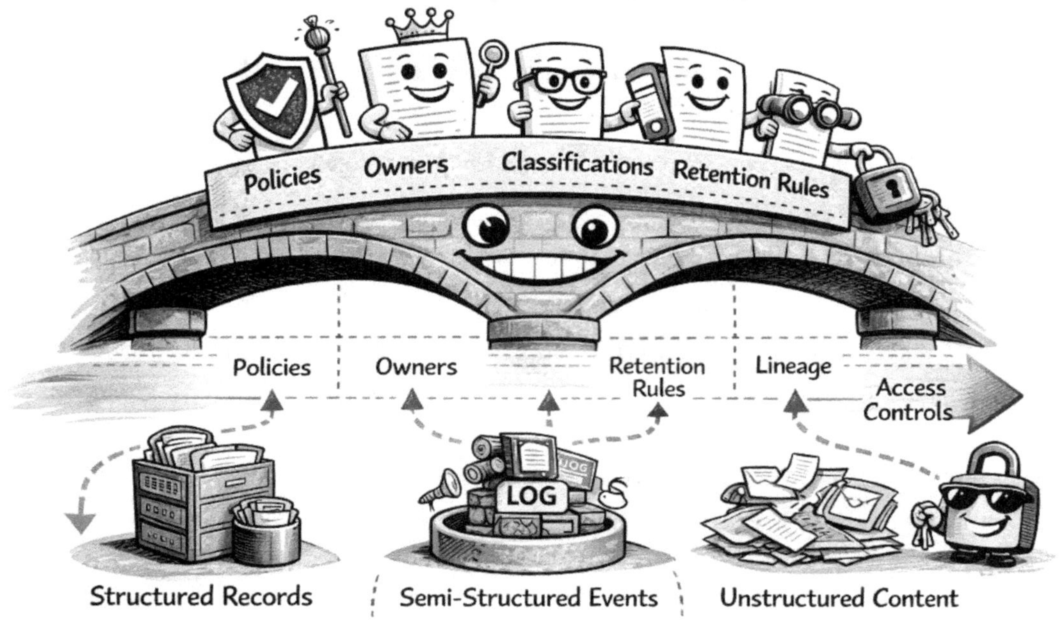

Governance must be cross-cutting, not repository-specific.

ARCHITECTURAL IMPLICATIONS

The Architecture Must Model Truth Chains, Not Just Data Stores

AI-ready architecture should model how business truth is assembled across assets. That means identifying which records, which documents, which events, and which narrative evidence together establish an answer that the enterprise can defend.

This shifts the design question from "Where is the data stored?" to "What assets collectively prove this business fact?" That is a much better architectural frame for governance.

For example, a control compliance answer might require:

- The structured control record.
- The policy section defining the control intent.
- The workflow events showing review dates.
- The evidence document attached to the last attestation.
- And the issue log showing open exceptions.

A trustworthy AI response should be able to retrieve, rank, and cite across that chain, with each asset carrying aligned governance metadata.

Access-aware Delivery Must Cross Asset Classes

Permission fidelity becomes more difficult when AI responses draw on multiple repositories. It is not enough to secure tables in a warehouse and separately secure documents in a content platform. The serving layer must ensure that the user or agent receives only content they are entitled to see, even when the answer spans multiple sources.

This requires identity-aware retrieval, policy propagation, and access trimming across structured and unstructured assets. It also requires care with derived outputs. A user who lacks access to the underlying investigation notes should not receive a generated summary that leaks their content indirectly.

Provenance Has to Survive Transformation

AI systems routinely transform data: they chunk documents, extract entities, generate embeddings, normalize events, create summaries, and join retrieved context with structured facts. Every one of those transformations risks breaking the provenance chain unless the architecture preserves source references and effective timestamps.

This is not optional. If the enterprise cannot show where an answer came from, which asset version was used, and whether that source was current at the time of use, it does not have defensible governance. It has generated text.

Freshness Standards Must Be Explicit

Structured systems often have clear update cycles. Unstructured repositories often do not. A policy document may be updated manually. A transcript may land immediately. A procedure wiki may have stale pages that look authoritative. An AI system that retrieves across all of them needs explicit freshness standards. That means declaring, by asset type and use case, what counts as current, authoritative, superseded, or advisory. It also means ranking assets by source authority, effective date, and publication status, not simply keyword similarity.

❖ FIGURE 41 – CROSS-ASSET TRUTH CHAIN

FAILURE MODES AND ANTI-PATTERNS

Split Stewardship

One team governs master data. Another governs document repositories. A third owns records retention. A fourth manages the AI assistant. No single group owns the end-to-end trust chain. This is one of the most common and damaging anti-patterns. Each team may perform its local responsibilities well, yet the overall system still fails because nobody owns cross-asset coherence.

Taxonomy Without Operational Linkage

Some organizations respond by building a broad enterprise taxonomy, but they never connect it to actual access policies, retention rules, or retrieval logic. The result is elegant terminology with little operational effect.

For AI, semantics must be executable. Terms, classifications, and relationships must influence how assets are discovered, ranked, filtered, served, and cited.

Repository-first Governance

Another anti-pattern is governing each repository in isolation and assuming interoperability will emerge later. It rarely does. Repository-native labels, folder permissions, and local retention rules are useful, but they do not create an enterprise governance model.

AI exposes this immediately because retrieval pipelines operate across repository boundaries. Local governance without cross-asset harmonization produces inconsistent outputs by design.

Orphaned Narrative Evidence

Enterprises often govern formal documents and structured records but ignore notes, transcripts, chat logs, and email threads unless they become legal exhibits. Yet those narrative assets frequently contain the rationale, caveat, or exception needed for correct interpretation.

Ignoring narrative evidence does not make it irrelevant. It only makes AI more likely to miss it, misuse it, or surface it without context.

KEY INSIGHT

The danger of split governance

Split governance does not merely slow AI programs down. It trains inconsistency into them. The model appears unreliable because the estate is architecturally incoherent.

Warning signs are usually visible before a major AI failure occurs:

- The same business concept has different owners depending on whether it appears in a table or a document.
- Policy PDFs are updated manually with no machine-readable effective date.
- Documents and records use different sensitivity classifications for the same process.
- Retention schedules are defined separately for case records and their supporting narratives.
- AI teams have to hand-curate "trusted folders" because enterprise governance metadata is incomplete.

⚠ **WARNING SIGN**

Policy documents governed by one team, and the related control data governed by another, is not a minor coordination issue. It is an architectural defect waiting to surface in an AI answer.

PRACTICAL APPLICATION

Start with High-Risk Cross-Asset Use Cases

Do not begin by trying to unify governance across the entire estate at once. Start where AI value and trust risk intersect most clearly. Good candidates include compliance Q&A, policy-aware service guidance, claims handling, customer dispute resolution, supplier risk assessment, and internal audit support.

In each case, map the assets the AI must use together. Identify the structured records, unstructured documents, semi-structured events, and narrative evidence required for a defensible answer or action.

Define the Cross-Asset Operating Model

At that point, governance needs to move from aspiration to operating model. The organization should define:

- Which asset classes are in scope.
- Who owns meaning across them.
- How classifications map across repositories.
- What provenance must be captured.
- How freshness is assessed.
- How exceptions are handled.
- How disputes are escalated.

Make Derived AI Assets Governable

A common mistake is to govern only original sources. In practice, AI systems create derived assets that matter operationally: chunks, embeddings, semantic labels, entity graphs, summaries, caches, and conversation traces. These must not become a shadow estate.

The rule should be simple: if a derived artifact influences retrieval, interpretation, or action, it must inherit governance from its sources and remain traceable to them.

Design for Disagreement

Cross-asset governance does not eliminate conflict. It makes conflict manageable. There will still be cases where a record says one thing, a policy says another, and a note documents a legitimate exception. Good architecture does not hide these tensions. It exposes them, preserves provenance, and routes them through stewardship and escalation.

That is how trust is built: not by pretending the estate is perfectly clean, but by making inconsistency visible, governable, and explainable.

TEMPLATES

Cross-Asset Governance Operating Model Canvas

Asset classes in scope

<asset classes covered by the policy or operating model, such as transactional records, master data, policy documents, contracts, events, tickets, emails, notes, transcripts, evidence attachments, and derived AI retrieval artifacts>

Governing principles

<core principles that define how assets should be governed across classes, including common meaning, declared authority, required ownership and classification, inherited controls, and treatment of narrative evidence>

Ownership model

<roles accountable for business meaning, technical enforcement, retention and legal hold interpretation, and use-case-specific trust and serving requirements>

Stewardship model

<steward roles responsible for structured data, content assets, process evidence, and reconciliation of cross-asset conflicts and control mappings>

Classification model

<enterprise classification scheme and supplementary tags applied across asset classes, including rules for mapping repository-native labels into the common model>

Retention model

<rules for retention based on business process and regulatory obligation, including alignment across linked assets and inheritance rules for derived AI artifacts>

Legal hold rules

<rules defining how legal holds propagate across linked assets, how derived AI artifacts are frozen or reproduced, and what sign-off is required for release>

Access control model

<rules for enforcing identity- and role-based access across repositories, retrieval-time access trimming, response-time protection, and handling of privileged content>

Provenance standard

<required provenance and traceability attributes for governed assets and derived objects, including source system, owner, authoritative status, effective date, version, lineage, and citation-ready identifiers>

Freshness standard	<rules defining freshness thresholds by use case and asset class, including treatment of effective dates, supersession, update latency, timestamps, authorship, and ranking by authority and recency>
Escalation path	<defined route for escalating metadata conflicts, meaning conflicts, classification or retention conflicts, legal hold issues, and unresolved cross-platform design problems>
Policy exceptions process	<rules for documenting, approving, reviewing, expiring, and revoking temporary exceptions, including required owner, rationale, scope, compensating controls, expiry date, and review trigger>
Success measures	<measures used to determine whether governance is improving, such as reduced conflicting answers, better metadata completeness, stronger citation coverage, reduced stale or unauthorized retrieval, and faster audit traceability>
Review cadence	<formal cadence for governance review, operational review, and immediate reassessment after regulatory change, litigation events, or material AI incidents>

CASE EXAMPLE

When Policy Documents Alone Could Not Define Compliance Truth

A global enterprise launched a compliance assistant for internal control owners. The goal seemed straightforward: allow users to ask questions such as, "What evidence is required for quarterly access reviews?" or "Is compensating evidence allowed when automated logs are unavailable?"

The team indexed the policy PDFs from a document repository and connected them to a retrieval layer. Early demonstrations were promising. The assistant returned articulate answers and cited policy language. Users were impressed.

Then production usage exposed a deeper problem.

The policy PDFs were governed by a central documentation team. The control records, attestation schedules, and exception logs lived in separate structured systems governed by compliance operations. The documentation team updated policy text quarterly. Compliance operations updated control applicability and evidence requirements more frequently when audit findings or regulatory interpretations changed. Exceptions were documented in tickets and workflow records that were not included in the assistant's retrieval scope.

As a result, the assistant answered from formally approved policy text that was often incomplete in operational terms. It told users that one form of evidence was sufficient, even when the control record had been tightened due to a recent issue. It failed to mention standing exceptions recorded in workflow data. In some cases, it cited a valid policy paragraph that no longer represented the effective operating expectation for a particular control population.

The assistant did not fail because the model hallucinated. It failed because governance was split across asset classes that jointly defined compliance truth.

The remediation required architectural change, not prompt tuning. The organization had to:

- Map each compliance question to the required truth chain across policy documents, control records, workflow events, and exception tickets.
- Define authoritative status by question type, not by repository prestige.
- Align classifications and access rules across the document and control systems.
- Capture effective dates and supersession metadata for policy content.
- Include exception records as governed narrative or event evidence where relevant.
- Require the assistant to cite not just policy text, but the linked control record and recent operational status where applicable.

Once that cross-asset governance model was implemented, answer quality improved sharply. More importantly, trust improved because users could see not only what the assistant answered but also why.

Closing Synthesis

AI is forcing enterprises to govern data according to business reality rather than storage convenience.

That reality is cross-asset. A row, a document, an event, and a narrative explanation may all be required to produce one trustworthy answer. When governance is fragmented across those assets, AI becomes the mechanism that exposes the fragmentation. Conflicting truth, missing context, and unsafe outputs are not random failures. They are the predictable result of split ownership, split classification, split retention, and broken provenance.

The architectural response is equally clear. Govern structured and unstructured data as one connected estate. Extend stewardship beyond tables to documents, relationships, and narrative evidence. Use metadata as the control plane that binds asset classes together. Design access-aware retrieval, provenance-preserving transformation, and freshness-aware ranking as enterprise responsibilities. Treat derived AI artifacts as governed objects, not implementation residue.

This is one of the clearest dividing lines between AI experimentation and AI-readiness. Experiments can survive on disconnected sources and local workarounds. Enterprise AI cannot. It requires unified governance because it operates on a unified business reality.

Key Takeaways

- Structured and unstructured assets often describe the same business fact, so they must be governed together.
- Split governance models are a major source of AI inconsistency, incomplete answers, and unsafe behavior.
- Cross-asset governance must cover ownership, classification, retention, access, provenance, and freshness.
- Metadata is the control plane that connects records, documents, events, relationships, and narrative evidence.
- Trustworthy enterprise AI depends on defensible truth chains, not isolated repositories.

CHAPTER 21: RESPONSIBLE AI STARTS UPSTREAM IN THE DATA ESTATE

Responsible AI is often discussed as if it begins at the point of model behavior: biased outputs, unsafe recommendations, inconsistent answers, or failures to escalate sensitive decisions. In practice, many of those downstream harms begin much earlier. They begin in the data estate.

An enterprise assistant does not invent all of its failures. Many are inherited. If the source estate is incomplete, the assistant will be incomplete. If policies are outdated, *their* guidance will be outdated. If definitions conflict across regions or business units, *their* answers will drift between interpretations. If low-authority documents are retrieved as if they were authoritative, the system will produce confident but unreliable guidance. If there is no review trigger for high-risk topics, the AI will continue past the point where a human should have stepped in. This is why responsible AI starts upstream. It starts with source coverage, semantic clarity, provenance, authority ranking, freshness controls, stewardship, and explicit escalation rules. These are not secondary hygiene issues. They are architectural determinants of safety, fairness, reliability, and trust. For enterprise architects, this changes the design question. The issue is not simply whether the model is accurate in a benchmark setting. The issue is whether the enterprise data estate has been organized so that AI systems can retrieve complete, current, permission-aware, context-rich, and defensible evidence for the task at hand. If that condition is not met, responsible AI will remain aspirational no matter how advanced the model appears.

WHY THIS MATTERS

Harm Rarely Starts Where It Becomes Visible

The visible failure usually appears at the answer layer. A manager asks an employee policy assistant about parental leave. A compliance analyst asks a control assistant whether a document retention obligation applies. A service representative asks a support copilot whether a customer qualifies for an exception. In each case, the harmful moment is the output: the wrong answer, the missing warning, the unsupported recommendation. But the root cause often sits upstream:

- A regional policy was never ingested.
- An outdated policy was not retired.
- The authoritative source was not labeled as authoritative.
- Conflicting definitions were left unresolved.
- The retrieval tier ranked convenience over trust.
- No rule required human review for sensitive cases.

The enterprise then misdiagnoses the problem as a model issue when the deeper failure was architectural.

Coverage Gaps Distort Behavior Even When Facts Are Technically Correct

Responsible AI is not just about eliminating falsehood. It is also about preventing omission, skew, and uneven representation. A system may produce answers that are factually grounded in its retrieved sources and still be irresponsible because the underlying source set is incomplete. That distinction matters. In enterprise environments, coverage matters as much as correctness. An AI system that has complete policies for headquarters staff but partial policies for frontline workers, contractors, or regional offices will generate systematically uneven support. It may appear reliable for the population best represented in the source estate and unreliable for everyone else. That is a fairness problem caused by data coverage, not merely by model reasoning.

KEY INSIGHT

Coverage matters as much as correctness

A correct answer from an incomplete evidence base can still be an irresponsible answer.

Freshness and Authority Shape Reliability

Two documents can say similar things while carrying very different decision weights. A draft memo is not equivalent to an approved policy. A local FAQ is not equivalent to a signed HR standard. A three-year-old benefits summary is not equivalent to this quarter's policy update. Yet many enterprise AI systems are still built on repositories that do not consistently encode source authority, approval status, effective date, supersession, or jurisdiction.

- When those controls are missing, the AI does not know which source should win. The result is not random error. It is structured unreliability. Low-authority, stale, or superseded content receives the same retrieval opportunity as reviewed and current content.

WARNING SIGN

A highly confident answer from a low-authority source

Confidence in tone is not evidence of trustworthiness. In enterprise AI, trust must come from source authority, provenance, and policy-aware retrieval.

Core Concepts

Data-Side Problems Materially Shape AI Outcomes

Enterprise AI systems operate through a chain: source creation, classification, ingestion, enrichment, indexing, retrieval, ranking, answer assembly, and user interaction. Failures introduced at any upstream stage propagate downstream. That propagation is especially dangerous because each layer can make the original defect harder to see.

- A missing document becomes a coverage gap.
- A coverage gap becomes retrieval bias.
- A retrieval bias becomes answer distortion.
- Answer distortion becomes an operational or ethical failure.

This is why responsible AI cannot be treated as a layer placed on top of the stack. It must be designed into the data estate itself.

Responsible AI Is Partly a Data Stewardship Problem

Most organizations already understand stewardship for analytics: owners, quality rules, definitions, controls, and lifecycle accountability. AI extends this need rather than replacing it. Stewardship must now cover not only tables and dashboards, but also policies, contracts, transcripts, knowledge articles, emails, playbooks, messages, and embedded business guidance. The stewardship question becomes more demanding: who ensures that the source set used by AI is complete enough, current enough, authoritative enough, and contextualized enough for a given use case? That is not a model governance question alone. It is a data stewardship question.

Key Insight

Responsible AI is partly a data stewardship problem

If nobody owns source completeness, authority, freshness, and review rules, then nobody owns a large share of AI risk.

Coverage, Imbalance, and Representational Risk

Coverage must be assessed against intended use, not against repository size. Ten thousand documents do not imply adequate support for a use case. What matters is whether the right topics, jurisdictions, user groups, time periods, and exception pathways are represented.

For example, an employee policy assistant may require coverage across:

- Corporate-wide policies.
- Country-specific employment rules.
- Union agreements.
- Contractor guidance.
- Manager-only procedural notes.
- Approved exception processes.
- Effective dates and superseded versions.

If one of those layers is missing, the assistant is not merely less helpful. It may be materially misleading for the populations affected by the gap.

Freshness Is a Control, Not a Convenience

Freshness is often treated as a performance tuning parameter. In responsible AI, it is a risk control. Some use cases tolerate older content. Others do not. HR policy, benefits eligibility, financial controls, legal obligations, safety procedures, and incident playbooks can change quickly enough that stale guidance creates real harm. Freshness, therefore, needs explicit policy:

- Acceptable staleness by use case.
- Effective dates and expiry logic.
- Supersession handling.
- Triggers for re-indexing or re-approval.
- User-visible temporal context.

Without those controls, the system may be technically functioning while being operationally unfit.

Authority Must Be Explicit in Metadata

Authority cannot remain implicit in folder location or institutional memory. It must be machine-readable. AI-ready metadata should distinguish:

- Draft versus approved.
- Local guidance versus enterprise standard.
- Advisory reference versus binding policy.
- Current versus superseded.
- Source system of record versus convenience copy.
- Stewarded content versus unmanaged content.

This is where metadata becomes the control plane for responsible AI. Without it, retrieval pipelines cannot rank responsibly, explain responsibly, or defer responsibly.

Human Review Belongs in the Data Contract

Not every answer should be fully automated. Some topics require escalation because the source base is incomplete, the evidence conflicts, the affected population is sensitive, or the consequences are material. These conditions should not be left to ad hoc prompt wording or assumed user caution. They should be specified in the data-serving contract. A sound AI data contract defines not only what the system may answer, but also when it must stop, qualify, cite, or escalate.

ARCHITECTURAL IMPLICATIONS

Treat Source Readiness as a First-Class Design Concern

Most AI programs spend too little time on source readiness and too much time on model interaction. The architectural sequence should be reversed. Before tuning prompts or experimenting with orchestration, the team should ask:

- Which sources are in scope?
- Which are authoritative?
- Which user groups and jurisdictions do they cover?
- Where are the known gaps?
- What freshness requirement applies?
- Which conflicts remain unresolved?
- What review triggers must be enforced?

That assessment is not overhead. It is the foundation of trustworthy AI.

Build Authority-Aware, Freshness-Aware Retrieval

Retrieval pipelines should not rank only by semantic similarity. They should incorporate enterprise trust signals. At a minimum, ranking logic should be capable of considering:

- Source authority level.
- Approval status.
- Effective date.
- Supersession state.
- Policy or jurisdiction relevance.
- User entitlement.
- Steward confidence.
- Evidence consistency.

This is especially important in high-impact use cases where a superficially relevant but low-authority source can distort the final answer.

Make Gaps and Conflicts Visible Instead of Hiding Them

Many systems are designed to smooth over ambiguity because fluent output feels more helpful. In enterprise settings, that instinct is dangerous. When evidence is partial or conflicting, the system should surface that state rather than resolve it invisibly. Architecturally, this means supporting:

- Explicit conflict markers.
- Coverage warnings.
- Source-count transparency.
- Citation-level explanations.
- Escalation states.
- Confidence grounded in evidence quality, not only model probability.

The goal is not conversational polish. The goal is defensible guidance.

Use Metadata to Enforce Responsible Delivery

Metadata should drive whether content is retrievable, how it is ranked, what it can support, and when it requires review. That includes:

- Classification and sensitivity tags.
- Intended use restrictions.
- Retention state.
- Jurisdiction.
- Effective date.
- Ownership and stewardship.
- Review cadence.
- Approval chain.
- Superseded-by relationships.

A repository without this metadata may still store information. It does not yet support responsible AI delivery.

Design Review Triggers as Operating Controls

Escalation should not depend on the user noticing risk. The system should recognize predefined conditions and switch modes. For example:

- Topic falls into legal, medical, regulatory, or employment-sensitive category.
- No current authoritative source is retrieved.
- Sources conflict on an active policy.
- The user belongs to a population affected by known coverage gaps.
- The requested action would change entitlements, pay, access, or compliance status.
- Retrieved evidence is older than the permitted freshness threshold.

These are architectural controls because they depend on well-structured metadata, governed retrieval, and serving-layer policy enforcement.

❖ FIGURE 42 – UPSTREAM-TO-DOWNSTREAM RISK CHAIN

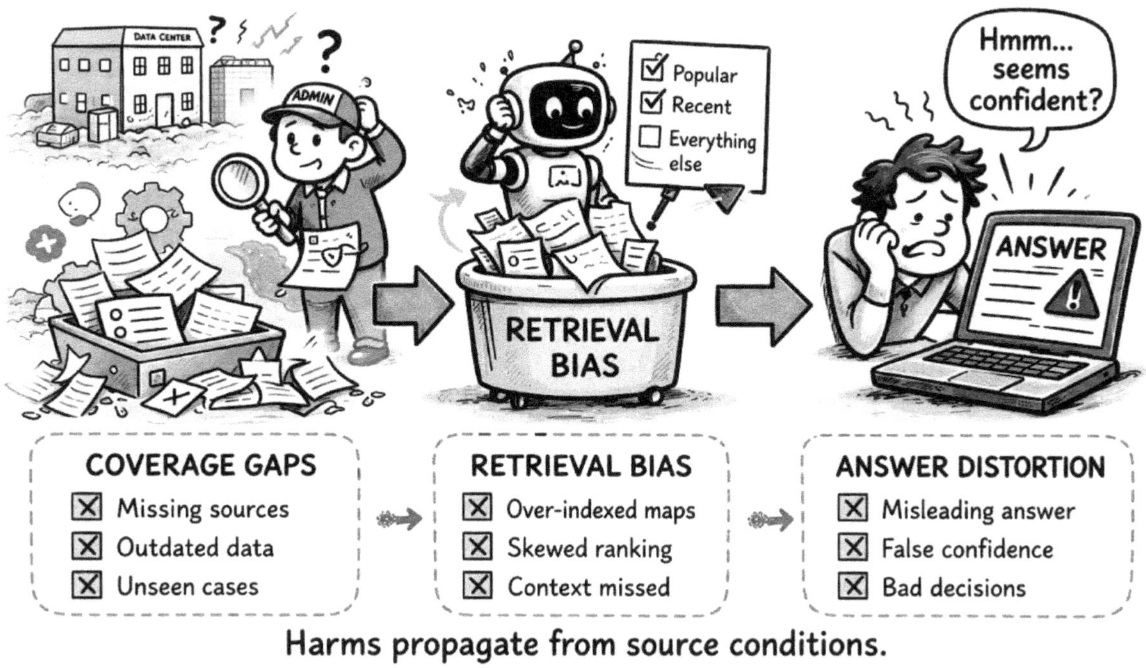

FAILURE MODES AND ANTI-PATTERNS

Assuming Repository Presence Equals Responsible Readiness

Organizations often point to SharePoint sites, knowledge bases, file stores, collaborative workspaces, or document management systems and assume that policy content is, therefore, available to AI. It is not. Presence in a repository is not the same as readiness for grounded, governed, explainable use.

The missing layers are usually metadata, authority designation, version control, jurisdiction tagging, access fidelity, and lifecycle governance.

Optimizing for Answer Rate Instead of Safe Answer Rate

Teams celebrate when the assistant answers a high percentage of user questions. That metric can be actively misleading. A responsible system should sometimes decline, defer, or escalate. An assistant who answers everything is often one who hides uncertainty, ignores gaps, or retrieves weak evidence.

The correct question is not "How often did it answer?" but "How often did it answer appropriately for the available evidence and risk level?"

Treating Stale Content as a Minor Issue

In many analytics settings, staleness is inconvenient. In AI guidance settings, it can be harmful. Outdated leave policies, obsolete control procedures, retired pricing rules, or superseded legal guidance can create systematic misdirection. Staleness should, therefore, be treated as a governance breach, not a cosmetic defect.

Failing to Model Sensitive Population Impacts

Coverage gaps do not affect all users equally. If policies are most complete for full-time domestic employees and weakest for contractors, part-time workers, acquisitions, or employees in smaller jurisdictions, then the AI system will distribute quality unevenly. That is both an operational and ethical failure.

Leaving Escalation to Prompt Wording

Many teams try to solve risk through instructions such as "recommend contacting HR for important matters." That is insufficient. Escalation must be driven by machine-readable triggers tied to topic, authority, freshness, conflict, and coverage conditions. Otherwise, the system will still answer when it should stop.

Practical Application

Start with a Responsible-Source Assessment for Each Use Case

Responsible AI cannot be assessed generically across the whole estate. It must be anchored to a concrete use case. A procurement policy assistant, executive research copilot, engineering runbook assistant, and claims decision support tool each require different source coverage, trust thresholds, freshness rules, and escalation controls. A practical assessment should answer five questions:

- What decisions or recommendations can this AI influence?
- Which user groups are affected?
- Which sources are authoritative for those decisions?

- Where are the known coverage gaps, imbalances, and conflicts?
- Under what conditions must the system escalate?

Put the Checklist into the Delivery Lifecycle

The checklist is most useful when tied to formal delivery gates:

- Use-case intake.
- Source onboarding.
- Pre-production architecture review.
- Controlled pilot release.
- Post-launch monitoring review.
- Periodic governance refresh.

This turns responsible AI from a principles statement into an operating model.

Design a Review-Trigger Model

The review-trigger model should be explicit enough to implement and easy enough to audit. It should classify requests into at least three states:

- **Answer directly**: current authoritative evidence is available and risk is low.
- **Answer with qualification**: evidence is partial but still useful, with clear caveats and citations.
- **Escalate**: evidence is missing, conflicting, stale, or high-risk.

❖ FIGURE 43 – HUMAN REVIEW TRIGGER MODEL

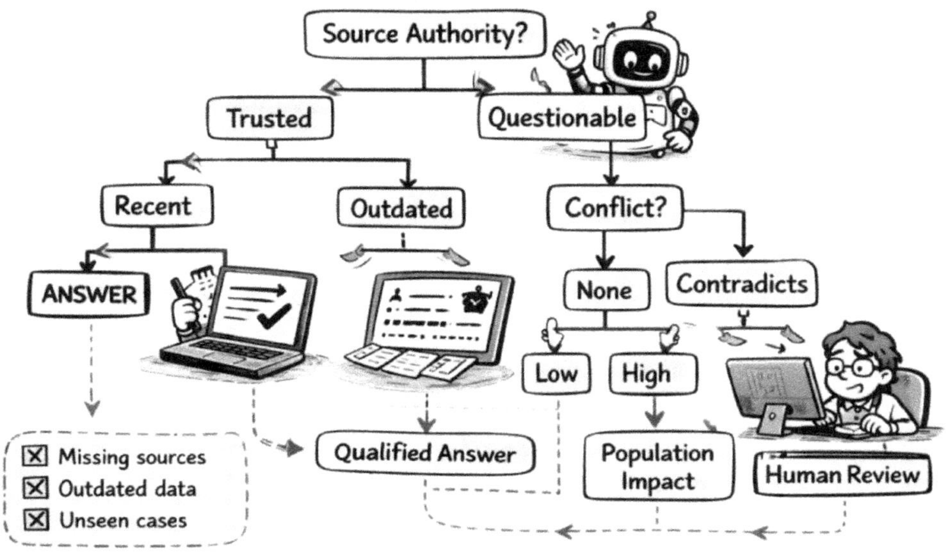

Templates

Responsible Data for AI Checklist

Use case	<name and description of the assistant, copilot, or AI scenario being assessed>
Affected user groups	<user populations, roles, teams, or stakeholder groups affected by the use case and its outputs>
Source coverage assessment	<assessment of how completely the relevant policies, documents, records, and guidance sources are covered for this use case, including areas of strong and weak coverage>
Known source imbalances	<known imbalances in source representation, such as stronger coverage for some geographies, populations, channels, document types, or business scenarios than others>
Authority levels by source	<tiering or ranking of source types by authority, from highest-authority approved sources to lower-authority supporting or non-authoritative materials>
Freshness risk	<assessment of how sensitive the use case is to outdated content, including areas where stale, unreviewed, or weakly superseded content creates material risk>
Conflicting source risk	<assessment of the likelihood and impact of conflicting guidance across sources, summaries, interpretations, or versions>
Sensitive population impacts	<populations, jurisdictions, employee groups, customer groups, or other cohorts for whom errors, omissions, or bias would create disproportionate harm, inequity, or legal exposure>
Review triggers	<conditions that require escalation, additional review, or refusal to provide automated guidance, such as missing authoritative sources, conflicts, stale content, sensitive topics, coverage gaps, or materially consequential outcomes>
Escalation workflow	<defined process for how the system should respond when automated guidance is insufficient, including evidence summary, explanation of insufficiency, routing path, logging, and stewardship follow-up>
Monitoring indicators	<metrics used to monitor retrieval quality, evidence quality, conflict detection, stale-source use, user corrections, overrides, escalation trends, and coverage gaps>
Owner	<role, team, or jointly accountable leaders responsible for the use case and its source fitness>
Review board	<governing body or cross-functional review group responsible for oversight, escalation review, policy alignment, and risk management>

Next review date	<date or cadence for the next formal review, including any event-based triggers for earlier reassessment>

Case Example

Responsible Automation Means Knowing When Not to Answer

A global enterprise launches an employee policy assistant to reduce HR ticket volume. The assistant is connected to the company's policy repository, HR knowledge articles, and selected manager guidance. Early testing looks promising. Most common questions are answered quickly, and employee satisfaction appears high.

Three months later, problems begin to surface. Employees in the United States receive broadly accurate answers about parental leave. Employees in Germany receive reasonable but incomplete guidance. Employees in several Asia-Pacific locations receive inconsistent answers depending on how the question is phrased. In some cases, the assistant cites a global leave summary that was intended only as a high-level orientation document. In other cases, it retrieves an older regional FAQ that predates a policy revision. Managers receive answers that mix employee entitlement language with manager approval process language, creating confusion about who can authorize exceptions. The visible symptom is inconsistency. The actual causes are upstream:

- Localized policies were incomplete in the indexed source set.
- Some current regional supplements had not been ingested.
- Historical documents were not consistently tagged as superseded.
- Authority levels were not encoded in metadata, so approved policies and convenience summaries competed in retrieval.
- No escalation rule existed for jurisdictions with known coverage gaps.
- No freshness threshold blocked older policy documents from influencing answers.

The assistant was not failing because it could not generate fluent text. It was failing because the data estate had not been made responsible for the use case.

The remediation effort required architectural, not merely conversational, changes. The organization introduced jurisdiction tags, policy effective dates, supersession links, and authority tiers. It limited retrieval for entitlement questions to approved policy and reviewed knowledge sources. It established a coverage map by region and employee type. It added a review trigger: if no current authoritative local policy is retrieved, the assistant must stop short of direct guidance and escalate to regional HR.

The result was not that the assistant answered more questions. In fact, it answered fewer questions directly. But the answers it did provide became more trustworthy, and the escalations became more meaningful. That is what responsible AI looks like in an enterprise setting: not maximal automation, but governed automation aligned to evidence quality and risk.

Closing Synthesis

Responsible AI does not begin with a model card, a red-team exercise, or a policy statement issued after deployment. It begins in the upstream design of the data estate. If sources are incomplete, AI will be incomplete. If definitions conflict, AI will inherit that ambiguity. If authoritative content is not distinguishable from convenience content, retrieval will be unreliable. If freshness is unmanaged, guidance will drift out of policy. If sensitive populations are underrepresented, support quality will be uneven. If no escalation conditions exist, the system will continue past the boundary where human judgment is required.

For enterprise architects, that is the central lesson: responsibility is not only a property of model behavior. It is a property of data readiness, metadata discipline, source governance, and serving contracts. The organizations that scale trustworthy AI will be the ones that treat source management, authority modeling, freshness control, provenance, and review triggers as core architecture.

Downstream harms often look like answer problems. In enterprise reality, many are data-estate problems that became visible only at the answer layer. The right response is not to ask the model to be more careful. It is to make the estate more governable, more explicit, more complete, and more accountable.

Key Takeaways

- Many AI harms begin upstream as coverage gaps, stale content, weak authority signals, and unresolved source conflicts.
- Responsible AI depends on source-management discipline, not just model-side safeguards.
- Coverage matters as much as correctness because incomplete evidence creates distorted outcomes.
- Freshness, authority, provenance, and review triggers must be encoded in metadata and data-serving contracts.
- The goal is not maximum automation; it is trustworthy automation that knows when to answer, qualify, or escalate.

Chapter 22: The Policy Layer: Retention, Legal Hold, Privacy, and Records

Enterprise AI does not operate outside policy. It operates inside it.

That point sounds obvious, yet many AI programs behave as if retention schedules, legal hold obligations, privacy requirements, minimization rules, and records controls are downstream governance concerns to be reconciled after a retrieval layer or assistant has already been deployed. That is backward. In an AI-serving architecture, policy is not an external brake. It is part of the design.

An enterprise can build a technically impressive assistant that retrieves across contracts, policies, emails, tickets, transcripts, and reports. But if that assistant surfaces content past its permitted lifecycle, indexes records under hold as if they were ordinary knowledge, exposes personal data beyond legitimate purpose, or cannot prove why a response was based on a given source, then the architecture is not ready for enterprise use. It is merely functional.

The policy layer answers a set of architectural questions that AI systems cannot avoid. What content may be retained? What content must be deleted? What content must be preserved even if it would otherwise be disposed of? What content may be indexed for ordinary retrieval? What content may be shown to a specific user, model, or agent for a specific purpose? What evidence must exist to prove that those controls operated as intended?

These are not legal footnotes. They are data design inputs.

The mature enterprise view is simple: AI-serving systems must honor the same lifecycle, obligation, and evidentiary controls that govern the data estate itself. If the enterprise policy model says a document is retained for records purposes but not appropriate for general knowledge retrieval, the architecture must enforce that distinction. If a legal hold suspends deletion, the architecture must preserve the asset without turning it into a broadly discoverable answer source. If privacy rules require minimization, then minimization must shape ingestion, enrichment, storage, retrieval, and response construction.

Policy-aware AI architecture is, therefore, not a compliance wrapper. It is a condition of trust.

WHY THIS MATTERS

AI Amplifies Policy Mistakes

In traditional systems, a policy mistake may remain localized. A file is kept too long in one repository. A record is misclassified in one application. A report includes fields it should not have shown. In AI systems, the blast radius is larger. An indexing pipeline can copy restricted content into a retrieval layer. A summarization service can synthesize across records with different handling obligations. An agent can act on content that should have been excluded from its operating context altogether.

AI does not merely consume data. It recombines, ranks, summarizes, and operationalizes it. That makes policy fidelity far more important than in passive storage environments.

Retrieval Without Lifecycle Awareness Creates False Confidence

Many organizations assume that if content still exists somewhere, it is fair game for retrieval. That is a dangerous assumption. Content may exist because it is subject to a retention rule, a records requirement, or a hold obligation. None of those conditions means the content is suitable for general-purpose discovery by a knowledge assistant.

A repository is not a serving contract. Persistence is not permission. Retention is not endorsement.

High-stakes Use Cases Need Evidence, Not Good Intentions

In regulated and litigious environments, it is not enough to say that privacy was considered or that deletion was intended. The enterprise must be able to show what rule applied, where it was enforced, who approved exceptions, what source was used, whether that source was under hold, whether redaction was applied, and whether access restrictions were honored at the moment of retrieval.

That requirement places policy squarely inside architecture. Evidence has to be designed into metadata, lifecycle controls, audit trails, and system boundaries. It cannot be reconstructed reliably from memory after an incident.

Different AI Consumers Need Different Policy Envelopes

A search assistant for internal policy documents, a legal review assistant, a customer service copilot, and an autonomous claims-handling agent do not deserve the same data access. Their trust thresholds differ. Their acceptable use of retained content differs. Their need for personal data differs. Their evidentiary burden differs.

The policy layer, therefore, shapes serving contracts by consumer type. It is not enough to secure the repository. The enterprise must define which policies apply to which AI consumer under which purpose and with what restrictions.

Core Concepts

Retention Is a Lifecycle Rule, Not a Storage Accident

Retention defines how long an asset must or may be kept based on business, legal, operational, or regulatory requirements. In AI architecture, that rule must be represented in machine-usable form. It cannot remain buried in a PDF policy manual or encoded only in the behavior of a records team.

For AI-serving purposes, retention metadata typically needs at least:

- Retention category.
- Triggering event.
- Disposition date or review date.
- Disposition action.
- Exception state.
- Authoritative owner.

Without those attributes, the retrieval layer cannot distinguish current operational knowledge from content merely being retained.

Legal Hold Suspends Disposition, Not Judgment

A legal hold changes the handling of content under obligation. It prevents destruction or alteration that would otherwise occur through normal lifecycle controls. It does not automatically make the content suitable for ordinary retrieval, assistant grounding, or training. That distinction matters because many organizations accidentally treat "preserved" as "available." In reality, held material may need stronger restrictions than ordinary content because its preservation exists for evidentiary reasons, not operational knowledge use.

Key Insight

Legal hold is not general-purpose knowledge

Content preserved under legal hold exists because the enterprise must keep it, not because the enterprise should surface it broadly. Preserve and retrieve are different architectural states.

Privacy Is About Purpose, Necessity, and Exposure

Privacy in AI-serving environments is not limited to access control. It includes purpose limitation, data minimization, redaction, masking, audience restriction, reuse restriction, and output control. A privacy-aware architecture asks:

- Why is this content being prepared for AI use?
- What personal or sensitive attributes are actually needed?
- Can the use case operate on redacted or masked forms?
- Should the model or assistant see the raw content, a transformed version, or no content at all?
- Are outputs prevented from re-exposing unnecessary personal information?

This is where policy becomes operational design. The answer may differ between indexing, retrieval, summarization, and action-taking.

Records Management Defines Evidentiary and Lifecycle Obligations

Records are not just old documents. They are assets with business, legal, or regulatory significance that require controlled retention, defensible disposition, and often stricter provenance. In AI systems, records discipline matters because answers may rely on artifacts that carry official meaning.

When a system cites a policy, contract clause, case record, or regulatory communication, the enterprise needs to know whether that source is an authoritative record, a draft, a convenience copy, a superseded version, or a retained-but-obsolete artifact. Without that distinction, AI can sound precise while being wrong in a legally important way.

Minimization Belongs Upstream

Minimization is often discussed as a response-time concern. That is too late. By the time sensitive content is already duplicated into chunk stores, vector indexes, caches, or intermediate pipelines, the architecture has already expanded risk. Minimization should influence:

- What gets ingested.
- What gets enriched.
- What gets chunked.
- What gets indexed.
- What fields are carried forward.
- What versions are retained for serving.
- What outputs may include.

The strongest architecture removes unnecessary exposure before retrieval ever begins.

Policy Metadata Must Be First-Class Metadata

If metadata is the control plane for AI, policy metadata is part of that control plane. Every retrievable asset should carry enough policy state to support correct use by the serving layer. That usually includes classification, privacy markers, retention category, lifecycle status, hold status, records designation, permitted use, jurisdiction where relevant, and access inheritance. Without policy metadata, the AI stack is forced to guess. Mature enterprises do not let retrieval guess.

ARCHITECTURAL IMPLICATIONS

The Policy Layer Must Span the Lifecycle

Policy is not a checkpoint between storage and retrieval. It spans the entire lifecycle from creation through disposition. The architecture should reflect that continuity explicitly.

❖ FIGURE 44 – POLICY CONTROL OVERLAY

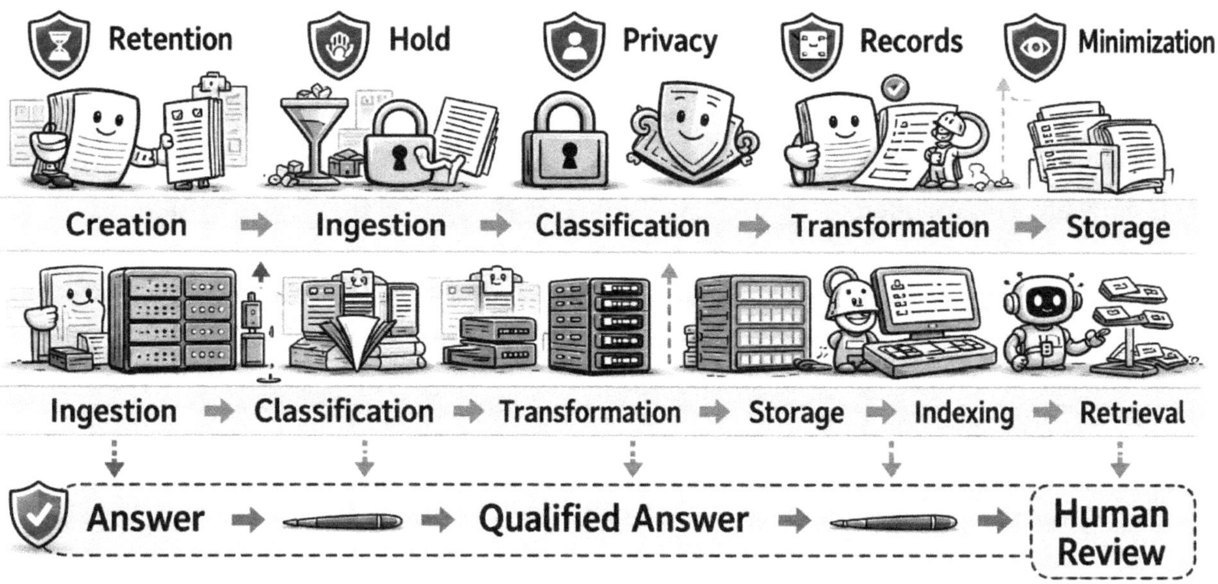

A useful way to think about this is as a horizontal control layer that cuts across creation, ingestion, classification, transformation, storage, indexing, retrieval, serving, audit, and disposition. Every stage either preserves policy meaning or corrupts it. There is no neutral stage.

Lifecycle State Must Travel with the Asset

An AI-serving system should not need to infer whether a document is current, archived, retained, under review, restricted, or held. That state should be represented explicitly and propagated through downstream systems.

If a content pipeline strips away retention category, hold flag, or privacy class when generating chunks or embeddings, then the serving layer loses the ability to make correct decisions. This is one of the most common architectural failures in AI indexing programs: rich source controls are replaced by thin technical metadata that is good enough for search relevance but not good enough for governed use.

Ordinary Retrieval and Preservation Retrieval Must Be Separated

The architecture should distinguish at least two patterns:

- Ordinary operational retrieval for assistants, copilots, analysts, and agents.
- Controlled evidentiary or legal retrieval for authorized review processes.

Those patterns do not share the same eligibility rules, ranking logic, user populations, or disclosure expectations. Conflating them creates both legal and operational risk.

A sound design often uses separate eligibility policies, separate indexes or logical partitions, separate query paths, and distinct audit expectations. The point is not technical elegance. The point is avoiding accidental reuse of preserved material in the wrong context.

Deletion Events Must Propagate to AI Layers

If the source system deletes or restricts content, downstream AI layers must honor that change quickly and verifiably. This includes:

- Search indexes.
- Vector stores.
- Caches.
- Materialized summaries.
- Chunk repositories.
- Fine-tuning or adaptation stores where applicable.
- Downstream feature or serving layers.

⚠ **WARNING SIGN**

AI index retains deleted or restricted content

If content is deleted, reclassified, or access-restricted in the source but remains searchable in the AI layer, the architecture is out of control. The problem is not just stale data. It is broken policy propagation.

Policy Enforcement Needs Multiple Control Points

No single enforcement point is sufficient. Mature architectures usually apply policy at several layers:

- At ingestion, by excluding ineligible content.
- At enrichment, by masking or minimizing fields.
- At indexing, by attaching policy attributes and partitioning content correctly.
- At retrieval, by filtering based on user, purpose, lifecycle state, and hold state.
- At response construction, by preventing unsafe synthesis or output leakage.
- At audit, by recording what was considered, retrieved, shown, and acted on.

Defense in depth matters because enterprise policies are rarely binary. The same asset may be retained, restricted to a narrow purpose, visible only to certain roles, and prohibited from certain forms of transformation.

Records and Policy Need Explicit Ownership

Policy-aware design fails when architects assume that "governance" will handle the hard decisions later. Someone must own retention categories. Someone must define what counts as a record. Someone must interpret whether legal hold content is eligible for any AI use. Someone must define minimization rules for each use case. Someone must sign off on exceptions.

In practice, ownership often spans legal, privacy, records, security, and data governance, but the architecture still needs a clear decision model. Ambiguity in decision rights becomes ambiguity in system behavior.

Failure Modes and Anti-Patterns

Treating Policy as Post-Ingestion Cleanup

This is the most common anti-pattern. Teams build ingestion and indexing first, then try to filter risky content later. By then, the content may already be chunked, copied, enriched, embedded, cached, and operationalized.

Key Insight

Policy by design, not policy by cleanup

If policy enters after indexing, the architecture is already compensating for a design mistake. The safest content is the content that was never inappropriately ingested in the first place.

Assuming Retained Means Useful

A retained document may exist for records reasons while being obsolete for operational guidance. If an assistant surfaces a superseded policy memo because it was retained properly, the assistant may still mislead the user. Good records hygiene does not automatically produce good retrieval quality.

This is where temporal correctness matters. The system must distinguish current authority from historical preservation.

Flattening Lifecycle Distinctions in the Index

Some teams create a universal content index where every document becomes the same kind of retrievable object. That destroys critical distinctions such as:

- Draft vs final.
- Record vs convenience copy.
- Current vs superseded.
- Held vs ordinarily retained.
- Public-internal vs restricted.
- Operational knowledge vs evidentiary preservation.

A universal index is easy to explain and dangerous to run.

Minimization Only at the User Interface

Masking output at the UI is useful, but insufficient. If raw sensitive content was already exposed to enrichment services, ranking models, or summarization steps, the architecture has already exceeded the minimum necessary exposure. Minimization must happen earlier.

No Auditable Evidence Path

If an enterprise cannot answer these questions, it does not have a defensible policy-aware AI architecture:

- Why was this source eligible?
- What version was retrieved?
- What policy state did it have at retrieval time?
- Was it under hold?
- Was it a record?
- What masking rules were applied?
- Which user or agent accessed it?
- Under what purpose and authorization?

Exception-driven Governance

Some organizations attempt to scale through waivers, manual exclusions, and case-by-case approvals. That may be unavoidable during early pilots, but it does not scale. Durable AI architecture encodes normal policy decisions as default system behavior and reserves exceptions for genuinely exceptional cases. Exception-driven governance is a sign that the control model is not yet architectural.

PRACTICAL APPLICATION

Start with Policy-Bearing Asset Classes

Do not begin by indexing everything. Begin with asset classes whose policy treatment is understood. For example:

- Approved policies and procedures.
- Finalized contracts.
- Controlled knowledge articles.
- Case records with explicit eligibility rules.
- Operational documentation with clear ownership.

Avoid early expansion into email, collaborative notes, or mixed-purpose content until lifecycle and privacy rules are sufficiently mature.

Build a Policy Eligibility Model for AI Use

For each asset class and use case, define:

- Whether the content may be ingested for AI.
- Whether it may be indexed for ordinary retrieval.
- Whether it may be retrieved only under special authorization.
- Whether it may be summarized.
- Whether it may be used for agentic action.
- Whether it requires masking, redaction, or transformed views.
- Whether it is excluded entirely.

This turns broad policy into serving rules.

Represent Policy as Metadata and Service Logic

The architecture should implement policy through both metadata and decision services. Metadata carries the state. Policy services evaluate eligibility at runtime or pipeline time.

A practical pattern is:

- Source systems publish lifecycle and classification metadata.
- Ingestion maps source categories to enterprise policy categories.
- Policy services evaluate ingestion and retrieval eligibility.
- Serving layers enforce user, purpose, and context restrictions.
- Audit services record decisions and evidence.

Design for Review, Not Only Automation

Some content cannot be resolved safely by automated rules alone. For example:

- Ambiguous records designation.
- Uncertain privacy sensitivity.
- Matter-related hold scope.
- Mixed documents containing both reusable guidance and privileged material.

Architectures should allow human review checkpoints where policy state is uncertain. This is not a sign of immaturity. It is a sign of realism.

❖ FIGURE 45 – LIFECYCLE CONTROL MAP

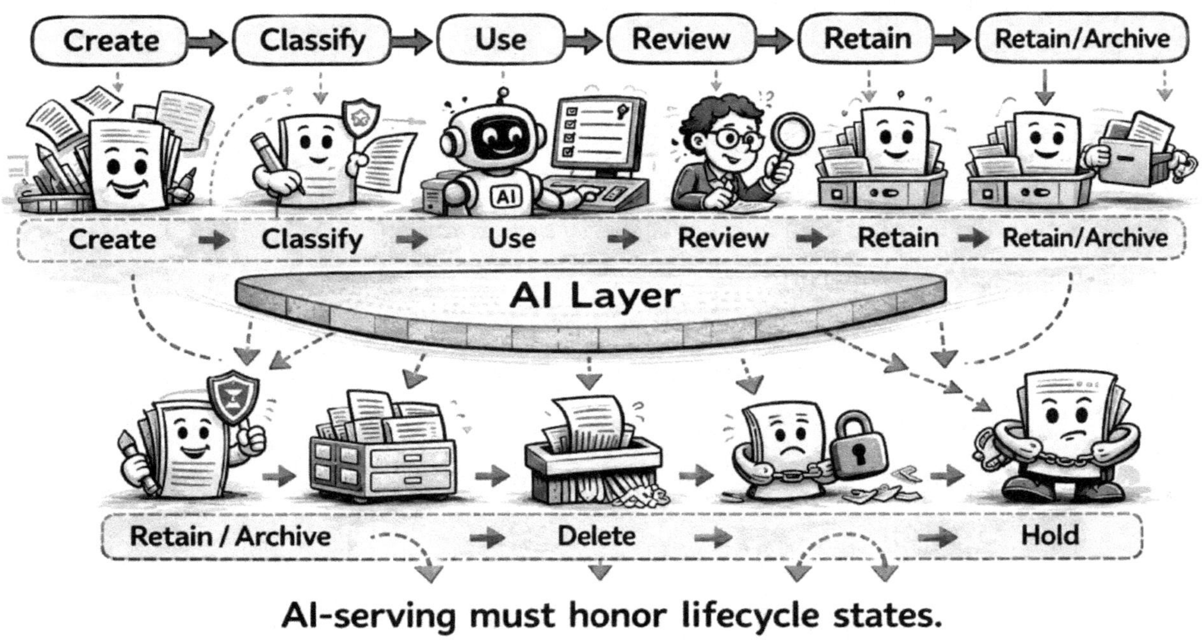

TEMPLATES

Policy Control Checklist for AI-Ready Data

Asset/use case	<asset type, content set, or AI use case to which the policy and governance rules apply>
Policy category	<policy domains or control areas relevant to the asset or use case, such as legal, records, privacy, confidentiality, or evidentiary preservation>
Retention rule	<rule defining how long each relevant asset class must be retained, including supersession, contract-term, matter-linkage, or regulatory conditions>
Hold rule	<rule defining how legal hold, preservation obligations, or similar restrictions override normal deletion and retrieval behavior>
Privacy rule	<rule defining when personal data, employee information, customer details, or other sensitive facts may be processed, by whom, and for what purpose>
Classification rule	<required classification categories used to distinguish authoritative, draft, archived, privileged, hold-preserved, or convenience-copy content>
Minimization requirement	<rule defining which content is eligible for general retrieval and which content must be excluded or restricted to reviewed pathways>
Redaction/masking requirement	<rule defining what sensitive or unnecessary information must be masked, removed, or excluded before content is made available for retrieval or reuse>
Access restriction	<rule defining which user populations may access the assistant or content, including stricter restrictions for privileged, hold-preserved, or matter-specific materials>
Audit evidence required	<audit data that must be captured for each access or response event, such as user identity, matter context, purpose, source identifiers, classifications, hold status, masking, and citations>
Exceptions process	<process required to approve exceptions, including who must approve, what must be documented, and how scope and review dates are controlled>
Enforcement point	<points in the lifecycle where controls must be applied, such as ingestion, indexing, retrieval, response generation, or downstream propagation>
Owner	<roles, leaders, or functions jointly accountable for policy approval, operational governance, and technical enforcement>

Validation date	<review cadence or date on which the artifact was last validated or must next be reapproved, including event-driven triggers for earlier review>

CASE EXAMPLE

Legal Review Assistant with Lifecycle-Aware Retrieval

Consider a legal review assistant built to help in-house counsel analyze contract language, policy obligations, and prior matter materials. The enterprise has decades of contracts, matter files, legal memos, investigation records, and policy documents. Some items are active knowledge sources. Some are retained records. Some are under legal hold. Some contain personal data or privileged analysis. Some are obsolete but retained for statutory reasons.

A naïve implementation builds a single search-and-retrieval layer across all legal repositories. The result looks powerful. The assistant can answer broadly and cite many sources. But the design is flawed. Suppose counsel asks, "Show me the company's current fallback position on indemnity carve-outs in supplier agreements." The assistant retrieves:

- A current approved playbook.
- An old negotiation memo retained as a record.
- A matter file preserved under hold.
- A superseded guidance note that still exists because its retention period has not expired.

The answer sounds comprehensive. It is also dangerous. The old memo may no longer reflect current policy. The held matter file should not have entered ordinary retrieval. The superseded guidance should have been ranked out or excluded. Personal data in the matter file may be unnecessary for the question. Privileged analysis may now be exposed too broadly.

A policy-aware design handles this differently. First, the source content is classified into operational guidance, record copy, draft, archived history, and hold-preserved matter content. Second, ordinary retrieval is limited to current approved guidance and explicitly eligible precedent sources. Third, held material is preserved in a separate controlled path available only for authorized evidentiary review. Fourth, obsolete but retained material remains in the estate for records compliance but is tagged as ineligible for general assistant grounding. Fifth, privacy and privilege rules require redaction or exclusion of sensitive matter details unless the specific user, matter, and purpose justify access. Sixth, every answer logs which policy state each source had at retrieval time. Now the assistant can still support counsel effectively, but within the enterprise policy model. It retrieves what is current, permitted, and relevant. It preserves what must be preserved. It excludes what should not enter ordinary knowledge use. That is the architectural distinction the legal function needs. Preserve everything required. Retrieve only what is allowed.

Closing Synthesis

The policy layer is not an administrative overlay on top of AI-Ready Data. It is part of the architecture that makes AI-Ready Data possible. Retention decides whether content remains in the estate. Legal hold decides whether normal disposition is suspended. Privacy decides what may be prepared, exposed, and reused for a given purpose. Records controls decide what must remain authoritative, traceable, and defensible. Minimization ensures the enterprise carries forward only what is necessary. Auditability proves that the system did what it was supposed to do.

The architectural lesson is clear. Enterprises should stop treating policy as a late-stage filter applied after ingestion and retrieval mechanics are already fixed. Policy belongs upstream, encoded in metadata, system boundaries, serving contracts, and lifecycle-aware control logic.

The strongest AI-serving environments will not be the ones with the biggest index or the broadest retrieval surface. They will be the ones who know exactly which content is current, which is preserved, which is restricted, which is minimized, which is authoritative, and which is out of bounds. That is what makes the data estate trustworthy to humans, defensible to auditors, and safe for AI.

A policy-aware architecture is slower only at the beginning. After that, it is faster, cleaner, and more durable than constant exception handling. It replaces ad hoc judgment with repeatable control. It gives assistants and agents better source material. It gives leaders clearer accountability. And it gives the enterprise a way to scale AI without quietly breaking the obligations that govern its data.

Key Takeaways

- Retention, legal hold, privacy, and records are architectural inputs, not downstream compliance checks.
- Preserved content is not automatically eligible for ordinary AI retrieval.
- Privacy and minimization must shape ingestion and indexing, not only user-facing output.
- Policy metadata has to survive every transformation if AI-serving is to remain trustworthy.
- Durable enterprise AI depends on lifecycle-aware retrieval, explicit enforcement points, and auditable evidence.

CHAPTER 23: WHO OWNS AI-READY DATA?

AI-Ready Data does not emerge from tooling. It emerges from clear ownership of source quality, metadata, semantic meaning, policy controls, and AI-serving obligations.

That distinction is one of the most important operational truths in enterprise AI. Organizations often assume that once a modern data platform, content repository, vector index, catalog, or copilot framework is in place, AI-Ready Data will somehow follow. It does not. Tools can store, index, classify, rank, retrieve, and serve. They cannot decide what a document means, whether a policy is authoritative, which definition should govern a business term, who is accountable for freshness, or what level of evidence an AI system must provide before its answer is trusted. **Those are ownership questions.**

The reason so many promising pilots stall is not simply poor model output. It is that no one has been given explicit authority to govern the conditions under which enterprise data becomes usable by AI. Source teams assume platform teams will handle it. Platform teams assume governance will define the rules. Governance assumes domain leaders will clean up their own assets. Security assumes permissions are already being applied correctly upstream. The result is a technically active but organizationally ownerless system.

AI-Ready Data, therefore, requires an ownership model that is layered, explicit, and enforceable. The enterprise must know who owns the business meaning of a domain, who stewards the metadata, who operates the platform, who governs policy, who enforces security, who defines semantic standards, who manages freshness, and who is accountable for the final AI-serving contract. Without that clarity, the architecture will remain incomplete no matter how advanced the tooling appears.

WHY THIS MATTERS

AI Consumes More Than Data Quality

Traditional data ownership models were built for reporting, integration, and compliance. Those models usually focused on data quality at the source, lineage into the warehouse, and access control around analytics consumption. AI systems require more.

A knowledge assistant does not merely need correct text. It needs authoritative text. An analyst copilot does not merely need a trusted table. It needs business definitions, current lineage, metric logic, and clear intended use. An action-taking agent does not merely need a document store. It needs policy-aware access, confidence thresholds, freshness controls, escalation rules, and evidence it can cite.

This is why high-quality data for analytics can still be unusable for AI. The problem is often not accuracy in the narrow sense. It is absent context, missing ownership, undefined semantics, weak provenance, poor permission fidelity, and unclear serving obligations.

Ownership Is What Turns Repositories into Usable Assets

Most enterprises already have plenty of content. Policies live in collaboration platforms. Contracts sit in document repositories. Product rules are buried in wikis. Customer interaction histories appear across CRM, case systems, and email archives. Logs and event streams capture operational truth. Master data hubs hold key entities. Yet AI systems still fail to answer basic questions consistently. The missing ingredient is not always ingestion. It is ownership. A repository becomes an AI-ready asset only when someone is accountable for at least five things:

- Whether the asset is authoritative.
- Whether its meaning is defined.
- Whether its metadata is complete.
- Whether its use is policy-compliant.
- Whether its delivery to AI meets a defined trust contract.

If those accountabilities are diffuse, the asset may exist, but it is not ready.

Scaling Fails Where Pilots Tolerate Ambiguity

Pilots often survive on heroics. A small team manually selects a set of documents, hand-curates a glossary, fixes bad permissions, tunes retrieval, and answers stakeholder questions in real time. This can create the illusion that the architecture works. It does not scale because the real operating model has not been built. Once the pilot expands across domains, the same unresolved questions surface everywhere. Who approves new source inclusion? Who defines document authority? Who resolves conflicting definitions? Who owns stale content removal? Who signs off on service levels for AI answers? Who investigates a grounded but wrong response caused by a bad source? If no one can answer these questions quickly, the pilot remains a demo rather than becoming an enterprise capability.

KEY INSIGHT

Ownership Is Universal, Accountability Disappears

Saying that everyone owns AI-Ready Data usually means no one is specifically accountable for source quality, semantic clarity, metadata completeness, freshness, or AI-serving behavior. Enterprise AI requires named responsibility, not shared aspiration.

Core Concepts

Ownership Must Exist at Multiple Layers

A central mistake in AI programs is the search for a single owner of "AI-Ready Data." There is no such person or team. Ownership is layered because the responsibilities are layered.

The business owner is accountable for the domain's intent, criticality, and business correctness. The steward is accountable for data and content hygiene, metadata completeness, issue management, and operational follow-through. The platform owner is accountable for ingestion, storage, indexing, delivery, observability, and runtime reliability. The governance owner is accountable for policies, standards, exceptions, and compliance alignment. The security owner is accountable for access models, permission fidelity, and identity-aware delivery. The semantic owner is accountable for definitions, taxonomies, relationships, and disambiguation. The freshness owner is accountable for update expectations and stale-content controls. The AI-serving owner is accountable for retrieval behavior, evidence design, trust thresholds, and consumer-specific service levels.

These are not redundant roles. They are different responsibilities that must connect through a common operating model.

Key Insight

Ownership Is Layered, Not Singular

AI-Ready Data cannot be owned by one team alone. Business owners, stewards, platform teams, governance leaders, security leaders, semantic owners, freshness owners, and AI-serving owners each hold distinct responsibilities that must work together as an operating model.

Platform Teams Cannot Own Business Meaning

Platform teams can provide catalogs, pipelines, search services, vector stores, semantic layers, policy engines, and observability tooling. They cannot define what "active customer" means in a regulated business context. They cannot decide which policy document supersedes an older procedure. They cannot determine whether a transcript reflects an approved process or an informal practice. They cannot arbitrate whether a product term in one division is equivalent to a term in another.

Business meaning belongs to the domain. This matters because AI systems are especially sensitive to ambiguous language. A report can tolerate some semantic slippage if its users already understand the context. A knowledge assistant cannot. It will retrieve and synthesize whatever the architecture presents as relevant. If business meaning is not explicitly owned, the system will operate on ambiguity at scale.

Domain Teams Cannot Alone Own Cross-Enterprise Standards

The opposite mistake is to assume that if each domain owns its data, the enterprise problem is solved. It is not. Domain autonomy without enterprise standards produces local correctness and enterprise inconsistency. One team defines "customer" at the household level. Another defines it at the contract level. A third defines it as any party with an open case. Meanwhile, document metadata varies by repository, sensitivity labels are unevenly applied, retention behavior differs, and access patterns are modeled inconsistently.

AI systems expose these inconsistencies faster than traditional analytics because they operate across domains and across content types. A cross-enterprise assistant may pull policy from one repository, a transaction rule from a data product, and procedural guidance from a wiki. If standards for metadata, semantics, policy, and delivery are not shared, the user experiences a single broken answer even though each domain believes it acted reasonably.

That is why domain ownership must sit within an enterprise architecture and governance framework. Local ownership is necessary. Enterprise standardization is also necessary.

Stewardship Must Be Explicit, Funded, and Measured

Stewardship is often praised and rarely operationalized. Enterprises routinely declare that stewards exist, then assign the role as a part-time administrative burden with no dedicated capacity, no service levels, and no metrics. That is not stewardship. That is wishful labeling.

In an AI-ready environment, stewardship must cover both structured and unstructured assets. A steward may need to monitor failed metadata enrichment, unresolved glossary collisions, stale documents in authoritative collections, broken lineage links, retrieval defects, misclassified content, and unresolved access exceptions. That work is operational, not ceremonial.

If stewardship is real, it has funded capacity, named responsibilities, measurable outputs, and escalation authority. If it is not funded and measured, it will be sacrificed the moment delivery pressure rises.

Decision Rights Matter as Much as Responsibilities

Ownership is not real unless it includes decision rights. A role without authority is merely a suggestion.

The enterprise must be explicit about who decides definitions, who approves access patterns, who sets quality thresholds, who grants exceptions to policy, who approves authoritative sources, who defines freshness SLAs, and who owns remediation when AI output fails because the underlying asset was wrong, stale, or ambiguous.

Many programs document roles but avoid hard decisions on authority. That preserves political comfort while guaranteeing operational confusion. AI-Ready Data cannot be governed on implied authority.

Freshness and Authority Are First-Class Ownership Concerns

Enterprises often focus ownership discussions on data quality and access while neglecting freshness and source authority. For AI, these are central.

A document can be perfectly written, properly classified, and technically retrievable, yet still be unsafe if no one knows whether it remains current. Similarly, a source can be accurate in content yet unusable if there is no named authority stating whether it is the governing version.

This is especially common in policy-heavy environments, where old procedures, draft guidance, approved standards, and informal notes coexist in the same content estate. AI systems will retrieve from what they are given. If the architecture does not distinguish current authority from historical residue, the user gets a plausible answer without defensible grounding.

⚠ **WARNING SIGN**

Missing Owners for Freshness and Authority Is a Major Risk

A source may be accurate, accessible, and well indexed, yet still be unsafe for AI use if no one is accountable for whether it is current and authoritative. When freshness and document authority lack named owners, retrieval systems can produce grounded answers that are still wrong.

ARCHITECTURAL IMPLICATIONS

The Architecture Must Encode Ownership, Not Merely Describe It

Ownership should not live only in meeting notes, governance decks, or organizational charts. It must be represented in the architecture itself.

That means core metadata for data products, documents, APIs, events, and semantic assets should include named owners, steward assignments, authority status, freshness expectations, policy classification, permissible use, and escalation path. Catalogs should expose this. Lineage systems should reference it. Retrieval services should use it. AI-serving layers should enforce it.

If ownership is not machine-visible, it cannot consistently influence discovery, ranking, policy enforcement, or remediation. Human understanding alone is not enough once the system scales.

AI-Serving Introduces a New Ownership Boundary

❖ FIGURE 46 – OWNERSHIP MAP ACROSS THE STACK

Traditional data architecture usually stops ownership at publication. A domain publishes a dataset, a document collection, or an API. After that, consumer teams are expected to use it appropriately.

AI changes that. AI-serving is not simple consumption. It is mediated interpretation and recomposition. The act of retrieval, grounding, ranking, summarization, citation, and action recommendation creates a new layer of responsibility.

Someone must own the contract between enterprise assets and AI behavior. That owner does not replace the domain owner or platform owner. Instead, the AI-serving owner defines how assets may be exposed to specific AI consumers, what evidence must accompany them, what confidence thresholds are acceptable, what fallback behaviors are required, and how defects are triaged.

This is one reason AI pilots often become trapped between data teams and application teams. The AI-serving layer is real, but no one has claimed it.

Decision Rights Should Be Modeled as Part of the Control Plane

A mature AI-ready architecture does not merely define assets. It defines who can decide what about those assets.

❖ FIGURE 47 – DECISION-RIGHTS MODEL

For example:

- The domain owner decides whether a source is authoritative for business interpretation.
- The semantic owner decides whether a term may be reused, mapped, deprecated, or split.
- The governance owner decides classification standards, retention alignment, and policy exceptions.
- The security owner decides access models and protected delivery rules.
- The platform owner decides technical patterns for ingestion, indexing, and runtime resilience.
- The AI-serving owner decides ranking inputs, citation requirements, consumer-specific trust thresholds, and answer suppression conditions.
- The steward coordinates remediation and operational follow-up when quality, freshness, or metadata obligations are not met.

Without a documented decision-rights model, defects will bounce endlessly between teams.

Architecture Should Differentiate Consumer Trust Contracts

Different AI consumers require different ownership and service expectations.

A knowledge assistant may be allowed to answer only from approved authoritative content, with visible citations and source dates. An analyst copilot may combine governed metrics, semantic definitions, and documented transformations, but should not infer policy. An executive briefing tool may use multiple curated sources but require human review for high-impact decisions. An operational agent may be permitted to act only when source provenance, policy checks, and transaction constraints all succeed.

These are not just product decisions. They are architecture decisions because they determine how data must be served, what metadata must exist, how policy is enforced, and which owner is accountable for each condition.

Failure Modes and Anti-Patterns

The Platform-As-Owner Fantasy

In this pattern, the enterprise creates a central AI or data platform team and quietly assumes that team will "own AI-Ready Data." The team stands up catalogs, pipelines, content connectors, vector indexing, retrieval services, and observability dashboards. It works hard and ships quickly.

Then the platform team discovers it cannot answer basic questions such as:

- Which of these policy documents is authoritative?

- Which business definition should govern the assistant's answers?
- Is this procedure current?
- Can these two terms be treated as equivalent?
- Who approves exposing this source to an executive copilot?
- What freshness threshold is acceptable for this domain?

The platform has capability but not authority. It can implement controls; it cannot invent business accountability. The result is technical progress without trustworthy scale.

Domain Autonomy Without Shared Standards

In this pattern, each domain is told to make its own assets AI-ready. Some do a respectable job locally. Others move slowly. Metadata quality varies. Definitions diverge. Document structures differ. Sensitivity tags are inconsistent. No common service-level expectations exist. Retrieval quality becomes impossible to reason about centrally because each domain exposes different signals.

This is often defended as agility. In practice, it produces fragmentation. AI becomes harder to trust precisely because every answer crosses inconsistent ownership models.

Stewardship as Volunteer Labor

This pattern is common and expensive. The enterprise names stewards but gives them no dedicated time, no review cadence, no metrics, and no escalation route. Metadata gaps persist. Freshness issues accumulate. Document owners are unknown. Glossary disputes linger. AI incidents recur because no one is accountable for cleanup.

This anti-pattern is especially damaging in unstructured estates. The content appears abundant, but nobody curates authority, lifecycle, or meaning. The assistant then retrieves what exists rather than what should be used.

Governance as Approval Theater

Some organizations respond to AI risk by creating larger committees. Definitions require months of review. Access approvals depend on disconnected workflows. Quality issues are logged but not remediated. Exceptions are discussed but not resolved. Everyone is involved, but no one is decisively accountable.

The appearance of governance increases while actual control decreases. AI-Ready Data requires embedded, operational governance that can act at the speed of architecture, not governance theater that exists mainly to distribute blame.

No Owner for Freshness or Source Authority

This is one of the most dangerous and least discussed failures. Retrieval pipelines often optimize for relevance, not authority. If two documents score similarly, the system may surface the wrong one unless authority and freshness signals are explicit and governed.

A user then receives an answer that is grounded in a document, cited properly, and still wrong because the cited source should not have been used. The system appears trustworthy while actually failing a basic architectural obligation.

Practical Application

Establish a Layered Ownership Model

A practical program begins by assigning ownership across the major responsibilities of AI-Ready Data. The goal is not to create more committees. It is to remove ambiguity.

At *a* minimum, every critical domain or asset should have named accountability for:

- Business correctness.
- Stewardship and remediation.
- Platform operation.
- Governance and policy alignment.
- Security and permission fidelity.
- Semantic definition and relationship management.
- Freshness and lifecycle expectations.
- AI-serving contract and consumer fit.

These assignments should be recorded in metadata and in operating procedures, not just in slides.

Use a Decision-Rights Model, Not Just a Role List

A role list tells you who is present. A decision-rights model tells you who decides.

For each critical question, the enterprise should designate one primary decision owner and define consultation paths. Typical decision areas include authoritative-source designation, business definition approval, quality threshold setting, metadata standard conformance, sensitivity classification, access pattern approval, freshness SLA setting, retrieval suppression rules, citation requirements, and defect remediation ownership.

When incidents occur, this model prevents endless routing between teams.

Fund Stewardship as an Operating Capability

Stewardship must appear in budget, staffing, performance expectations, and governance cadence. A named steward without funded time is not a control; it is a placeholder.

Practical stewardship metrics may include metadata completeness, unresolved glossary conflicts, percentage of authoritative documents with current owners, percentage of critical assets with freshness SLAs, policy-classification coverage, retrieval defect resolution time, and percentage of AI-serving assets with documented escalation routes.

What gets measured gets maintained. What is merely declared gets ignored.

Make Ownership Machine-Visible

Ownership should be stored as metadata attached to assets and services. For example, a governed document collection should expose its business owner, steward, authority status, review cadence, sensitivity class, freshness SLA, semantic mappings, and approved AI use cases. A structured data product should expose its domain owner, steward, semantic owner, lineage references, policy classification, access constraints, and allowed serving contexts.

This allows catalogs, retrieval systems, observability platforms, and AI gateways to enforce or at least expose ownership-aware behavior.

TEMPLATES

AI-Ready Data Ownership Charter

Domain/asset	<name of the domain, asset class, or governed content area to which the operating model applies>
Business owner	<senior business leader accountable for determining authoritative business content and its approved operational use>
Steward	<named steward responsible for coordinating issue logging, triage, remediation, and closure across participating owners>
Platform owner	<leader accountable for ingestion, indexing, enrichment, runtime delivery, and observability patterns for the platform>
Governance owner	<leader accountable for classification, retention alignment, policy interpretation, and governance exception handling>

Security owner	<leader accountable for access patterns, permission inheritance, identity alignment, and protected delivery controls>
Semantic owner	<leader accountable for glossary definitions, concept mappings, disambiguation rules, and domain meaning>
Freshness owner	<leader accountable for review intervals, staleness rules, expiry handling, and suppression of outdated content>
AI-serving owner	<leader accountable for retrieval rules, citation requirements, trust thresholds, answer behavior, and AI-serving controls>
Decision rights	<clear allocation of approval authority across business, semantic, governance, security, platform, freshness, AI-serving, and stewardship responsibilities>
Escalation route	<defined path for escalating defects, policy conflicts, access issues, semantic disputes, and unresolved governance concerns>
Service levels	<operational service expectations for review cadence, metadata completeness, defect triage, permission synchronization, and stale-content suppression>
Metrics owned	<named measures used to monitor authority coverage, freshness compliance, metadata quality, retrieval quality, citation behavior, access-control health, and remediation performance>
Review cadence	<formal schedule for operational review, governance review, and event-driven reassessment after material incidents or major changes>
Sign-off	<required approvers whose approval formally authorizes the operating model, controls, and accountability structure>

Case Example

What Looked Like a Model Problem Was Really an Ownership Problem

A large enterprise launches an internal knowledge assistant for service representatives. The pilot looks promising in demonstrations. It retrieves policy documents, procedure guides, product notes, and knowledge articles from several repositories. Early testers are impressed that the assistant can answer questions in plain language and provide citations.

Then real use begins.

Representatives notice that answers about the same issue vary by phrasing. In one case, the assistant cites an old procedure document that had not been formally retired but had been superseded months earlier. In another, it retrieves a current policy but interprets a product term using an outdated glossary definition from a different business unit. In a third case, it correctly finds the latest article but fails to recognize that a linked exception rule applies only to one customer segment.

The technical team initially treats these as retrieval-tuning problems. They adjust chunking, ranking, and prompts. Some improvement follows, but the defects continue. Eventually, the deeper issue becomes obvious.

Nobody owns document quality across the contributing repositories. Nobody owns the enterprise glossary terms used by the assistant. Nobody owns the freshness SLA for critical policy content. The service domain assumed the content platform team would clean this up. The platform team assumed the domain would identify authoritative sources. Governance assumed existing records policies were enough. Security ensured access controls were broadly correct, but that did nothing to determine which source should be trusted. The assistant product owner could tune the system, but could not declare one source authoritative over another.

The project stalls not because the model is weak, but because ownership is absent at the exact points where AI trust depends on it.

The recovery plan is architectural, not cosmetic. The enterprise creates a charter for the service knowledge domain. It designates a business owner for authoritative policy use, a named steward for metadata and issue follow-through, a semantic owner for glossary alignment, a freshness owner for document review cycles, and an AI-serving owner for answer behavior and citation standards. Authoritative collections are tagged explicitly. Superseded content is either retired or demoted from retrieval eligibility. Freshness SLAs are enforced. Term collisions are resolved in the semantic layer. Retrieval now uses authority and freshness as ranking and suppression signals, not just keyword or embedding similarity.

Only after those ownership controls are in place does the assistant become reliable enough to scale.

This case illustrates a broader lesson: what looks like a model problem is often an ownership problem encoded in architecture.

Closing Synthesis

Who owns AI-Ready Data is the wrong question if it implies a single accountable party. The right question is: who owns each obligation required to make enterprise data discoverable, interpretable, governed, trusted, and safe for AI use?

The answer must be layered.

Business domains must own business meaning and source intent. Stewards must own operational quality and remediation. Platform teams must own the technical capabilities that make readiness possible. Governance must own standards and policy alignment. Security must own access-aware delivery. Semantic owners must resolve ambiguity. Freshness owners must prevent stale truth from masquerading as current truth. AI-serving owners must define the contract by which enterprise assets are exposed to assistants, copilots, and agents.

When these roles are explicit, funded, measurable, and encoded in metadata, AI-readiness becomes durable. When they are vague, overlapping, or assumed, pilots remain fragile no matter how impressive the tooling looks.

Enterprise AI does not scale on optimism. It scales on named accountability built into the architecture.

Key Takeaways

- AI-Ready Data depends on explicit ownership of meaning, metadata, policy, freshness, and serving obligations.
- No single team can own AI-Ready Data end to end; ownership must be layered by responsibility.
- Platform teams enable readiness, but they cannot own business meaning or source authority.
- Stewardship must be funded, measured, and operationalized across structured and unstructured assets.
- The fastest way to stall an AI pilot is to leave freshness, document authority, and remediation without named owners.

Chapter 24: AI-Ready Data Products

A data product becomes AI-ready when it is not only consumable, but interpretable, governed, discoverable, permission-aware, explainable, and fit for explicit AI use cases. That distinction matters. Enterprises already have many assets they call data products: curated tables, published dashboards, feature sets, event streams, document collections, APIs, and domain marts. Some are well engineered. Some are well documented. Some are widely reused. But most were designed for human analysts, downstream applications, or batch reporting. They were not designed to support grounded answers from a knowledge assistant, evidence-backed responses from an executive briefing tool, or controlled decision support for an enterprise agent.

An analytics-ready product answers a familiar question: Can a consumer use this asset reliably for reporting, integration, or analysis? An AI-ready product must answer a much harder question: can an AI system use this asset in a way that remains interpretable, bounded, trustworthy, explainable, and aligned to policy?

That requires a stronger contract. The contract must describe not only what the product contains, but what it means, where it came from, how fresh it is, who is allowed to access it, which use cases it supports, which use cases it must not support, and what evidence an AI system should return when it uses it. In other words, AI-ready productization is where data architecture, metadata, semantics, governance, and service design meet.

This chapter argues that AI-Ready Data products are one of the most practical ways to move from scattered AI experimentation to repeatable enterprise capability. They reduce one-off pipeline sprawl. They make governance reusable instead of reactive. They give AI consumers clearer serving contracts. They force ownership. They make trust visible.

They also introduce discipline. Not every dataset deserves product treatment. But where AI use cases depend on repeatable, governed reuse, product thinking is no longer optional.

Why This Matters

The Enterprise AI Bottleneck Is Usually Upstream

Organizations often assume that once data is cleaned, centralized, or indexed, AI systems will be able to use it safely. In practice, this is rarely true. AI systems are unforgiving consumers. They amplify ambiguity, stale content, hidden permissions, inconsistent definitions, and missing provenance. A human analyst may notice that a table column is overloaded, that a policy document is superseded, or that a glossary term is disputed. A language model will not reliably make those distinctions unless the architecture makes them explicit. This is why data product discipline matters more in the AI era than it did in the analytics era. AI systems consume at scale, across modalities, often in real time, and often without the tacit institutional knowledge that human experts bring to interpretation. The product must, *therefore,* carry the context that humans used to supply informally.

AI Consumers Need Stronger Assurances Than Analytics Consumers

A dashboard team may tolerate imperfect lineage documentation if the metric definition is stable and the audience is trained. A knowledge assistant answering employee policy questions cannot. An agent recommending next actions in a service workflow cannot. An executive briefing tool synthesizing data across market reports, contracts, forecasts, and operational metrics cannot.

These consumers need more than data availability. They need:

- Explicit intended use.
- Restricted use boundaries.
- Authority ranking among sources.
- Semantic context.
- Access-aware delivery.
- Freshness expectations.
- Citation rules.
- Confidence or trust indicators.
- Named owners and stewards.

Without those elements, the organization does not have an AI-ready product. It has a data asset that may be useful, but is not safe to operationalize through AI.

Product Thinking Reduces Bespoke AI Plumbing

In many enterprises, AI pilots create a parallel integration layer: custom connectors, ad hoc embeddings, private taxonomies, isolated indexes, prompt-specific retrieval hacks, undocumented filters, and fragile access workarounds. Each team builds its own interpretation of "trusted data." Each model team creates its own partial metadata. Each assistant carries its own retrieval logic. The result is expensive, opaque, and difficult to govern.

AI-Ready Data products reverse this pattern. They shift work upstream into reusable contracts. Instead of every AI team rebuilding meaning, trust signals, and controls, those elements are published once at the product level and consumed many times. That is a major architectural advantage.

Core Concepts

From Dataset to Product

A dataset is a collection of data. A product is a managed offering with defined consumers, a service contract, ownership, lifecycle expectations, and support commitments.

That distinction is foundational.

A table in a warehouse may be technically clean and widely queried, yet still fail product criteria. It may have no named owner, no documented intended use, no steward, no refresh commitment, no semantic definitions, and no restriction on how it should be used. Such an asset may be useful, but it is not governable at scale for AI consumption.

Key Insight

A dataset is not a product

A dataset becomes a product only when it has a defined purpose, target consumers, ownership, service expectations, and an explicit contract for safe use.

For AI, the product contract must be even richer. It must make interpretation and trust machine-usable, not merely human-assumed.

The AI-Ready Product Contract

An AI-ready data product extends classic product elements such as ownership, quality, and service levels with AI-specific requirements.

Those requirements include six layers.

Core content or data

This is the payload: records, documents, events, embeddings inputs, curated excerpts, metrics, or knowledge objects. It can be structured, semi-structured, unstructured, or mixed.

Metadata

Metadata carries discoverability, lineage, timestamps, policy bindings, stewardship, source authority, quality indicators, and retrieval attributes. In AI settings, metadata is not documentation on the side. It is part of the serving mechanism.

Semantic layer

This includes definitions, business terms, canonical entities, ontology links, policy interpretations, and relationship context. Without this layer, AI systems often retrieve correctly and still answer incorrectly because they cannot disambiguate meaning.

Controls

Controls define classification, access rules, retention, legal constraints, privacy handling, regional boundaries, and delivery restrictions. AI must inherit these controls at consumption, not after the fact.

Trust signals

Trust signals indicate source authority, freshness status, approval state, review date, known limitations, confidence bounds, and citation expectations. These are essential when an AI system must explain why it answered in a certain way.

Service contract

The service contract defines target consumers, allowed and prohibited uses, interface expectations, performance characteristics, support model, escalation path, and retirement criteria.

KEY INSIGHT

AI-ready products carry trust metadata

If a consumer cannot determine source authority, freshness, provenance, sensitivity, and intended use, the product is not ready for trustworthy AI consumption.

Intended Use and Restricted Use Belong in the Definition

One of the most important differences between analytics-oriented products and AI-ready products is that intended use and restricted use must be explicit. This is not legal decoration. It is architectural guidance. Consider a policy corpus in HR. It may be appropriate for:

- Answering employee questions about leave, travel, conduct, or benefits enrollment.
- Guiding managers toward the correct policy reference.
- Supporting policy search and citation.

It may be inappropriate for:

- Generating personalized legal advice.

- Inferring employee risk categories.
- Recommending disciplinary action.
- Making eligibility determinations without a human review step.

If those boundaries are not part of the product contract, every consuming team will invent its own assumptions. Some will be too permissive. Others will be too restrictive. Neither scales.

Not Every Dataset Should Become a Product

Productization introduces overhead: ownership, stewardship, documentation, monitoring, and lifecycle management. That overhead is justified only when the asset has repeated value across use cases, domains, or teams. A temporary extract for a one-time analysis does not need full product treatment. A stable, cross-domain source used by multiple copilots, retrieval systems, and operational agents probably does.

A useful rule is simple: productize where reuse, risk, and semantic dependency are all high. That usually includes:

- Policy and knowledge corpora.
- Mastered business entities.
- Governed event streams.
- Curated customer, supplier, employee, and asset views.
- Regulated reporting definitions.
- Operational decision-support datasets.
- Reference data and business glossaries used by AI systems.
- Source-authoritative document collections with explicit citation requirements.

Architectural Implications

Productization Shifts Work from Model Teams to the Data Estate

When AI-ready product design is done well, model teams do less compensating work. They do not need to guess which source is authoritative. They do not need to reverse engineer whether a document is current. They do not need to invent an access policy wrapper. They do not need to create a parallel glossary inside the prompts and retrieval code. That is the correct architectural direction. The enterprise data estate should publish meaning, trust, and control upstream.

The Product Must Support Multiple AI Serving Patterns

Different AI consumers need different delivery contracts. A knowledge assistant may require:

- Chunkable content.

- Citation-ready source references.
- Access-aware retrieval.
- Source ranking.
- Freshness and supersession signals.

An analyst copilot may require:

- Metric definitions.
- Lineage to source systems.
- Join guidance.
- Semantic aliases.
- Controlled access to derived and raw layers.

An action-taking agent may require:

- Explicit allowed actions.
- Transactional boundaries.
- Machine-readable policy constraints.
- Auditable provenance.
- Stronger latency and freshness guarantees.

An AI-Ready Data product should, *therefore,* be designed with consumer classes in mind, not with a vague promise of "reuse." Reuse without service design usually becomes ambiguity at scale.

Product Metadata Must Be Operational, Not Ceremonial

Many organizations have product catalogs full of static descriptions that were written once and never used in delivery. That is not enough. For AI, metadata must be live and enforceable. It should drive:

- Discovery and ranking.
- Retrieval filtering.
- Authorization checks.
- Freshness thresholds.
- Citation rendering.
- Lineage display.
- Deprecation handling.
- Monitoring and support routing.

If the metadata cannot affect runtime behavior, it will not reliably protect AI outcomes.

❖ FIGURE 48 – AI-READY PRODUCT ANATOMY

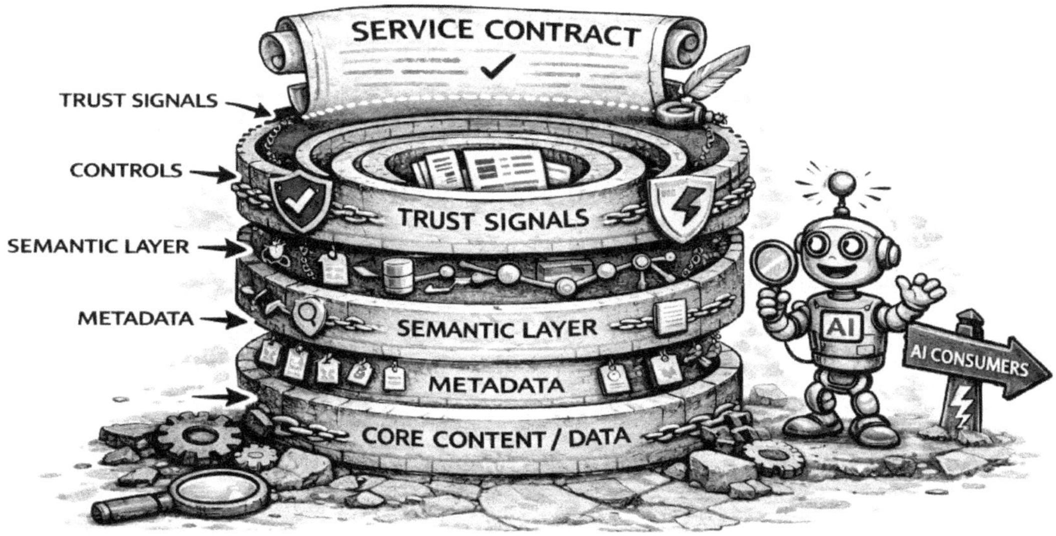

Product Lifecycle Is Part of Architecture

An AI-ready product is not published once and forgotten. It requires lifecycle stewardship.

The lifecycle includes:

- Design.
- Publish.
- Consume.
- Monitor.
- Improve.
- Retire.

At design time, the team defines purpose, consumers, semantics, controls, and trust requirements. At publish time, the product is cataloged and exposed through approved interfaces. During consumption, usage patterns and retrieval outcomes are observed. Monitoring tracks drift, stale sources, access anomalies, and support issues. Improvement updates content, metadata, policy bindings, or semantic coverage. Retirement removes or deprecates the product safely, with successor guidance where needed.

❖ FIGURE 49 – PRODUCT LIFECYCLE

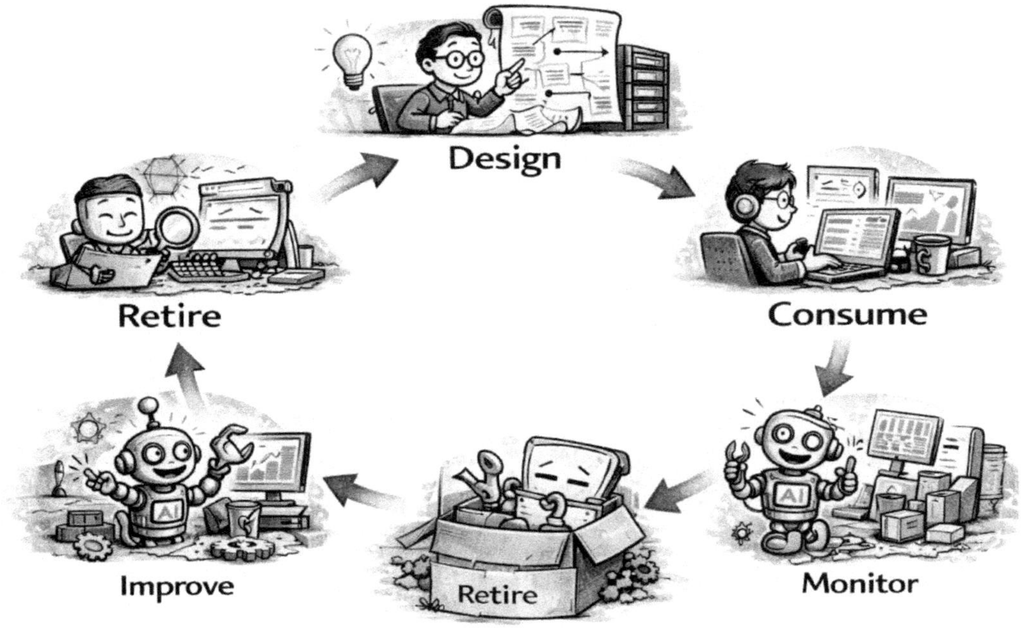

FAILURE MODES AND ANTI-PATTERNS

Calling Anything Reusable a Product

One of the most common anti-patterns is linguistic inflation. A team publishes a dataset, labels it "reusable," and assumes the work is done. But reuse is not a product characteristic by itself. Many assets are reused in an unmanaged way.

⚠ WARNING SIGN

"Reusable" data with no owner, SLA, or intended use statement

That is not an AI-ready product. It is unmanaged dependency disguised as strategy.

Treating Documentation as Optional

AI systems expose every missing definition. If a product contains "active employee," "customer," "high risk," "net revenue," or "policy exception" without governed meaning, AI consumers will fill gaps with statistical approximation. That is unacceptable in enterprise settings.

Separating Retrieval Design from Product Design

Some teams treat retrieval as a downstream implementation detail. They publish content, then let every assistant team decide how to chunk it, rank it, filter it, and cite it. This produces inconsistent answers from the same source estate.

Retrieval quality is an architectural responsibility. Product owners should specify document granularity, supersession handling, source authority, citation references, metadata enrichment expectations, and freshness behavior where AI use cases depend on them.

Ignoring Restricted Uses

A product definition that lists only approved use cases is incomplete. AI systems are often used in adjacent or unintended workflows. The absence of restricted-use guidance invites overreach.

Productizing Low-Value Assets

Not every data asset merits product overhead. Over-productization creates catalog clutter, stewardship fatigue, and diluted governance attention. The discipline works only when applied selectively and rigorously.

Assuming Access Control at the Repository Is Enough

A SharePoint folder permission, warehouse role, or API token is not a sufficient AI access model. AI-ready delivery may need content-level filtering, field suppression, jurisdiction-aware controls, group-based policy inheritance, and output constraints. Product design must account for how access is preserved in AI-mediated consumption.

Practical Application

Where to Start

Most organizations should not begin by trying to convert the entire data estate into products. They should start with a small number of high-value, high-risk, repeatedly used domains where AI consumption is already happening or clearly planned.

Good initial candidates include:

- HR policy and employee knowledge.
- Customer support knowledge.
- Finance definitions and management reporting logic.
- Legal and contracting knowledge.
- Regulated product information.

- Core entity and reference data.
- Operational event streams used in copilots or agents.

The selection criteria should be explicit:

- Repeated cross-team reuse.
- Clear AI demand.
- Meaningful governance requirements.
- Stable business ownership.
- Enough source maturity to support stewardship.

Minimum Viable AI-Ready Product Components

A practical minimum for an AI-ready data product includes:

- A defined purpose.
- Named owner and steward.
- Target AI consumers.
- Authoritative source list.
- Semantic definitions.
- Sensitivity classification.
- Access model.
- Refresh expectations.
- Provenance and citation approach.
- Allowed uses.
- Restricted uses.
- Quality indicators.
- Review cadence.
- Retirement criteria.

That minimum is not bureaucratic overhead. It is the operating contract that lets multiple AI teams consume the same asset without rebuilding trust from scratch.

Product Design Questions Architects Should Force Early

Before publishing an AI-ready product, architects should force clarity on five questions:

- What decision or interaction is this product meant to support?
- Which AI consumers are allowed to use it, and under what trust threshold?
- What evidence must accompany answers or recommendations?

- What uses are prohibited even if technically possible?
- Who is accountable when the product becomes stale, ambiguous, or unsafe?

These questions reveal whether the organization is designing for production or merely publishing data hopefully.

TEMPLATES

AI-Ready Data Product Template

Product name	<name of the governed data, content, or knowledge product>
Purpose	<business purpose of the product and the role it is intended to play for AI assistants, search experiences, or operational workflows>
Target AI consumers	<AI assistants, copilots, search experiences, service workflows, or other approved consumers intended to use the product>
Business owner	<senior business leader accountable for the product's purpose, authority, and approved use>
Steward	<named steward or supporting stewardship roles responsible for product quality, governance coordination, and ongoing maintenance>
Included assets	<documents, records, registers, supplements, FAQs, or other governed assets included within the product scope>
Authoritative sources	<systems, repositories, or publication platforms designated as the authoritative sources for the product>
Definitions/semantic assets	<business glossary terms, taxonomies, ontologies, mappings, or other semantic assets required to support correct interpretation and retrieval>
Sensitivity/classification	<security, confidentiality, or jurisdictional sensitivity classification that applies to the product and its contents>
Access model	<how access is controlled and enforced, including role-based, group-based, document-level, section-level, or region-aware restrictions>
Refresh SLA	<required time within which published or approved changes must be reflected in the catalog, retrieval layer, or serving layer>

Provenance/citation approach

<required method for tracing answers back to source evidence, including citation fields, canonical links, and handling of superseded sources>

Allowed uses

<approved AI-supported uses of the product, such as question answering, guidance, search, summarization, or workflow support>

Restricted uses

<prohibited or tightly controlled uses that the product must not support because of risk, policy, legal, or governance constraints>

Quality indicators

<metrics or indicators used to assess product quality, such as completeness, approval status, freshness, citation coverage, ambiguity, conflict status, or retrieval precision>

Review cadence

<schedule for operational, governance, semantic, or event-driven review of the product>

Known limitations

<documented coverage gaps, technical constraints, structural issues, or exclusions that affect current product fitness>

Support contact

<mailbox, channel, team, or service contact responsible for product support and issue handling>

Retirement criteria

<conditions under which the product should be retired, replaced, or migrated, including continuity requirements for governance, citations, controls, and semantic integrity>

Case Example

HR Policy as an AI-ready Product

A global enterprise wants to deploy an employee HR assistant and a manager guidance copilot. The raw material already exists across the organization: handbook PDFs, regional leave policies, travel rules, code of conduct documents, manager playbooks, exception request forms, and FAQ pages. Historically, employees searched these manually. HR service teams answered repeated questions by email and ticket.

At first glance, this looks like a straightforward retrieval problem. Index the documents, connect a model, and answer questions. In practice, it is a product design problem.

The organization discovers several issues immediately:

- Multiple policy versions exist across repositories.
- Some documents are global, others region-specific.

- Several FAQs summarize policy but are not authoritative.
- Some content is manager-only.
- Effective dates are inconsistent.
- Terms such as employee, contractor, dependent, and leave have local legal nuances.
- Older documents are retained for records purposes but should not guide current answers.

The enterprise responds by creating an AI-ready HR Enterprise Policy Knowledge Product.

What changed when the domain adopted product discipline

First, the HR policy team became the business owner, with a named steward accountable for operational quality.

Second, authoritative sources were explicitly ranked. Legal-approved policy publications outranked summary FAQs. Global policy documents were linked to local variants by jurisdiction metadata. Superseded content was retained for records and audit, but was marked non-default for retrieval.

Third, semantic assets were attached. The glossary defined key terms. A policy taxonomy organized content by topic, audience, and jurisdiction. Relationship mappings connected FAQs to the governing policy sections they summarized.

Fourth, the access model was tightened. Manager-only documents were filtered by identity group. Sensitive sections were excluded from general employee responses. Regional content was served according to the user's jurisdiction.

Fifth, provenance rules were made mandatory. The assistant was required to return the policy title, section, effective date, and source reference in every substantive answer. If no authoritative source was found, the assistant was instructed to defer rather than improvise.

Sixth, restricted uses were made explicit. The assistant could explain policy, summarize rules, and route employees to the correct process. It could not determine legal entitlement, assess misconduct, recommend disciplinary action, or provide personalized legal advice.

The result

The result was not merely better retrieval. It was a safer and more scalable operating model.

HR no longer had to approve each new assistant as a custom integration project because the domain had published a governed product with reusable controls and trust signals. Retrieval behavior became more consistent across channels. Employees received answers with evidence. Managers got guidance within defined bounds. Governance became embedded in the product instead of retrofitted into each consuming application. This is the real value of AI-Ready Data products. They turn fragile AI projects into governed consumption of well-defined enterprise assets.

CLOSING SYNTHESIS

AI-Ready Data products are one of the clearest expressions of mature enterprise AI architecture.

They convert raw availability into governed usability. They replace informal assumptions with explicit contracts. They make semantics, controls, freshness, provenance, and intended use visible to both human and machine consumers. They reduce bespoke pipeline sprawl by moving interpretation and trust upstream. They create a scalable unit for ownership, reuse, and operational accountability.

But discipline is essential. A product label cannot compensate for missing stewardship, weak semantics, or absent controls. A dataset does not become AI-ready because it is published in a catalog or indexed for search. It becomes AI-ready when its contract is strong enough for enterprise AI systems to consume it safely, repeatedly, and explainably.

That is why product thinking matters here. The enterprise does not need more disconnected AI data feeds. It needs a governed portfolio of products that know what they are for, who they are for, what they mean, what they permit, and how they should be trusted.

This is the architectural shift. AI-Ready Data is not just an integration outcome. It is a product discipline.

KEY TAKEAWAYS

- AI-Ready Data products require stronger contracts than analytics-only products, including meaning, trust, control, and explicit use boundaries.
- Intended use, restricted use, provenance, and trust signals must be part of the product definition, not added later.
- Product thinking reduces one-off AI pipeline sprawl by publishing reusable semantics, controls, and service expectations upstream.
- Not every dataset should become a product; productization is most valuable where reuse, risk, and semantic dependency are high.
- A data product is AI-ready only when it is consumable, interpretable, governed, discoverable, permission-aware, explainable, and fit for explicit AI use cases.

Chapter 25: Federated Delivery: Platform Teams, Domain Teams, and Centers of Excellence

AI-Ready Data does not scale through heroic central teams, nor does it scale through unmanaged local autonomy. It scales through a federated operating model. In that model, shared platform capabilities, common controls, and enterprise standards are centralized where reuse matters most, while ownership of business meaning, data quality, stewardship, and operational accountability remains with the domains that create and use the data.

This distinction is not administrative. It is architectural. Enterprise AI depends on discoverability, semantic consistency, permission fidelity, lineage, provenance, and retrieval quality. Those capabilities cannot be rebuilt independently by every line of business without generating fragmentation, duplicated cost, inconsistent controls, and uneven trust. At the same time, no central team can fully understand the operational meaning, lifecycle, exceptions, and business consequences of every customer, product, claim, shipment, contract, interaction, policy, or case record across the enterprise.

The right answer is, *therefore,* not to choose between centralization and decentralization. It is to divide responsibilities deliberately. The enterprise platform should provide common services. Domain teams should own meaning and stewardship. Governance and security teams should embed policy and control. A center of excellence should accelerate adoption, provide methods, and remove friction without becoming the permanent owner of everything.

Federated delivery is how organizations move from isolated AI experiments to repeatable, governed enterprise capability.

Why This Matters

AI-Ready Data Requires Both Scale and Context

Traditional data operating models were often designed for reporting, integration, and application support. AI-ready data introduces a different burden. Now the enterprise must support assistants, copilots, and agents that retrieve across structured and unstructured assets, reason over multiple sources, honor access constraints, surface evidence, and act within governed boundaries.

That changes the operating requirement. The organization no longer needs only pipelines and storage. It needs metadata services, semantic services, policy services, retrieval services, evidence services, and access-aware delivery contracts. Those services benefit from centralization because they must behave consistently. Yet their value depends on accurate local meaning, authoritative sources, and domain stewardship, which cannot be abstracted away.

A global metadata layer without domain accountability becomes stale. Domain accountability without shared metadata services becomes incoherent. AI fails in both cases, for different reasons.

Centralization Alone Becomes a Bottleneck

Many enterprises begin by creating a strong central data or AI team. This often helps at first. Standards are defined, platforms are procured, and shared controls are established. But as demand grows, the model starts to crack.

Every domain queues for onboarding. Every glossary term requires central review. Every retrieval pattern becomes a custom implementation. Every exception request lands with the same overburdened team. Delivery slows. Business teams circumvent the platform. Local solutions emerge in spreadsheets, file shares, bespoke vector stores, departmental knowledge bases, and isolated prompt applications. Centralization that was intended to create order instead creates delay.

Full Decentralization Creates Drift and Risk

Some organizations react by pushing responsibility outward. They tell each domain to build its own pipelines, metadata model, retrieval stack, chunking strategy, classification scheme, access model, and evaluation process. This may increase speed briefly, but it does not scale safely.

Now customer means one thing in sales, another in service, and a third in finance. One domain attaches lineage; another does not. One team enforces source ranking; another retrieves whatever is nearest. One team uses business-approved definitions; another indexes raw documents with no stewardship. Identity propagation is uneven. Retention rules are interpreted differently. Evidence and citations vary by application. What appears to be agility is really unmanaged variance.

For enterprise AI, unmanaged variance is not a local inconvenience. It is a trust problem.

Core Concepts

Federated Delivery Is a Separation-of-Responsibilities Model

Federated delivery is not an org-chart slogan. It is a decision framework for allocating responsibilities across five major groups:

- Platform teams.
- Domain teams.

- Governance teams.
- Security teams.
- AI enablement or center of excellence teams.

The question is not who is important. The question is who should own what.

The platform team owns shared technical capabilities that should be built once and reused many times. The domain team owns business meaning, source authority, stewardship, and quality expectations. Governance owns policy interpretation, control design, and compliance alignment. Security owns identity, access, protection, and assurance mechanisms. The center of excellence enables patterns, coaching, templates, and adoption acceleration.

When those boundaries are clear, delivery speeds up because teams stop rebuilding the same infrastructure and stop waiting on the wrong group for the wrong decisions.

Shared Services Should Be Centralized Where Consistency Matters

Some capabilities should rarely be reinvented by domains:

- Enterprise metadata catalog and metadata APIs.
- Identity propagation and entitlement integration.
- Data classification and policy tagging services.
- Lineage capture services.
- Common ingestion and enrichment frameworks.
- Document parsing and content normalization services.
- Retrieval orchestration services.
- Evaluation harnesses for retrieval quality and groundedness.
- Observability, usage telemetry, and audit services.
- Standard serving interfaces for different AI consumers.

These are plumbing capabilities. They should be stable, reusable, observable, and governed centrally because inconsistency at this layer creates systemic risk.

Meaning Must Remain Local

Domains must retain ownership of the business meaning that makes data trustworthy:

- Authoritative source designation.
- Business definitions and approved semantic mappings.
- Stewardship workflows.

- Freshness expectations.
- Quality thresholds.
- Exception handling.
- Sensitivity interpretation in context.
- Domain-specific retrieval relevance signals.
- Approved usage boundaries for domain content.

A central team can standardize the framework for expressing these things. It cannot author them credibly for every business area. That is the core principle of federated delivery: the enterprise can centralize the mechanism, but it must federate the meaning.

Centers of Excellence Enable, They Do Not Absorb Responsibility

A center of excellence is often created to accelerate AI adoption. This is useful when done correctly. It becomes harmful when it becomes a shadow delivery organization or a permanent decision bottleneck.

The right center of excellence does four things well:

- Defines reference patterns.
- Creates reusable templates and accelerators.
- Coaches delivery teams.
- Helps govern exceptions and capability maturity.

It does not become the long-term owner of every domain's data product, metadata model, retrieval flow, or business semantic decision.

Standards and Templates Increase Speed

In immature organizations, standards are often treated as governance overhead. In mature organizations, standards are delivery accelerators. A domain moves faster when it does not need to invent:

- Its metadata schema.
- Its document onboarding checklist.
- Its retrieval evaluation rubric.
- Its source-authority declaration format.
- Its access-control design pattern.
- Its lineage minimums.
- Its evidence and citation contract.
- Its exception submission process.

The best federated models standardize the things that should not vary, while preserving flexibility where the business context genuinely differs.

KEY INSIGHT

Centralize the plumbing, federate the meaning

Build shared metadata, identity, policy, lineage, retrieval, and observability services once. Keep business definitions, source authority, stewardship, quality rules, and operational accountability in the domains. The enterprise moves faster when mechanisms are centralized and meaning is not.

ARCHITECTURAL IMPLICATIONS

The Operating Model Becomes Part of the Architecture

Architects often treat operating model questions as downstream governance matters. For AI-Ready Data, this is a mistake. Ownership boundaries directly affect architecture quality.

If no one owns domain semantics, the metadata layer degrades. If no shared retrieval service exists, applications diverge in ranking behavior and evidence quality. If the security model is not delivered as a reusable service, access-aware retrieval becomes inconsistent. If the governance model is manual and advisory only, policy enforcement will arrive too late.

The operating model is, *therefore,* part of the architecture. It determines where control points live, how services are consumed, who approves change, and how trust is sustained.

Platform Teams Should Publish a Service Catalog

The platform team should not operate as an opaque internal provider that delivers custom work by request. It should publish a clear service catalog that domain teams can consume.

That catalog typically includes services such as:

- Source onboarding and connector frameworks.
- Metadata registration and schema publication.
- Glossary and semantic linking services.
- Classification and policy tagging apis.
- Identity-aware indexing and retrieval.
- Lineage instrumentation.
- Content extraction and chunking pipelines.

- Ranking and citation services.
- Evaluation tools for retrieval quality.
- Standard serving endpoints for assistants, copilots, and agents.
- Audit logs, telemetry, and operational dashboards.

This matters because reuse reduces chaos. Domains need to know what exists, when to use it, what standards apply, and what service-level expectations govern the interaction.

❖ FIGURE 50 – SERVICE CATALOG MAP

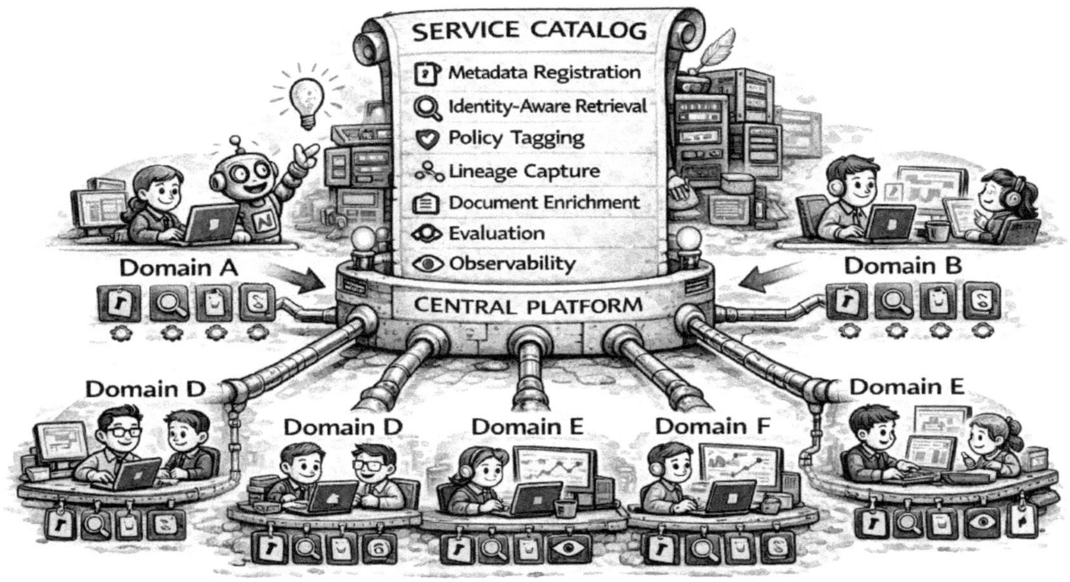

Domain Teams Should Publish Accountable Data Products and Knowledge Assets

A domain should not merely "provide data." It should publish governed, semantically described, access-aware assets that can be consumed by humans and AI systems.

For structured assets, that means clear definitions, source provenance, acceptable use, freshness expectations, and lineage. For unstructured assets, that means authoritative repositories, stewardship, document classification, content quality expectations, retention alignment, and retrieval inclusion rules. For semi-structured assets, that means events and payloads are described well enough to support interpretation and downstream grounding.

Domains do not need to build the shared machinery. They do need to stand behind the meaning and quality of what enters that machinery.

Governance Must Be Embedded as an Operating Role, Not an Approval Committee

In a federated model, governance cannot live as an after-the-fact review board. Governance needs an active delivery role. That role includes:

- Defining control objectives.
- Specifying required metadata fields.
- Establishing minimum lineage requirements.
- Defining classification and retention obligations.
- Approving standard evidence patterns.
- Managing policy exceptions.
- Measuring control adoption across domains.

Governance owns the rule framework. Platform operationalizes the controls. Domains comply and steward locally. That is different from centralized governance trying to inspect every asset one by one.

Security Must Provide Reusable Control Services

Security should not be limited to periodic audits or access review meetings. For AI-Ready Data, security must provide operational capabilities that can be consumed by the platform and domains:

- Identity federation.
- Entitlement resolution.
- Policy enforcement points.
- Encryption and protection services.
- Secrets and key management.
- Activity logging.
- Anomaly detection.
- Data loss prevention integration.
- Access-aware retrieval interfaces.

If security is purely advisory, domain teams will improvise. Improvised security in retrieval systems is one of the fastest paths to enterprise AI failure.

AI Enablement Should Accelerate Adoption Without Becoming an Empire

AI enablement teams or centers of excellence are most useful when the organization is learning how to industrialize patterns. They should curate reference architectures, train teams, document good practices, run office hours, maintain evaluation frameworks, and coordinate maturity roadmaps.

They should not become the permanent owner of every deployment. The longer the center of excellence owns delivery, the less accountable the domain and platform teams become. The goal of enablement is capability diffusion, not capability hoarding. What a center of excellence should and should not do:

Should do:

- Define reference patterns for AI-Ready Data delivery.
- Provide reusable templates, controls, and accelerators.
- Coach platform and domain teams.
- Run maturity assessments and exception reviews.
- Curate evaluation methods and lessons learned.

Should not do:

- Own all domain semantics.
- Build every pipeline or retrieval flow.
- Act as the long-term steward for business content.
- Replace governance or security ownership.
- Become the only team allowed to make AI decisions.

A center of excellence succeeds when other teams become more capable and less dependent on it over time.

Federated Accountability Should Be Explicit

❖ FIGURE 51 – FEDERATED OPERATING MODEL

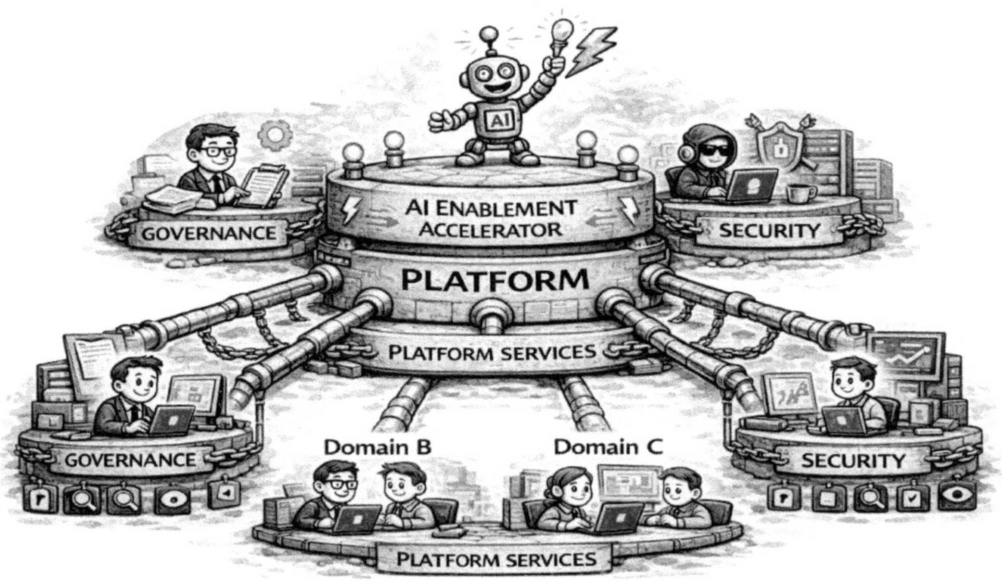

The federated model should be formalized through a responsibility map, usually with named accountabilities. Ambiguity is expensive. It causes duplicate work, delayed decisions, and avoidable control failures.

For example:

- Platform is accountable for metadata APIs, retrieval infrastructure, common observability, and service reliability.
- Domains are accountable for term definitions, source authority, stewardship, and business-level quality.
- Governance is accountable for control design, policy interpretation, and exception review.
- Security is accountable for access models, identity propagation, and protective controls.
- AI enablement is accountable for patterns, training, and adoption support.

This should not live as a buried spreadsheet. It should be a visible operating contract.

Failure Modes and Anti-Patterns

The Central Hero Team

In this model, one central team owns platform engineering, metadata, semantics, governance coordination, retrieval, and application delivery. It becomes the intake point for every request.

This model appears coherent but collapses under demand. The central team becomes a bottleneck. Domains disengage from stewardship because they assume the central team now "owns data." Platform backlogs grow. Local workarounds spread.

The problem is not a lack of talent. The problem is the concentration of responsibilities that do not belong together.

Every Domain Builds a Stack

Here, each domain is told to operate independently. One builds its own catalog extension. Another builds a separate vector store. Another defines its own metadata fields. Another uses a different approach to chunking, source ranking, or permission inheritance.

This creates local speed and enterprise incoherence. The organization then discovers that cross-domain assistants cannot reconcile meaning, citations are inconsistent, access behavior varies, and evaluation results do not compare cleanly. The cost of later harmonization is far greater than the cost of early shared services.

⚠ **WARNING SIGN**

Every domain invents its own metadata and retrieval rules

When domains create their own metadata fields, chunking logic, source-authority rules, citation conventions, and ranking strategies, the enterprise is not scaling. It is fragmenting. This is an early warning sign that the platform team is providing too little usable shared capability or too little adoption support.

The Center of Excellence Becomes a Shadow Owner

A center of excellence can accidentally become a permanent parallel organization. It starts by helping teams pilot AI use cases. Then it owns the retrieval framework, the evaluation process, the semantic mappings, the document onboarding, and the business-use prioritization. Soon, no team moves without it.

This reduces local capability growth and creates strategic dependence on a team that was supposed to be temporary or catalytic. The organization confuses enablement with central ownership.

Governance Is Advisory Only

When governance only publishes policy documents but does not shape delivery patterns, teams interpret rules inconsistently. Some assets are classified correctly; others are not. Some retrieval flows preserve evidence and source authority; others do not. Some domains capture minimum metadata; others skip it to move faster.

AI-ready governance has to be operational. It must be present in templates, service gates, control checks, metadata requirements, and exception processes.

Security Is Bolted on at the End

Many AI failures are not caused by model quality. They are caused by access mistakes. A retrieval layer that ignores document-level permissions, a summarization service that leaks across entitlements, or a knowledge assistant that surfaces stale restricted content can destroy trust faster than a poor answer.

Security cannot arrive only after the demo works. Identity, authorization, and protection have to be part of the federated model from the start.

Practical Application

Start with a Responsibility Inventory

A practical federated transformation begins by inventorying all capabilities required for AI-Ready Data delivery. Most enterprises discover that responsibilities are currently mixed, duplicated, or missing.

Typical capability groups include:

- Ingestion and source onboarding.
- Metadata capture and publishing.
- Glossary and taxonomy services.
- Ontology and relationship management where needed.
- Lineage instrumentation.
- Classification and retention tagging.
- Identity and access propagation.
- Content extraction and enrichment.
- Retrieval, ranking, and evidence generation.
- Evaluation and testing.
- Serving interfaces and product contracts.
- Observability and audit.
- Stewardship and issue management.

For each capability, assign an owner, a service model, and a consumption path.

Define the Service Boundaries

Next, make service boundaries concrete. A good test is simple: Could a new domain onboard without negotiating bespoke architecture?

If the answer is no, the service model is too vague.

For example, a platform service boundary might state that any domain can register a source, publish required metadata, inherit standard classification workflows, use enterprise chunking and enrichment defaults, define domain-specific relevance boosts, and consume access-aware retrieval through a standard API. That is clear. It allows reuse without stripping away domain control.

Standardize the Templates That Matter

Templates are a major force multiplier. A federated model should provide standard artifacts for:

- Domain onboarding.
- Asset registration.
- Source-authority declaration.
- Retrieval inclusion and exclusion rules.
- Metadata minimums.
- Access model mapping.
- Evidence and citation design.
- Exception and waiver requests.
- Stewardship escalation.
- Quality and freshness targets.

These templates should be lightweight enough to use and strong enough to enforce architectural consistency.

Fund Shared Services Centrally and Stewardship Locally

The funding model matters more than many architects admit. Shared platform services usually require central funding because domains will underinvest in enterprise capabilities whose value is distributed. Domain stewardship, however, should usually be funded by the domains because it is inseparable from operational ownership.

This funding split reinforces the federated model. The enterprise pays for common infrastructure. The business pays for local meaning and stewardship.

Measure the Model with Operating KPIs

A federated model should be measured through indicators that reveal whether shared capability and local accountability are both working. Useful metrics include:

- Percentage of priority domains onboarded to shared metadata services.
- Percentage of AI-consumable assets with required metadata minimums.
- Coverage of identity-aware retrieval.
- Percentage of authoritative sources explicitly designated.
- Retrieval evaluation scores by domain.
- Policy exception volume and resolution time.
- Stewardship issue resolution time.
- Percentage of domain assets with lineage visibility.
- Reuse rate of platform services versus bespoke implementations.

If the enterprise measures only platform uptime or only domain output volume, it will miss the health of the federated model.

TEMPLATES

Federated Operating Model Worksheet

Shared platform capabilities	<common enterprise platform services and reusable capabilities provided centrally, such as metadata, ingestion, parsing, retrieval, lineage, observability, evaluation, and standard AI-serving interfaces>
Domain-owned responsibilities	<responsibilities owned by business domains, such as defining terms, designating authoritative sources, assigning stewards, setting quality thresholds, approving inclusion rules, resolving disputes, validating relevance, and remediating stale or ambiguous content>
Governance-owned responsibilities	<responsibilities owned by governance functions, such as defining metadata minimums, control objectives, classification, retention, provenance, evidence standards, lineage expectations, waiver processes, and adherence measures>
Security-owned responsibilities	<responsibilities owned by security functions, such as identity federation, entitlement integration, access-model design, protection controls, monitoring, restricted-content handling, and validation of access-aware delivery>
AI enablement / COE role	<responsibilities of the AI enablement team or center of excellence, such as publishing reference architectures, supporting onboarding, maintaining starter kits, running design reviews, curating evaluation methods, capturing lessons learned, and reducing long-term dependency through capability transfer>
Service catalog	<standard shared services available to domains and teams, such as source onboarding, metadata publishing, semantic linking, policy tagging, identity-aware indexing, retrieval, citation, lineage, evaluation, observability, serving APIs, and stewardship workflows>
Standard templates required	<required templates, forms, and checklists that domains and teams must use, such as onboarding checklists, asset registration, authoritative source declarations, metadata minimums, access mappings, evidence contracts, stewardship assignments, exceptions, and maturity assessments>
Escalation and exception process	<defined process for submitting, assessing, reviewing, approving, recording, and tracking exceptions, including business rationale, technical

	impact, policy implications, security implications, expiration dates, and review triggers>
Funding model	<approach for funding shared platform services, domain stewardship, governance, security, AI enablement, and any chargeback or showback model for premium services>
KPI ownership	<allocation of key performance indicators across platform, domains, governance, security, AI enablement, and executive sponsorship, including the measures each is accountable for>
Maturity roadmap	<staged maturity progression for federated delivery, describing how the organization moves from fragmented practices to standardized, federated, scaled, and optimized operating models>
Risks and mitigations	<key risks to the federated operating model and the corresponding mitigations needed to reduce bottlenecks, inconsistency, weak stewardship, policy drift, access failures, dependency on central teams, underfunding, or poor standards adoption>

CASE EXAMPLE

Federated Delivery Turns Local Knowledge into Enterprise-Scale AI

A multinational organization in manufacturing, distribution, and after-sales service faced a common problem. It had strong regional businesses, numerous content repositories, and several central teams responsible for data, security, and digital transformation. It also had growing demand for AI assistants: a field-service copilot, a procurement knowledge assistant, a regulatory document summarizer, and an executive operational briefing tool.

The first attempt was highly centralized. A central AI program team tried to ingest documents, normalize metadata, define relevance rules, and build retrieval pipelines for every region and function. Within six months, the team had produced promising pilots but had become a bottleneck. Regional teams complained that important local content was being misclassified. Product documentation from one region used different terminology from another. Central engineers lacked the context to determine which maintenance bulletin overrode which local procedure. Security reviews were slow because every access pattern required custom interpretation.

The organization then moved to a federated model.

The platform team centralized the capabilities that needed consistency: metadata registration, identity integration, policy tagging, lineage capture, retrieval orchestration, citation generation, and observability. It published these as shared services with documented onboarding patterns.

The domain teams in service operations, procurement, regulatory affairs, and manufacturing retained ownership of business meaning. Each domain designated authoritative sources, appointed stewards, mapped domain terminology to the enterprise glossary, defined freshness expectations, and declared which content was approved for AI retrieval and which was out of scope.

Governance defined the required metadata minimums, evidence rules, retention-aligned handling patterns, and exception process. Security integrated entitlement propagation into the retrieval layer so regional access controls remained intact. The AI center of excellence created templates for source onboarding, retrieval evaluation, and stewardship workflows, then coached teams during their first two delivery cycles.

The effect was immediate. Onboarding time for new sources dropped because domains no longer negotiated unique plumbing. Retrieval quality improved because domain stewards could tune source authority and relevance rules within a common framework. Security incidents decreased because access-aware retrieval was shared rather than improvised. Most importantly, trust improved. Users could see where answers came from, which sources were authoritative, and who in the business stood behind them.

The organization did not centralize understanding. It centralized the capabilities required to make local understanding usable at an enterprise scale.

Closing Synthesis

AI-Ready Data demands an operating model that is both disciplined and realistic. Central teams are necessary, but not sufficient. Domain ownership is essential, but not sufficient. Governance and security are foundational, but they cannot function only as reviewers. A center of excellence is valuable, but only if it accelerates capability instead of absorbing it.

The federated model works because it respects the nature of enterprise data. Shared infrastructure benefits from standardization. Business meaning does not. Policy needs consistency. Stewardship needs proximity. Retrieval needs central services. Trust needs local accountability.

This is why federated delivery is not a compromise position between two organizational extremes. It is the architecture-aligned operating model for AI-Ready Data at enterprise scale.

When done well, it achieves four outcomes at once. It reduces bottlenecks. It lowers inconsistency. It embeds control. And it keeps accountability attached to the people who actually understand the data.

That is how enterprises move from scattered AI enthusiasm to governed, explainable, repeatable delivery.

Key Takeaways

- AI-Ready Data scales through federated delivery, not pure centralization or pure decentralization.
- Centralize shared platform services, but keep business meaning, source authority, and stewardship in the domains.
- Governance and security must operate as embedded delivery functions, not after-the-fact reviewers.
- A center of excellence should accelerate and standardize adoption without becoming the permanent owner of delivery.
- The strongest federated models use service catalogs, templates, explicit accountability, and measurable operating KPIs.

CHAPTER 26: ADOPTION, LITERACY, AND ORGANIZATIONAL CHANGE

Enterprise AI programs often describe adoption as a downstream concern. The architecture team designs the platform, the governance team defines controls, the product team launches a copilot, and someone else is expected to "drive usage." That view is wrong. In an AI-ready enterprise, adoption is not a communications problem. It is an architectural outcome shaped by trust signals, workflow fit, literacy, stewardship behaviors, and operating model design.

A system can be technically elegant and still fail in practice. It can expose citations, enforce permissions, use authoritative sources, and provide lineage, yet remain underused because users do not know how to interpret source-aware answers. It can deliver grounded outputs, yet still be rejected because business teams cannot distinguish between a defensible answer and a merely fluent one. It can provide high-quality retrieval, yet still disappoint because stewards do not understand that keeping content current is now part of model-era operations.

This chapter argues that adoption must be designed with the same seriousness as ingestion, metadata, governance, and retrieval. If the organization does not understand how to trust, use, steward, and improve AI-Ready Data, even excellent architecture will underperform. The enterprise does not scale trustworthy AI simply by building the right data foundation. It scales trustworthy AI when people know what the system is doing, what evidence supports it, what its boundaries are, and what their role is in keeping it reliable.

WHY THIS MATTERS

Adoption Determines Whether Architecture Produces Value

Many enterprise data programs have lived through the same pattern: the platform is built, the controls are in place, and usage remains shallow. In the AI era, that pattern becomes more dangerous because poor adoption does not merely reduce return on investment. It actively distorts perceptions of quality, trust, and architectural adequacy.

When users do not understand source-aware AI, they often misdiagnose the problem. If an assistant answers cautiously and cites three sources, some users interpret that as a weakness rather than a strength. If an analyst copilot refuses to answer because the user lacks access to the underlying documents, the behavior may be described as broken rather than governed. If an agent requests confirmation before taking action, leaders may see friction instead of control. Without literacy, the organization penalizes precisely the design properties that make enterprise AI trustworthy.

Trust Is Not Automatic, Even When Controls Exist

Trust in enterprise AI is not produced by interface polish or model fluency. It is produced by repeated exposure to evidence, consistency, and understandable boundaries. People trust systems that make their reasoning inspectable. They trust systems that behave predictably across cases. They trust systems that show when they are uncertain, when they are restricted, and when they are drawing from stale or low-authority material.

This matters especially in data-rich enterprises where users have learned, often correctly, to be skeptical. They have seen conflicting reports, undocumented logic, stale dashboards, shared drives full of outdated documents, and policy changes not reflected in downstream systems. In that environment, trust must be earned. That requires architecture that exposes provenance and governance, and organizational change that teaches people how to interpret those signals.

AI Changes What "Data Literacy" Must Include

Traditional data literacy focused on metrics, dashboards, definitions, and basic analytic reasoning. That remains necessary, but it is no longer sufficient. In an AI-ready environment, users must also understand source ranking, authority, temporal validity, access-aware retrieval, semantic ambiguity, and the difference between generated phrasing and evidentiary support. This is not a niche concern for specialists. Executives need to know when a briefing tool is summarizing authoritative records versus inferred commentary. Analysts need to know how to challenge a grounded answer and when to escalate a missing source. Stewards need to understand that content quality now affects retrieval quality, not just human search. Architects need to design trust signals into the serving layer, not assume users will discover them on their own.

CORE CONCEPTS

Trust Adoption Depends on Clarity and Evidence

Users adopt enterprise AI when they can answer four questions quickly:

- What sources did this answer use?
- Why were those sources considered authoritative?
- Is the answer current enough for my task?
- What should I do if the answer appears wrong or incomplete?

These questions are architectural and organizational at the same time. The platform must surface source, lineage, timing, and policy context. The organization must teach users what those signals mean and how to act on them.

A trustworthy system does not ask users to accept hidden processes. It makes trust inspectable. That is especially important for AI consumers because the interface can easily create a false sense of certainty. A polished paragraph with a confident tone can conceal weak evidence. Conversely, a concise answer with citations may be far more reliable. Adoption depends on teaching users to value the latter.

KEY INSIGHT

Trust is taught as well as built

Trustworthy design is necessary, but not self-explanatory. Users must be taught how to read citations, interpret source authority, recognize freshness limits, and distinguish grounded answers from plausible language. Organizations that skip this step often conclude that the system lacks quality when the real issue is that the trust model was never made legible.

Users Need Literacy About Source-Aware AI, Not Just Prompts

Too much AI training begins and ends with prompting tips. That is inadequate for enterprise use. Prompting may help users express questions, but it does not teach them how to assess answer reliability. Source-aware AI literacy should include:

- How retrieval works at a conceptual level.
- What authoritative versus merely accessible content means.
- Why permissions affect answer completeness.
- How temporal correctness changes interpretation.
- How citations, snippets, and provenance should be reviewed.
- When to accept, challenge, verify, or escalate an answer.

This is not deep model science. It is operational literacy for working safely with grounded systems. A claims analyst using a policy assistant does not need to understand transformer internals. But that analyst does need to know that a recent endorsement may override an older policy clause, that access restrictions can hide relevant documents, and that the absence of a citation is a trust signal in itself.

KEY INSIGHT

What data literacy means in the AI era

In the AI era, data literacy includes the ability to evaluate source-backed answers, understand how governance and permissions shape retrieval, recognize ambiguity and stale context, and use evidence trails rather than fluent language as the basis for trust.

Stewards and Owners Need New Habits and Incentives

In traditional environments, content stewardship was often episodic. A policy page could remain stale for months without obvious operational consequences. In an AI-ready environment, that same page may become a highly ranked grounding source for hundreds of daily interactions. The cost of poor stewardship rises sharply.

Data owners, content owners, and stewards, therefore, need new operating habits:

- Maintaining authoritative-source designations.
- Reviewing stale or duplicative content.
- Improving metadata completeness.
- Resolving conflicting definitions.
- Monitoring retrieval failures and escalation patterns.
- Participating in adoption reviews, not only governance reviews.

Incentives must change with these responsibilities. If teams are measured only on content volume or system uptime, stewardship will remain secondary. If they are measured on answer trust, source freshness, policy compliance, and resolution speed for content defects, behavior changes.

Change Management Should Be Tied to Operating Model Shifts

Successful AI adoption rarely comes from training alone. It comes from aligning training with decision rights, workflows, service ownership, and escalation paths.

If a business assistant now answers policy questions from governed sources, who owns the answer quality when citations are contradictory? If an executive briefing tool combines structured KPIs with unstructured management commentary, who decides what counts as an authoritative source? If an analyst copilot reduces manual report assembly, how are review controls updated? These are operating model questions, not simply enablement questions.

Organizations often fail here by treating rollout as a launch campaign. They communicate benefits, schedule demos, and provide office hours, but they do not redefine who curates source sets, who reviews trust metrics, who approves workflow changes, or who funds ongoing stewardship. Adoption then stalls because the tool exists, but the operating model around it does not.

Measured Adoption Is a Design Feedback Loop

Adoption should not be measured as raw usage alone. Logins and prompt counts are weak signals. They show curiosity, not trust.

Useful adoption measures include:

- Percentage of answers opened with citations.
- Rate of source-click-through by role.
- Escalation frequency and resolution time.
- Reuse rate of trusted answers in downstream work.
- Percentage of low-confidence answers abandoned.
- Frequency of stale-source incidents.
- Changes in time-to-complete for target workflows.
- User-reported trust by scenario, not generic satisfaction.

These measures create a feedback loop between architecture and user behavior. If analysts ignore citations, the problem may be literacy, interface design, or poor citation usefulness. If stewards face repeated escalations on ambiguous terminology, the issue may be *a* missing semantic context. If executives stop using a briefing assistant after three weeks, the workflow may not fit their meeting cadence. Adoption metrics should, *therefore,* be treated as architectural signals.

Architectural Implications

Adoption Must Be Designed into the Serving Layer

The serving layer should expose the information users need to trust and use the system correctly. This includes:

- Source citations that are visible, not buried.
- Source type and authority labeling.
- Freshness indicators.
- Confidence framing tied to evidence, not opaque scores.
- Access-aware explanations when answers are incomplete.
- Pathways for feedback, challenge, and escalation.

A grounded answer without inspectable evidence creates dependency without trust. A grounded answer with unusable citations creates friction without clarity. The architecture must support a human judgment loop.

Workflow Fit Matters as Much as Model Quality

Adoption rises when AI appears inside the work itself rather than beside it. An analyst copilot that lives outside the reporting workflow may see sporadic usage. The same capability embedded in a research, reconciliation, or variance-analysis workflow is more likely to become habitual.

This has direct architectural consequences. Data-serving contracts should be designed for the task context. A knowledge assistant may prioritize breadth and discoverability. An analyst copilot may require stronger source filtering, tabular grounding, and citation granularity. An operational agent may require action logs, approval gates, and policy-bound execution paths. The architecture should, *therefore,* not aim for a single generic answer experience. It should support differentiated trust patterns for different consumers.

Literacy Design Should Align to Role

Not everyone needs the same training because not everyone interacts with AI-Ready Data in the same way.

❖ FIGURE 52 – ADOPTION DEPENDENCY MODEL

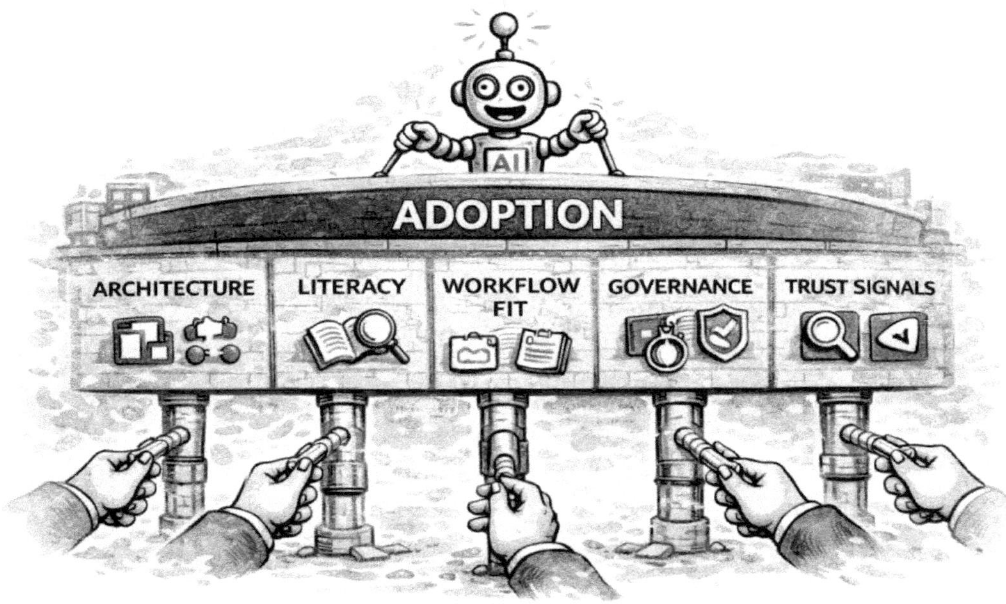

Executives need decision-use literacy: how to judge whether a briefing is grounded, current, and policy-safe. Architects need design literacy: how metadata, semantics, provenance, and access controls shape answer quality. Stewards need stewardship literacy: how content maintenance affects ranking, grounding, and trust. Analysts need working literacy: how to challenge, verify, and reuse answers responsibly. End users need practical literacy: when to trust, when to verify, and how to escalate.

Governance Signals Should Be Made Visible

Governance often remains hidden in enterprise tools. Users see the output but not the safeguards. In AI systems, that invisibility is counterproductive. When a tool refuses to answer, limits scope, or asks for confirmation, the system should make the governing reason legible. Examples include:

- "This answer excludes restricted HR content."
- "The most recent approved policy is from February 12; older drafts were ignored."
- "Two definitions of customer conflict across domains; using the Finance-approved definition for this answer."
- "No authoritative source found after the retention cutover date."

These are not merely usability features. They reinforce the enterprise trust model.

❖ FIGURE 53 – ROLE-BASED LITERACY MAP

FAILURE MODES AND ANTI-PATTERNS

Treating Adoption as a Launch Campaign

A common anti-pattern is to treat adoption as awareness plus training. The organization announces the tool, runs demos, distributes prompt tips, and expects behavior to change. It rarely does. Without workflow redesign, ownership changes, and trust education, users return to old habits: emailing subject matter experts, downloading spreadsheets, searching shared drives, or bypassing the governed assistant entirely.

Measuring Activity Instead of Trust

Another anti-pattern is celebrating volume. Thousands of prompts may look impressive while users still copy answers into side channels, ignore citations, and verify everything manually. That is not adoption. That is trial usage under uncertainty. The key question is not whether users interacted with the tool. It is whether they integrated it into real work under the organization's trust and governance model.

Assuming Users Understand Grounded Answers

Many teams believe that if citations are present, users will naturally know how to use them. In reality, some users never click them, some treat them as ornamental, and some assume citation presence means guaranteed correctness. All three behaviors are risky.

> ⚠ **WARNING SIGN**
>
> **Users treat grounded answers like magic**
>
> When users stop asking where the answer came from, whether the source is authoritative, or whether the content is current, the organization has created dependence without literacy. Grounded answers should reduce blind trust, not increase it.

Leaving Stewards Outside the Adoption Loop

A system grounded in enterprise content will reflect the strengths and weaknesses of that content. If content owners are not involved in rollout, quality issues persist and confidence declines. The business may blame the assistant when the real defect sits upstream in metadata, taxonomy, or stale source material.

Confusing Resistance with Irrationality

Users are often portrayed as resistant to change when they are actually reacting rationally to unclear trust conditions. If the assistant cannot explain why it chose a source, if terminology conflicts remain unresolved, or if workflow benefits are vague, skepticism is reasonable. Good change management does not try to overpower skepticism. It uses it as input to improve architecture and operating design.

PRACTICAL APPLICATION

Designing Adoption Into Delivery

Adoption becomes durable when it is treated as part of delivery, not as a post-launch support activity. In practice, that means every AI-Ready Data initiative should move through adoption design in parallel with source onboarding, metadata enrichment, policy mapping, and retrieval testing. The question is not whether users will be trained after the system is built. The question is whether the system, its workflows, and its operating model are being shaped so that people can trust it, interpret it, and improve it.

A practical starting point is to define the target user decisions and actions before discussing enablement. For each major AI consumer, the team should ask: what is this user expected to do differently because this capability exists? An executive may be expected to begin a briefing with a grounded summary instead of waiting for a manually assembled pack. An analyst may be expected to start research with cited answers rather than opening five systems and reconstructing context by hand. A steward may be expected to review authoritative source labels and stale content as part of a recurring operating rhythm. These are behavior changes, not feature descriptions. If the desired behavior is unclear, adoption will remain vague and difficult to measure.

The next step is to identify the trust conditions required for that behavior to happen. Users do not adopt enterprise AI because it is available. They adopt it when the cost of relying on it feels lower than the cost of bypassing it. That usually requires visible citations, clear authority indicators, freshness cues, understandable failure states, and a simple way to challenge or escalate questionable answers. If those trust conditions are missing, more training will not solve the problem. The architecture and interface need to make trustworthy use easier than skeptical workarounds.

Teams should then redesign the workflow around the capability rather than placing the capability beside the workflow. This is where many programs fail. They introduce a copilot, but leave the old approval paths, review templates, and performance expectations unchanged. Users are told to use the new tool, but success is still measured according to the old manual process. The result is predictable: people treat the AI system as optional. Practical adoption work, *therefore,* includes changing templates, review checkpoints, escalation routes, and team norms so that source-aware AI becomes part of how work is actually performed.

Role-based literacy should be introduced as task-specific instruction rather than broad AI awareness. Executives need to know how to interpret grounded briefings and when to ask for stronger evidence. Analysts need to know how to inspect sources, resolve ambiguity, and judge whether an answer is sufficiently defensible for downstream use. Stewards need to understand how metadata, duplication, stale content, and unresolved terminology degrade trust. Architects and platform teams need to read usage and trust metrics as design feedback, not just support noise. The practical aim is not to make everyone an AI expert. It is to make each role competent in the trust and governance behaviors relevant to its responsibilities.

Finally, adoption should be reviewed using operational evidence, not launch enthusiasm. In the first weeks of deployment, the team should examine whether users open citations, whether escalations cluster around specific sources or terms, whether certain roles abandon answers more often than others, and whether the workflow actually gets faster or more reliable. These are the signals that show whether the organization is learning to work with AI-Ready Data. When adoption is weak, the response should not default to "more communications." It should begin with a harder question: which part of the architecture, workflow, trust model, or role literacy is making correct use harder than it should be?

That is the practical discipline. Build the capability. Design the trust signals. Change the workflow. Teach the role-specific behaviors. Measure what people actually do. Then feed those findings back into the architecture. In an AI-ready enterprise, adoption is not the final mile. It is part of the system.

TEMPLATES

AI-Ready Data Adoption Plan

Capability	<name of the capability, assistant, or copilot being assessed>
Primary purpose	<main purpose of the capability, including the kind of questions, analysis, drafting, or support it is intended to provide>
Stakeholder adoption profile	<set of stakeholder groups whose behavior, trust, literacy, workflows, and review cycles must be shaped for successful adoption>
Stakeholder group	<specific user group, sponsor group, steward group, platform group, or adjacent business audience affected by the capability>
Desired behavior change	<specific shift in behavior expected from this stakeholder group when the capability is adopted successfully>
Current behavior	<how this stakeholder group works today before adoption of the capability>
Trust barriers	<main reasons this stakeholder group may hesitate to adopt or rely on the capability>
Literacy needs	<knowledge this stakeholder group needs in order to use the capability appropriately, interpret trust signals, and understand limits>
Workflow changes	<changes required in the stakeholder group's day-to-day workflow, decision process, or review process once the capability is introduced>
Training materials required	<guides, demos, checklists, labs, references, or other materials needed to support this stakeholder group's adoption>
Adoption metrics	<measures used to track whether this stakeholder group is adopting the capability effectively and safely>
Communication cadence	<planned frequency and format of communication, reviews, office hours, tips, or sponsor updates for this stakeholder group>
Feedback loops	<mechanisms used to capture issues, trust concerns, usability problems, source gaps, and repeated overrides from this stakeholder group>

Owner	<role, team, or leader accountable for enabling adoption and addressing issues for this stakeholder group>
Review schedule	<cadence for formally reviewing adoption progress, trust barriers, and remediation needs for this stakeholder group>

CASE EXAMPLE

Adoption Fails When Trust Is Not Designed Into the Workflow

A global manufacturer launched an analyst copilot intended to help finance and operations analysts answer recurring business questions. The architecture was strong. The copilot used governed access controls, authoritative ERP and planning data, approved policy documents, and a business glossary. Answers included citations to both structured records and unstructured explanatory documents. The retrieval layer filtered out drafts and stale content. By most technical measures, the system was sound.

Yet adoption was disappointing. Analysts continued to build answers manually. They opened dashboards, searched email chains, asked colleagues for context, and assembled commentary in spreadsheets and slide notes. Leadership interpreted the low usage as evidence that the copilot was not good enough. A review began, and the first instinct was to tune the model and rework retrieval.

But the deeper analysis showed a different picture. First, analysts did not understand how to use source-aware answers. Many assumed that a cited answer still needed to be rebuilt manually from scratch because they did not trust what counted as sufficient evidence. Second, the citation experience was technically present but behaviorally weak. Analysts viewed the answer, but rarely opened the sources. Third, managers continued to request final polished commentary rather than first-draft sourced analysis, so the workflow had not changed. Fourth, several content owners did not realize that old operational memos were still discoverable and competing with newer approved guidance.

The organization responded in four ways. It introduced role-based literacy sessions focused not on prompting, but on how to evaluate grounded answers. Analysts were taught how to inspect source authority, freshness, and semantic scope. Managers were taught to ask, "What evidence supports this interpretation?" rather than, "Can you rewrite this in a more confident tone?" Stewards were trained on how source labeling and stale content affected answer trust. It also changed the workflow. Analysts were expected to begin recurring variance research in the copilot, review the cited evidence, and only then move into narrative drafting. The review template for management packs was updated so that source-backed commentary was explicit. This made trust behavior part of the work, not an optional extra step. Next, the platform team improved trust signals. It added clearer authority labels, surfaced "most recent approved source" indicators, and provided more legible explanations when answers were incomplete due to permissions or source gaps.

Finally, stewardship was operationalized. High-value source collections were reviewed monthly. Conflicting definitions were escalated into glossary governance. Stale documents were demoted or retired.

Within a quarter, the pattern changed. Prompt volume alone did not rise dramatically, but meaningful adoption did. Analysts started using the copilot earlier in the workflow. Citation open rates increased. Time-to-first-draft fell. Managers reported greater confidence in the evidence trail. The lesson was clear: the original problem was not bad architecture. It was an incomplete adoption design.

Closing Synthesis

Enterprise AI-readiness is often described in technical terms: metadata, retrieval, semantics, policy, provenance, access control, and serving design. All of that is necessary. None of it is sufficient on its own.

The organization must also learn how to work with AI-Ready Data. It must understand what trustworthy evidence looks like in an AI-mediated interaction. It must train different roles differently. It must align stewardship behavior with retrieval reality. It must redesign workflows so that grounded answers are actually usable. It must measure adoption as a signal of trust, literacy, and design fit rather than a vanity count of interactions.

The most mature enterprises will recognize that adoption is part of architecture. They will not separate platform design from literacy, or governance from behavior, or trust signals from operating model. They will build systems that are not only technically defensible, but organizationally legible. That is what allows AI-Ready Data to become a durable enterprise capability rather than a temporary demonstration.

Key Takeaways

- Adoption is not a downstream communications task; it is an architectural design concern.
- Users need literacy in source-aware, evidence-based AI use, not just better prompts.
- Stewards and owners must adopt new habits because content quality now directly shapes AI trust.
- Change management only works when tied to workflow, ownership, and operating model shifts.
- Adoption metrics should measure trust, evidence use, and workflow integration, not just activity.

CHAPTER 27: CURRENT-STATE ASSESSMENT

No credible AI-ready transformation begins with implementation. It begins with a ruthless assessment of the current estate across sources, metadata, semantics, content, governance, identity, and readiness for safe retrieval. That framing is the right starting point because most enterprises are not constrained first by model choice. They are constrained by an estate that was never designed to support secure discovery, semantic interpretation, policy-aware delivery, defensible retrieval, or explainable use by AI systems.

This matters because organizations are often tempted to build the roadmap they want rather than the roadmap their architecture will support. They assume that because data exists, it is usable. They assume that because content lives in enterprise repositories, it is retrievable in a trustworthy way. They assume that because there is a data catalog, metadata is sufficient. They assume that because access controls exist in source systems, those controls will carry cleanly into AI workflows. Those assumptions are wrong often enough to derail transformation.

A current-state assessment is, *therefore,* not an administrative exercise. It is an architectural act of truth-telling. It forces the enterprise to confront uneven readiness across domains, exposes the real blockers to trustworthy AI, and replaces optimism with evidence. Done well, it prevents fantasy-roadmap design. Done badly, it produces a glossy maturity report that hides the very issues that will later surface as poor answers, citation failures, access leaks, stale outputs, or brittle agent behavior.

The objective is not to grade the enterprise for its own sake. The objective is to produce a heatmap of where AI-ready capability actually exists, where it is weak, and where investment will create usable progress.

WHY THIS MATTERS

Assessment Is the Difference Between Ambition and Architecture

AI programs fail when leaders fund use cases that assume capabilities the estate does not possess. A team may propose a policy assistant, a sales copilot, a contract risk summarizer, or an operations agent. On paper, each looks plausible. In practice, each depends on a very specific combination of structured data quality, document accessibility, metadata coverage, semantic consistency, access-aware retrieval, freshness control, and lineage evidence.

Without a current-state assessment, the organization confuses aspiration with readiness. It plans for enterprise-scale AI while operating with departmental metadata, fragmented content repositories, undocumented business concepts, and inconsistent ownership.

Most Organizations Misdiagnose the Real Problem

Many enterprises believe their primary blocker is data quality in the narrow reporting sense: missing values, inconsistent fields, duplicate records, and delayed feeds. Those problems matter, but they are rarely the only or even the biggest obstacle for AI. For many AI use cases, the harder problems are elsewhere:

- Documents are scattered across uncontrolled repositories.
- File names carry more meaning than metadata.
- Policy classification is inconsistent.
- Content has no authoritative source signal.
- The same business term means different things by domain.
- Access entitlements cannot be enforced at retrieval time.
- Lineage stops at ingestion rather than extending to serving.
- Stewards are named in governance decks but not operationally accountable.

These are not model problems. They are architecture and operating model problems.

Assessment Must Be Domain-Based

Enterprise-wide abstractions are useful for principles, but not for readiness decisions. "The company has a catalog" tells you almost nothing. "The claims domain has glossary coverage for its core entities, authoritative document sources for policy interpretation, and lineage to downstream retrieval products" tells you something actionable. Assessment must, *therefore,* be performed at the domain level. Sales, finance, HR, legal, supply chain, service, risk, and operations may live in the same enterprise, but they do not have the same source patterns, stewardship quality, semantic maturity, content sprawl, policy obligations, or retrieval requirements. AI-readiness is uneven by nature. The assessment must reveal that unevenness rather than averaging it away.

Use-Case Pressure Should Shape Depth

Not all domains require the same assessment depth. A low-risk knowledge assistant for internal process guidance does not demand the same rigor as an action-taking agent in claims adjudication or trade exception handling. The more consequential the use case, the more exacting the assessment must be. Use-case pressure helps determine which dimensions deserve the deepest inspection:

- If citation quality matters, provenance and source authority need more scrutiny.
- If the assistant will surface personal data, security and policy fidelity must be assessed in detail.
- If the use case depends on the current operational state, freshness, and event flow become central.
- If the use case crosses domains, semantic alignment and entity resolution become decisive.

The right question is never, "How mature is the enterprise overall?" The right question is, "How ready is this domain, for this class of AI use case, under these trust requirements?"

Core Concepts

Current-State Assessment Is an Architectural Inventory of AI-Readiness

A real assessment examines more than data stores. It examines the full estate required for trustworthy AI use:

Source reality

What systems, repositories, message streams, APIs, and file stores actually contain the needed facts and context? Which are systems of record? Which are merely copies, extracts, or convenience stores?

Metadata reality

What metadata exists, where is it maintained, how complete is it, and does it influence actual discovery, ranking, lineage, and policy enforcement? Metadata is not a catalog screenshot. It is the control plane that determines whether AI can discover, interpret, and trust what it retrieves.

Semantic reality

Are business terms defined? Are synonyms managed? Are key entities resolved consistently across systems? Are relationships explicit or left for downstream interpretation? AI systems amplify semantic ambiguity. If the enterprise does not settle meaning upstream, the assistant settles it downstream, often incorrectly.

Content reality

What unstructured content matters? Where does it live? Is it classified? Is it current? Is there an authoritative version? Can it be chunked and cited sensibly? Repositories are not readiness. Stored documents are only potential assets until they are governed, enriched, and made retrievable with context.

Governance and identity reality

Can policy, privacy, retention, legal hold, and access rights be enforced consistently across structured and unstructured sources? Are identities and entitlements resolvable at serving time, not just in source applications?

Retrieval reality

Can the estate support chunking, enrichment, ranking, freshness, source authority, access filtering, and citation generation in a defensible way? Retrieval quality is not a model-side patch. It is an architectural outcome.

Maturity Must Be Scored by Dimension, Not Assumed by Reputation

A domain with excellent structured data may still be weak in semantics and unstructured content. A domain with well-managed documents may still lack retrieval safeguards. A domain with strong ownership may still have poor freshness control. That is why a dimensional score matters. It prevents a strong capability in one area from masking a critical weakness in another. Leaders usually overestimate:

- How well enterprise content is classified.
- How complete metadata coverage really is.
- How clear ownership and stewardship actually are.
- How transferable source-system permissions are into AI delivery.
- How current supposedly authoritative documents really are.
- How consistent business definitions are across domains.
- How much retrieval trust can be improved later without upstream redesign.
- The output should be a heatmap, not a report.

Narrative findings are useful, but the primary output should be visual and comparative. A heatmap forces prioritization. It shows where domains are strong, where they are weak, and where use-case fit is highest. A long report can conceal reality in prose. A heatmap exposes it at a glance.

❖ FIGURE 54 – CURRENT-STATE ASSESSMENT FRAMEWORK

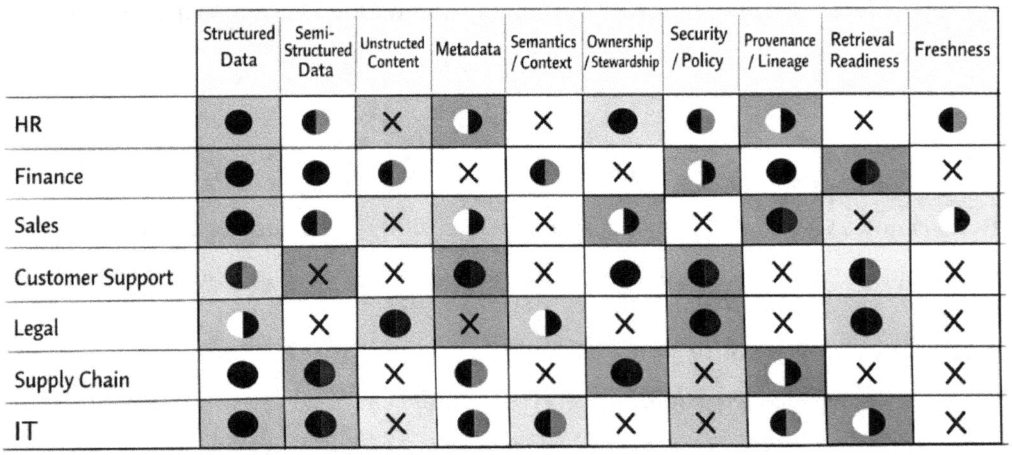

ARCHITECTURAL IMPLICATIONS

The Roadmap Must Follow Evidence, Not Politics

Once the assessment exposes uneven readiness, the roadmap should not be driven by executive preference alone. It should be driven by where the estate can support trustworthy value with manageable remediation. A domain with moderate business demand but strong metadata, clear ownership, and retrievable authoritative content may be a better first target than a politically visible domain with severe semantic ambiguity and document sprawl.

Domain Architecture Becomes the Unit of Change

This is one reason federated delivery models matter. Enterprise standards can define the scoring model, but readiness itself emerges in domains. The remediation actions are usually domain-specific:

- Define critical business entities.
- Establish content authority rules.
- Close metadata gaps.
- Rationalize repositories.
- Name accountable stewards.
- Map entitlements into serving layers.
- Instrument freshness and lineage.

The assessment should, therefore, feed domain roadmaps, not only enterprise strategy decks.

AI-serving Contracts Must Be Designed from the Findings

The assessment should directly shape data-serving contracts for different AI consumers. A knowledge assistant may tolerate moderate freshness latency but require strong citation fidelity. An analyst copilot may need richer structured semantics and metric definitions. An agent may require transaction-safe interfaces, policy gates, audit trails, and narrow source authority. Current-state assessment is the point where the enterprise decides what each class of AI consumer is realistically allowed to rely on.

Metadata and Semantics Become First-Order Investment Targets

In many enterprises, the assessment reveals that the next dollar should not go first into another model experiment or another vector index. It should go into business glossaries, taxonomies, entity definitions, source authority models, repository rationalization, document classification, and steward accountability. This often surprises leadership because those investments look less glamorous than AI pilots. They are, nonetheless, what make AI usable at scale.

Failure Modes and Anti-Patterns

Enterprise-Average Maturity

An enterprise average hides the only thing that matters: variation. If legal is strong in content control, sales is strong in CRM structure, and HR is weak in metadata, the average tells you nothing about safe use-case selection.

Source Inventory Without Retrieval Assessment

Many assessments stop at listing systems and repositories. That is incomplete. An AI-ready assessment must ask whether sources can be interpreted, filtered, ranked, cited, and governed in real use. A source that cannot support those functions may still be valuable operationally, but it is not yet AI-ready.

Treating Content as an Afterthought

Teams often assess databases in detail and documents superficially. This is backward for many enterprise AI use cases. Policies, contracts, procedures, meeting records, exception notes, product documentation, and correspondence often contain the business meaning the model needs most. If those assets are unmanaged, the use case is weaker than it appears.

Assuming Ownership Where None Exists

A named executive sponsor is not the same as operational stewardship. If nobody curates definitions, resolves content disputes, approves source authority, or owns freshness expectations, the estate is not ready, no matter how polished the architecture diagram looks.

Premature Roadmap Certainty

One of the clearest warning signs is the statement, "We already know our current state." Enterprises that say this usually know their platforms, not their readiness. They know where data is stored, not whether it is usable for grounded and governed AI.

⚠ WARNING SIGN

We already know our current state

Treat this statement as a risk indicator. It often means:

- Platform inventory is being mistaken for readiness assessment.
- Assumptions are replacing evidence.
- Content sprawl has not been examined.
- Stewardship accountability is presumed, not tested.
- Semantic inconsistency has been normalized.
- Retrieval trust has never been measured under real user entitlements.

Assessing Without Use-Case Pressure

A generic maturity survey produces generic results. The assessment only becomes useful when tested against concrete use cases with explicit trust thresholds, policy constraints, and freshness expectations.

Practical Application

How to Run the Assessment

A practical current-state assessment usually runs in four passes.

Pass 1: Define domains and candidate use cases

Select a manageable set of business domains and identify the highest-value AI use cases for each. Make the use cases concrete enough to test trust requirements. "Copilot for customer service resolution guidance" is useful. "Use AI in customer service" is not.

Pass 2: Score readiness dimensions

Score each domain against the core dimensions:

- Structured data readiness.
- Semi-structured readiness.
- Unstructured content readiness.
- Metadata quality and coverage.
- Semantic/context maturity.
- Ownership and stewardship.
- Security and policy readiness.
- Provenance and lineage.
- Retrieval readiness.
- Freshness.

Use a simple scale, but make the criteria specific. A three-level or five-level model is fine. Ambiguous scoring is worse than coarse scoring.

Pass 3: Validate with workshops and evidence

Run structured workshops with domain owners, architects, platform teams, governance leads, and operational stewards. Ask for evidence, not sentiment. Look at sample repositories, metadata completeness, glossary coverage, access patterns, lineage records, and retrieval traces where available.

Pass 4: Produce a heatmap and remediation plan

Do not end with findings alone. Produce a heatmap, identify the top blockers by domain, and translate them into architectural actions. The best assessments result in a sequenced remediation backlog, not a maturity presentation.

KEY INSIGHT

The assessment workshop questions that matter most

Ask these questions in every domain:

- What business decisions or actions will the AI use case influence?
- Which sources are authoritative, and who says so?
- What critical context exists only in documents, messages, or notes?
- What metadata is missing that would prevent trustworthy retrieval?
- Which business terms are ambiguous across systems or teams?
- How are permissions enforced today, and how would they be enforced in AI delivery?
- How would a user know whether an answer is current?
- Can the domain explain where a retrieved fact came from?
- Who is accountable for content quality, semantic clarity, and policy interpretation?
- What would make this use case unsafe or untrustworthy if deployed now?

❖ FIGURE 55 – DOMAIN HEATMAP FOR PRIORITIZATION

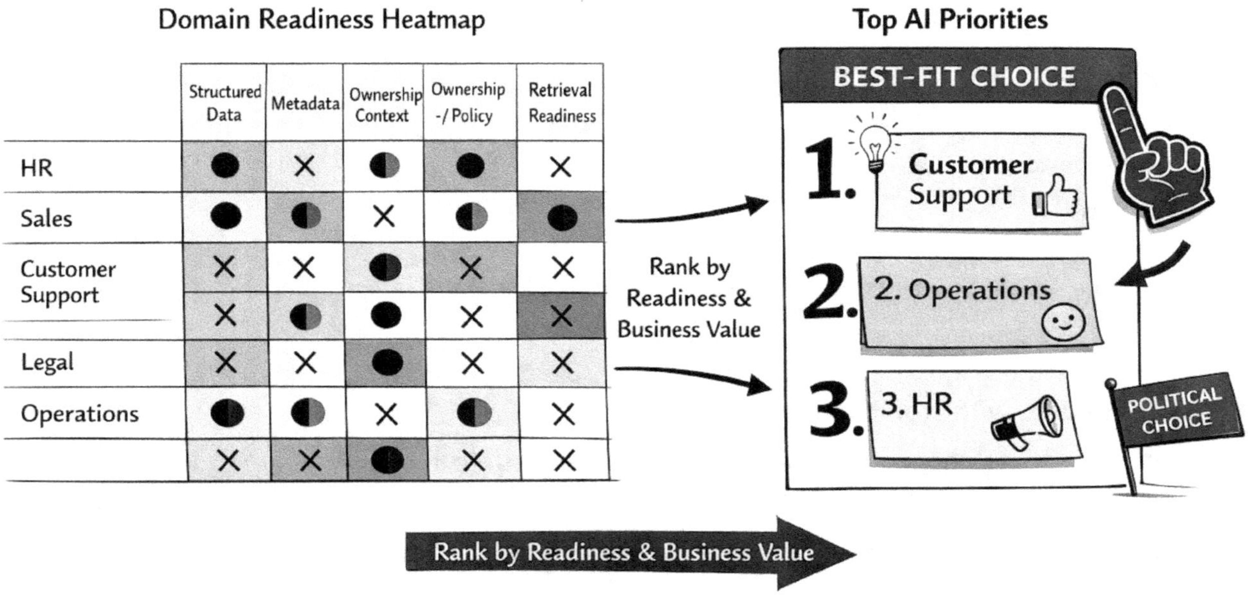

What a Good Heatmap Reveals

A good heatmap does not simply identify the lowest scores. It reveals patterns. For example:

- Several domains may be weak in metadata even when structured data is strong.
- Regulated domains may score well on policy but poorly on retrieval design.

- Customer-facing domains may have rich unstructured content but poor stewardship.
- Operations domains may have strong freshness but weak semantics.

Those patterns tell the enterprise where to establish shared capabilities and where to target domain-specific remediation.

Templates

AI-Ready Current-State Scorecard

Domain	<name of the business domain being assessed>
Core use cases	<primary AI assistants, copilots, or workflows this domain is intended to support>
Structured data readiness score	<readiness score for structured data in the domain, such as 1/5 through 5/5, with brief justification if needed>
Semi-structured readiness score	<readiness score for semi-structured data in the domain, such as events, logs, messages, or payloads, with brief justification if needed>
Unstructured content readiness score	<readiness score for documents, articles, guides, notes, or other unstructured content in the domain, with brief justification if needed>
Metadata score	<readiness score for metadata quality and completeness, including authority flags, ownership tags, and descriptive metadata>
Semantic/context score	<readiness score for shared business meaning, terminology consistency, ontology support, and contextual interpretation>
Ownership/stewardship score	<readiness score for business ownership, stewardship clarity, and operational accountability across the domain>
Security/policy score	<readiness score for access control, retrieval-time enforcement, policy alignment, and protection of sensitive content>
Provenance/lineage score	<readiness score for traceability from source through transformation, enrichment, indexing, and AI output>
Retrieval readiness score	<readiness score for chunking, ranking, citation design, authority-aware retrieval, and suppression of obsolete content>

Freshness score	<readiness score for update timeliness, publication reliability, and confidence that current content is served>
Overall maturity level	<overall maturity classification for the domain, such as not ready, emerging, partially ready, or deployment-ready>
Key blockers	<main issues preventing higher readiness, such as content sprawl, weak authority rules, incomplete metadata, inconsistent terminology, fragmented stewardship, permission gaps, or weak provenance>
Recommended next actions	<priority actions needed to improve readiness, governance, semantics, retrieval quality, permissions, and traceability>
Sponsor	<senior business sponsor accountable for supporting the domain's readiness improvement>
Assessment date	<date on which the readiness assessment was completed>

Case Example

The Current-State Assessment Revealed a Knowledge Problem, Not Just a Data Problem

A mid-size enterprise began its AI program with confidence. It had a modern cloud data platform, an enterprise reporting estate, a serviceable catalog, and several well-run data engineering teams. Leadership assumed that the major effort would be improving data quality for a few operational datasets and then connecting an assistant to existing repositories.

The current-state assessment told a different story.

The company selected three domains for review: customer support, product compliance, and sales operations. On structured data, the results were respectable. Customer and product records were broadly usable. Operational pipelines were stable. Basic technical metadata existed. Freshness for core systems was acceptable.

The real problem emerged elsewhere.

In customer support, the assistant would need to rely on troubleshooting guides, escalation notes, release bulletins, and policy exceptions. Those materials lived across a knowledge base, shared drives, collaboration spaces, and team-maintained folders. Duplicate versions were common. Some documents had no owner. Many had no effective date. Several contradicted one another. File location was being used as a proxy for trust.

In product compliance, the challenge was even sharper. Requirements interpretation existed partly in formal policy documents, partly in annotated spreadsheets, and partly in email threads between compliance specialists and product managers. The enterprise had data, but not a governed knowledge estate.

In sales operations, metric definitions appeared consistent until the assessment workshop compared dashboard logic, CRM field use, compensation rules, and deal desk guidance. "Closed," "booked," and "active customer" did not mean the same thing across workflows.

The assessment changed the roadmap immediately.

Leadership had expected to fund indexing, model tuning, and interface work. Instead, the first investments went into:

- Metadata completion for content assets.
- Domain-level stewardship assignment.
- Source authority rules.
- Business glossary and semantic alignment.
- Repository rationalization.
- Retrieval design with access-aware ranking and citation patterns.

The most important discovery was not that the company had bad data. It was that it lacked the metadata, ownership, and content discipline required for trustworthy AI. Once that became visible, the roadmap became realistic. Within months, the enterprise was no longer asking, "Which model should we deploy first?" It was asking, "Which domain can now support trustworthy retrieval and governed use?" That was the more mature question.

Closing Synthesis

Current-state assessment is where enterprise AI stops being aspirational and becomes architectural. It is the discipline that exposes whether the estate can support grounded, explainable, policy-aware, access-aware, domain-relevant AI.

It prevents fantasy-roadmap design by replacing general confidence with domain evidence. It surfaces the weaknesses leaders most often underestimate, especially in content, metadata, semantics, and stewardship. It forces the organization to assess readiness where it actually lives: inside domains, under specific use-case pressure, with real trust thresholds and policy obligations. And it produces the only output that matters at this stage: a heatmap that guides prioritization.

Organizations that skip this step usually move faster in the first quarter and slower in every quarter after that. They build prototypes on assumptions, then spend months compensating for missing context, poor retrieval, weak provenance, and governance gaps that should have been identified at the start.

Organizations that do this well move differently. They accept uneven readiness. They choose domains based on fit, not politics. They invest early in metadata, semantics, stewardship, and content authority. They align architecture to the actual demands of trustworthy AI rather than to the excitement of the moment.

That is how an enterprise begins to redesign its data estate for repeatable, governed AI at scale.

Key Takeaways

- A current-state assessment is not optional; it is the architectural starting point for any credible AI-ready transformation.
- The biggest blockers are often metadata, semantics, stewardship, and document sprawl, not conventional data quality alone.
- Readiness must be assessed by domain and against concrete use cases, not as an enterprise average.
- The right output is a heatmap tied to remediation actions, not a generic maturity report.
- The assessment should directly shape roadmap priorities, data-serving contracts, and domain investment decisions.

Chapter 28: Prioritizing Use Cases and Choosing the First Domains

The first domains in an AI-Ready Data program should not be chosen by excitement, visibility, or executive curiosity alone. They should be chosen where business value, data suitability, trust requirements, and transformation feasibility align. That is the difference between a first wave that compounds learning and one that institutionalizes technical debt.

This matters because early AI choices are rarely isolated experiments. They shape funding patterns, architectural norms, control expectations, and political narratives. If the first use case succeeds for the wrong reasons, the organization learns the wrong lesson. If it fails because the team chose a glamorous but unready domain, the organization may conclude that the technology is immature when the real problem was poor domain selection.

In enterprise settings, the first wave is not just a product decision. It is an architectural commitment. The initial use case determines which data domains are forced into the spotlight, which metadata gaps are exposed first, which governance controls are tested, which serving patterns are normalized, and which stakeholders gain confidence or lose it.

The right starting point is, therefore, not simply the most valuable idea. It is the most valuable viable idea.

Why This Matters

Enterprises often say they are prioritizing AI by business value. In practice, many are prioritizing by executive visibility, vendor demos, or the loudest internal sponsor. That is how organizations end up starting with use cases that look impressive in a steering committee but collapse under real trust, permission, and provenance requirements.

A use case can be commercially attractive and still be a poor first move. For example, a revenue-facing sales assistant may promise obvious upside, but if product collateral is inconsistent, pricing rules are fragmented, CRM semantics are weak, and entitlement boundaries are unclear, the assistant will become a machine for scaling ambiguity. The business will see activity, but not reliable value.

By contrast, internal enterprise use cases often provide a better first proving ground. They are closer to authoritative internal sources, easier to constrain, and more forgiving than external or high-profile uses. They let the organization build the muscles that matter: metadata enrichment, access-aware retrieval, source ranking, citation discipline, lineage capture, and policy-aware delivery. Those are reusable capabilities. They should be built where learning is fast and harm is controlled.

That is why first-wave prioritization is an enterprise architecture decision. It determines whether the organization builds a reusable AI-Ready Data foundation or a pile of disconnected pilots.

KEY INSIGHT

A good pilot teaches the right lessons

A first pilot should do more than prove that a model can answer questions. It should reveal whether the organization can identify authoritative sources, enrich them with metadata, enforce permissions, track provenance, and serve answers with defensible evidence. A pilot that succeeds without teaching those disciplines is a misleading success.

CORE CONCEPTS

Attractive Use Cases Are Not Always Suitable Starting Points

The first filtering mistake is to confuse attractiveness with suitability.

Attractiveness is usually expressed in business language: large user population, visible pain point, executive attention, or measurable upside. Suitability is architectural: source quality, metadata maturity, semantic clarity, governance complexity, and trust tolerance.

A use case is a strong first-wave candidate only when both are present.

This is where many programs go wrong. They assume that if a use case is important, the architecture can simply be made to work around it. In reality, the first wave should favor conditions that make disciplined learning possible. If the team must solve every hard problem at once—identity, entity resolution, retention, content quality, fine-grained authorization, citation fidelity, semantic ambiguity, and freshness—then the use case is not a pilot. It is a transformation program disguised as a demo.

Internal Enterprise Use Cases Are Usually the Best Proving Ground

Internal enterprise use cases often outperform external or highly visible uses as starting points for one reason: they let the organization learn under constraint. Examples include:

- Internal policy and procedure Q&A.
- Service desk knowledge copilots.
- Contract clause retrieval for internal legal teams.
- Engineering runbook assistants.
- Controlled analyst research copilots using governed internal content.

These use cases still require serious architecture. They still demand permission fidelity, provenance, version control, and source authority. But they usually avoid the immediate reputational and legal exposure of customer-facing responses or executive-level synthesis across many partially governed domains.

The goal is not to stay internal forever. The goal is to start where the enterprise can build reliable patterns before moving into more exposed terrain.

Domain Readiness Matters as Much as Business Demand

A domain is not ready because people want to use it. A domain is ready when its data can be discovered, interpreted, governed, and served with confidence.

For first-wave AI prioritization, domain readiness should be assessed across at least five dimensions:

Structured readiness

Are the core entities, identifiers, and transactional records stable enough to support grounding, joins, filters, and context assembly?

Unstructured readiness

Do the documents, policies, notes, transcripts, and knowledge assets exist in authoritative form, with clear ownership and manageable duplication?

Metadata readiness

Can sources be classified, ranked, filtered, explained, and governed through usable metadata such as owner, effective date, document type, sensitivity, business term mapping, and source authority?

Governance readiness

Can the domain support retention rules, access control, privacy obligations, and defensible traceability?

Operational readiness

Is there stewardship, sponsorship, and a realistic path to improve defects discovered during implementation?

Business demand without domain readiness creates theater. Domain readiness without business demand creates shelfware. The first domains should have enough of both to justify investment and enough control to produce trustworthy outcomes.

Quick Wins Must Still Build Reusable Capability

The phrase "quick win" has damaged many architecture programs because it is often interpreted as "something small and easy." That is not the right standard.

A quick win should be defined as a use case that can produce value quickly while forcing the organization to build capabilities it will need again. Those capabilities include source inventory, metadata enrichment, trust scoring, access-aware retrieval, semantic normalization, evidence presentation, and domain stewardship.

A quick win that depends on manual curation, special-case permissions, or one-off prompt tricks is not a win. It is a local workaround.

First-Wave Choices Shape Credibility and Direction

Early wins produce more than momentum. They shape the political map of the program.

If the first use case is well chosen, the enterprise learns that trustworthy AI depends on architectural discipline. Stakeholders see why metadata, semantics, provenance, and governance matter. The program earns credibility by being correct, explainable, and useful.

If the first use case is poorly chosen, the enterprise learns the opposite lesson. It may conclude that speed matters more than source authority, that answers without citations are acceptable, or that cleanup can happen later. Those lessons are expensive to unlearn.

KEY INSIGHT

Value vs feasibility vs trust risk

High-value use cases often sit in the zone of highest trust risk and greatest implementation complexity. A disciplined prioritization method forces all three dimensions into the decision at once. Value alone is not enough. Feasibility alone is not enough. Low risk alone is not enough. The first wave should sit where meaningful value can be delivered without outrunning the organization's control capabilities.

ARCHITECTURAL IMPLICATIONS

Prioritization Must Be Tied to Data-Serving Contracts

Different AI consumers require different serving contracts. A knowledge assistant can often operate with bounded retrieval and citation requirements. An analyst copilot may need richer joins, freshness controls, and semantic disambiguation. An executive briefing tool requires synthesis across sources with strong temporal correctness and explicit evidence. An action-taking agent requires all of that plus policy-aware execution controls.

That means use-case prioritization is inseparable from data-serving design. Before selecting a first-wave use case, the architecture team should be able to answer:

- What evidence must the system show?
- What freshness window is acceptable?
- What sources are authoritative?
- What permissions apply at retrieval time?
- What confidence or abstention behavior is required?
- What audit trail must be retained?

A use case whose serving contract the organization cannot yet meet is not a first-wave candidate, even if the business case is strong.

Domain Choice Determines Which Architectural Muscles Are Built First

Choosing an internal policy Q&A assistant forces the organization to solve authoritative document identification, effective-date metadata, version control, citation design, and permission-aware retrieval.

Choosing a sales assistant forces it to solve customer-account entity resolution, content freshness, product hierarchy semantics, pricing governance, contract interpretation boundaries, and regional entitlement complexity.

Choosing executive intelligence forces it to solve cross-domain synthesis, source conflict handling, temporal reconciliation, access-aware summarization, and high-consequence trust calibration.

Each of those is valuable. The question is not whether those capabilities matter. The question is which set of capabilities should be forced first.

For most enterprises, the right answer is to begin where the capability gaps are real but bounded.

Prioritization Should Reward Reuse, Not Local Optimization

A good first-wave domain creates assets that survive the first use case:

- Business glossary extensions.
- Taxonomies for document type and source authority.
- Content quality rules.
- Stewardship roles.

- Access-aware retrieval patterns.
- Citation and evidence standards.
- Provenance logging.
- Ranking signals and trust labels.

These are enterprise assets, not pilot artifacts. That is why reuse potential must be an explicit part of prioritization.

Domain Selection Should Be Sequenced, Not One-Off

The first domain should not be selected in isolation. It should be chosen as the first move in a sequence. A sound sequence often looks like this:

- Start with a bounded internal use case in a domain with strong source authority.
- Expand into a related domain that reuses the same metadata, governance, and retrieval patterns.
- Move into higher-value and higher-risk domains only after proving that trust, lineage, and permission controls hold under pressure.

This approach creates compounding architectural value instead of a collection of disconnected experiments.

Failure Modes and Anti-Patterns

Choosing the Most Visible Use Case Instead of the Most Viable One

This is the most common early error. The organization chooses a board-facing, revenue-facing, or customer-facing scenario because it appears strategic. In reality, it is often too dependent on immature cross-domain integration, too exposed to trust failure, and too difficult to govern in the time available.

⚠ Warning Sign

Choosing the most visible use case instead of the most viable one

Visibility is not evidence of readiness. A high-visibility use case amplifies every weakness in metadata, provenance, permissions, and source quality. If the first deployment must defend every answer to the executive committee, the program may be starting several stages too late.

Treating Domain Demand as Proof of Domain Readiness

Business users frequently ask for AI in the domains where they feel the most friction. That signal matters, but it does not prove architectural readiness. Sometimes the most painful domains are painful precisely because their semantics are unstable, their content is fragmented, and their ownership is unresolved.

High demand can justify eventual investment. It does not automatically justify first-wave selection.

Optimizing for Speed at the Expense of Control

Programs under pressure often strip away the very elements that make enterprise AI trustworthy: citations, confidence boundaries, source filtering, access-aware retrieval, retention controls, and quality thresholds. This creates faster demos and weaker systems.

The problem is not only risk. It is also learning. A pilot that bypasses governance and metadata does not prepare the enterprise for scale.

Assuming Documents in Repositories Are Ready for AI

Many first-wave mistakes come from repository optimism. Teams assume that because thousands of documents exist in SharePoint, Teams, drives, or content platforms, they already have a knowledge base.

They do not.

Documents are not AI-ready merely because they are stored somewhere. They need ownership, authority signals, duplication control, effective dates, classification, permission fidelity, and suitable retrieval design. Without those, the system retrieves volume rather than truth.

Ignoring Reuse Potential

Some pilots create local value but no durable architecture. They rely on hand-selected files, manually maintained answer sets, or hard-coded filters that no other domain can reuse.

These pilots are seductive because they appear successful. But they leave the enterprise no closer to a governed, reusable AI-Ready Data estate.

PRACTICAL APPLICATION

A Disciplined Prioritization Method

A practical prioritization model should score candidate use cases across four weighted dimensions:

- **Business value:** magnitude of the problem, user adoption potential, measurable outcome.
- **Feasibility:** source quality, data accessibility, domain ownership, implementation complexity.
- **Trust and control readiness:** provenance, permissions, risk profile, explainability requirements.
- **Reuse potential:** likelihood that the metadata, governance, and serving patterns will be reused elsewhere.

This is not a spreadsheet exercise for its own sake. It is a forcing mechanism. It prevents the organization from skipping the hard but necessary questions.

❖ FIGURE 56 – USE-CASE PRIORITIZATION MATRIX

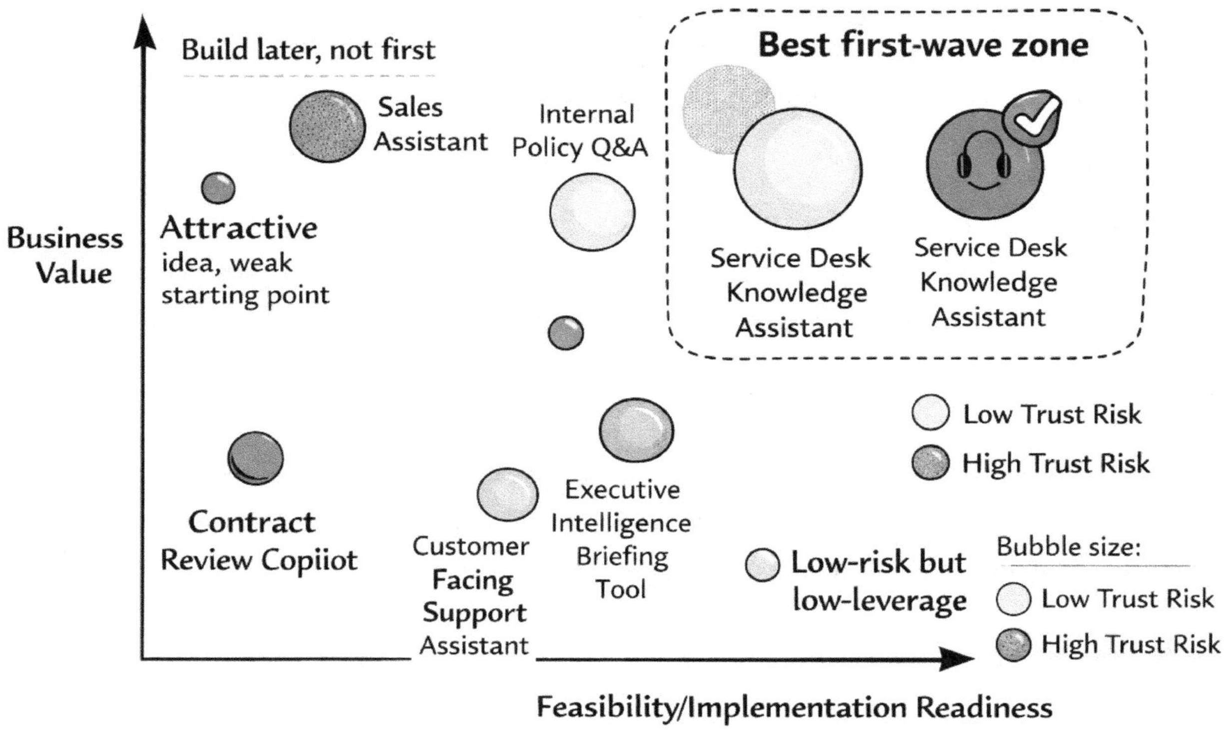

A Domain Selection Framework

After scoring the use case, the team should compare candidate domains using a structured set of architectural questions:

- Are authoritative sources identifiable?
- Is the domain vocabulary stable enough for semantic interpretation?
- Are permissions understandable and enforceable?
- Are effective dates, lineage, and ownership visible?
- Is there enough stewardship to fix defects discovered during rollout?
- Can the domain support a strong citation model?
- Will the implementation produce reusable metadata and governance patterns?

❖ FIGURE 57 – DOMAIN SELECTION FRAMEWORK

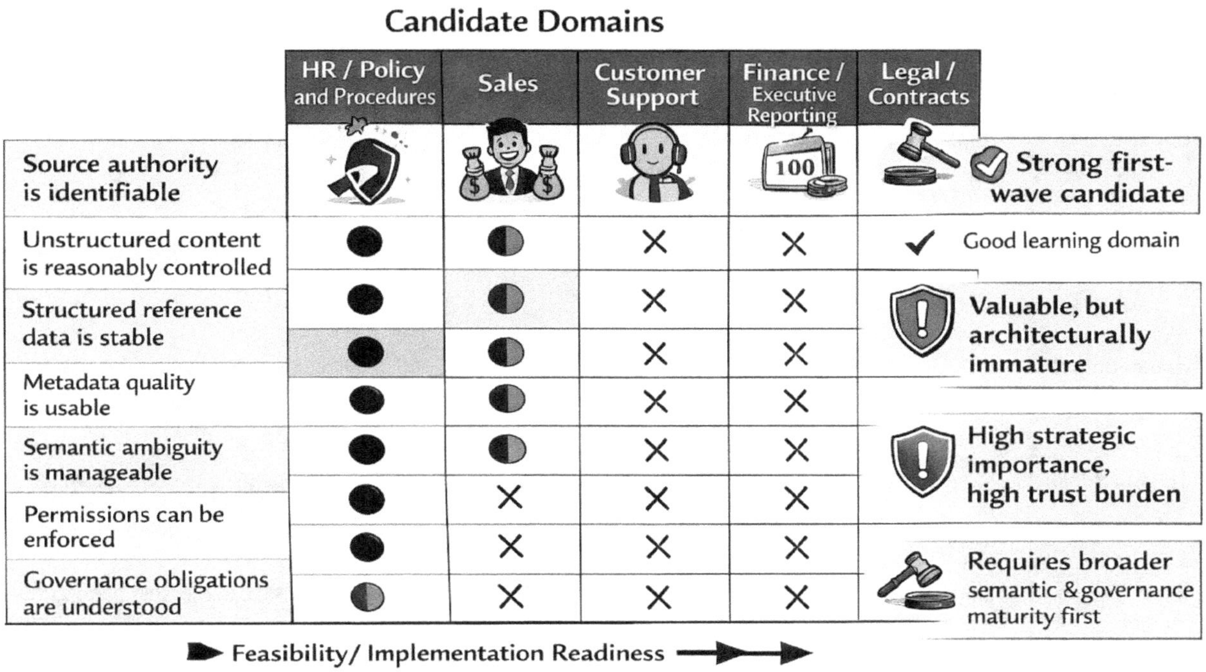

TEMPLATES

Use Case Prioritization Model

Use case name	<name of the proposed AI assistant, copilot, or use case being evaluated>
Business objective	<business outcome the use case is intended to improve, such as speed, consistency, productivity, auditability, or decision support>
Target users	<primary user groups, roles, or teams expected to use the capability>
Data domains required	<business domains, data sources, content types, and metadata needed for the use case to function effectively>
Structured readiness	<assessment of how ready the required structured data is, including key strengths and limitations>
Unstructured readiness	<assessment of how ready the required unstructured content is, including document quality, governance, and availability>

Metadata readiness <assessment of how complete and reliable the metadata is, including authority, ownership, effective dates, and semantic linkage>

Governance risk <level of governance, compliance, or control risk associated with the use case if answers are wrong, incomplete, or outdated>

Security/privacy complexity <level of security, privacy, access-control, and entitlement complexity involved in supporting the use case safely>

Trust sensitivity <degree to which the use case depends on highly trustworthy, cited, abstaining, and evidence-backed answers>

Reuse potential <degree to which the patterns, controls, and architecture developed for this use case can be reused across future assistants or copilots>

Time to value <expected speed at which the organization can deliver meaningful business value from the use case>

Executive sponsorship <strength of senior-business support and likelihood of visible leadership backing>

Overall score <overall prioritization score for the candidate use case, using the organization's chosen scoring method>

Recommendation <recommended sequencing decision, such as start here, first wave, second wave, later wave, or do not select yet>

Notes <additional rationale explaining why this use case is or is not a good candidate at the current stage of AI-Ready Data maturity>

CASE EXAMPLE

Choose the First Use Case That Builds the Right AI Architecture

Consider a regulated enterprise deciding between three first-wave options: internal policy Q&A, a sales assistant, and executive intelligence.

At first glance, the sales assistant appears to have the strongest headline business case. It touches revenue, supports a large user group, and fits a familiar narrative about AI-driven growth. Executive intelligence appears even more strategic because it speaks directly to leadership decision-making. Internal policy Q&A looks less exciting.

But architecture changes the answer.

The internal policy Q&A use case has a bounded user population, a controlled source set, and a clear requirement for authoritative answers. It forces the organization to solve document authority, approval state, effective dating, permission-aware retrieval, and citation design. Those are not side issues. They are core AI-Ready Data capabilities. The use case also exposes common enterprise weaknesses—duplicate documents, obsolete versions, missing ownership, weak classification—in a manageable setting where defects can be corrected.

The sales assistant is powerful, but it asks too much too early. It requires stable customer and account semantics, reconciled product information, current pricing logic, approved messaging, contract interpretation boundaries, and fine-grained entitlements. It also creates behavioral risk because users may act on imperfect advice in live commercial situations. This can absolutely become a major second-wave or third-wave capability, but it is usually a poor place to learn the basics of governed retrieval and evidence-based response.

Executive intelligence is the most dangerous first-wave choice. It requires synthesis across many domains whose definitions, reporting cycles, and permissions differ. It is highly exposed to stale or conflicting information. It invites over-trust because the audience is senior. It also creates strong political pressure to make the system appear broader and smarter than the underlying data estate can safely support.

The disciplined choice is internal policy Q&A.

That choice does not mean the enterprise lacks ambition. It means the enterprise understands sequence. First, prove that authoritative sources can be identified, governed, retrieved, cited, and explained. Next, extend those patterns into domains with more structured complexity and greater actionability, such as sales. Only then move into high-synthesis, high-consequence scenarios such as executive intelligence.

This is how serious enterprises scale trustworthy AI: not by starting with the flashiest use case, but by starting with the use case that builds the right architecture.

Closing Synthesis

The first AI-ready domains should be selected with the same discipline used for any other core architectural decision. The question is not which use case sounds most impressive. The question is which use case lets the enterprise create real value while building reusable capabilities for trust, governance, metadata, semantics, and delivery.

That is why not every attractive use case is a good starting point. It is why internal use cases often make the best first proving ground. It is why domain readiness matters as much as business demand. It is why quick wins must still build reusable capability. And it is why first-wave choices shape both political credibility and architectural direction.

A weak first choice teaches the organization to confuse demos with readiness. A strong first choice teaches the organization how to build an AI-Ready Data estate.

The enterprises that scale trustworthy AI will not be the ones that start with the loudest use case. They will be the ones that start where value, feasibility, trust, and reuse align—and then expand deliberately from there.

Key Takeaways

- The best first AI use case is not the most exciting one; it is the most valuable viable one.
- Internal, bounded enterprise use cases usually provide the safest and most educational first proving ground.
- Domain readiness must be assessed across structured data, unstructured content, metadata, governance, and operating ownership.
- Quick wins are only worth pursuing if they create reusable architectural capability.
- First-wave choices shape not only outcomes, but the enterprise's long-term standards for trust, evidence, and control.

CHAPTER 29: DESIGNING THE TARGET STATE

A target state is useful only if it can be built. That sounds obvious, yet many enterprise AI target-state exercises fail at precisely this point. They produce attractive diagrams, broad capability lists, and ambitious narratives, but they do not describe the first executable architecture. They describe aspiration without constraint. The result is predictable: teams debate abstractions, vendors map products to boxes, and implementation stalls because no one can answer the simplest question—what exactly are we building first, for whom, with what controls, and under whose authority?

For AI-Ready Data, the target state must do more than point toward modernization. It must translate business ambition into concrete architectural decisions. It must define which source classes matter first, what metadata must be captured, how semantics will be expressed, how governance will be enforced, how retrieval will work, which AI consumers are in scope, and which operating assumptions are non-negotiable. It must also define what is not being built yet. This is why the first target state should not be a theoretical end-state. It should be the first durable state. Durable means it can support real use cases, survive audit and operational scrutiny, and expand without being replaced. If the first design only works as a pilot architecture, it is not a target state. It is a temporary scaffold.

In practical terms, target-state design for AI-Ready Data is the act of choosing the first architectural shape that makes trustworthy AI possible. It is constrained by use case, informed by enterprise reality, and structured to enable later growth. That is the design discipline this chapter addresses.

WHY THIS MATTERS

The Wrong Target State Creates Expensive Motion Without Progress

Enterprises rarely fail because they lack diagrams. They fail because their diagrams do not encode operational truth.

A target state that says "connect all enterprise data to AI" is not a target state. It is a slogan. A target state that shows repositories flowing into a vector store and then into a copilot is not a target state either, unless it also shows classification, source authority, identity propagation, semantic interpretation, lineage, freshness handling, and who owns the delivery path. Without those elements, the architecture may generate answers, but it will not generate trust. This matters because AI systems are unforgiving of architectural ambiguity. Analytics platforms can sometimes tolerate loose business definitions, delayed metadata curation, and partial lineage. AI systems cannot. A retrieval experience is only as trustworthy as its source eligibility rules. A grounding answer is only as defensible as its provenance. An agent action is only as safe as its permission model and policy context. When the target state leaves these issues vague, implementation teams improvise them later. That is when inconsistency, risk, and rework enter the estate.

The First Executable State Sets the Trajectory

The first real target state becomes precedent. It shapes how teams think about metadata, how governance is embedded, how content is prepared, how trust is evaluated, and how future use cases are admitted.

If that first state is well designed, later expansion becomes a disciplined extension. Analyst copilots can inherit semantic assets built for a knowledge assistant. Executive briefing tools can inherit source authority rules, citation patterns, and trust thresholds. Action-taking agents can inherit identity and policy foundations rather than bypass them.

If the first state is poorly designed, every later use case becomes a special case. Teams create separate ingestion paths, local glossaries, duplicate embeddings, inconsistent entitlements, and fragmented measures of quality. What begins as one pilot quickly becomes five architectures held together by enthusiasm.

AI-ready Architecture Must Show Control as Well as Capability

A mature target state is not just a capability map. It is a control map. That means the architecture must show how the organization will know what data exists, what it means, who may use it, when it can be surfaced, what the source of truth is, how evidence is preserved, and how quality and risk are monitored over time. Capability without control creates adoption risk. Control without capability creates delay. The target state must join them.

KEY INSIGHT

Design the first durable state, not the perfect future

The target state is not a fantasy of full enterprise convergence. It is the first architecture that can be governed, operated, and expanded. If the design cannot survive real implementation trade-offs, it is not a target state.

CORE CONCEPTS

Constrained Scope Is a Design Strength

The first principle of target-state design is constraint. A target state must be narrow enough to implement and broad enough to matter. That usually means constraining along four dimensions:

Use case

Start with a concrete AI consumer and a bounded task. "Enterprise knowledge assistant for HR and policy questions" is designable. "AI for employee productivity" is not.

Domain

Choose the domains whose semantics, authority, and controls are needed first. Early scope should favor domains where business meaning is important, source ownership is identifiable, and answer risk can be managed.

Source class

Specify which kinds of sources will participate in the first state: structured systems of record, document repositories, knowledge platforms, event streams, or collaboration content. Not every source class needs to be admitted in phase one.

Trust contract

Define what the AI system must be able to prove. Must it cite authoritative sources? Must it respect document-level ACLs? Must it distinguish policy-effective dates from publication dates? Must it refuse when confidence or evidence is insufficient? Those are architectural decisions, not prompt decisions.

Constraint is not a weakness. It is what makes a target state executable.

A Target State Is a Set of Decisions, Not a Picture

The second principle is that a target state must encode decisions that downstream teams can act on. At *a* minimum, it must answer the following:

- Which data and content classes are in scope?
- What metadata standard will govern discovery, ranking, trust, and lineage?
- What semantic layer will reduce ambiguity?
- How access control and identity will propagate?
- What governance obligations must be enforced before delivery?
- Which retrieval and grounding patterns are allowed?
- What AI consumer types are supported?
- Which platform assumptions are fixed and which remain flexible?
- Who owns each capability operationally?

A diagram may summarize these choices, but it cannot substitute for them.

The First Target State Must Enable Later Expansion

The third principle is extension by design. Phase one should not attempt to serve every AI consumer, but it must avoid blocking later ones. For example, a knowledge assistant may initially need document retrieval with citations and permission-aware search. An analyst copilot will later need that, plus governed access to structured metrics, semantic definitions, and aggregation logic. An executive copilot will need curated summarization across authoritative sources with temporal correctness and business context. If the first target state ignores metadata standardization, domain semantics, or provenance models because "the first use case only needs documents," it quietly guarantees rework later.

A good first target state, *therefore,* chooses shared foundations even when the immediate use case could get by without them.

Principles Matter More Than Tool Names

A tool choice may accelerate delivery, but it is not the architecture. The architecture is the set of invariants that should remain true even if platforms evolve. For example:

- Metadata must drive discoverability, policy, trust, and lineage.
- Access control must remain source-faithful through retrieval and serving.
- Semantic interpretation must be explicit enough to reduce ambiguity.
- Governance must cover structured and unstructured assets together.
- Retrieval must prioritize authority, freshness, and explainability rather than raw similarity alone.

If those principles are clear, the organization can implement them on different platforms. If those principles are absent, naming tools only hide the design gap.

Architectural Implications

The Target State Must Name the Major Layers

A practical AI-ready target state usually includes at least five layers.

Source classes

These include structured systems of record, semi-structured operational feeds, and unstructured repositories such as knowledge bases, policies, contracts, transcripts, and collaborative content. Each source class carries different preparation and control requirements.

Control layer

This spans classification, retention, privacy, legal hold, lineage, entitlement mapping, source authority designation, stewardship, and monitoring. It is not a sidecar. It must cut across every stage.

Semantic layer

This layer includes glossary terms, taxonomies, ontologies where needed, canonical entities, relationship models, and domain definitions. It is the mechanism that lets AI systems interpret terms consistently across sources.

❖ FIGURE 58 – TARGET-STATE REFERENCE ARCHITECTURE

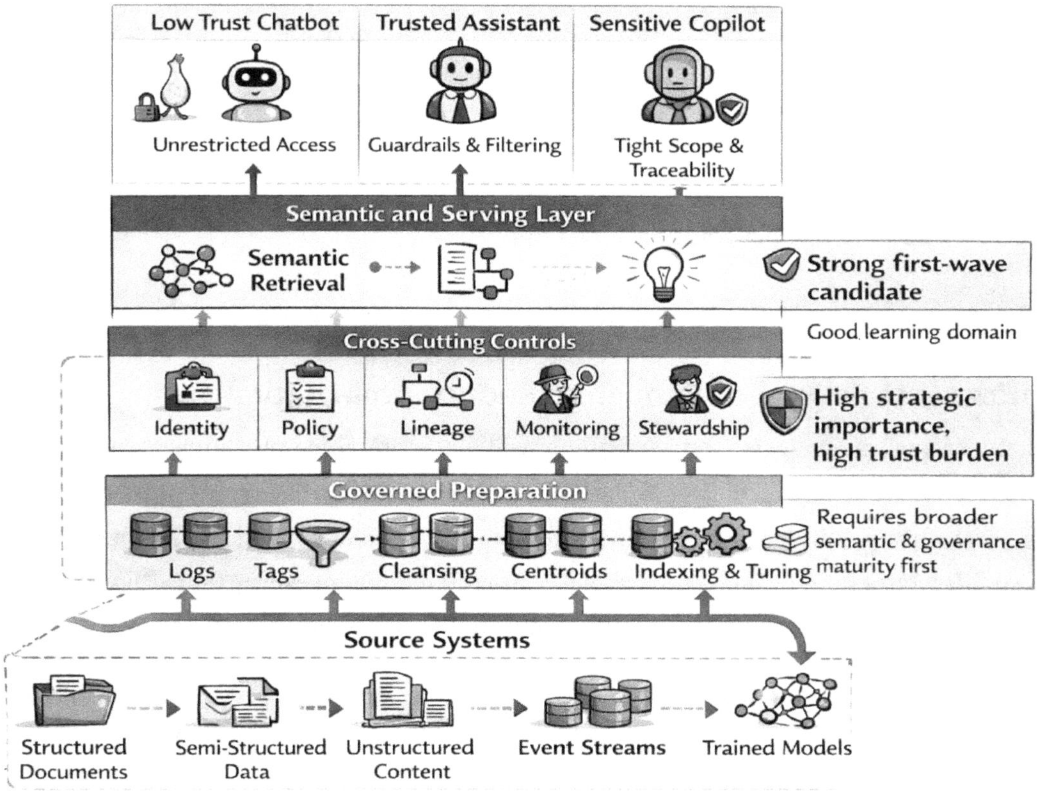

Retrieval and grounding layer

This includes content preparation, chunking strategy, enrichment, indexing, ranking, access-aware retrieval, freshness handling, source weighting, and citation generation.

Serving layer

This is where AI consumers interact with the estate: knowledge assistants, analyst copilots, executive briefings, or agents. Each requires a different contract for evidence, latency, actionability, and refusal behavior.

Metadata Standard Is Not Optional

The target state must specify what metadata is mandatory in phase one. Without that, discoverability and trust become inconsistent. A workable phase-one metadata standard often includes:

- Business title and description.
- Domain and subdomain.
- Asset type and source system.
- Owner and steward.
- Classification and handling requirements.
- Record status and retention disposition.
- Source authority designation.
- Effective date and last-updated date.
- Provenance and transformation lineage.
- Permitted use and excluded use.
- Semantic tags and linked glossary terms.
- Quality status and review cadence.

This is not bureaucratic overhead. It is the minimum data needed to make AI delivery defensible.

Semantics Must Be Explicit Enough to Reduce Ambiguity

Target-state design must decide how meaning will be represented. In some cases, glossary-plus-taxonomy is enough. In others, entity resolution and ontology patterns are necessary because the same business term means different things in different operational contexts. "Customer," "member," "subscriber," "account holder," and "policyholder" are not interchangeable just because users speak as if they are. If the target state does not specify how such ambiguity is handled, the AI layer will absorb the confusion and reflect it back as plausible but wrong answers.

Governance Must Be Visible in the Design

If governance is implied but not shown, teams will treat it as deferred work. That is dangerous in AI programs because the serving experience is often built faster than the control model. The target state should, therefore, make governance concrete:

- Which classifications exclude assets from retrieval.
- Which content requires human approval before inclusion.
- How retention and legal hold affect serving eligibility.
- How privacy obligations constrain chunking, enrichment, and logging.
- How exceptions are approved.
- How audit evidence is produced.

KEY INSIGHT

What target-state diagrams usually leave out

Most target-state diagrams show ingestion, indexing, and serving. They do not show content eligibility rules, stewardship checkpoints, authority scoring, temporal validity, policy inheritance, or operational ownership. Those omissions are not cosmetic. They are the difference between a demo and an enterprise architecture.

Operating Assumptions Belong Inside the Target State

A reference architecture with no operating assumptions is structurally incomplete. The target state should specify:

- Which teams own source onboarding.
- Who curates domain semantics.
- Who approves source eligibility.
- How retrieval quality is measured.
- How policy changes propagate.
- What support model applies when AI answers are disputed.
- Which incidents trigger rollback or source suppression.

Without those assumptions, the architecture has no executable governance.

WARNING SIGN

A reference architecture with no operating assumptions

If no team can explain who owns metadata quality, source eligibility, retrieval tuning, or policy enforcement, the target state is not ready. It is only a diagram.

FAILURE MODES AND ANTI-PATTERNS

Designing the Universal Future State First

Some organizations try to design the architecture that will eventually support every assistant, copilot, and agent. This usually produces a maximalist model with no sequence, no delivery logic, and no acceptance criteria.

The remedy is to design the first durable state first. Expansion should be an architectural property, not an initial scope commitment.

Equating Repositories with Readiness

Another common mistake is assuming that because content exists in SharePoint, Teams, file shares, ticketing systems, or knowledge platforms, it is ready for AI retrieval. It is not.

Content may be stale, duplicative, weakly titled, missing owners, improperly permissioned, devoid of effective dates, or semantically ambiguous. A target state that ignores content preparation and source authority modeling will produce noisy answers and erode trust quickly.

Over-Indexing on the Retrieval Engine

Teams often spend too much time choosing vector databases, ranking approaches, or LLM orchestration layers before defining authority rules, metadata, access propagation, and semantic normalization.

Retrieval quality is an architecture problem, not a product shopping problem. The engine matters, but it sits downstream of more fundamental decisions.

Treating Governance as a Later Phase

This usually appears as, "Let us prove value first, then we will add controls." In enterprise AI, that sequencing is backward. The ability to prove value depends on the controls being present. If users cannot trust source provenance, access fidelity, or citation behavior, adoption will stall no matter how fluent the model seems.

Failing to Distinguish AI Consumer Types

A knowledge assistant, analyst copilot, executive summarizer, and action-taking agent do not share the same contract.

A knowledge assistant may safely answer only from curated authoritative content with citations. An analyst copilot may need governed access to metrics and calculation logic. An executive tool may require summarization across multiple sources but with stricter source weighting and temporal controls. An agent may need write-back permissions, transactional safeguards, and policy-aware decision constraints. A target state that collapses these into "AI applications" is too vague to implement responsibly.

Practical Application

How to Design the First Target State

A practical sequence looks like this.

Step 1: Anchor on one business objective

The objective should be concrete enough to test. For example, reduce time to answer employee policy questions while increasing answer consistency and citation quality.

Step 2: Select in-scope use cases

Choose a small number of user journeys, not a broad persona statement. For example:

- Employees ask benefits and leave-policy questions.
- HR operations staff answer escalated policy questions.
- Managers validate policy obligations for employee actions.
- Step 3: Identify domains and source classes.

Select only the domains and content needed to answer those journeys. Then classify source types: policy repository, HR knowledge base, intranet guidance pages, selected system-of-record tables for organization and eligibility context.

Step 4: Define the trust contract

Specify what the system must do to be acceptable:

- Cite authoritative sources.
- Respect existing permissions.
- Distinguish current policy from superseded policy.
- Refuse when no authoritative evidence exists.
- Log evidence for review.

Step 5: Choose foundational cross-use-case capabilities

Even if phase one is narrow, include the metadata, semantic, and governance foundations that later copilots will need. This is where future-proofing belongs.

Step 6: Write the operating model

Document who approves onboarding, who owns semantics, who tunes retrieval, who monitors trust metrics, and who resolves disputes.

Step 7: State what is deferred

A good target state has a disciplined "not yet" section. That prevents accidental scope expansion and protects implementation quality.

Making the Target State Testable

A good target state must be testable before it is fully built. That means writing acceptance criteria such as:

- The assistant answers only from approved authoritative sources.
- Every answer includes citations that resolve to visible source passages.
- Superseded policies are excluded or clearly labeled.
- Users do not receive grounded answers from content they are not entitled to view.
- Disputed answers can be traced to retrieval logs, source versions, and ranking rationale.

If the target state cannot be translated into test criteria, it is still too abstract.

❖ FIGURE 59 – CURRENT-TO-TARGET TRANSITION

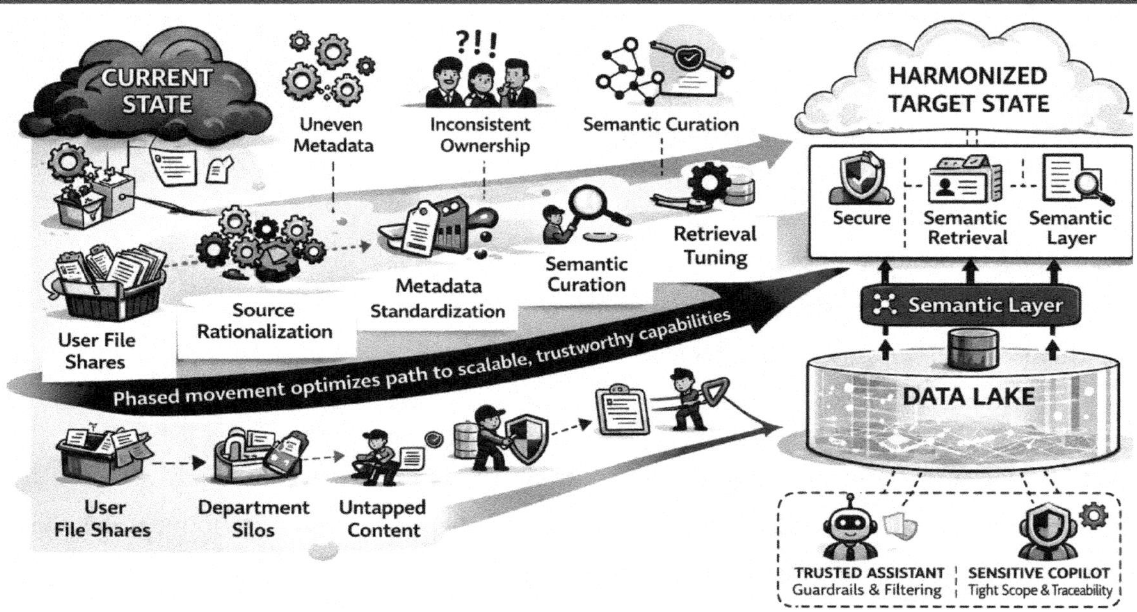

TEMPLATES

Target-State Blueprint Template

Strategic objective	<primary architectural and business objective the initiative is intended to achieve, including the target AI capability and the reusable foundations it should create>
In-scope use cases	<AI assistants, copilots, workflows, or retrieval scenarios explicitly included within the current initiative scope>

In-scope domains	<business domains, policy areas, or subject areas covered by the architecture and operating model>
Core architecture principles	<foundational design principles that must guide the architecture, such as use-case grounding, metadata-driven control, source-faithful access enforcement, semantic clarity, authoritative-source prioritization, explainability, platform agnosticism, and phased extensibility>
Source classes	<types of source content, records, reference data, notifications, or metadata feeds included in the architecture>
Metadata standard	<mandatory metadata fields and control attributes required for assets to be discoverable, governed, retrievable, and safe for AI use>
Semantic strategy	<glossary, taxonomy, synonym management, entity resolution, ontology, or other semantic methods required to support correct interpretation and disambiguation>
Governance model	<governance structure, approval responsibilities, exception handling, audit expectations, and pattern-compliance mechanisms that govern the architecture>
Identity/access model	<approach for identity federation, ACL inheritance, access filtering, derived-asset controls, and audit logging for access-sensitive retrieval and serving>
Retrieval/grounding pattern	<retrieval and answer-grounding design, including metadata use, semantic retrieval, authority-aware ranking, date filtering, chunking, enrichment, evidence-based generation, citation requirements, and abstention behavior>
AI consumer types	<phased or approved categories of AI consumers, such as assistants, copilots, or briefing tools, that the architecture is intended to support over time>
Platform assumptions	<assumptions about systems of record, metadata synchronization, identity federation, shared governance patterns, observability, and optional tooling flexibility>
Operating model	<allocation of responsibilities across platform teams, domain teams, security, governance, and product ownership, including review cadence>
KPIs	<key performance indicators used to measure citation quality, acceptance, unresolved queries, permission safety, retrieval quality, freshness, onboarding speed, dispute resolution, and user trust>
Phase 1 scope	<initial delivery scope, including included domains, source restrictions, interaction mode, citation requirements, and any limitations on actions or structured context>

Deferred items	<capabilities, domains, integrations, or operating-model expansions explicitly postponed to later phases>
Risks	<key delivery, governance, metadata, access-control, semantic, stakeholder, or stewardship risks that could undermine the architecture if not addressed>
Approval signatures	<required approvers whose sign-off is needed to authorize the architecture, controls, and rollout>

Case Example

Designing the First Target State for an Enterprise Knowledge Assistant

Consider a large enterprise that wants to launch an internal knowledge assistant. Executives describe the ambition broadly: employees should be able to ask natural-language questions about policy, process, and company guidance. The temptation is to treat this as a generalized enterprise search problem with an LLM on top.

That would be a mistake.

The architecture team instead narrows the first target state to a specific business outcome: provide authoritative answers to employee HR and corporate policy questions, with citations, while creating reusable control and semantic foundations for later analyst and executive copilots.

Current-state reality

The organization has:

- Policy documents in multiple SharePoint sites.
- HR knowledge articles in a service platform.
- Manager guidance pages on the intranet.
- Organizational data in an HRIS.
- Inconsistent ownership of older documents.
- No common authoritative-source flag.
- Effective dates present in some policies but missing in others.
- Glossary work underway but not systematically linked to content.

In other words, the current state contains useful material but is not AI-ready.

Target-state decisions

The team makes several critical choices.

They restrict source classes

Only authoritative policy repositories, approved HR knowledge articles, and selected organization-reference data enter phase one. Open collaboration spaces, emails, and notes are excluded.

They define source authority explicitly

Each admitted source is assigned an authority status, owner, steward, and review cadence. Duplicate policy copies in informal repositories are excluded from retrieval.

They implement a mandatory metadata minimum

No document is eligible for grounded answering unless it has domain, owner, effective date, supersession status, and classification populated.

They add a lightweight semantic layer

Terms such as leave, absence, manager, contingent worker, employee type, and business travel are normalized through a glossary and taxonomy so retrieval and answer generation do not rely solely on document phrasing.

They make access source-faithful

If a manager-only guidance page exists, the assistant may use it only for users with the right entitlement. No centralized index is allowed to weaken source permissions.

They define the serving contract

The assistant must cite the exact policy or knowledge article used, distinguish current from historical policy, and abstain when no approved authoritative answer exists.

Why this design enables expansion

At first glance, this may seem overbuilt for a simple knowledge assistant. It is not.

Because the team standardized metadata, created authority rules, and introduced a usable semantic layer, they now have foundations for the next two consumer types.

An analyst copilot can later use the same domain definitions and ownership model when structured HR measures are introduced. An executive copilot can later summarize policy change impacts using the same authoritative-source logic and effective-date discipline. The first target state was not universal, but it was expandable by design.

What they deliberately deferred

They did not include every content repository. They did not support free-form enterprise search. They did not allow agentic actions. They did not onboard broad structured-data domains. Those choices protected quality and made the initial state executable. That is the essence of good target-state design: build the first architecture that can be trusted, then extend it with discipline.

CLOSING SYNTHESIS

Designing the target state is not an exercise in architectural imagination. It is an exercise in architectural commitment.

The target state for AI-Ready Data must describe the first executable state in which enterprise AI can operate with trust, control, and semantic clarity. It must be constrained enough to build, specific enough to govern, and durable enough to extend. It must identify source classes, metadata standards, semantic strategy, governance obligations, retrieval patterns, AI consumer contracts, and operating ownership. And it must say what will wait.

The strongest target states are not the most ambitious. They are the most coherent. They connect business purpose to data architecture without hand-waving. They make metadata operational. They treat governance as a design layer. They distinguish among AI consumer types. They preserve platform flexibility by being precise about principles.

If the current-state assessment tells you where you are, and the roadmap tells you how you will move, then the target state tells you what you are actually trying to build. For enterprise AI, that target cannot be a vague promise of intelligence. It must be a governed, contextualized, evidence-bearing data architecture that can serve AI repeatedly and safely at scale.

KEY TAKEAWAYS

- The target state must define the first executable AI-ready architecture, not a distant ideal.
- A usable target state specifies metadata, semantics, governance, retrieval, access, and ownership explicitly.
- The first design should be narrow in scope but intentional in laying foundations for later expansion.
- Capability without control is not an enterprise target state; the architecture must show both.
- Principles outlast tool choices, so design the invariants first and let platforms implement them.

CHAPTER 30: SEQUENCING THE TRANSFORMATION

Enterprise AI programs rarely fail because the organization lacked enthusiasm, budget, or model access. They fail because the transformation sequence was wrong. Teams rush to index content, launch assistants, and demo retrieval-driven experiences before they have stabilized core sources, enforced permissions, defined ownership, or established the metadata needed for trustworthy interpretation. The result is predictable: pilot debt, governance rework, weak trust, and an expanding cleanup burden.

AI-ready transformation is, therefore, not only a question of what capabilities to build. It is a question of when to build them. Sequence is strategy. In enterprise architecture, the order of operations determines whether each investment compounds or whether each new use case exposes another missing prerequisite. A retrieval layer built on top of unmanaged repositories does not create readiness. It industrializes ambiguity. A copilot connected to poorly described data products does not improve decision quality. It scales misinterpretation. An agent allowed to act on operational systems before evidence, policy, and provenance are reliable does not create efficiency. It creates risk.

The practical lesson is simple but often ignored: capabilities must be built in dependency order. Stabilize first. Govern early. Add context before scale. Treat grounding as an architectural discipline. Operationalize with controls. Then scale on purpose. When the sequence is right, each wave leaves behind reusable assets: better metadata, clearer ownership, stronger policy enforcement, more trustworthy retrieval, more durable delivery patterns, and a more mature operating model. That is what separates AI experimentation from enterprise transformation.

WHY THIS MATTERS

AI Adoption Magnifies Architectural Mistakes

Traditional data modernization could tolerate a surprising amount of disorder because many downstream consumers were trained analysts, data engineers, or report developers. They understood the caveats. They knew which tables to trust and which fields to ignore. They carried tribal knowledge that compensated for architectural gaps.

AI systems do not operate that way. They consume what is made available to them. They depend on metadata, permissions, semantic clarity, freshness controls, and source authority to distinguish signal from noise. When those controls are missing, AI does not politely abstain. It produces answers, rankings, summaries, and actions anyway.

That changes the economics of sequencing. A missing glossary in an analytics estate may create confusion for a handful of analysts. The same missing context in an enterprise assistant can generate thousands of incorrect interpretations in a month. A weak permission model in a legacy document repository may remain mostly invisible in manual workflows. The same weakness in an AI retrieval pipeline becomes an enterprise-wide exposure event.

Rework Is More Expensive After Rollout

Many organizations assume they can "start with a pilot" and fix structure later. In practice, later is the most expensive time to fix anything. Once users depend on an assistant, every change to chunking, classification, source authority, metadata inheritance, or access logic becomes disruptive. Once executive sponsors have seen adoption numbers, slowing the rollout to repair architecture feels like backtracking. Once developers have built application logic around a weak retrieval layer, technical debt becomes organizational debt. This is why sequencing matters. Not because architects prefer order, but because the wrong order locks in failure patterns.

Trust Is Built Upstream

Trust is not created by better phrasing in the interface. It is created upstream in the data estate. Users trust AI systems when answers are traceable, current, access-aware, and semantically coherent. They distrust them when the same question yields conflicting answers, citations point to obsolete documents, or permissions are enforced inconsistently.

The transformation sequence must, *therefore,* prioritize the things that produce trust before the things that increase exposure. This is the opposite of how many pilot programs are structured. Many enterprises expand usage first and attempt to add control later. That inversion is one of the defining mistakes of AI transformation.

Core Concepts

Sequence Is Not Project Management Trivia

In an AI-ready transformation, sequence is not a scheduling convenience. It is an architectural principle. Certain capabilities only work reliably when the capabilities beneath them are already in place.

Retrieval quality depends on source stability, metadata completeness, semantic enrichment, and permission fidelity. Explainability depends on provenance, citation design, temporal correctness, and source authority logic. Action-taking agents depend on stronger controls still: identity, entitlement checks, policy enforcement, auditability, and bounded operating contracts.

This means there is a natural dependency chain in the transformation. Ignoring that chain produces rework. Respecting it produces compounding value.

The Six Transformation Waves

A practical way to manage this dependency chain is to organize the journey into six waves:

- **Stabilize**: Rationalize critical sources, establish content hygiene, reduce duplication, define authoritative systems, and fix the most dangerous access inconsistencies.
- **Govern**: Apply classification, retention, privacy, provenance, legal constraints, and access-aware delivery patterns across structured and unstructured assets.
- **Contextualize**: Build the semantic and metadata layer: business definitions, glossaries, taxonomies, entity models, relationship mapping, source descriptions, freshness signals, and usage intent.
- **Ground**: Build trustworthy retrieval and evidence patterns: chunking, enrichment, ranking, source authority, citation behavior, temporal filtering, and evaluation.
- **Operationalize**: Turn successful patterns into governed services and products with delivery contracts, monitoring, support processes, steward workflows, and change management.
- **Scale**: Extend to more domains, more consumers, and more complex AI experiences while preserving the control model and reusing the capability assets created in earlier waves.

These waves are not strictly linear in the sense that one must be completed globally before another begins anywhere. They are ordered in the sense that a domain should not scale downstream capabilities until upstream prerequisites are strong enough.

KEY INSIGHT

Pilot debt: what it is and how it forms

Pilot debt is the accumulated architectural and operating burden created when an organization launches AI use cases on top of sources, metadata, permissions, or governance structures that are not ready for repeated enterprise use.

Pilot Debt Usually Forms in Five Ways

- Indexing repositories before resolving source authority.
- Exposing content before permission inheritance is trustworthy.
- Adding semantic labels manually in the application instead of fixing them in the data estate.
- Measuring adoption before measuring answer quality and traceability.
- Treating one-off enrichment logic as a permanent foundation.

Pilot debt feels fast in the first month and expensive in every month after that.

Wave Checkpoints Matter

Each wave needs explicit exit criteria. Without them, organizations claim progress because code was written or a pilot was launched, while the actual architectural dependency remains unresolved.

A useful checkpoint asks questions such as these:

- Are authoritative sources explicitly designated?
- Are entitlements preserved from source to retrieval layer?
- Can important content be classified consistently?
- Do business terms have agreed definitions in the chosen domain?
- Can answers cite current, approved, and access-appropriate sources?
- Is there a named owner for the capability after go-live?

If the answer is no, the wave is not complete. Movement to the next wave should be a decision, not a drift.

Reusable Assets Are the Real Output

The goal of each wave is not merely to enable one use case. It is to leave behind reusable capability. A domain-level taxonomy, a citation pattern, an access-aware ingestion service, a provenance schema, a stewardship workflow, or a retrieval evaluation harness should all serve future use cases as well.

This is what makes transformation durable. Each wave lowers the cost and increases the safety of the next one.

Architectural Implications

Stabilize and Govern Before Scaling Retrieval

Many organizations want retrieval first because retrieval is visible. It powers demos. It creates immediate user interaction. It gives sponsors something to see. Architecturally, however, retrieval is downstream of source readiness.

If the source layer is unstable, duplicated, weakly governed, and full of unlabeled exceptions, retrieval will faithfully amplify those weaknesses. Indexing more content does not solve ambiguity. It multiplies it. Ranking cannot compensate for the absence of source authority. Prompt design cannot compensate for broken permissions. Vector search cannot repair poor lifecycle control.

That is why the first architectural implication is blunt: do not scale retrieval until the sources, permissions, and minimum governance controls are dependable enough to deserve scale.

Metadata and Context Cannot Be Deferred

A common excuse is that metadata can be improved later, once usage patterns are known. This is usually a mistake. Metadata is not decorative documentation. It is operating logic for AI systems.

Without metadata, systems cannot reliably answer questions such as:

- Which source is authoritative?
- How current is this content?
- Is this content approved for this audience?
- Which business term does this field or paragraph actually represent?
- Which document supersedes which prior version?
- Should this evidence be used for summary, recommendation, action, or not at all?

Deferring metadata means deferring answer quality, policy enforcement, trust scoring, and explainability. In effect, it means building a retrieval pipeline without the control plane that makes it enterprise-safe.

Ownership and Operating Model Must Appear Early

Architects sometimes treat ownership as a later governance concern, to be assigned once the platform proves its value. That is backward. Early ownership is necessary precisely because transformation creates cross-domain decisions that nobody will make by accident.

Who decides source authority when SharePoint, a contract repository, and a line-of-business system disagree? Who owns the glossary for customer-facing service interactions? Who approves a retrieval policy that excludes draft legal memos from general assistant use? Who decides whether an action-taking agent may rely on a summary or must verify against a system of record?

These are not implementation details. They are operating-model decisions. If they are unresolved, architecture becomes a proxy battleground for organizational ambiguity.

Different Consumers Require Different Sequencing Tolerances

A knowledge assistant that answers internal policy questions can often be introduced earlier than an operational agent that updates customer records. The latter requires much stronger assurance around identity, authorization, transaction controls, auditability, and exception handling.

This means sequencing must also account for consumer type. Low-risk read-heavy experiences may begin once grounding is reliable in selected domains. Write-capable agents should wait until operational contracts, policy enforcement, and escalation paths are proven. The transformation is not one line. It is a set of controlled maturity paths sharing the same architectural foundation.

❖ Figure 60 – Wave Roadmap

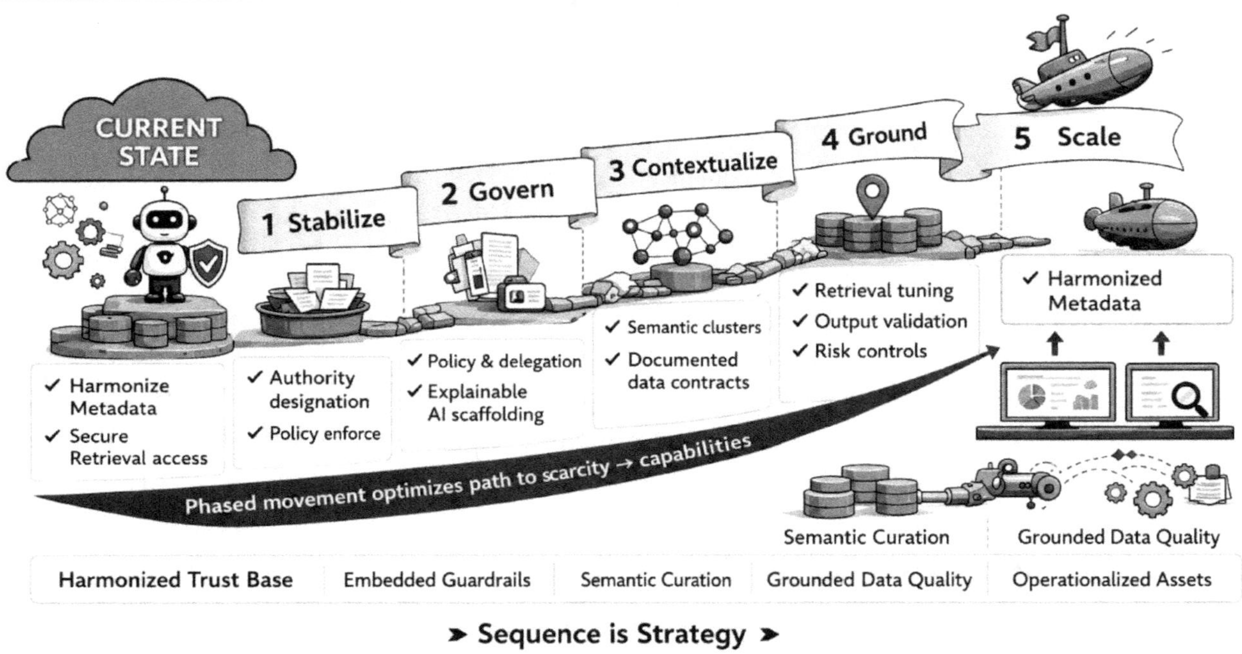

❖ Figure 61 – Dependency Chain

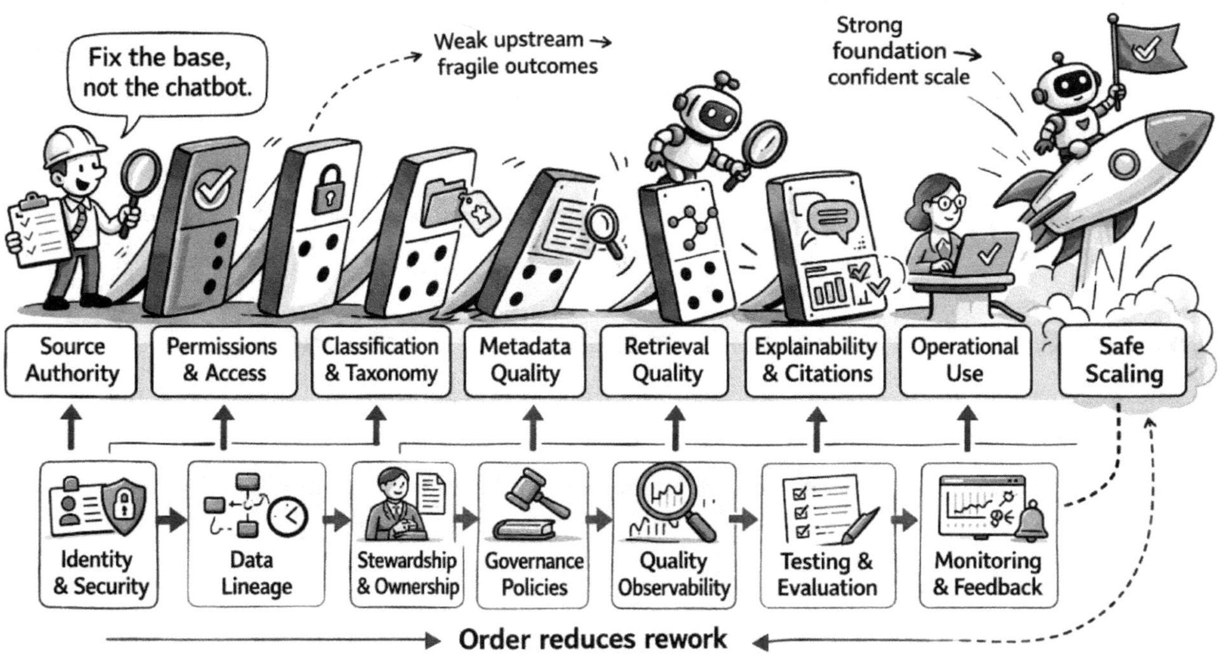

Failure Modes and Anti-Patterns

Retrieval-First Transformation

This is the most common failure mode. The organization chooses an appealing use case, indexes everything it can reach, and starts tuning prompts and ranking models. Only after inconsistent answers appear does it begin to ask which sources are authoritative, whether permissions were preserved, whether obsolete content is contaminating results, or whether key terms mean different things across business units.

This anti-pattern mistakes technical connectivity for readiness.

Governance After Adoption

Here the team argues that strict governance would slow momentum, so the pilot proceeds with "temporary" exceptions. Draft documents are included. Classification is incomplete. Retention logic is ignored. Legal hold content is not cleanly separated. Sensitive content relies on application-side filtering instead of source-aligned controls.

The team tells itself this is acceptable because the rollout is small. Then the pilot succeeds, executive interest grows, and the temporary shortcuts become the production baseline. The program now faces a choice between slowing expansion or institutionalizing weak controls.

Metadata as a Documentation Project

Some enterprises do recognize the importance of metadata, but they treat it as a catalog exercise disconnected from runtime use. Terms are documented, but retrieval pipelines do not use them. Data products have descriptions, but ranking logic does not consider source authority or freshness. Ownership fields exist, but stewardship workflows are not operational.

Metadata that does not influence runtime behavior is not functioning as a control plane. It is merely archived intention.

Scaling Usage Before the Estate Is Ready

Once initial adoption appears, there is pressure to connect more repositories, more users, more use cases, and more actions. The program mistakes breadth for maturity.

This is where transformation programs often become fragile. Scaling multiplies unresolved defects. Weak permission inheritance becomes a larger security risk. Thin metadata becomes a wider trust problem. Unclear ownership becomes a support and change-management crisis.

⚠ WARNING SIGN

Scaling usage before fixing metadata and permissions

If adoption metrics are rising faster than metadata completeness, permission fidelity, and source authority coverage, the program is not maturing. It is accumulating risk.

Typical warning signs include:

- user growth without corresponding steward assignment
- more indexed content without authoritative source designation
- faster answer times but weaker citation quality
- broader connector coverage with rising access exceptions
- pilot praise from demos paired with high manual review behind the scenes

When those signals appear together, scale should pause.

One-Off Implementation Logic

Teams under delivery pressure often solve readiness gaps inside the application layer. They hand-code synonym lists, exclusion rules, exception paths, and trust rankings for a single assistant. This may rescue the immediate pilot, but it leaves nothing reusable behind. The next use case starts over, often solving the same problem differently. A transformation program that does not leave reusable assets is not transforming the estate. It is funding isolated workarounds.

PRACTICAL APPLICATION

Use the Waves to Plan, Not Just to Describe

The six-wave model is most useful when turned into a planning mechanism. Each target domain should have a wave plan with named owners, explicit prerequisites, decision gates, and exit criteria. That plan should be reviewed by architecture, governance, security, and business leadership together.

The essential discipline is this: every wave must deliver business value, but it must also leave behind reusable capability. If a wave delivers a pilot but leaves no durable metadata, policy, evaluation, or operating assets, it has not improved enterprise readiness enough.

The Six Transformation Waves

Wave 1: Stabilize

Fix source chaos. Reduce duplication. Designate authoritative systems. Correct the most material permission inconsistencies. Establish basic ingestion reliability.

Wave 2: Govern

Apply classification, retention, privacy, provenance, and access-aware policy handling across priority assets. Make governance executable, not advisory.

Wave 3: Contextualize

Define business meaning. Build glossaries, taxonomies, entity relationships, source descriptions, freshness semantics, and intended-use metadata.

Wave 4: Ground

Implement retrieval, enrichment, ranking, citation, and evaluation patterns that produce defensible answers rather than merely plausible ones.

Wave 5: Operationalize

Turn successful patterns into services, data products, operating playbooks, support models, and monitored production controls.

Wave 6: Scale

Expand by reusing the assets from the earlier waves, not by rebuilding them domain by domain.

How to Apply Wave Checkpoints

A practical enterprise sequence often looks like this:

A first domain is selected not because it is easy, but because it is valuable and governable. Core sources are rationalized. A small set of content types is prioritized. Permission inheritance is verified. Domain definitions are agreed. Retrieval is evaluated against representative questions. Citations are tested for temporal correctness and source authority. Operational ownership is assigned. Only then is the use case expanded.

This does not eliminate iteration. It improves iteration quality. Teams still learn by doing, but they learn in a bounded architecture rather than in an uncontrolled sprawl.

Transformation Wave Planning Canvas

Use the following canvas for each wave in each priority domain. The point is to force dependency awareness, not just to capture status. The example below is fully populated for an illustrative domain: enterprise HR policy and employee knowledge.

What Good Sequencing Looks Like in Practice

A well-sequenced transformation does not spend a year on abstract architecture before delivering anything. It delivers in waves, but it chooses wave objectives carefully.

In the first wave, value may come from source rationalization that immediately improves search relevance and reduces support tickets. In the second, governance controls may unblock a previously risky use case. In the third, metadata and semantic context may reduce conflicting answers enough to support executive sponsorship. In the fourth, retrieval evaluation may provide the evidence needed to industrialize a platform pattern. In the fifth, operationalization may create a supportable service catalog. In the sixth, scale may accelerate because teams are reusing proven assets rather than improvising.

The transformation, *therefore,* balances pragmatism with discipline. It does not postpone value. It sequences value.

TEMPLATES

Transformation Wave Planning Canvas

Wave number/name	<name and sequence number of the transformation wave or implementation stage>
Objective	<primary objective of this wave and the capability foundation it is intended to establish>
Capabilities delivered	<capabilities, controls, metadata assets, semantic assets, and operating-model elements expected to be delivered in this wave>
Domains included	<business domains, functions, or subject areas included within the scope of this wave>
Prerequisites	<conditions, earlier-wave deliverables, controls, or dependencies that must already be in place before this wave can begin successfully>
Key milestones	<major checkpoints, deliverables, agreements, enrichments, validations, or sign-offs that mark meaningful progress through the wave>
Exit criteria	<measurable conditions that must be satisfied before the wave can be considered complete and before progression to the next wave is allowed>
Risks	<key delivery, governance, semantic, stewardship, metadata, structural, or organizational risks that could prevent the wave from succeeding>

Owners	<named roles or functions accountable for domain ownership, product ownership, architecture, governance, stewardship, and other responsibilities within the wave>
KPIs	<key performance indicators used to measure completion quality, metadata quality, authority coverage, retrieval performance, consistency improvement, or operational responsiveness during this wave>
Reusable assets produced	<standards, workflows, templates, patterns, metadata models, semantic assets, or control approaches created in this wave that can be reused in other domains or later waves>
Governance approvals needed	<approvals required from governance, security, legal, business, or other control functions before the wave can proceed or be closed>
Decision gates	<formal go or no-go conditions, threshold checks, or blocking issues that determine whether expansion, progression, or broader rollout is permitted>
Timeline	<planned duration and phase breakdown for the wave, including how time is allocated across major activities>

CASE EXAMPLE

Sequence the Foundations Before You Scale Retrieval

A multinational insurance company decided to launch an internal knowledge assistant for claims, underwriting, and policy servicing. Leadership wanted speed. The team chose a retrieval-first approach: connect document repositories, ingest policy manuals, index procedural guides, and fine-tune ranking from early user feedback.

The initial pilot looked promising. Employees liked natural-language search. Executives saw higher engagement than they expected. The program was quickly approved for broader rollout across operations.

Within weeks, problems appeared.

Claims agents received answers that mixed current policy rules with superseded regional exceptions. Underwriters were shown references from draft guidance that had never been approved for enterprise use. Service teams got different answers to the same question because identical content existed in multiple repositories with different update histories. Most serious of all, permission behavior was inconsistent. In some cases, retrieval results respected source permissions. In others, inherited access logic broke during ingestion because repository structures were not mapped consistently.

The technology was not the real problem. The sequence was.

The company had treated repository connectivity as readiness. It had not settled source authority between claims operations, legal policy management, and regional business units. Effective dates were inconsistent. Supersession relationships were largely absent. Classification for sensitive procedural content was incomplete. Glossary terms such as "claim closure," "adjudication," and "coverage exception" were used differently across functions. Ownership of the assistant existed, but ownership of the underlying content rules did not.

The program paused expansion and stepped back.

First, it reduced the source footprint. Instead of indexing every accessible repository, it designated authoritative policy sources by function and geography. Second, it repaired permission inheritance and made access validation a release gate rather than a best-effort check. Third, it created metadata requirements for effective dates, owner, approval status, jurisdiction, and supersession. Fourth, it established a cross-functional operating group including claims, underwriting, legal, security, and information governance. Fifth, it rebuilt retrieval evaluation around business-critical questions rather than generic relevance scores.

Only after those controls were in place did the company scale again.

The second rollout was slower in appearance and much stronger in outcome. Citation quality improved. Conflicting answers fell sharply. Sensitive content exposure risk dropped. Domain stewards had a formal path to resolve ambiguity. Most importantly, the assets created for the insurance policy domain were reused for compliance content and producer support knowledge.

The case demonstrates the central lesson of this chapter: when retrieval is implemented before metadata, permissions, and ownership are reliable, the program eventually has to return to those foundations anyway. The only question is whether it does so before scale or after damage.

Closing Synthesis

AI-ready transformation succeeds when it is sequenced as an architectural progression rather than pursued as a collection of disconnected pilots. The right question is not, "What assistant can we launch next?" The right question is, "What capability should we build next so that future assistants, copilots, and agents become safer, cheaper, and more trustworthy to deploy?"

That is why stabilization comes before broad retrieval. Governance comes before mass exposure. Context comes before confident interpretation. Grounding comes before operational dependence. Operationalization comes before scale.

This sequence is not bureaucratic caution. It is the fastest route to durable enterprise value because it minimizes rework and maximizes reuse. Each wave should leave behind assets that the next wave can depend on: authoritative-source patterns, permission models, classification rules, glossaries, semantic mappings, citation logic, evaluation harnesses, stewardship workflows, support playbooks, and delivery contracts.

Enterprises that follow this path do not eliminate iteration. They make iteration cumulative. They do not build a new workaround for every pilot. They improve the estate itself. That is the real transformation.

In the end, sequencing is not about slowing AI down. It is about building the conditions under which AI can be trusted to scale.

Key Takeaways

- The order in which AI-ready capabilities are built determines whether the program compounds value or compounds rework.
- Retrieval should not scale ahead of source stability, permission fidelity, governance, and metadata.
- Ownership and operating model decisions must be established early because architectural ambiguity is usually organizational ambiguity.
- Transformation should proceed in waves with explicit checkpoints and exit criteria, not as uncontrolled pilot expansion.
- Every wave should leave behind reusable capability assets so the enterprise data estate becomes progressively more AI-ready.

CHAPTER 31: MEASURING AI-READINESS AND BUSINESS PROGRESS

AI-ready transformation should not be measured by how many prompts were submitted, how many assistant sessions occurred, or how many model calls were processed. Those numbers may describe activity, but they do not describe readiness. They do not tell an architecture team whether enterprise data is becoming more discoverable, more interpretable, more governable, more trusted, or more reusable for AI-driven work.

That distinction matters. Enterprises routinely mistake AI motion for AI progress. A dashboard may show rising assistant adoption while the underlying answers still lack reliable citations, use stale content, violate intended-use boundaries, or depend on a narrow and brittle set of sources. In such environments, usage can go up while trust goes down.

A serious AI-Ready Data program measures something different. It measures whether the data estate is becoming fit for secure discovery, semantic interpretation, governed retrieval, grounded response generation, and accountable operational use. It measures whether the organization is reducing ambiguity, increasing evidence quality, improving policy fidelity, shortening the path from question to defensible answer, and creating reusable data products that multiple AI consumers can depend on. That is the real signal of progress, and it is the standard this chapter uses.

WHY THIS MATTERS

Metrics Shape Architecture

Enterprises build what they measure. If they measure model throughput, they will optimize throughput. If they measure chatbot traffic, they will optimize traffic. If they measure answer quality, evidence quality, policy compliance, freshness, and reuse, they will build architectures that support trustworthy AI.

This is not a reporting issue. It is an architectural control issue. A team that reports only usage may postpone hard work on metadata enrichment, source authority models, citation design, access-aware retrieval, document lifecycle controls, and semantic harmonization across domains. A team that reports readiness and trust cannot postpone those things, because those capabilities are what move the metrics.

Executive Confidence Is Earned Through Evidence

Executives rarely lose confidence in AI because they dislike the idea of automation. They lose confidence because the system cannot consistently answer basic questions with defensible evidence. They see outputs that sound polished but are not clearly grounded in approved sources. They notice contradictions across answers. They discover that different functions define the same term differently. They learn that a response cited a stale policy or a draft document. Trust falls sharply after that.

The remedy is not a better demo. The remedy is measurement that makes trust visible.

When a transformation team can show that authoritative source coverage has increased from 42 percent to 81 percent in a priority domain, that freshness compliance for retrieved content has moved from 61 percent to 93 percent, and that citation coverage for executive-facing answers has risen from 48 percent to 97 percent, skepticism changes form. The conversation is no longer, "Are these tools real?" It becomes, "Which domains are ready next, and what risks remain?"

Leading Indicators Matter More Than Anecdotes

Lagging indicators matter, but they arrive too late to guide architectural decisions. By the time a business leader complains that an assistant produced a weak answer in a board-preparation workflow, the architecture problem has already happened upstream.

Leading indicators provide earlier control. They reveal whether authoritative sources are onboarded, whether metadata is complete enough to support ranking and filtering, whether retrieval freshness rules are being met, whether evidence appears with answers, whether policy filters are firing correctly, and whether users actually accept or override the system's cited outputs.

These are not peripheral signals. They are the earliest measurable signs that the data estate is becoming fit for trustworthy AI.

Core Concepts

Readiness Is Not a Single Score

Enterprises often ask for one maturity score. That is understandable and dangerous. AI-readiness is multidimensional. A domain can be strong in source onboarding and weak in semantic consistency. It can be strong in access control and weak in freshness discipline. It can be strong in citation coverage and weak in outcome adoption. A single composite score may be useful for summary reporting, but it should never replace the underlying measures. A better model is a layered measurement across four levels:

- **Technical signals:** source coverage, metadata completeness, classification coverage, freshness compliance, permission propagation, schema or content normalization, and semantic tagging.

- **Trust signals:** citation coverage, evidence acceptance, source authority alignment, answer traceability, contradiction rate, and temporal correctness.

- **Operational outcomes:** reuse across use cases, reduction in manual document hunts, lower escalation rates, faster answer resolution, higher analyst productivity, and fewer governance exceptions.

- **Business outcomes:** reduced cycle time, lower compliance risk exposure, faster onboarding, improved service resolution, better decision latency, or measurable revenue and cost effects.

Technical signals should roll upward into trust signals, then into operational outcomes, and finally into business outcomes. That is the only defensible way to tell the story of progress.

Trust Is Measurable

Many organizations talk about trust as if it were subjective. It is not fully subjective. Trust can be observed through measurable properties of the answer, the evidence, and the retrieval path. Trust becomes measurable when you ask questions such as:

- Did the answer include citations?
- Were those citations from approved, authoritative sources?
- Were the cited sources current enough for the use case?
- Could the answer be traced to a retrieval event, source object, and policy decision?
- Did users accept the answer without needing manual revalidation?
- Were contradictions detected across cited sources?
- Did the answer stay within the user's access boundaries?

Once these are measured, trust stops being a feeling and becomes an operating discipline.

Domain-Based Measurement Is Essential

AI-readiness is not uniform across the enterprise. The customer domain, finance domain, legal domain, manufacturing domain, and HR domain will not move at the same pace, nor should they be judged by identical thresholds.

Domain-based metrics matter for three reasons.

First, domains own meaning. Business definitions, policies, freshness expectations, and source authority rules are domain-specific. Second, domains carry different risks. A legal policy assistant and a marketing copy assistant do not operate under the same trust threshold. Third, domains expose uneven architecture debt. One domain may have a strong glossary and clean stewardship model but weak unstructured content hygiene. Another may have rich documents and strong records controls but fragmented metadata.

A domain-based readiness model makes these differences visible rather than hiding them behind enterprise averages.

Business Progress Must Be Traced Back to Readiness

It is tempting to report business outcomes only: faster case resolution, shorter onboarding time, reduced analyst effort. Those matter, but they are not enough by themselves.

Without the readiness chain behind them, business improvements become hard to explain and harder to repeat. If service resolution time improves, leadership should be able to see which readiness factors enabled it: perhaps stronger knowledge-source coverage, tighter freshness control, higher citation coverage, and better semantic mapping of product and incident terms.

This linkage matters for scaling. Otherwise, the enterprise gets isolated wins instead of repeatable capability growth.

KEY INSIGHT

Vanity Metrics to Avoid

- Total prompt volume
- Total assistant sessions
- Number of users who tried the tool once
- Average response length
- Token consumption reported as a success metric
- Number of documents ingested without quality qualification
- Number of models deployed without trust or outcome measures
- "Questions answered" without evidence-quality review
- Satisfaction scores without answer validation
- Productivity claims that are not tied to a measured workflow baseline

These metrics may be operationally interesting, but none of them proves AI-readiness.

What Trust Looks Like in Measurable Terms

Trustworthy AI in the enterprise is visible in the operating data. It appears when answers are grounded in approved sources, evidence is present by default, freshness rules are enforced, access boundaries are honored, and users rely on the output without repeated manual correction.

That means trust can be measured through indicators such as citation coverage, evidence acceptance rate, freshness compliance, authoritative-source share of retrieved content, contradiction rate, override rate, and policy exception frequency.

KEY INSIGHT

What Trust Looks Like in Measurable Terms

- A trustworthy AI data estate typically shows:
- High citation coverage for high-stakes answers
- High share of retrieved evidence from authoritative sources
- Low stale-evidence rate
- Low contradiction rate across cited sources
- High user acceptance of evidence-backed answers
- Low manual override rate for approved workflows
- Low policy-exception frequency
- Full traceability from answer to source, retrieval event, and access decision

If these are not improving, trust is not improving, regardless of traffic.

ARCHITECTURAL IMPLICATIONS

Measurement Must Be Built into the Architecture

These metrics cannot be reconstructed reliably at the end of the pipeline. They must be designed into the data estate.

That requires instrumentation across the full chain:

- Source onboarding and classification.
- Metadata capture and enrichment.
- Semantic labeling and glossary alignment.
- Access and policy enforcement.
- Retrieval events and ranking decisions.
- Citation generation.
- Answer consumption and user feedback.
- Workflow outcomes and business process telemetry.

If an architecture team cannot observe the path from source object to retrieval event to answer to workflow outcome, then it cannot govern AI at enterprise scale.

Metadata Is the Measurement Backbone

Most of the measures that matter depend on metadata.

Source coverage requires source inventories and authority labels. Freshness compliance requires timestamps, retention states, and lifecycle metadata. Citation quality requires source identifiers, provenance markers, and stable references. Policy compliance depends on classification tags, entitlement metadata, usage restrictions, and legal-hold markers. Domain readiness requires ownership, stewardship, glossary alignment, and lineage.

In other words, measurement quality is downstream of metadata quality. When metadata is thin, inconsistent, or optional, readiness measurement becomes speculative.

Different AI Consumers Require Different KPI Thresholds

A single metric can have multiple acceptable ranges depending on the consumer.

A general employee knowledge assistant may tolerate lower evidence density for low-risk internal guidance. An executive briefing tool should demand stronger freshness and source-authority controls. An analyst copilot should require clear provenance and traceable joins across structured and unstructured evidence. An action-taking agent should meet the highest threshold for policy fidelity, authorization, and explainability.

Therefore, KPI catalogs should define thresholds by consumer type, not just by metric name. An enterprise that applies one universal standard will either overconstrain low-risk use cases or underprotect high-risk ones.

Executive Dashboards Should Show Risk Reduction and Capability Growth

Executives do not need raw telemetry. They need a compact view of whether risk is falling and durable capability is rising.

A useful executive dashboard shows, by domain:

- Readiness stage.
- Authoritative source coverage.
- Freshness compliance.
- Citation coverage.

- Policy enforcement coverage.
- Reuse across use cases.
- Unresolved risk items.
- The operational workflows now supported.
- The business outcomes attributable to the improvement.

That framing matters. It turns reporting from AI theater into enterprise capability governance.

❖ FIGURE 62 – METRIC HIERARCHY

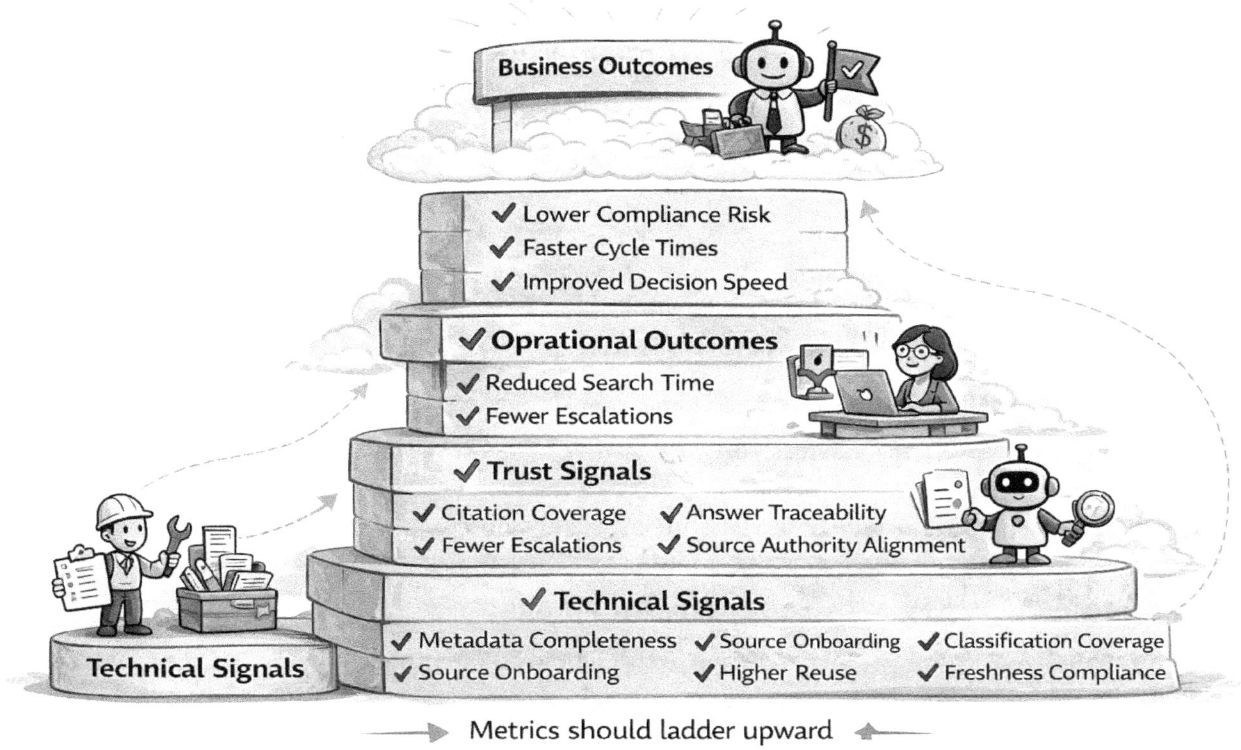

FAILURE MODES AND ANTI-PATTERNS

Reporting Activity Instead of Readiness

The most common anti-pattern is reporting usage as if usage proves value. It does not. Heavy usage may mean curiosity, mandate, novelty, or lack of alternatives. It may coexist with poor answer quality.

A team that reports sessions and queries without answer quality or evidence quality is reporting demand, not readiness.

⚠ **WARNING SIGN**

If the dashboard highlights queries, sessions, and active users but does not show answer quality, evidence quality, source authority, freshness, or policy fidelity, the organization is measuring AI demand rather than AI trustworthiness.

Measuring Only Lagging Incidents

Another failure mode is waiting for visible failures: an incorrect policy answer, a stale citation, a permissions breach, or a public executive complaint. These are important signals, but they are late signals.

Architects need leading indicators that detect readiness gaps before trust is damaged.

Using Enterprise Averages to Hide Domain Weakness

Enterprise averages flatter weak programs. An overall citation coverage rate of 82 percent may look healthy, while the legal domain sits at 41 percent and the product-service domain sits at 94 percent. The average hides the risk.

Readiness must be visible at the domain level and, for sensitive use cases, at the workflow level.

Treating Trust as Survey Sentiment Only

User surveys have value, but they are insufficient. People often report confidence based on style, speed, or interface polish. An answer can feel trustworthy while being weakly grounded.

Trust measurement must include observed evidence quality, not just perceived usefulness.

Overloading One KPI with Too Many Meanings

Organizations sometimes ask one metric to represent readiness, trust, quality, and business value simultaneously. This creates confusion. For example, "assistant effectiveness" becomes a vague basket containing usage, sentiment, answer speed, and adoption. Such measures are not actionable.

Each KPI should have one primary purpose, a clear owner, and a defined remediation action when it misses the threshold.

Failing to Baseline Before Rollout

Without a baseline, every improvement claim becomes rhetorical. Teams must measure the pre-AI state: manual search time, escalation rates, policy exception frequency, document hunt effort, evidence validation time, and time to produce decision support.

Only then can business progress be credibly shown.

Practical Application

Build a Domain Readiness Scorecard First

A sensible sequence is to start with priority domains rather than enterprise-wide abstraction. Choose domains where business value, information demand, and governance risk all justify disciplined measurement.

For each domain, define:

- The approved source inventory.
- The authoritative-source hierarchy.
- The expected freshness rules.
- The glossary and semantic dependencies.
- The target AI consumers.
- The minimum trust thresholds.
- The business workflows expected to benefit.

Then assign KPIs across the four levels: technical, trust, operational, and business.

Separate Readiness Reviews from Adoption Reviews

Adoption matters, but it should not be the first lens. A readiness review asks whether the architecture can safely support trustworthy AI. An adoption review asks whether users are engaging and where value is being realized.

When these are mixed together too early, leaders may pressure teams to chase usage before readiness is real.

Instrument Evidence Quality Explicitly

Most teams instrument latency before they instrument evidence. That order is wrong for enterprise AI.

Evidence quality should be observable through measures such as citation presence, citation relevance, authoritative-source share, freshness pass rate, and unresolved-answer rate. These should be available at answer, workflow, domain, and consumer-type levels.

Tie Every KPI to an Owner and Action

A KPI without an owner becomes background noise. A KPI without a defined action becomes theater.

If freshness compliance falls below the threshold, the action may be to suspend a domain from executive-facing use until indexing and lifecycle defects are corrected. If citation coverage dips, the action may be to block certain answer types until retrieval templates or source mappings are fixed. If policy exceptions rise, the action may be to review entitlements, classification tags, or repository connectors.

❖ FIGURE 63 – DOMAIN READINESS DASHBOARD

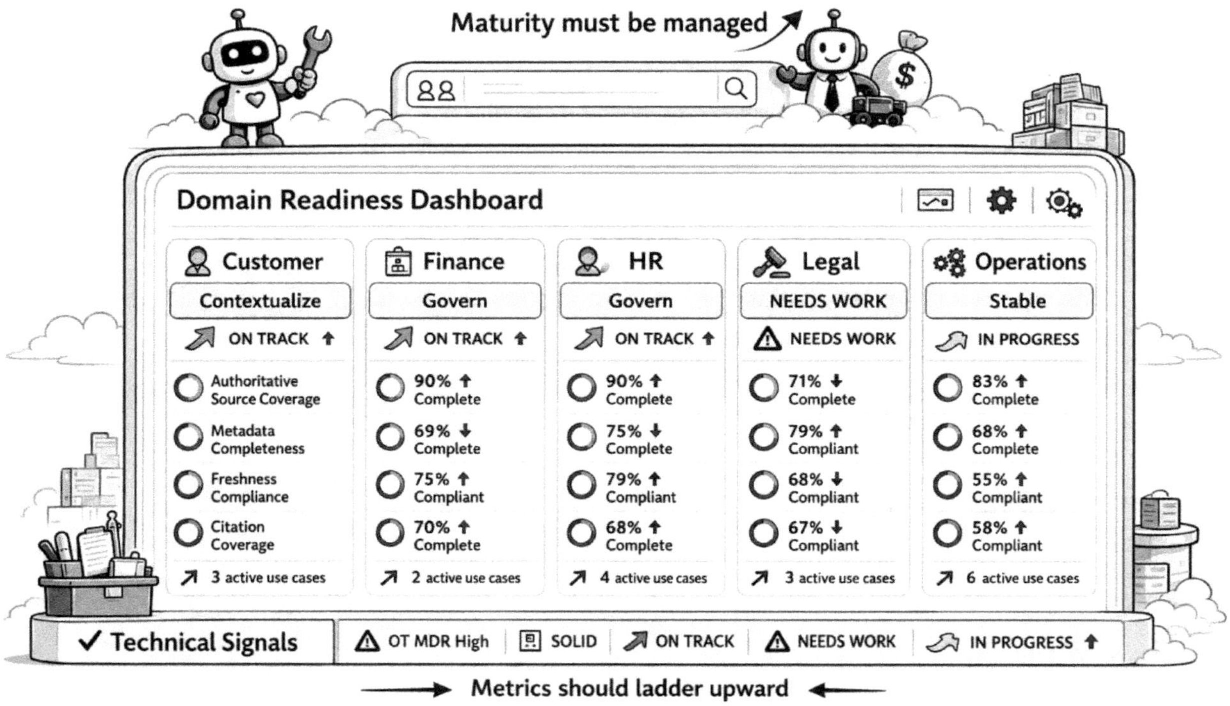

TEMPLATES

AI-Readiness KPI Catalog

KPI name <official name of the key performance indicator>

Definition <clear definition of what the KPI measures and how it is calculated in the context of AI-Ready Data, retrieval, trust, reuse, risk, or operational performance>

Type <classification of the KPI, such as technical, trust, operational, or business>

Why it matters <reason this KPI is important and what risk, capability, or business outcome it helps monitor or improve>

Data source <systems, logs, registries, scorecards, telemetry, audits, or records used to calculate and report the KPI>

Owner	<role, team, or jointly accountable leaders responsible for monitoring, improving, and acting on this KPI>
Baseline	<starting performance level for the KPI at the beginning of the measurement period or program>
Target	<desired future performance level and, where applicable, the time horizon in which it should be achieved>
Reporting cadence	<frequency with which the KPI is reviewed and reported, such as weekly, biweekly, monthly, or quarterly>
Thresholds	<red, amber, and green threshold ranges used to interpret KPI performance>
Red/amber/green logic	<rule used to determine KPI status, including how scoring, weighting, aggregation, or pass-rate logic is applied>
Action when below threshold	<required response, remediation, escalation, or gating action when KPI performance falls below the acceptable threshold>
Audience	<stakeholders, leaders, councils, boards, or teams that consume this KPI and use it for oversight, prioritization, or decision-making>

CASE EXAMPLE

Trust Grew When the Program Measured Readiness, Not Usage

A global enterprise launched an executive research assistant intended to help senior leaders prepare for account reviews, board updates, and transformation meetings. Early demos looked impressive. The assistant could summarize policies, surface account context, and produce briefings quickly. Yet the executive steering committee remained skeptical.

The reason was simple. The reporting pack emphasized the wrong metrics. It showed monthly active users, total assistant sessions, prompt volume, and average response latency. None of those measures answered the question executives actually cared about: why should they trust the output?

The transformation team reset the program around domain-based readiness and trust metrics.

They selected three priority domains for executive briefings: customer, finance, and policy. For each domain, they created an authoritative source inventory and defined freshness expectations. They then instrumented five measures that leaders could understand immediately:

- Authoritative source coverage.
- Freshness compliance.

- Citation coverage.
- Evidence acceptance rate.
- Unresolved-answer rate for high-stakes questions.

The first baseline was uncomfortable.

In the customer domain, only 46 percent of briefing-relevant content came from explicitly designated authoritative sources. In finance, freshness compliance on planning documents was 58 percent because archived drafts and superseded spreadsheets were still retrievable. In policy, citation coverage was only 52 percent for answers over a defined materiality threshold. The unresolved-answer rate was also high: when the system lacked adequate evidence, it still attempted to answer too often.

The team did not respond by tuning prompts or adding another model. They addressed the architecture.

They tightened source onboarding rules, marked authoritative repositories and document classes, enriched metadata for document status and effective date, improved semantic tagging for policy topics, and changed retrieval rules so stale or draft content was heavily down-ranked or excluded for executive-facing workflows. They also required citations for all answers in the targeted briefing workflows and introduced answer suppression when minimum evidence thresholds were not met.

Twelve weeks later, the dashboard told a different story.

Authoritative source coverage across the three domains rose from 46, 63, and 54 percent to 84, 88, and 91 percent. Freshness compliance improved to above 92 percent in all three domains. Citation coverage for executive-facing answers reached 98 percent. Unresolved-answer behavior improved because the assistant now declined low-evidence questions rather than fabricating continuity. Most importantly, executive staff reported a sharp decline in manual evidence checking before using outputs in briefing packs.

At that point skepticism changed. Leaders stopped asking how many sessions the assistant had processed. They started asking which adjacent domains could be brought to the same readiness standard. The team had not won confidence through novelty. It had won confidence through evidence, measurable control, and visible architectural improvement.

Closing Synthesis

The purpose of measurement in an AI-ready transformation is not to make the program look active. It is to make the program governable, explainable, and worth trusting.

That requires a metric system that starts with architecture, passes through trust, and ends in business outcomes. Technical signals matter because they show whether the estate is becoming fit for AI. Trust signals matter because they show whether the system deserves reliance. Operational outcomes matter because they show whether work is changing. Business outcomes matter because they show whether the transformation is earning its place.

The central discipline is to resist vanity. Activity is not readiness. Traffic is not trust. Adoption is not proof. Only a measured increase in source authority, semantic clarity, freshness discipline, evidence quality, policy fidelity, reuse, and business effectiveness demonstrates real progress.

Enterprises that get this right do more than build better dashboards. They create a management system for AI-ready architecture. They can show which domains are advancing, which are risky, which controls are strengthening, which workflows are now defensible, and which outcomes are becoming repeatable. That is what mature progress looks like.

Key Takeaways

- AI-ready progress should be measured through readiness, trust, reuse, safety, and business outcomes, not usage vanity.
- Technical metrics matter only when they ladder upward into trust signals, operational change, and business value.
- Trust is measurable through evidence quality, citation coverage, freshness, source authority, and traceability.
- Readiness must be assessed by domain because meaning, risk, and control requirements are not uniform across the enterprise.
- The best executive dashboards show capability growth and risk reduction, not just assistant traffic.

CHAPTER 32: WHAT GOES WRONG WHEN YOU LAYER AI ON TOP OF BAD DATA

When organizations place AI on top of unmanaged data estates, the result is not merely lower answer quality. The result is contradictory truth, security exposure, operational confusion, and rapid loss of organizational trust.

That is the point many enterprise programs miss. They treat AI failure as a model issue when it is often a data architecture issue. They assume that if the model is capable enough, it will somehow overcome stale content, conflicting definitions, weak metadata, broken permissions, absent lineage, and ungoverned repositories. It will not. It will amplify them.

A weak data estate does not produce one neat, obvious failure. It produces a family of failures that look different on the surface but share the same cause. One assistant gives outdated policy guidance. Another cites the wrong contract version. A third exposes information a user should never have seen. An agent takes an action based on an obsolete operating rule. A leadership copilot produces a polished summary that sounds coherent but blends incompatible definitions from finance, operations, and customer support. The outputs vary. The architectural defect is the same.

This chapter is about those predictable failures. Not abstractly, but as enterprise design realities. Hallucinations matter, but they are only one symptom. The deeper problem is that AI systems consume meaning, permissions, provenance, and context, not just bytes. If those are weak, fragmented, or missing, the AI layer becomes a force multiplier for confusion.

The most expensive outcome is not a wrong answer. It is a trust failure. Once users believe they must manually verify every response, the system has already lost its value. Adoption stalls, escalations grow, controls tighten, costs rise, and the organization concludes that "AI is not ready," when the actual truth is more precise: the data estate was not ready.

WHY THIS MATTERS

AI Failure Is Rarely Isolated

Traditional enterprise systems can often contain poor data quality within a bounded workflow. A bad field mapping may affect one report. A missing attribute may inconvenience one downstream team. AI changes the blast radius. It joins content across repositories, synthesizes across domains, and presents outputs in natural language with an authority that users may over-trust initially and distrust completely later. That is why bad data architecture creates predictable AI failures. The more broadly an AI system retrieves, reasons, summarizes, and recommends, the more it depends on the enterprise having solved foundational questions:

- Which source is authoritative?
- Which version is current?
- Which definition applies in this business context?
- Which users may see which content?
- What evidence supports this answer?
- What time period does this answer reflect?
- What should happen when sources conflict?

If the architecture cannot answer those questions consistently, the AI layer cannot answer them safely.

The Cost Is Larger Than Answer Quality

Many organizations underestimate the business cost of poor AI-readiness because they measure only model performance or pilot sentiment. They ignore the operational cost that begins after deployment.

Bad readiness drives rework. Teams spend time investigating why answers were wrong, which source was used, and whether exposure occurred. It drives manual verification. Users start cross-checking outputs against policy documents, data warehouses, email threads, or subject matter experts. It drives adoption loss. People stop using the system except for trivial tasks. It drives governance overhead. Risk, legal, and security teams respond by restricting access or slowing rollouts. It drives missed opportunity. High-value use cases never scale because the organization cannot defend the outputs.

In other words, weak data foundations raise cost and lower scale at the same time.

Prevention Is Cheaper Than Credibility Repair

An enterprise can fix many technical problems after launch. It is much harder to repair the perception that an internal AI system is unreliable, unsafe, or unpredictable. Credibility, once lost, is not restored by promising that the next version is better. It is restored only when users experience repeated evidence that the system now behaves with authority, consistency, and traceability.

That is why prevention is cheaper than credibility repair. It is less expensive to classify content, define semantic boundaries, establish source authority, instrument lineage, and enforce access-aware retrieval before rollout than to rebuild confidence after the first visible failures.

KEY INSIGHT

Trust breaks faster than it builds

A user will forgive one awkward answer from a new assistant. They will not forgive repeated contradictions on matters they believe the enterprise should know with certainty, such as policy, pricing, entitlements, customer commitments, or regulatory obligations. In practice, trust usually collapses suddenly, not gradually.

CORE CONCEPTS

Bad Data for AI Is Not the Same as Bad Data for Reporting

A dataset can be good enough for reporting and be unusable for AI. Reporting can tolerate rigid schemas, narrow questions, and human interpretation around gaps. AI often cannot. A generative or agentic system needs context that traditional analytics environments leave implicit. For AI, "bad data" includes:

- Content with no clear authority.
- Records with no business definition.
- Documents with no effective date.
- Repositories with broken or flattened permissions.
- Events with weak identity linkage.
- Retrieval indexes with poor chunking and no semantic enrichment.
- Sources with unknown freshness.
- Outputs with no evidence trail.
- Terms that mean different things in different domains.

This is why AI-Ready Data is not just clean data. It is contextualized, governed, interpretable, permission-aware, and operationally usable.

Hallucination Is Only One Failure Mode

Hallucination receives attention because it is visible: the model says something false. But many enterprise failures are subtler and often more dangerous.

- The assistant may retrieve a real document that is obsolete.
- It may use a legitimate definition from the wrong domain.
- It may summarize two authoritative sources that conflict because one has not yet been superseded.
- It may return content that the user is not entitled to see.
- It may recommend an action based on data that was current yesterday but invalid this morning.
- It may produce a defensible-sounding answer without showing the limits of evidence.

None of those are classic hallucinations. All are architectural failures.

Metadata Is the Control Plane

Metadata determines whether AI can discover, rank, filter, explain, and safely serve enterprise information. Without metadata, retrieval becomes pattern matching over undifferentiated content. With metadata, the enterprise can distinguish draft from approved, current from obsolete, policy from commentary, local exception from enterprise standard, customer-facing rule from internal note, and public knowledge from restricted material.

The key point is not merely that metadata is useful. It is that metadata governs AI behavior in practice. Source authority, classification, effective dates, lineage, ownership, intended use, sensitivity, policy tags, and semantic mappings are what make trustworthy AI possible.

Semantic Context Is What Prevents Contradictory Truth

Many AI failures originate not in poor storage or poor access, but in ambiguous meaning. "Customer" may mean account holder in one domain, legal entity in another, active subscriber in a third, and billing relationship in a fourth. "Revenue" may differ by finance policy, operational dashboard convention, and regional adjustment logic. "Policy" may mean HR policy, underwriting policy, or access-control policy, depending on the system. If these meanings are not modeled and surfaced, AI systems synthesize across them as if they were equivalent. That creates a contradictory truth: each source may be locally correct, but the combined answer is globally misleading.

Glossaries, taxonomies, ontologies, entity resolution, and relationship modeling are, therefore, not academic add-ons. They are operational controls against semantic failure.

Repositories Are Not Readiness

Many enterprises believe they are ready for AI because the relevant documents already exist in SharePoint, Teams, file stores, email archives, collaboration tools, or knowledge bases. This is a category mistake. Storage is not readiness. A repository does not guarantee:

- Clean extraction.
- Durable identifiers.
- Current-state tagging.
- Retention awareness.
- Access fidelity.
- Policy classification.
- Semantic enrichment.

- Source ranking.
- Chunk integrity.
- Citation-ready evidence.

Documents sitting in a repository are not AI-ready simply because they are digitally accessible. They must be prepared for trustworthy retrieval and governed use.

ARCHITECTURAL IMPLICATIONS

The Enterprise Must Design for Source Authority

AI systems should not treat all available content as equal. An architecture for trustworthy AI needs explicit source authority rules. A policy portal may outrank email attachments. Approved procedures may outrank team notes. Signed contracts may outrank draft statements of work. Master data records may outrank replicated extracts. Enterprise taxonomy definitions may outrank local spreadsheet labels. When those rules are absent, ranking becomes accidental. The system may retrieve the easiest text to parse, not the most authoritative source.

Freshness Must Be Designed, Not Assumed

Many AI failures are temporal. The answer would have been correct last quarter, before a pricing update, before a revised operating policy, before a merger, before a retention change, before a regulatory interpretation shifted. Freshness is not a cosmetic detail. It is part of the truth. Architecturally, this means the enterprise needs:

- Effective dates.
- Supersession logic.
- Publication states.
- Synchronization expectations.
- Re-indexing discipline.
- Stale-source detection.
- Answer experiences that make the temporal scope visible.

An answer without a time context is often an unreliable answer.

Retrieval Quality Is an Architecture Responsibility

Organizations frequently blame the model when retrieval is weak. But poor retrieval is often caused by upstream design choices: bad chunk boundaries, missing titles, absent document structure, no policy tags, broken citations, no version handling, no authority weighting, no domain-aware ranking, no access-aware filtering, and no distinction between canonical and convenience copies.

Retrieval quality is not merely an embedding problem. It is a design problem spanning content preparation, metadata, indexing, access control, ranking, and serving contracts.

Governance Must Span Structured and Unstructured Assets Together

Governance programs built for tabular analytics often break under AI because they ignore the assets AI uses most heavily: policies, procedures, transcripts, emails, notes, logs, messages, and knowledge articles. Yet these often carry the business meaning that structured systems do not fully capture. An AI-ready architecture must apply classification, retention, privacy, legal hold, provenance, and access controls consistently across structured and unstructured content. Otherwise, the AI system becomes the first place where those governance gaps become visible.

Different AI Consumers Need Different Data-Serving Contracts

A knowledge assistant answering employee questions does not require the same contract as an action-taking agent initiating workflow changes. An executive briefing tool does not require the same level of granularity as an analyst copilot performing cross-domain investigation. A customer-service assistant may need high recall with clear citations. A financial review copilot may need narrower retrieval with stronger source authority and stricter freshness guarantees. The implication is that there is no single "AI-ready" serving layer. There are multiple serving contracts, each with distinct thresholds for evidence, completeness, speed, permissions, and explainability.

❖ FIGURE 64 – FAILURE MAP

FAILURE MODES AND ANTI-PATTERNS

Contradictory Answers from Legitimate Sources

This is one of the most common and damaging patterns. Users ask a straightforward question and receive different answers depending on phrasing, source mix, or time of day. In many cases, the system is not inventing facts. It is surfacing conflicting but real artifacts from the estate. Typical causes include:

- Multiple policy versions with no supersession markers.
- Domain terms with unresolved ambiguity.
- Replicated data products with different refresh cycles.
- Local process documents presented as enterprise standards.
- No authority ranking between canonical and derivative sources.

Users experience this as unreliability. Architects should experience it as a semantic and metadata failure.

Security Exposure Through Flattened Retrieval

When documents are extracted and indexed without preserving permission fidelity, the AI layer can inadvertently widen access. Even if the user interface enforces identity, the retrieval layer may still expose content through snippets, citations, summaries, or vector search hits that were not access-trimmed correctly. This is not a minor bug. It is a structural governance breach. The damage is amplified because AI systems can summarize restricted content in natural language, making exposure more legible and actionable than a raw document leak.

Obsolete Truth Presented as Current Guidance

This failure is especially common in internal assistants. The answer is fluent, specific, and wrong only because it is old. A user asks for the travel approval rule, onboarding procedure, pricing exception path, or incident escalation standard and receives a response from an obsolete document that was never retired, never tagged as superseded, or never re-ranked below the current standard. This is why freshness controls matter. An enterprise that cannot distinguish current from historical guidance should not expect AI to do so reliably on its behalf.

KEY INSIGHT

The first month failure pattern

Week one often looks better than reality because early users ask easy questions, tolerate rough edges, and assume the system is learning. Weeks two through four reveal the real readiness gap. Harder questions arrive. Edge cases appear. Contradictions are compared in chat threads. Subject matter experts begin forwarding screenshots. Confidence drops much faster in this period than most program teams expect.

Incorrect Action Recommendations from Context-Poor Data

An agent or copilot may not produce a visibly false answer. Instead, it may recommend the wrong next step because the data lacks policy context, exceptions, dependency rules, or state transitions. For example, it may suggest closing a case that requires legal review, issuing a credit that exceeds delegated authority, or routing a request through an outdated process.

These failures are especially serious because they convert data ambiguity into operational action.

Explainability Gaps That Block Adoption

Some outputs are directionally useful but cannot be trusted because the system cannot show where the answer came from, which version it used, or what evidence it ignored. In high-value enterprise settings, that is often enough to stop adoption even when answer quality appears acceptable.

A system that cannot cite, trace, and bound its answer forces the user to become the control layer. That defeats the point of enterprise AI.

"We Will Fix Governance After the Pilot"

This almost always fails. Once teams see early value, the organization is tempted to scale before governance is embedded. The result is a growing retrieval footprint, inconsistent controls, and a larger remediation burden later. Governance is much harder to retrofit after indexes, prompts, connectors, and user expectations have already spread.

Treating Document Ingestion as Readiness

Bulk ingest is not a readiness milestone. It is merely the start of a control problem. Without classification, authority modeling, lifecycle tagging, and retrieval design, large-scale ingestion often worsens answer quality by increasing noise.

Using One Generic Retrieval Pipeline for Every Use Case

A single pipeline may be operationally convenient, but it is architecturally weak. Different consumers need different indexing, ranking, freshness, citation, and control rules. Standardization is useful at the capability level, not at the expense of serving fit.

Assuming SMEs Can Compensate for Architectural Weakness

Subject matter experts can identify bad answers during pilots. They cannot sustainably validate every production answer. Once users start depending on human backstopping, the AI system ceases to be scalable.

⚠ WARNING SIGN

Users start double-checking every answer manually

Once this becomes normal behavior, your issue is no longer model accuracy. It is loss of institutional confidence. The assistant has become an extra step rather than a source of leverage.

Practical Application

Start with Failure-Oriented Architecture Reviews

Many AI programs begin with capability excitement. A better starting point is failure analysis. Ask, before deployment:

- Where can the system retrieve multiple conflicting truths?
- Which sources are authoritative and how is that expressed?
- How are effective dates and supersession handled?
- What content should never be retrieved for this user group?
- Which terms are semantically ambiguous across domains?
- What evidence must every answer provide?
- What actions, if any, are allowed when evidence is incomplete?

This shifts design from optimistic enablement to controlled trustworthiness.

Establish a Source Hierarchy

For each use case, define a source hierarchy:

- System of record.
- Approved policy source.
- Domain-owned procedural source.
- Derived analytical source.
- Local working material.
- Conversational or informal source.

The hierarchy should shape indexing, ranking, and answer presentation. Do not let the retrieval engine decide authority by accident.

Make Freshness Visible

Every AI-serving pattern should include time logic. At a minimum:

- Effective date.
- Last reviewed date.
- Publication state.
- Superseded-by relationships.

Where freshness cannot be guaranteed, the answer should say so. A bounded answer is more trustworthy than a falsely confident one.

Build Access-Aware Retrieval End to End

Permission fidelity must survive extraction, enrichment, indexing, ranking, and response generation. If the control is applied only at the document store or only at the front-end experience, it is incomplete.

Introduce a Reusable Diagnostic Template

One practical way to operationalize failure learning is to standardize how issues are documented. Teams often record incidents as isolated bugs. That hides patterns. A better approach is to use a common diagnostic that captures not just what failed, but which architectural layer failed.

Use the Template to Find Recurring Causes

Over time, the template will reveal common root causes:

- Missing lifecycle metadata.
- Unresolved semantic ambiguity.
- Broken permission propagation.
- Weak source authority.
- Inconsistent refresh discipline.
- No answer-level explainability standard.

Those patterns should inform the roadmap more than isolated model tweaks.

❖ FIGURE 65 – COST-OF-POOR-READINESS MODEL

TEMPLATES

AI Failure Mode Diagnostic

Failure scenario
<brief description of the failure event, including what the assistant, copilot, or agent did wrong in a real or plausible business context>

Observed symptom
<visible behavior showing how the failure appeared to the user, such as incorrect guidance, wrong citation, outdated recommendation, or inconsistent answer>

User impact
<effect on the end user, employee, analyst, customer-facing worker, or manager who relied on the output>

Business impact
<effect on operations, trust, compliance, support burden, risk exposure, or process efficiency caused by the failure>

Root cause category
<primary failure category, such as stale content, weak metadata, semantic ambiguity, permission failure, poor supersession handling, or governance breakdown>

Source systems involved
<systems, repositories, indexes, portals, or platforms that contributed to the failure path>

Metadata factor
<metadata weakness that contributed to the failure, such as missing effective dates, approval state, owner, authority tags, or supersession markers>

Semantic factor
<semantic or contextual weakness that contributed to the failure, such as ambiguous terms, missing disambiguation, weak taxonomy, or absent domain context>

Governance factor
<governance or lifecycle weakness that contributed to the failure, such as poor archival rules, weak source authority controls, or lack of retrieval restrictions>

Security factor
<security, access, or scope-control issue that contributed to the failure, or statement of whether no direct security breach occurred but scope controls were still weak>

Freshness factor
<temporal or lifecycle weakness that contributed to the failure, such as stale indexing logic, lack of current-versus-obsolete distinction, or missing refresh and expiry rules>

Detectability
<assessment of how easy or difficult it is to notice the failure before or after user impact, such as low, medium, or high>

Severity
<assessment of the seriousness of the incident, such as low, medium, or high, including whether it was operational, financial, legal, or trust-related>

Immediate containment
<near-term actions required to stop recurrence quickly, such as removing content, tightening retrieval scope, adjusting ranking, or notifying users>

Long-term fix
<structural remediation needed to prevent recurrence, such as authority tiers, lifecycle metadata, supersession handling, domain-aware retrieval, or stronger answer evidence rules>

Owner	<role, team, or jointly accountable leaders responsible for containment, remediation, and prevention>
Review date	<date or cadence for post-incident review, follow-up validation, and governance oversight>

CASE EXAMPLE

An Internal Assistant Loses Credibility in Two Weeks

Consider a common enterprise pattern. A company launches an internal assistant to answer employee questions about operating procedures, travel rules, approvals, and policy exceptions. The rollout is positioned as low risk because it is internal and read-only. Leadership expects fast adoption because the problem seems simple: employees waste time searching for answers that already exist somewhere in the organization.

The first few days look promising. Users ask basic questions. The assistant responds fluently. Screenshots circulate showing quick wins. A program team interprets this as evidence that the architecture is sound.

Then the second week begins. An employee asks whether a regional manager can approve an expense override above a certain threshold. The assistant cites a policy PDF from the previous quarter and says yes. Another employee asks a similar question and gets a different answer, this time citing a newer finance operations page that says no, unless the request is routed through a revised control workflow. A third user asks for the escalation procedure and receives steps from a business-unit playbook that was never meant to apply enterprise-wide.

Now the issue is no longer isolated answer quality. Users begin comparing screenshots. Finance and HR teams receive forwarded outputs with comments such as, “Which one is right?” Subject matter experts spend time correcting the system informally. Some employees stop using the assistant and return to asking colleagues directly. Others continue using it, but only as a starting point, then manually verify everything themselves.

Within two weeks, the rollout has a credibility problem.

What actually went wrong

The model was not the main issue. The assistant failed because the data estate underneath it was not prepared for governed retrieval.

The policy library contained multiple valid-looking versions with inconsistent metadata.

The enterprise search layer lacked clear authority weighting.

Team-level guidance was indexed alongside approved policy.

Superseded documents were still retrievable.

Permissions were technically intact, but governance was weak enough that non-canonical sources still influenced answers.

Semantic distinctions between "approval," "exception," and "delegated authority" were not modeled consistently across finance and operations.

Each defect seemed manageable in isolation. Together, they produced contradictory truth.

Why trust collapsed so quickly

The assistant was deployed into a category of questions where users expect institutional certainty. Operating procedures and approval rules are not brainstorming topics. They are control topics. When an assistant is wrong there, users interpret the failure as evidence that the system is unsafe, not merely immature.

This is the essential lesson. Trust failure is the most expensive outcome because it turns every future improvement into a credibility recovery exercise. Even after the underlying defects are fixed, users remember the early contradiction.

What the enterprise should have done differently

A stronger rollout would have included:

- A limited source set containing only approved current policy.
- Explicit supersession handling.
- Authority ranking that excluded local playbooks from enterprise answers.
- Semantic disambiguation for approval-related terms.
- Answer citations showing effective dates.
- A pilot review process focused on high-risk contradiction scenarios rather than only general usefulness.

In other words, the organization should have treated internal policy guidance as a governed data-serving problem, not a search convenience problem.

Closing Synthesis

When AI is layered on top of bad data, the resulting failures are not mysterious. They are predictable expressions of architectural weakness. Poor source authority produces contradiction. Weak metadata produces bad retrieval. Missing semantic context produces ambiguity. Broken governance produces exposure. Weak freshness controls produce obsolete truth. Missing provenance produces explainability failure. And together they produce the business outcome that matters most: loss of trust.

This is why bad readiness cannot be dismissed as a quality nuisance. It is a structural limit on enterprise AI. Organizations do not scale trustworthy copilots, assistants, or agents by making models slightly better while leaving the data estate semantically fragmented, poorly governed, and operationally opaque. They scale trustworthy AI by redesigning the estate so that meaning, permissions, lineage, freshness, and authority are explicit and enforceable.

The central lesson is simple. Hallucination is only one thing that goes wrong. The broader problem is that unmanaged data estates generate unmanaged AI behavior. Once that behavior reaches employees, customers, or operations, the organization pays for it in rework, delay, caution, and credibility loss.

Prevention is, therefore, cheaper than repair. The enterprises that succeed will be the ones that treat AI-readiness as architecture, not aspiration. They will prepare data before they expose it. They will govern content before they index it. They will model meaning before they scale retrieval. And they will understand that trustworthy AI is built not on access to more data, but on the disciplined design of better data-serving conditions.

Key Takeaways

- Bad data architecture creates predictable AI failures long before model limits are reached.
- Hallucinations are only one failure mode; contradiction, exposure, staleness, and weak explainability are equally important.
- Trust failure is the most expensive outcome because users who verify everything manually no longer receive leverage from AI.
- Weak data foundations increase rework, investigation, governance burden, and missed scale at the same time.
- It is cheaper to build authority, metadata, semantics, freshness, and governance into the estate up front than to repair credibility after rollout.

CHAPTER 33: ANTI-PATTERNS THAT LOOK MODERN BUT FAIL IN PRODUCTION

Many enterprise AI failures begin as impressive demonstrations.

A team assembles a sleek chatbot. It answers policy questions from a document store, summarizes account activity from a few APIs, and produces fluent responses that appear intelligent enough to excite sponsors. In a controlled lab environment, the results look modern, fast, and inevitable. Then production realities arrive. Security asks how permissions are enforced. Legal asks which content is retained and which is excluded. Data governance asks which source is authoritative. Audit asks for lineage. Operations asks who owns defects, drift, and remediation. No one has good answers. The demo collapses under the weight of enterprise reality.

This is the pattern behind many AI programs that stall after early enthusiasm. The problem is rarely that the model is weak. The problem is that the surrounding data architecture was never designed for governed discovery, semantic interpretation, provenance, trust, or operational accountability. The architecture may look current because it uses embeddings, vector search, copilots, or agents. But modern components do not make a mature system.

In enterprise settings, the most dangerous AI anti-patterns are not the obviously reckless ones. They are the ones that look sophisticated enough to win funding. They borrow the language of modern AI architecture while skipping the hard dependencies that make production use safe and durable. They optimize for surface appeal and speed to demo rather than ownership, policy, metadata, and operating discipline. That is why naming anti-patterns matters. Once teams can recognize them, they can stop treating predictable failure as an unfortunate surprise and start treating it as an avoidable design flaw.

WHY THIS MATTERS

Demos Can Hide Structural Weakness

A polished proof of concept is often a poor indicator of production readiness. In fact, the easier a demo is to assemble, the greater the risk that key controls were bypassed. Enterprise AI systems only reveal their real architecture when they are forced to answer harder questions:

- Can they distinguish authoritative content from merely available content?
- Can they enforce source-specific permissions at retrieval time?
- Can they explain why one result was ranked above another?

- Can they show users evidence, citation, timestamp, and provenance?
- Can they support remediation when wrong answers appear?
- Can they prevent use in contexts where the data is incomplete, stale, or legally restricted?

If those questions have no design answer, the architecture is not modern. It is unfinished.

Anti-Patterns Waste More Than Money

These failures do not just waste pilot budgets. They damage trust in the wider transformation. Business leaders begin to believe AI itself is unreliable when the deeper problem is that the data estate was never prepared for AI consumption. Security and legal teams become more skeptical. Stewards become reactive instead of engaged. Good use cases get delayed because earlier initiatives normalized architectural shortcuts. That is why anti-patterns matter at the enterprise level. They are not isolated technical mistakes. They are force multipliers for organizational confusion.

Many Failures Are Predictable in Advance

The encouraging truth is that most of these failures are visible during architecture review. An experienced reviewer can often predict failure before a single production incident occurs. If ownership is missing, if policy mappings are undefined, if semantic context is absent, if ranking logic is opaque, if evidence is not exposed, then the downstream failure mode is already present. Production merely makes it visible.

Core Concepts

Modern-Looking Architecture Can Still Be Structurally Unsound

Enterprises often confuse novelty with maturity. A system that uses vector search, a foundation model, and a conversational interface may still be less production-ready than a simpler system with strong metadata, policy enforcement, authoritative sourcing, and operational ownership.

The architectural question is never, "Does it use current techniques?" The question is, "Can it produce trustworthy outcomes repeatedly under enterprise conditions?"

That distinction matters because AI-Ready Data is not simply cleaned or consolidated data. It is data that can be discovered, interpreted, filtered, ranked, governed, traced, and safely delivered to different AI consumers with appropriate evidence and controls.

Vector-First Patterns Often Skip Context

A common anti-pattern begins with embeddings and a vector store. Teams ingest whatever content is easiest to collect, chunk it mechanically, embed it, and call the retrieval layer complete. But vectors without metadata are not an architecture. Similarity alone cannot distinguish policy documents from outdated drafts, local guidance from enterprise standards, informal notes from approved procedure, or restricted content from broadly shareable content.

Embedding content may improve recall. It does not create business meaning, provenance, or governance.

Chatbot-First Patterns Often Skip Service Design

Another common anti-pattern begins with the interface. Teams decide that the goal is a chatbot, so they optimize for conversational experience before deciding what the system is actually authorized to do, which sources it may rely on, what evidence it must show, and what confidence or risk thresholds apply. The result is a polished interaction model wrapped around a weak trust model.

A good conversational interface cannot rescue a poor data-serving contract.

Pilot-First Patterns Often Skip the Operating Model

A pilot is supposed to reduce uncertainty. In many enterprises, however, pilots are used to postpone architecture. Teams treat governance, stewardship, remediation, and service ownership as later concerns. They assume success will create momentum and that the architecture can be fixed afterward.

Usually, the opposite happens. The pilot establishes expectations, shortcuts, and dependencies that become harder to unwind later. The organization inherits technical debt before it has agreed on standards.

Anti-Patterns Thrive Where Ownership Is Weak

Weak ownership is the breeding ground for every other failure. When no one owns source quality, metadata quality, retrieval outcomes, policy interpretation, or user remediation, anti-patterns multiply because no one has the authority or incentive to resolve them. In those conditions, AI becomes a layer of plausible output resting on unowned ambiguity.

KEY INSIGHT

Why Modernity Is Not Maturity

A production-grade AI architecture is not defined by whether it uses the latest model, vector index, agent framework, or orchestration pattern. It is defined by whether it can operate within enterprise constraints: source authority, permission fidelity, semantic clarity, policy enforcement, provenance, explainability, monitoring, and accountable ownership.

Modern components can accelerate a good architecture. They can also camouflage a bad one.

ARCHITECTURAL IMPLICATIONS

The Retrieval Layer Is an Enterprise Control Surface

Many teams still treat retrieval as a model-adjacent feature. In reality, retrieval is a major architectural control surface. It determines which content is eligible, which content is prioritized, which policies are enforced, and what evidence reaches the user. That means retrieval cannot be separated from metadata, classification, business semantics, and access control.

An enterprise retrieval layer should answer at least these questions:

- Which sources are authoritative for which types of questions?
- Which metadata attributes influence filtering and ranking?
- How are freshness and supersession handled?
- How are entitlements preserved from source to response?
- How are citations and timestamps exposed?
- How are unresolved ambiguities escalated?

If the architecture cannot answer those questions, the retrieval layer is not enterprise-ready.

Semantic Context Is Not Optional Decoration

Without a semantic layer, AI systems confuse related but distinct business concepts. They treat "customer," "account holder," "subscriber," "member," and "party" as interchangeable. They fail to recognize temporal changes in policy. They merge structured indicators with unstructured commentary without understanding their relationship. They surface information that is syntactically relevant but semantically misleading.

Glossaries, taxonomies, ontologies, entity resolution, and business rules are not academic extras. They are the mechanisms that reduce ambiguity and make grounded reasoning possible.

Governance Must Span Structured and Unstructured Data Together

Anti-patterns often appear because governance remains focused on tables while enterprise meaning lives in documents, notes, transcripts, messages, and workflow content. A production AI system must handle both worlds together. The architecture must understand not only the record in a warehouse, but also the policy document that explains its treatment, the retention rule that constrains its use, the case note that changes its interpretation, and the entitlement model that limits who may see it.

Treating unstructured content as a secondary concern is one of the fastest ways to build a system that looks complete and fails under real use.

❖ FIGURE 66 – HEALTHY PATTERN VS FLASHY ANTI-PATTERN

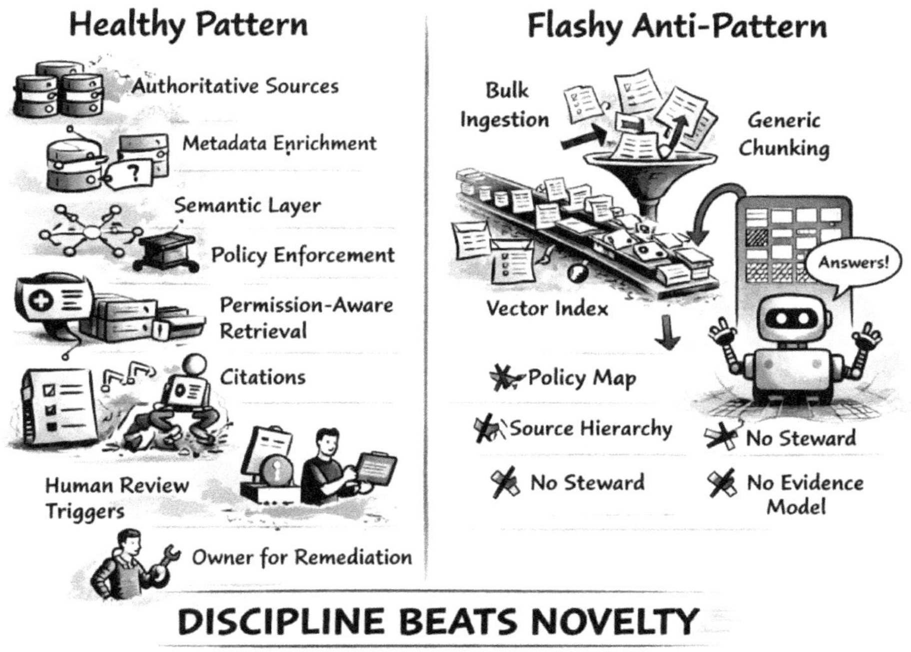

Different Consumers Require Different Serving Contracts

A search assistant, an analyst copilot, an executive briefing system, and an action-taking agent should not share the same trust assumptions. The assistant may tolerate lower confidence if it always cites evidence and stays advisory. The action-taking agent may require strong source authority, narrow scope, explicit approvals, and human review triggers. Architectures fail when they assume one generalized AI pattern can serve all consumers equally well.

FAILURE MODES AND ANTI-PATTERNS

The Vector-First Shortcut

This pattern starts by ingesting content into embeddings and assumes similarity search will sort out relevance. It often ignores document status, business criticality, authority level, version lineage, and intended use.

Why it fails in production: Because similarity is not trust. The system retrieves adjacent content, not necessarily authoritative content. Drafts compete with approved policies. Local workarounds outrank enterprise standards. Users receive plausible answers with no clear basis for trust.

Healthy alternative: Build vector retrieval on top of metadata-enriched content with source hierarchy, document lifecycle status, classification, freshness rules, and semantic tags.

The Chatbot-First Facade

This pattern treats the interface as the product. Teams prioritize conversational fluency, tone, and quick answers before defining the data contract.

Why it fails in production: Because the user experience hides the absence of enterprise controls. Once users depend on it, unresolved issues emerge: unsupported question types, hidden policy conflicts, unverifiable answers, and inconsistent permissions.

Healthy alternative: Design the service contract first. Define supported decisions, evidence requirements, answer boundaries, prohibited uses, and escalation paths before optimizing the interface.

The Pilot-First Escape Hatch

This pattern uses "it is just a pilot" as a reason to defer stewardship, standards, logging, remediation, and policy integration.

Why it fails in production: Because pilots shape future architecture. Once the organization sees value, the pressure shifts from "Should we continue?" to "How quickly can we scale?" At that point, shortcuts become liabilities and politically difficult to undo.

Healthy alternative: Treat even small pilots as governed slices of the target state. Scope narrowly, but do not suspend ownership or trust requirements.

The Repository Equals Readiness Assumption

This pattern assumes that because documents exist in SharePoint, Teams, file shares, or a content platform, they are ready for AI retrieval.

Why it fails in production: Because storage is not readiness. Repositories contain duplicates, drafts, orphaned content, conflicting versions, inconsistent permissions, and unclear lifecycle status. AI amplifies those issues instead of solving them.

Healthy alternative: Curate retrieval-ready collections with lifecycle metadata, ownership, authority ranking, classification, and exclusion rules.

The Metadata-Light Stack

This pattern captures minimal metadata because teams want to move quickly. They may keep only title, URL, and raw content.

Why it fails in production: Because metadata governs discoverability, ranking, lineage, policy enforcement, freshness, and explainability. Without it, the architecture cannot distinguish approved from obsolete, public from restricted, or canonical from duplicate.

Healthy alternative: Treat metadata as the control plane. Capture source system, owner, classification, sensitivity, authority, effective date, review status, supersession relationship, business domain, and intended use.

The One-Size-Fits-All Trust Model

This pattern uses the same retrieval and response logic for all consumers, from lightweight assistants to action-oriented agents.

Why it fails in production: Because different consumers require different evidence, confidence thresholds, control points, and intervention paths. A response acceptable for exploration may be unacceptable for execution.

Healthy alternative: Define distinct serving contracts by consumer type, risk level, and actionability.

The Ownership Vacuum

This pattern launches an AI capability with a project team but no durable service owner, data steward, or remediation workflow.

Why it fails in production: Because defects accumulate with nowhere to go. Users report wrong answers. Source teams disagree. Outdated documents remain indexed. No one owns retraining, reclassification, policy updates, or root-cause analysis.

Healthy alternative: Assign named owners for source quality, retrieval quality, policy interpretation, operations, and user issue resolution.

The No-Evidence Response Pattern

This pattern values fluent answers over visible proof. The system returns conclusions but hides sources, timestamps, ranking rationale, or confidence context.

Why it fails in production: Because enterprise users need defensible output, not polished prose. Without visible evidence, trust becomes a matter of style rather than architecture.

Healthy alternative: Expose citations, source identity, effective date, confidence framing, and where relevant, the exact policy or record basis for the answer.

KEY INSIGHT

The Anti-Pattern Catalog

Use this catalog during reviews to name what is going wrong early:

- Vector-first shortcut
- Pilot-first escape hatch
- Metadata-light stack
- Ownership vacuum
- Chatbot-first facade
- Repository equals readiness
- One-size-fits-all trust model
- No-evidence response pattern

The value of the catalog is not taxonomy for its own sake. It gives teams a shared language for intervention before the architecture hardens.

❖ FIGURE 67 – HEALTHY PATTERN VS FLASHY ANTI-PATTERN

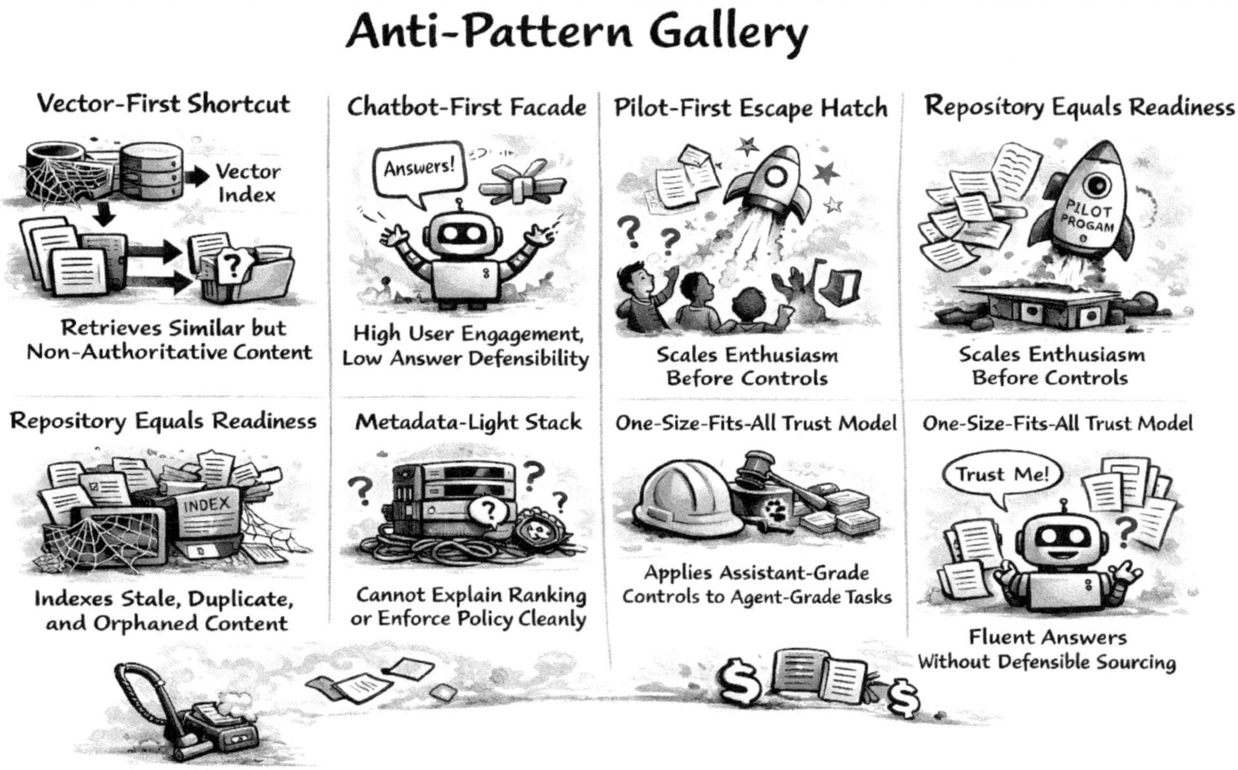

⚠ WARNING SIGN

A proof of concept with no steward, no policy map, and no trust model is not an early success. It is an early warning.

PRACTICAL APPLICATION

Use Architecture Review to Stop Predictable Failure

Anti-patterns become expensive when they are discovered through incidents rather than design review. The practical response is to institutionalize a small set of architecture questions that force hard dependencies into the open. Those questions should be asked before launch, before scale-out, and whenever a team proposes a new AI consumer against enterprise data.

TEMPLATES

AI Architecture Review Questions

Authoritative source question	<definition of the canonical system, repository, or governed publication for each answer type, including source precedence, override conditions, and whether the use case is blocked when no authoritative source can be named>
Metadata governance question	<metadata fields that govern eligibility, filtering, and ranking, such as classification, owner, lifecycle status, effective date, geography, product line, business domain, sensitivity, and approval state>
Freshness handling question	<rules for how effective dates, publication dates, superseded content, stale records, refresh cadence, invalidation logic, and unconfirmed freshness are handled architecturally>
Permission fidelity question	<definition of how source permissions are preserved through indexing, enrichment, retrieval, and response generation, including identity source, entitlement logic, and exception handling>
Evidence exposure question	<definition of which citations, timestamps, excerpts, provenance elements, and confidence cues are shown to users so they can inspect the basis of the answer>
Semantic layer question	<definition of the glossary, taxonomy, ontology, business rules, and entity model used to reduce ambiguity, distinguish similar concepts, resolve aliases, and handle temporal or jurisdictional variation>
Remediation ownership question	<named accountable owners for retrieval defects, source disputes, stale content, policy conflicts, and user escalations, including response times, triage paths, and correction propagation>
Prohibited uses question	<explicit statement of where the system must not be used, such as regulated determinations, legal interpretations, customer communications, financial decisions, operational execution, or other domains with insufficient evidence or scope>
Human review trigger question	<thresholds and conditions that require escalation to human review, such as low evidence density, conflicting sources, stale authoritative content, high-impact decisions, policy-sensitive topics, or state-changing actions>

Trust metrics question	<metrics used to demonstrate trustworthiness, such as citation click-through, grounded-answer rate, stale-answer rate, unauthorized retrieval incidents, unresolved ambiguity rate, remediation cycle time, and user-reported trustworthiness>
Accepted technical debt question	<explicit record of current shortcuts, gaps, or deferred controls, such as missing metadata, partial source coverage, incomplete semantic mapping, deferred retention controls, coarse permissions, or manual remediation>
Risk approval question	<named business owner, architecture lead, security reviewer, and governance authority who approved the current state and accepted the documented risk in writing>

CASE EXAMPLE

The Demo That Everyone Loved

A global services company built a policy chatbot for internal employees. The prototype used a modern foundation model, vector search over several document libraries, and an elegant conversational interface. In demos, employees asked questions about travel policy, remote work allowances, and expense rules. The chatbot answered quickly and sounded authoritative. Leaders praised it as a breakthrough in enterprise knowledge access.

The project team presented usage metrics from a controlled pilot group. Average response time was low. User satisfaction in demos was high. The initiative looked ready for rollout.

The review that stopped it

Then the enterprise review began.

Security asked how the system preserved document-level permissions across SharePoint sites, HR repositories, and local team folders. The answer was incomplete. Some permissions were inherited during indexing, but group changes were not guaranteed to propagate quickly. There was no clear explanation for how exception cases would be handled.

Governance asked which travel policy source was authoritative. The team had indexed the corporate policy portal, regional HR sites, country-specific exception documents, archived FAQs, and old presentation decks. No one had defined source precedence. In some cases, the system retrieved a country-level exception document before the current enterprise baseline. In others, an outdated FAQ outranked the approved policy page because it used more similar phrasing.

Legal asked how retention and legal hold rules applied to indexed content. The team had no complete inventory of which repositories contained policy records versus informal guidance. Some indexed content should not have been part of the retrieval corpus at all.

Architecture asked how freshness worked. The answer was that nightly indexing would "mostly keep things current." But there was no logic for superseded policies, no effective-date interpretation, and no mechanism to warn users when retrieved content might be obsolete.

Operations asked who would own remediation when employees reported incorrect answers. The project team had planned to handle issues during launch, but there was no permanent service owner, no stewarding model, and no service-level expectation for corrections.

Finally, audit asked what evidence employees would see. The chatbot showed a link to a source page, but not document status, effective date, authority level, or conflicting-source alerts. In other words, it sounded confident without exposing the information necessary to justify confidence.

Why it failed enterprise review

Nothing in this case failed because the model was incapable. The failure came from architecture. The system had the classic traits of a flashy anti-pattern:

- Chatbot-first design.
- Repository equals readiness.
- Metadata-light retrieval.
- No source hierarchy.
- Weak freshness model.
- Incomplete permission fidelity.
- No named remediation owner.
- No evidence-centered trust design.

The demo worked in the lab because the questions were curated, the content was semi-familiar, and the social setting rewarded fluency. It failed enterprise review because the architecture could not support defensible production use.

What the healthy redesign looked like

The company did not abandon the use case. It redesigned the service. First, it narrowed the scope to travel policy only, instead of all HR knowledge. Second, it defined authoritative sources by policy domain and geography. Third, it curated the retrieval corpus to exclude drafts, archived presentations, and local guidance that lacked approval status. Fourth, it enriched content with metadata for owner, policy status, effective date, jurisdiction, and supersession relationship. Fifth, it enforced permission fidelity directly from source entitlements. Sixth, it changed the interface so every answer showed source, effective date, authority tier, and direct citation. Seventh, it introduced a human review trigger whenever sources conflicted or the question implied a regulated employment decision. Finally, it assigned a durable service owner with stewardship support. The resulting system was less flashy. It was also trustworthy.

Closing Synthesis

Enterprise AI anti-patterns persist because they are easy to mistake for progress. They use modern components, move quickly, and produce outputs that appear sophisticated. But many of them are structurally unsound because they depend on the very things the enterprise has not yet made explicit: authority, metadata, semantics, policy, stewardship, and accountable operations.

That is why architecture review is so important. Most of these failures can be predicted before launch. When a team cannot explain authoritative sourcing, permission fidelity, freshness, semantic context, or remediation ownership, the problem is not hidden. It is already present. Production will merely expose it in a more expensive way.

The deeper lesson is that trustworthy AI does not emerge from novelty alone. It emerges from disciplined data architecture. Enterprises do not scale AI by piling models and interfaces on top of ungoverned repositories. They scale it by building a governed, contextualized, explainable data estate that can support retrieval, reasoning, and action safely over time.

In that sense, anti-patterns are useful. They remind us that the appearance of modernity is cheap, while architectural maturity is earned. The teams that succeed are not the ones with the flashiest demos. They are the ones disciplined enough to make trust visible in the design.

Key Takeaways

- Modern AI components do not compensate for weak source authority, metadata, policy, or ownership.
- Vector-first, chatbot-first, and pilot-first approaches often fail because they skip enterprise dependencies.
- Most AI production failures are predictable during architecture review.
- Trustworthy AI requires evidence, provenance, permission fidelity, freshness, and semantic clarity.
- Naming anti-patterns gives enterprises a practical way to intervene before demo success becomes production failure.

Chapter 34: From Dashboards to Agents

For most of the modern data era, enterprise information delivery has been built around a simple premise: people go to the data. They open reports, inspect dashboards, compare trends, and decide what to do next. The interface may have improved, the refresh cycle may have accelerated, and the visual layer may have become more sophisticated, but the operating assumption has remained stable. Human users pull information from systems designed to summarize the state of the business.

That assumption is now changing.

Enterprises are moving toward a model in which AI systems do not merely present information, but assemble context, interpret conditions, recommend responses, and, in bounded cases, initiate actions. In this world, intelligence is no longer only something a user retrieves. It is increasingly something the system delivers, explains, and operationalizes within the flow of work.

This is not a user-interface trend. It is an architectural shift.

A dashboard can tolerate a surprising amount of ambiguity beneath the surface. An agent cannot. A dashboard can expose metrics and leave interpretation to a manager. A copilot can summarize those metrics and propose next steps, but it still operates mainly through suggestion. An agent crosses a more serious threshold. Once a system can trigger a workflow, create a case, escalate an incident, apply a hold, send a communication, or change a parameter, the required standards for trust, lineage, semantic precision, policy enforcement, and control increase materially.

Dashboards remain useful. In many enterprises, they will remain indispensable for years. But dashboards no longer define the future state alone. Organizations now have to architect for multiple consumption modes at once: reports for formal review, dashboards for exploration, copilots for interpretation, and bounded agents for governed action. The move from passive insight to active intervention raises the bar for AI-readiness because the architecture beneath the interface must now support not only visibility, but explanation, recommendation, and controlled execution.

The transition from dashboards to agents is, therefore, not a story about replacing business intelligence with generative AI. It is a story about redesigning the enterprise data estate so that AI-mediated systems can consume data and content with sufficient context, governance, evidence, and control to be trusted in real operations.

WHY THIS MATTERS

Dashboards Solved One Class of Problem

Dashboards emerged because organizations needed shared visibility. Executives needed KPI packs. Managers needed trend lines. Operations teams needed drill-down views into backlog, throughput, defects, or service levels. Dashboards gave the enterprise a common lens on performance.

That model still matters. A board pack still requires stable numbers. A finance review still requires reconciled metrics. An operations director still needs a trusted view of service levels and exceptions. Nothing about AI changes the need for visible, defensible, shared metrics.

But dashboards solve a narrower problem than many organizations now face. They answer, “What is happening?” They sometimes help with, “Where should I look next?” They are far less effective at answering, in real time, “What does this mean in this context, for this user, right now, and what should happen next?”

AI-Mediated Intelligence Changes Speed, Format, and Expectation

The moment AI becomes part of the delivery model, three things change.

First, speed changes. A weekly KPI pack becomes a daily exception narrative. A monthly service review becomes near-real-time issue detection. A human no longer has to go find the information before beginning interpretation.

Second, format changes. Instead of a static view, the user receives contextual explanation, prioritized anomalies, recommended next steps, and links to supporting evidence. The output becomes conversational, narrative, and task-oriented rather than purely visual.

Third, expectation changes. Once a system can summarize conditions and recommend action, business users quickly expect it to notice more, personalize more, and respond more proactively. The enterprise moves from descriptive analytics toward guided intervention.

That expectation shift is precisely why architecture matters. It is one thing to misread a chart. It is another for a system to confidently recommend the wrong remediation or trigger the wrong action because it retrieved stale policy, misidentified the customer, ignored access restrictions, or lacked event-level context.

The Transition Period Is Unavoidable

Very few enterprises will move directly from dashboards to fully autonomous agents. The realistic pattern is coexistence. Some domains will remain report-centric because of regulation, auditability, or business conservatism. Others will adopt copilots first, especially where interpretation bottlenecks are more painful than execution bottlenecks. A smaller number will progress to bounded agents in operational contexts where the action space is narrow, the control framework is strong, and the cost of delay is material. During this period, enterprises must support both legacy and emergent consumption modes. The same underlying data estate may need to power an executive dashboard, an analyst copilot, a service operations assistant, and a bounded remediation agent. That is why the architecture cannot be optimized for one interface alone.

Core Concepts

Reports, Dashboards, Copilots, and Agents Are Not Interchangeable

The mistake many organizations make is treating these as points on a simple maturity ladder. They are better understood as distinct interaction models with different trust contracts.

- A report is scheduled, static, and formal. Its value is consistency.
- A dashboard is interactive, visual, and exploratory. Its value is self-service visibility.
- A copilot is contextual, conversational, and assistive. Its value is interpretation, explanation, and recommendation in the flow of work.
- An agent is goal-directed and action-capable within bounded permissions. Its value is not just insight, but intervention.

The data demands increase at each stage, but the control demands increase even faster.

Key Insight

Dashboard, Copilot, or Agent?

A dashboard shows state.

A copilot interprets state.

An agent responds to state.

The architectural distinction is decisive. If the system only visualizes metrics, the enterprise needs trustworthy data products and shared metric definitions. If the system explains, recommends, or acts, it also needs richer metadata, stronger semantic controls, evidence-aware retrieval, policy enforcement, and explicit operating boundaries.

The architectural distinction is decisive. If the system only visualizes metrics, the enterprise needs trustworthy data products and shared metric definitions. If the system explains, recommends, or acts, it also needs richer metadata, stronger semantic controls, evidence-aware retrieval, policy enforcement, and explicit operating boundaries.

Agents Need Stronger Controls Than Assistants

An assistant can be wrong and still be recoverable if the user can inspect evidence, question the conclusion, and decide not to proceed. An agent changes the risk model because the output may become an input to operational execution.

That does not mean every agent is dangerous. It means every agent must be bounded.

A bounded agent has a defined scope, a limited action set, clear approval gates, auditable evidence, permission-aware retrieval, and reversible or compensating actions where appropriate. It is not simply a more capable chatbot. It is a controlled operational component.

The enterprise must, therefore, distinguish between:

- Systems that provide answers.
- Systems that provide recommendations.
- Systems that prepare actions for approval.
- Systems that execute predefined actions under policy.

These are materially different architectural categories.

Passive Insight and Active Intervention Require Different Readiness

Traditional BI readiness emphasizes data quality, consistency, dimensional modeling, and performance for query workloads. Those remain necessary. They are not sufficient.

An AI system that recommends or acts must also understand business meaning, source authority, temporal correctness, permission fidelity, and intended use. It must know whether a policy is current, whether a document is superseded, whether a customer identifier maps to the same entity across systems, whether a recommended action is allowed in this region, and whether a user is entitled to see or execute that action.

In other words, the path from dashboard to agent is not simply a change in presentation. It is a change in the burden of proof.

❖ FIGURE 68 – CONSUMPTION EVOLUTION

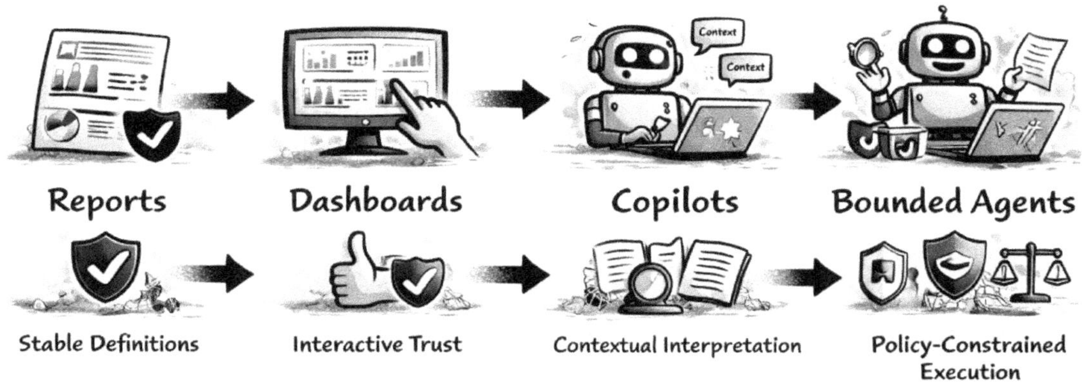

ARCHITECTURAL IMPLICATIONS

The Serving Layer Must Become Consumer-Specific

One of the central ideas in AI-ready architecture is that different AI consumers require different data-serving contracts. This chapter makes that principle concrete.

A dashboard can consume curated metrics and drill paths. A copilot often needs those same metrics plus business definitions, source notes, recent events, policy context, and narrative-ready metadata. An agent may need all of that plus machine-readable rules, action constraints, approval states, execution interfaces, and full audit capture.

This means the enterprise cannot treat "the data layer" as a single undifferentiated asset. It needs serving patterns aligned to consumption mode.

For example:

- A dashboard-serving contract may prioritize metric consistency and refresh cadence.
- A copilot-serving contract may prioritize explanation, citation, and role-aware personalization.
- An agent-serving contract may prioritize action eligibility, permission fidelity, execution safety, and traceability.

The same domain may expose multiple contracts from the same underlying sources.

Metadata Becomes Even More Important as Systems Become More Active

When human users inspect charts, they often supply missing context from experience. When AI systems interpret and act, that missing context has to be made explicit.

Metadata is what allows the system to rank trusted sources, filter by recency, interpret business terms, preserve lineage, enforce policy, and explain why a recommendation was made. Without strong metadata, copilots become shallow summarizers and agents become unsafe automations.

In dashboard-centric architecture, metadata often remains underdeveloped because the semantic load is carried by report designers and experienced users. In agent-oriented architecture, that approach breaks down. The system itself must have enough context to operate correctly without relying on tacit institutional knowledge.

Unstructured and Semi-Structured Sources Become Operational Inputs

A dashboard can often function on structured warehouse data alone. A copilot or agent usually cannot.

Why is inventory delayed? The answer may involve structured shipment data, semi-structured events from logistics APIs, email correspondence from a supplier, a revised operating procedure, and a service ticket note documenting a temporary workaround. The meaning required for action is spread across data types.

That is why AI-ready architecture must treat unstructured content and semi-structured events as first-class enterprise assets. The system needs governed access to policy documents, procedures, knowledge articles, contracts, transcripts, messages, and event streams, not merely because they are useful for summarization, but because they often contain the constraints under which action is allowed.

Control Boundaries Must Be Explicit

An agent should never "figure out" its own operating perimeter from vague text alone. The enterprise must define:

- What the agent is allowed to do.
- Under what conditions.
- Against which systems.
- With what approval steps.
- Under which role entitlements.
- With what logging and exception handling.

This requires a formal control boundary between recommendation and execution.

❖ FIGURE 69 – HUMAN-IN-LOOP VS AGENT-IN-LOOP

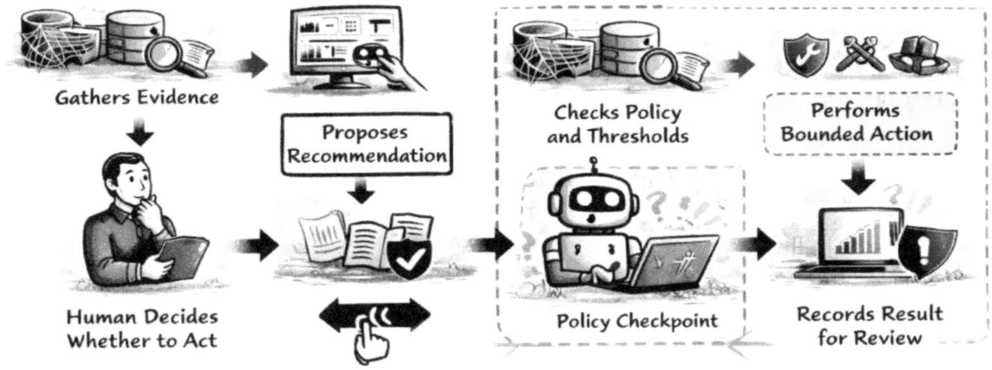

Governance Must Move Closer to Runtime

In a dashboard world, governance is often experienced as design-time control: definitions, certified metrics, approved reports, and access rules. In an agent world, governance also becomes runtime control.

The system must determine whether the retrieved source is authoritative, whether the requested action is allowed, whether the context is complete enough to proceed, and whether human approval is mandatory. Governance cannot remain a static oversight function. It has to be embedded in retrieval, decision support, and action orchestration.

KEY INSIGHT

What changes when AI can act

When AI can act, the architecture must answer five questions before execution:

- Is the information current enough?
- Is the source authoritative enough?
- Is the context complete enough?
- Is the user or agent permitted enough?
- Is the action bounded enough?

If any of these answers is unclear, the system should stop at recommendation, not proceed to execution.

FAILURE MODES AND ANTI-PATTERNS

Treating an Agent as a More Powerful Dashboard

This is one of the most common and most dangerous mistakes. The organization assumes that because it has decent dashboards, it is close to agentic capability. It is not.

A dashboard can survive with inconsistent definitions so long as expert users know how to interpret them. An agent cannot. A dashboard can link to a policy manual. An agent must know which policy version applies. A dashboard can expose a customer count with minor lag. An agent deciding whether to trigger outreach or escalate a service issue must know whether the customer record is current, matched correctly, and legally usable for that purpose.

The anti-pattern is not ambition. It is category confusion.

⚠ WARNING SIGN

Treating an agent as a more powerful dashboard

A warning sign appears when the organization says:

"We already have the data in dashboards, so the agent should be easy."

What usually follows is brittle retrieval, vague permissions, weak lineage, missing exception handling, and false confidence in action recommendations. Dashboard visibility is not evidence of agent readiness.

Over-Rotating to Interface Innovation While Neglecting Serving Architecture

Some enterprises invest heavily in conversational interfaces, orchestration tools, or workflow wrappers without upgrading the underlying data estate. The result is a polished front end connected to semantically weak, poorly governed, poorly contextualized data.

This produces systems that sound capable but cannot reliably justify their output.

Failing to Distinguish Wrong Answer Risk from Wrong Action Risk

A misleading narrative summary may waste time. A wrong action may trigger customer harm, compliance exposure, financial loss, or operational disruption. These are not the same risk class.

A mature architecture distinguishes them explicitly. It does not collapse them into a generic "AI risk" category.

Ignoring Coexistence During Transition

Another failure mode is trying to force every user into the newest interface. Enterprises still need dashboards, periodic reports, and formal review packs. In many cases, these remain the primary system of record for governance and oversight, even while copilots or agents emerge around them.

The right design principle is coexistence with progressive elevation, not abrupt replacement.

PRACTICAL APPLICATION

Choosing the Right Interaction Model

The practical question is not, "How do we deploy agents?" It is, "Which interaction model best fits this use case given its decision pattern, risk profile, and control needs?"

That decision should be made explicitly, not through hype or vendor defaults.

A useful starting framework is:

- Choose a dashboard when the user needs stable visibility and self-directed exploration.
- Choose a copilot when the user needs explanation, summarization, prioritization, or contextual recommendation.
- Choose a bounded agent when the action space is narrow, policy can be encoded, evidence can be captured, approvals are clear, and the cost of delay justifies controlled automation.

Designing for Escalation, Not Only Automation

A sound enterprise pattern is staged authority.

At stage one, the system summarizes and cites.

At stage two, it recommends and prioritizes.

At stage three, it prepares actions for approval.

At stage four, it executes only the small subset of actions that are low-risk, well-bounded, reversible, and fully policy-constrained.

This progression is important because it allows the organization to improve data quality, semantics, permissions, and governance in parallel with increasing operational ambition.

Example Design Questions Architects Should Ask

When evaluating whether a use case should move beyond dashboards, ask:

- Is the core need visibility, interpretation, or action?
- What evidence must accompany any recommendation?
- Which content sources define policy or operating constraints?
- What freshness threshold makes the recommendation trustworthy?
- Which actions require approval, and which can be safely automated?
- How will the system explain what it did and why?
- How will a user challenge, override, or reverse the outcome?

These are architecture questions, not merely product questions.

TEMPLATES

Decision Framework — Dashboard, Copilot, or Agent

Use case	<name of the operational, analytical, or AI-supported workflow being assessed>
Primary user	<main user role, team, or leadership group expected to rely on the use case>
Frequency	<how often the use case is expected to run or be used, such as daily, intraday, weekly, or event-driven>
Need for explanation	<degree to which the use case requires transparent explanation of outcomes, drivers, and supporting evidence>
Need for personalization	<degree to which outputs should be tailored by role, region, product line, business unit, or other user context>
Need for proactive alerting	<degree to which the system must initiate alerts or surface issues without waiting for users to inspect a dashboard or report>
Need for recommendation	<degree to which the system should propose likely actions, next-best steps, or remediation options based on evidence and constraints>
Need for action execution	<degree to which the system should prepare, initiate, or execute actions, and whether those actions require human approval>
Risk of wrong answer	<level of business, operational, financial, or trust risk created by incorrect explanations, diagnoses, or narratives>
Risk of wrong action	<level of business, operational, financial, compliance, or customer risk created by incorrect or premature actions>

Best-fit interaction model	<recommended interaction pattern, such as assistant, copilot, bounded agent, or another controlled model, including where human approval is required>
Controls required	<governance, data, retrieval, security, approval, audit, rollback, and policy controls required for safe operation of the use case>
Notes	<additional implementation guidance, scope constraints, or target-state clarification, especially where phased rollout or limited autonomy is recommended>

CASE EXAMPLE

From Dashboards to Copilots to Bounded Agents

An operations leadership team at a national distributor has historically relied on weekly KPI packs. Every Monday, leaders review fulfillment rates, backorders, on-time shipment percentages, warehouse exceptions, and customer service escalations. The process is disciplined, but slow. By the time a trend becomes visible in the pack, the operational damage has often already spread across regions.

The first attempt to modernize focused on a richer dashboard. The new dashboard was more interactive and refreshed daily. It improved visibility, but managers still had to inspect the data, identify anomalies, join information from several systems, and decide who needed to act. The bottleneck moved, but it did not disappear.

The next step was not a full agent. It was a daily exception copilot.

Each morning, the system assembled a narrative for operations leadership: where service-level thresholds were being missed, which facilities showed unusual backlog growth, which suppliers were involved, whether the issue was local or systemic, and which known operational constraints applied. Crucially, every narrative linked back to supporting evidence: shipment events, warehouse throughput metrics, supplier notices, current operating procedures, and recent incident notes.

This changed the operating cadence. Instead of spending the first part of the day finding the problem, leaders began with a synthesized explanation of the problem.

But the most valuable shift came when the architecture supported bounded action preparation. For repeatable scenarios, the system could prepare remediation steps: draft a regional escalation, create a logistics review case, assemble impacted order lists, and suggest customer outreach priority. It did not execute these actions automatically. A human operations lead still approved them.

That approval boundary mattered. The organization had enough trust in the data to support recommendations and workflow preparation, but not enough appetite to allow unreviewed remediation. This was the correct design choice.

The architecture supporting this transition looked very different from the architecture supporting the original KPI pack. It required:

- Unified entity mapping across orders, shipments, facilities, suppliers, and customers.
- Event ingestion from logistics systems for near-real-time state changes.
- Governed retrieval from operating procedures and supplier communications.
- Freshness metadata to prevent outdated policy use.
- Role-aware access controls so managers only saw authorized regional detail.
- Citation and lineage capture for every narrative claim.
- Workflow integration to prepare, but not execute, remediation actions.
- Full audit records of what the system recommended and what humans approved.

The result was not "AI replacing dashboards." The result was a layered operating model. The weekly KPI pack still existed for formal review. The dashboard still existed for exploration. The copilot handled daily interpretation. Bounded agent functions prepared operational responses within explicit control limits.

This is what enterprise transition usually looks like in practice: not replacement, but architectural expansion with progressively stronger trust and control.

Closing Synthesis

The move from dashboards to agents is not a cosmetic evolution in enterprise analytics. It is a change in what the enterprise expects its information systems to do. Dashboards help users inspect the business. Copilots help users interpret the business. Agents, if they are to be trusted, must help the business respond within clearly governed limits.

That progression raises the standard for readiness.

An enterprise can build successful dashboards on top of curated metrics and experienced human interpretation. It cannot safely build copilots and agents on that basis alone. Once systems begin to explain, recommend, and act, the data estate must provide far more than clean records and performant queries. It must provide business meaning, provenance, temporal correctness, permission fidelity, policy context, retrieval quality, and action boundaries.

This is why the architectural question matters more than the interface question. The real issue is not whether the front end looks like a dashboard, a chat panel, or a task agent. The real issue is whether the enterprise has designed its data, metadata, semantics, governance, and serving patterns to support the trust contract implied by that interface.

Dashboards remain useful. They remain necessary. But they are no longer the sole design center for enterprise information delivery. Organizations now need an architecture that can support passive insight and active intervention at the same time. They need to serve human readers, AI interpreters, and bounded operational agents from a data estate designed for explanation, control, and repeated trustworthy use.

That is the path forward: not abandoning dashboards, but architecting beyond them.

Key Takeaways

- Dashboards remain important, but they no longer define the enterprise future state by themselves.
- Copilots and agents impose higher requirements for semantics, metadata, lineage, governance, and runtime control.
- The move from insight to action changes the burden of proof from visibility to explainable, policy-bounded intervention.
- Agents are not more powerful dashboards; they are operational components that require explicit control boundaries.
- The right target architecture supports coexistence across reports, dashboards, copilots, and bounded agents during transition.

CHAPTER 35: THE AI-READY ENTERPRISE

The AI-ready enterprise is not the one with the most AI tools. It is the one whose data, content, metadata, semantics, governance, and operating model make trustworthy AI repeatable.

That distinction matters more than most organizations admit. Many enterprises now have pilots, copilots, model subscriptions, vector indexes, and a growing list of "AI use cases." Yet very few can answer the harder architectural questions. Which sources are authoritative for a given answer? Which records, documents, and events can an agent access under policy? What business meaning is attached to a field, phrase, clause, or identifier? How does the system know whether a source is current, superseded, restricted, or legally held? What evidence can be shown when an AI-generated recommendation affects a customer, employee, regulator, or financial decision?

An enterprise becomes AI-ready when those questions have reliable answers.

This is not a project milestone. It is not the successful deployment of a chatbot, the fine-tuning of a model, or the centralization of a few high-value datasets. It is an enterprise condition. It describes a state in which structured data, semi-structured signals, and unstructured content can be discovered, interpreted, governed, trusted, and served to different AI consumers with the right controls, context, and proof.

In that state, AI becomes repeatable because trust becomes repeatable. Retrieval is not improvised. Semantics are not inferred from raw column names. Governance is not a review gate at the end. Policy is not detached from delivery. Provenance is not optional. The enterprise has designed a durable substrate for intelligence.

That is the architect's task in the AI era.

KEY INSIGHT

What the Destination Looks Like

An AI-ready enterprise has the following traits:

- Authoritative sources are known and ranked.
- Metadata drives discovery, access, freshness, lineage, and trust.
- Business meaning is explicit, not buried in tribal knowledge.
- Structured and unstructured data are governed together.
- AI consumers receive data through defined serving contracts.
- Outputs are explainable, source-aware, and policy-conformant.
- Ownership and stewardship are operational, not symbolic.
- New AI use cases can be added without rebuilding the estate each time.

The destination is not more tools. The destination is coherence.

WHY THIS MATTERS

AI Failure Is Usually a Data-Estate Failure

Enterprises often misdiagnose AI failure as a model problem. In practice, many failures begin much earlier. The model may be capable, but the surrounding estate is not prepared to support secure discovery, semantic interpretation, permission-aware retrieval, provenance, freshness control, and operational accountability.

A reporting environment can answer known questions from curated facts. An AI system often has to navigate ambiguity, combine evidence across sources, and explain why it chose one answer over another. That demands more than quality scores on tables. It demands architectural readiness.

Consider three common examples.

A policy assistant retrieves an obsolete benefits document because no freshness and supersession metadata were attached to the content.

A sales copilot summarizes a customer incorrectly because "customer," "account holder," and "subscriber" are treated as interchangeable across systems.

An operations agent takes action on a service case using data it can technically reach but is not permitted to use in that context because access policy was enforced at the application layer, not the data-serving layer.

None of these are primarily model failures. They are failures of metadata, semantics, policy design, and delivery architecture.

AI-Readiness Is Now a Competitive Operating Condition

As AI moves from experimentation into operational use, the enterprise data estate becomes a strategic limiter. Organizations with coherent metadata, governed content, and clear ownership can add new assistants, copilots, and agents faster because the substrate already exists. Organizations without that substrate pay the same penalty on every initiative: rediscovery, reclassification, recontextualization, repipeline, and reapproval.

The cost is not only speed. It is also risk. Enterprises that cannot demonstrate provenance, explainability, and policy fidelity will be forced to keep AI shallow. They may permit drafting but not recommendation. Summarization but not action. Search but not decision support. That may be prudent in the short term, but it is not a scalable end-state.

The Real Target Is Governed Reuse

The end goal is not one successful AI deployment. The end goal is a governed, contextualized, explainable, secure, and reusable enterprise data estate that can support trustworthy AI repeatedly and at scale.

That is why AI-readiness must be understood as an enterprise condition rather than a sequence of disconnected solutions.

CORE CONCEPTS

AI-Readiness Is an Architectural State

AI-Ready Data is not simply clean data. Data can be complete, reconciled, and fit for reporting while still being unusable for AI. If it lacks business meaning, provenance, intended-use constraints, permission fidelity, and freshness controls, it is not ready for trustworthy interpretation or action.

Architecturally, AI-readiness means the estate can do five things consistently:

- Discover relevant data and content.
- Interpret them with shared semantic meaning.
- Govern them with embedded policy and lifecycle control.
- Serve them appropriately to different AI consumers.
- Explain outputs with defensible evidence and traceability.

If any one of those capabilities is missing, the enterprise may still deploy AI, but it will not deploy trustworthy AI at scale.

The Enterprise Trust Model Must Span All Data Shapes

Traditional enterprise architecture often separates structured data from documents, messages, transcripts, and collaboration content. AI collapses that distinction. A customer dispute may depend on transaction records, CRM notes, contract language, service transcripts, and email approvals. An executive briefing may combine financial tables, operating metrics, market commentary, and internal board materials. An agent may need master data, event streams, policy documents, and workflow history within the same reasoning cycle.

That means structured, semi-structured, and unstructured assets must converge under a unified trust model.

The model should answer the same questions regardless of format:

- What is this asset?
- What does it mean?
- Where did it come from?
- Who owns it?
- Who may use it, and for what purpose?
- How current is it?
- What other assets does it relate to?
- Can it be cited or relied upon?
- What obligations apply to retention, privacy, legal hold, or records management?

If the enterprise can answer those questions only for tables, it is not AI-ready.

Metadata Is the Control Plane

Metadata is not documentation attached to the side of the platform. It is the control plane for AI.

It determines whether assets are discoverable, understandable, governable, rankable, and explainable. It carries lineage, classification, freshness, ownership, source authority, business definitions, policy tags, retention state, and usage constraints. It also enables the evidence layer that distinguishes defensible output from plausible output.

Without robust metadata, retrieval quality degrades. Policy enforcement becomes brittle. Citations become decorative rather than meaningful. Agents become unsafe because they cannot distinguish between authoritative and merely accessible sources.

Semantics Reduce Ambiguity Before the Model Sees the Data

Many AI failures are rooted in unresolved business ambiguity. Enterprises often assume the model will "figure out" whether member means customer, subscriber, covered person, or policyholder. That is a poor architectural bet.

Glossaries, taxonomies, ontologies, entity resolution, and relationship models are not academic overhead. They reduce ambiguity before retrieval and reasoning occur. They allow the system to understand that a contract amendment supersedes a prior clause, that a household may contain multiple customers, or that a service entitlement depends on both product and region.

The more regulated, distributed, and terminology-heavy the enterprise, the more essential semantic architecture becomes.

Different AI Consumers Need Different Serving Contracts

A knowledge assistant, an analyst copilot, an executive briefing tool, and an action-taking agent do not need the same thing. A knowledge assistant may tolerate some ambiguity if it cites its sources and stays within low-risk informational use. An analyst copilot needs consistent definitions, controlled joins, temporal correctness, and governed access to analytical context. An executive briefing tool needs source ranking, narrative compression, conflict handling, and clear confidence signals. An agent that takes action needs stronger guarantees: policy-aware access, workflow boundaries, approved source sets, action eligibility rules, and audit-grade traceability.

AI-ready enterprises do not expose one undifferentiated data layer to all of them. They design serving contracts.

Architectural Implications

The Target State Is Layered but Coherent

The architecture of an AI-ready enterprise should not become a patchwork of disconnected retrieval components, ad hoc content pipelines, and isolated semantic projects. It should converge into a coherent set of layers.

❖ FIGURE 70 – AI-READY ENTERPRISE END-STATE

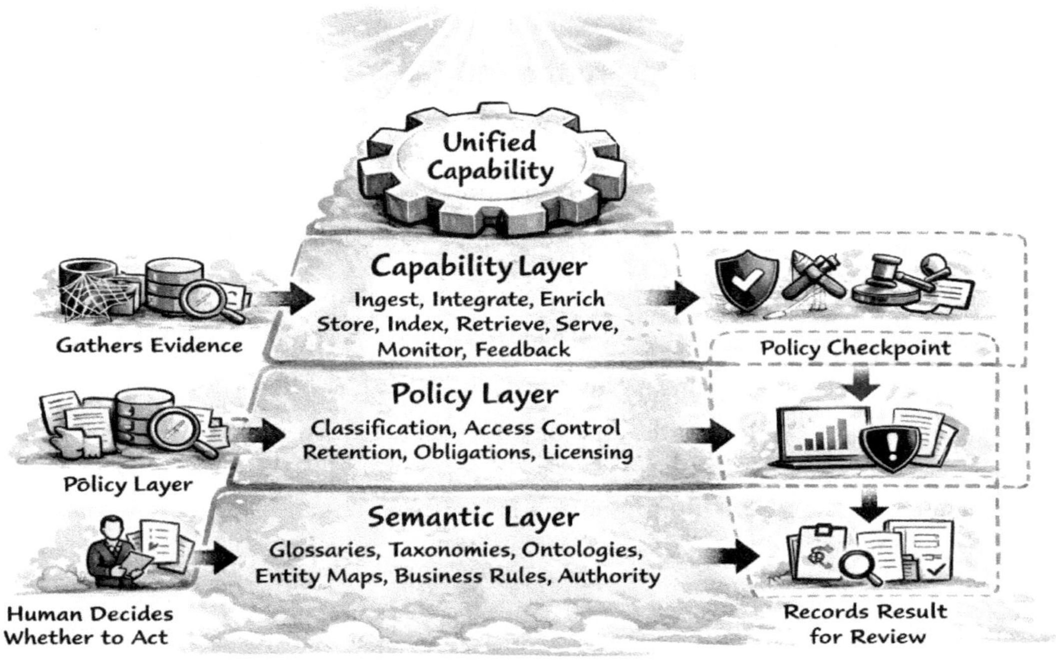

A useful way to think about that end-state is through four integrated layers:

Capability layer. Data and content ingestion, integration, enrichment, storage, indexing, retrieval, serving, monitoring, and feedback.

Policy layer. Classification, access control, privacy rules, retention, legal hold, records obligations, licensing restrictions, and intended-use constraints.

Semantic layer. Glossaries, taxonomies, ontologies, entity resolution, relationship maps, business rules, and source authority models.

Operating layer. Ownership, stewardship, decision rights, service management, quality management, review forums, and lifecycle governance.

These are not separate programs. They are coordinated aspects of one architecture.

Unstructured Content Must Be Engineered, Not Merely Stored

Many enterprises still treat unstructured content as a repository problem. If policies are in SharePoint, contracts in a content system, tickets in a service platform, and emails in mailboxes, leadership assumes the organization "has the knowledge." It does not. It has files.

AI-ready enterprises engineer content for use. They classify it, extract structure from it, preserve authorship and effective dates, detect supersession, attach source authority, enforce permissions, manage retention state, and prepare it for high-quality retrieval and citation. They also distinguish between content that may support explanation, content that may support summarization only, and content that must never be used for AI grounding at all.

Retrieval Quality Belongs in Architecture

Retrieval quality is often treated as a tuning exercise. It is more fundamental than that.

Architectural responsibility includes:

- Defining authoritative source hierarchies.
- Segmenting content by use eligibility.
- Choosing chunking and enrichment patterns that preserve meaning.
- Carrying security context through indexing and retrieval.
- Designing freshness and supersession logic.
- Exposing provenance and citation-ready source references.
- Monitoring retrieval outcomes and failure patterns.

If retrieval is inaccurate, stale, over-permissive, or semantically shallow, the model will amplify those weaknesses.

Governance Must Move Upstream

Governance for AI cannot be a downstream review function. It has to shape how assets are modeled, tagged, stored, indexed, served, and monitored.

That means governance is embedded in architecture and operations:

- Policy metadata is attached close to the source.
- Retention and legal obligations travel with content.
- Privacy classification informs retrieval eligibility.
- Stewardship workflows include unstructured assets.
- Exceptions are visible and time-bound.
- New AI use cases must declare purpose, source set, trust threshold, and action boundary.

This is what it means to treat governance as a design layer rather than a compliance checkpoint.

KEY INSIGHT

The Architect's Mandate in the AI Era

The architect's job is no longer just to move and model data. It is to design a durable substrate for trustworthy intelligence.

That mandate includes:

- making business meaning explicit
- unifying trust across data shapes
- ensuring access-aware delivery
- designing for provenance and explainability
- defining serving contracts by AI consumer type
- embedding policy and governance into flow, storage, retrieval, and use
- building an operating model that survives beyond the pilot

FAILURE MODES AND ANTI-PATTERNS

Mistaking Repository Presence for Readiness

The most common anti-pattern is assuming that because content exists, it is ready. Repositories do not provide semantic clarity, permission fidelity, freshness, or source authority on their own. A document library full of duplicates, drafts, and obsolete versions is not a knowledge base.

Treating Metadata as Optional Decoration

Enterprises often invest heavily in models and interfaces while neglecting ownership metadata, business definitions, lineage, retention status, and source authority. The result is AI that sounds fluent but cannot defend itself.

Building Isolated AI Pipelines by Use Case

Another common failure is constructing separate ingestion, indexing, and policy logic for each use case. This creates short-term wins and long-term disorder. Every new assistant re-solves the same architectural problems. Over time, policy drifts, quality measures diverge, and trust collapses under inconsistency.

Leaving Semantics Unresolved

When key terms vary across business units, products, and regulations, failure to reconcile them becomes a direct AI risk. The model may bridge ambiguity with probability. The enterprise must bridge it with architecture.

Overexposing Data to Agents

Organizations sometimes move too quickly from informational copilots to action-taking agents without strengthening serving contracts. An agent does not simply need access. It needs bounded authority, verified source sets, policy controls, temporal awareness, and auditability. Without those, speed becomes unmanaged risk.

Bolting Governance on After Deployment

When privacy, retention, records, and legal obligations are addressed only after pilots are live, enterprises face painful rework. Indexed content has to be reclassified. Sources have to be excluded retroactively. Audit trails are incomplete. Trust from risk and legal functions erodes quickly.

PRACTICAL APPLICATION

Start by Defining the Enterprise Condition You Are Trying to Reach

Do not begin with a tool selection exercise. Begin by describing the target condition.

What must be true for the enterprise to say it is AI-ready in a meaningful sense? Which sources must be governable? Which semantic ambiguities must be resolved? Which policies must be enforced in delivery? Which AI consumers matter first? Which domains are high-value and high-consequence?

Those answers become the basis for sequencing.

❖ FIGURE 71 – MATURITY END-STATE MAP

A practical maturity path often looks like this:

Fragmented. Data and content are siloed; ownership is unclear; AI pilots rely on narrow extracts.

Searchable. Basic discovery and indexing exist; metadata is partial; governance is uneven.

Contextualized. Semantic definitions, ownership, and source authority improve; retrieval becomes more reliable.

Governed. Policy, lifecycle, and access-aware delivery are embedded across structured and unstructured assets.

Reusable. Common serving patterns, metadata controls, and trust measures support multiple AI use cases.

Agent-ready. High-assurance serving contracts, action boundaries, provenance, and auditability enable controlled automation.

The progression is staged, but it must be intentional.

KEY INSIGHT

90-Day Starting Moves for the Reader

In the next 90 days:

- pick two domains, not ten
- identify authoritative sources and their owners
- define required metadata for AI use
- classify the highest-value content repositories
- resolve the most dangerous business term ambiguities
- establish one governance forum that includes architecture, risk, legal, and domain owners
- design one serving contract for a low-risk assistant and one for a higher-trust copilot
- measure retrieval quality before expanding scope

The objective is not to "launch AI." It is to make trustworthy AI reproducible.

TEMPLATES

90-Day AI-Ready Enterprise Action Agenda

Executive objective	<primary enterprise objective to be achieved, including the minimum viable architecture, governance controls, and ownership model required for trustworthy AI within the defined timeframe>
Priority domains	<business domains selected for initial focus, including knowledge, policy, compliance, or operational domains with measurable business impact>
Immediate assessment actions	<initial actions required to understand current state, including source inventory, AI use-case discovery, terminology conflict mapping, permission and retention review, and retrieval risk assessment>
Metadata actions	<actions required to assign ownership, define mandatory metadata, establish source-ranking logic, identify glossary and relationship gaps, and create a metadata improvement backlog>
Governance actions	<actions required to define source eligibility, embed privacy and records controls, document approval paths, and establish exception handling with appropriate review cadence>
Content actions	<actions required to classify repositories, identify obsolete or duplicate content, enrich high-value documents, and prepare citation-ready trusted source sets>
Ownership actions	<actions required to assign executive sponsorship, domain ownership, data ownership, stewardship, decision rights, and cross-functional working governance>
First use cases	<initial AI assistants, copilots, or workflows selected for early delivery, including any source authority, citation, grounding, or freshness constraints>
Risks to contain	<key risks that must be actively controlled during the initial phase, such as restricted-content exposure, stale retrieval, semantic conflict, weak auditability, or ungoverned index proliferation>
Metrics to establish	<measures that must be defined early to track ownership coverage, metadata coverage, retrieval quality, stale-content risk, glossary conflict resolution, and citation or lineage quality>
Sponsors	<senior executives and business leaders who provide sponsorship, oversight, and decision support for the initiative and its priority domains>
Review date	<date or checkpoint at which progress is formally reviewed and scaling decisions are made based on control maturity, retrieval quality, and reuse readiness>

Case Example

Global Enterprise in Its Third Year of AI Modernization

A global enterprise in its third year of AI modernization provides a useful composite example.

Three years earlier, it looked familiar: customer data spread across CRM, billing, service, and regional systems; policy and product knowledge scattered across document libraries; service transcripts stored but rarely reused; legal and compliance content isolated from operational delivery; and a growing set of AI pilots built on local extracts and ungoverned indexes.

The first generation of pilots produced mixed results. A policy assistant cited outdated documents. A service copilot gave inconsistent answers because product terminology differed by region. An executive summary tool blended draft materials with final performance reports because source authority was never modeled.

The turnaround did not begin with a new model. It began with an architectural reset.

The enterprise selected three priority domains: customer service, product and policy knowledge, and compliance guidance. It established domain owners, named stewards, and created a common metadata standard for AI grounding. That standard required authority level, effective date, supersession status, classification, access policy, owner, steward, lineage reference, and intended-use tags.

It then addressed semantics. The company had historically used customer, member, subscriber, and account holder in ways that overlapped but were not equivalent. A semantic working group aligned glossary entries, relationship rules, and entity mappings across the first three domains. That work reduced a major source of ambiguity in both retrieval and downstream recommendations.

At the same time, the enterprise re-engineered its treatment of unstructured content. Instead of indexing entire repositories wholesale, it curated approved source classes. Final policy documents, approved knowledge articles, and governed transcript summaries were admitted to AI grounding. Draft content, personal mailboxes, redundant local files, and unresolved records under hold were excluded or quarantined. Supersession logic prevented outdated documents from outranking current policy.

Serving contracts were then differentiated. The employee knowledge assistant was allowed a broad search across approved informational content, but it had to provide citations and freshness indicators. The service copilot received a narrower contract with stronger product, entitlement, and case-context controls. A limited agent for service follow-up was allowed to draft actions but not execute them unless confidence, policy, and approval conditions were satisfied.

By year three, the enterprise had not achieved perfection, but it had reached a meaningful end-state. New AI use cases no longer started from zero. Priority domains had known authoritative sources. Metadata coverage was visible and managed. Unstructured content was governed as an enterprise asset. Semantic ambiguity was reduced in the most consequential terms. Retrieval quality was measured as an architectural KPI. Risk, legal, and compliance functions participated upstream rather than reacting downstream.

Most importantly, trust became portable. The organization could now extend AI into new workflows without rebuilding the estate each time.

That is what an AI-ready enterprise looks like in practice. Not frictionless. Not tool-centric. Architecturally coherent.

Closing Synthesis

The AI-ready enterprise is not defined by enthusiasm, investment level, or the number of AI experiences it can demonstrate. It is defined by whether trustworthy AI can be repeated across domains without improvising the foundations each time.

That requires a change in architectural ambition. The task is no longer to prepare data only for reporting, dashboards, or isolated machine learning pipelines. The task is to create a governed, contextualized, explainable, secure, and reusable enterprise data estate that can support assistants, copilots, and agents with appropriate trust controls.

In that estate, structured, semi-structured, and unstructured assets are treated as parts of one governed knowledge substrate. Metadata acts as the control plane. Semantic context reduces ambiguity before the model reaches the data. Governance is embedded in architecture and operations. Retrieval quality is designed, not hoped for. Different AI consumers receive different serving contracts. Ownership and stewardship are visible and enforceable.

This is why AI-readiness is an enterprise condition, not a project outcome.

For the architect, the message is clear. The mandate in the AI era is not to add intelligence to a weak substrate. It is to design the substrate so intelligence can be trusted.

Key Takeaways

- The AI-ready enterprise is defined by repeatable trust, not by the number of AI tools it has deployed.
- AI-readiness is an enterprise condition that depends on metadata, semantics, governance, and operating model discipline.
- Structured, semi-structured, and unstructured data must converge under one trust model for AI to scale safely.
- Retrieval quality, provenance, and access-aware delivery are architectural responsibilities, not model-side afterthoughts.
- The architect's role is to build a durable, governed substrate for trustworthy intelligence across many use cases.

INDEX

Access-aware delivery, 23, 242, 262
  auditability, 244
  classification and sensitivity, 239
  delivery, 244, 263
  discovery Becomes Easier Than Navigation, 237
  end-to-end Enforcement Is Required, 241
  identity propagation, 239
  inference Creates Exposure Even Without Direct Document Access, 237, 238
  permission drift, 239
  permission fidelity, 252
  revocation latency, 242
  security Errors Become Scalable and Repeatable, 238
  the AI-serving Layer Is Part of the Security Architecture, 240
Access-aware retrieval. See Access-aware delivery:retrieval
Adoption
  adoption, 331, 341, 344, 345, 347, 348, 350, 351, 391, 397, 413, 426
  literacy, 342, 343, 346
  organizational change, 344
  trust adoption, 342
  workflow Fit Matters as Much as Model Quality, 345
Agent-ready data. See AI readiness:agent-ready
Agents
  aI-mediated Intelligence Changes Speed, Format, and Expectation, 446
  choosing the Right Interaction Model, 453
  control Boundaries Must Be Explicit, 450
  dashboards Solved One Class of Problem, 446
  designing for Escalation, Not Only Automation, 453
  example Design Questions Architects Should Ask, 454
  passive Insight and Active Intervention Require Different Readiness, 448
  the Serving Layer Must Become Consumer-Specific, 449
  the Transition Period Is Unavoidable, 447
AI failure modes
  aI Failure Is Rarely Isolated, 419
  bad Data for AI Is Not the Same as Bad Data for Reporting, 421
  establish a Source Hierarchy, 427
  introduce a Reusable Diagnostic Template, 428
  prevention Is Cheaper Than Credibility Repair, 420
  repositories Are Not Readiness, 422
  start with Failure-Oriented Architecture Reviews, 427
  the Cost Is Larger Than Answer Quality, 420
  use the Template to Find Recurring Causes, 428
AI readiness
  agent-ready, 17, 18
  AI-ready data, 21, 28, 36, 37, 47, 59, 61, 68, 196, 293, 307, 313, 320, 322, 325, 378
  analytics-ready, 16
  as architectural condition, 31
  assess Current Assets Against Dimensions, 35
  assess Domains Against the Right Readiness Target, 22
  build the Minimum Evidence Standard, 35
  by data class, 30
  define Readiness by Consumer and Data Class, 35
  from Twelve Dashboards to One Daily Briefing, 23
  GenAI-ready, 16
  introduce a Readiness Maturity Model, 35
  maturity Models Matter Because Transformation Must Be Sequenced, 31
  ML-ready, 16
  quality Is Necessary, but Not Sufficient, 30
  readiness ladder, 17
  report-ready, 4, 15
  score What Traditional Assessments Missed, 22
  start with an Enterprise Definition, 35
  the Architecture Must Serve Machine Interpretation, Not Just Human Access, 18
  the Consumer Has Changed, 14
  the Interaction Model Has Changed, 14
  the Meaning of, 15
  the Risk Surface Has Changed, 15
AI-ready data. See AI readiness
AI-ready data products, 321, 330
  from Dataset to Product, 313
  intended Use and Restricted Use Belong in the Definition, 314
  not Every Dataset Should Become a Product, 315
  product Design Questions Architects Should Force Early, 320
  product Thinking Reduces Bespoke AI Plumbing, 312
  productization Shifts Work from Model Teams to the Data Estate, 315
  the Enterprise AI Bottleneck Is Usually Upstream, 311, 312
  the Product Must Support Multiple AI Serving Patterns, 315
  where to Start, 319
AI-ready enterprise, 469
  aI Failure Is Usually a Data-Estate Failure, 460
  aI-readiness Is an Architectural State, 461

aI-readiness Is Now a Competitive Operating Condition, 461
global Enterprise in Its Third Year of AI Modernization, 470
semantics Reduce Ambiguity Before the Model Sees the Data, 463
start by Defining the Enterprise Condition You Are Trying to Reach, 467
the Real Target Is Governed Reuse, 461
Analytics-ready data. See AI readiness:analytics-ready
Anti-patterns, 421, 429, 434
aI Architecture Review Questions, 441
allowing Plausible Language to Substitute for Evidence, 254
answer-layer Filtering Only, 243
assessing Without Use-Case Pressure, 358
assuming Documents in Repositories Are Ready for AI, 371
assuming Retained Means Useful, 290
assuming SMEs Can Compensate for Architectural Weakness, 426
assuming Users Understand Grounded Answers, 348
broad Indexing Under a Service Account, 242
building Isolated AI Pipelines by Use Case, 466
building One Readiness Standard for Every AI Use Case, 22
building Vague, Low-Semantic Relationship Models, 149
calling Anything Reusable a Product, 318
canonical Model Absolutism, 203
chatbot-first facade, 435, 438
choosing the Most Visible Use Case Instead of the Most Viable One, 370
coarse Labels Replacing Real Permissions, 243
conflating User Permission with Consumer Permission, 232
confusing Data Quality with AI Usability, 8
confusing Naming Conventions with Meaning, 134
confusing Resistance with Irrationality, 348
contradictory answers, 424
demos Can Hide Structural Weakness, 433
designing Taxonomies No One Will Use, 134
designing the Universal Future State First, 383
domain Autonomy Without Shared Standards, 305
duplicate Drift, 89
enterprise-average Maturity, 357
equating Repositories with Readiness, 384
evaluate Only with Generic Benchmarks, 219
event Streams with No Semantic Contract, 203
every Domain Builds a Stack, 333
failing to Baseline Before Rollout, 412
failing to Distinguish Authoritative from Supporting Sources, 162
failing to Distinguish Wrong Answer Risk from Wrong Action Risk, 452
failing to Model Sensitive Population Impacts, 278
forcing Every Use Case into One Store, 189
governing Sources but Not Answers, 254
hiding Temporal Ambiguity, 162
hiding Uncertainty, 149
ignore Temporal Correctness, 219
ignoring Coexistence During Transition, 453
ignoring Conflicting Definitions, 134
ignoring Restricted Uses, 319
ignoring Reuse Potential, 371
ignoring Temporal Correctness, 34
ignoring Transformation Opacity, 162
incorrect Action Recommendations from Context-Poor Data, 425
leaving Content Ungoverned Because It Is Messy, 189
leaving Escalation to Prompt Wording, 278
leaving Semantics Unresolved, 466
letting Source Teams Invent Semantics Independently, 74
many Failures Are Predictable in Advance, 434
measuring Only Lagging Incidents, 412
mistaking Data Accumulation for Enterprise Understanding, 47
modern-looking Architecture Can Still Be Structurally Unsound, 434
no Auditable Evidence Path, 290
no Excluded-Use Discipline, 204
no-evidence response pattern, 439
obsolete Truth Presented as Current Guidance, 425
one-off Implementation Logic, 398
one-size-fits-all trust model, 439
optimizing for Answer Rate Instead of Safe Answer Rate, 278
optimizing for Speed at the Expense of Control, 371
optimizing Only for Query Performance, 61
orphaned Narrative Evidence, 265
over-focusing on Model Selection, 21
over-Indexing Low-Value Noise, 90
over-relying on Logs as Explanation, 75
over-rotating to Interface Innovation While Neglecting Serving Architecture, 452
pilot-first escape hatch, 435, 438
premature Roadmap Certainty, 358
preserving Hidden Logic and Tribal Knowledge, 47
productizing Low-Value Assets, 319
reporting Activity Instead of Readiness, 411
saaS Onboarding by Connector Convenience Alone, 204
scaling Usage Before the Estate Is Ready, 397
security Is Bolted on at the End, 334
stale but plausible content, 90
the Central Hero Team, 333

the Demo That Everyone Loved, 442
tool Sprawl Without Capability Design, 176
treating AI as Just Another BI Channel, 254
treating Content as an Afterthought, 358
treating Document Ingestion as Readiness, 426
treating Documentation as Optional, 318
treating Domain Demand as Proof of Domain Readiness, 370
treating Payload Capture as Readiness, 73
treating Policy as Post-Ingestion Cleanup, 289
treating Repositories as Knowledge Architecture, 21
treating Semantics as Optional Documentation, 133
treating Stale Content as a Minor Issue, 278
unowned Content, 89
use Architecture Review to Stop Predictable Failure, 441
using Enterprise Averages to Hide Domain Weakness, 412
using Prompt Logic to Compensate for Missing Data Design, 61
weak Audit Design, 233
Anti-patterns:, 105
Business meaning. See Semantic context:business meaning
Capability pillars
al Failures Are Usually Capability Failures Across the Architecture, 170
capability Pillars Assessment, 178
cross-cutting Controls Matter as Much as the Pillars Themselves, 172
centralize What Must Be Common, 173
how to Assess the Current Capability Pillars, 177
ingestion Must Preserve Meaning, Not Just Move Bytes, 174
mapping Two Use Cases onto One Architecture, 178
serving Patterns Must Reflect the Consumer, 176
sources Are Broader Than Databases, 174
the Model Is Organized into Capability Pillars, 171
traditional Readiness Models Do Not Go Far Enough, 170
Centre of excellence. See Federated delivery:center of excellence
Converged patterns, 191, 192
al Questions Are Structurally Different from Reporting Questions, 183
choose a Primary Pattern, Then Add Supporting Patterns Deliberately, 190
content, 185
design for Coordinated Serving, Not Isolated Storage, 186
different Structures Solve Different Enterprise Problems, 184
graph, 146, 148, 150, 189
orchestration, 184, 188
relational, 184, 186
start with Workload Decomposition, 190
vector, 434, 437
Copilots. See also Serving contracts:analyst copilots
Cross-asset governance. See Governance:cross-asset
Current-state assessment, 355, 362
assessment Is the Difference Between Ambition and Architecture, 353
assessment Must Be Domain-Based, 354
domain Architecture Becomes the Unit of Change, 357
how to Run the Assessment, 359
maturity Must Be Scored by Dimension, Not Assumed by Reputation, 356
most Organizations Misdiagnose the Real Problem, 354
the Roadmap Must Follow Evidence, Not Politics, 356
use-case Pressure Should Shape Depth, 354
what a Good Heatmap Reveals, 360
Dashboards. See also Agents
Data structures
al Changes the Consumption Contract, 41
al Workloads Expose Embedded Assumptions, 44
consumer-specific Data Contracts Become Essential, 46
design Intent Does Not Disappear, 42
every Structure Now Needs Compensating Controls, 45
excellent Reporting, Poor Policy Assistance, 50
file Repositories: Built for Storage and Collaboration, 44
lakes: Built for Accumulation and Flexibility, 43
legacy Success Can Hide AI Weakness, 42
start with a Structure-By-Structure Assessment, 48
the Architecture Must Separate Storage from Serving, 45
traditional Data Structure Suitability Assessment, 49
Document repositories
document Enrichment Checklist, 108
enrichment Must Make Enterprise Meaning Explicit, 104
inventory Must Precede Ingestion, 102
most Enterprise Meaning Lives Outside Rows and Columns, 98
permissions Must Remain Intact Across Transformation, 105
repositories Create a False Sense of Readiness, 98
storage Location Does Not Equal Semantic Readiness, 99
treat Curation as a Funnel, Not a One-Time Cleanup, 108
Evidence model. See Retrieval:evidence model

Explainability. See Provenance:explainability
Federated delivery
center of excellence, 334
centers of Excellence Enable, They Do Not Absorb Responsibility, 328
centralization Alone Becomes a Bottleneck, 326
define the Service Boundaries, 335
domain teams, 300
federated Accountability Should Be Explicit, 332, 333
federated delivery, 326, 338
federated Operating Model Worksheet, 337
full Decentralization Creates Drift and Risk, 326
meaning Must Remain Local, 327
platform teams, 299, 329
security Must Provide Reusable Control Services, 331
shared Services Should Be Centralized Where Consistency Matters, 327
standardize the Templates That Matter, 335
standards and Templates Increase Speed, 328
start with a Responsibility Inventory, 335
the Operating Model Becomes Part of the Architecture, 329
GenAI-ready data. See AI readiness:GenAI-ready
Glossaries. See Semantic context:glossary
Governance, 34, 75, 106, 147, 175, 177, 202, 251, 255, 256, 257, 260, 261, 291, 305, 331, 334, 346, 382, 384, 426, 451, 465, 467
aI Consumes Business Reality, Not Storage Categories, 259
behavior control, 250
content governance, 203, 255
cross-asset, 261, 267
define the Cross-Asset Operating Model, 266
design for Disagreement, 267
evidence Is Part of the Answer, 251
layer 4: Consumer-specific Policy, 255
legal hold, 285
lifecycle awareness, 88, 121, 279, 287, 290, 317
make Derived AI Assets Governable, 266
minimization, 286, 290
policy layer, 287
privacy, 286
records management, 286
retention, 285
runtime AI controls, 255
separate Knowledge Permission from Action Permission, 253
start with High-Risk Cross-Asset Use Cases, 266
the Architecture Must Model Truth Chains, Not Just Data Stores, 263
when Policy Documents Alone Could Not Define Compliance Truth, 268
Grounding. See Retrieval:grounding
Integration patterns, 204, 205
aI Operates Across Fragmented Enterprise Reality, 195
API access, 201
canonical layers, 199
integration Is a Meaning-Preserving Discipline, 197
pattern Choice Is Not Arbitrary, 198
replication, 202
saaS and Collaboration Platforms Are Part of the Real Architecture, 199
shadow copies, 201
source onboarding, 205
Knowledge graphs
convergence Beats Purity, 145
define Entity Classes and Match Strategies Explicitly, 150
entity resolution, 143, 147, 150
knowledge graphs, 143
relationship intelligence, 141, 186
relationship types, 144
relationship-rich Use Cases Justify the Investment, 142
resolved identity, 142
temporal truth, 149
Legal hold. See Governance:legal hold
Measurement
business progress, 408
evidence quality, 218, 413
executive Confidence Is Earned Through Evidence, 405
executive Dashboards Should Show Risk Reduction and Capability Growth, 410
leading indicators, 406
measurement, 407, 409, 410, 412, 413, 414
metrics Shape Architecture, 405
operating KPIs, 336
readiness Is Not a Single Score, 406
scorecards, 23, 361, 413
Metadata, 58, 72, 106, 114, 117, 118, 120, 123, 177, 200, 229, 250, 262, 274, 276, 291, 316, 357, 381, 395, 397, 438, 449, 466
aI Needs More Than Access, 113
AI-serving, 100, 116
as control plane, 4, 32, 86, 160, 175, 186, 422, 462
as retrieval infrastructure, 217
authorization truth, 241
business, 115
how to Use the Standard, 121
metadata poverty, 119
metadata-aware ranking, 213
minimum viable standard, 121, 122
operational, 116
policy, 115, 287
prioritize Enrichment Where AI Value and Risk Are Highest, 122

runtime relevance, 117
technical, 115, 120
ML-ready data. See AI readiness:ML-ready
Models
not first limiting factor, 3
Ontologies. See Semantic context:ontology
Ownership
aI Consumes More Than Data Quality, 297
decision rights, 300, 303
ownership, 134, 289, 298, 299, 301, 302, 303, 304, 306, 307, 308, 344, 358, 395, 435, 439
stewardship, 264, 273, 300, 305, 307, 336
use a Decision-Rights Model, Not Just a Role List, 306
Permission fidelity. See Access-aware delivery:permission fidelity
Pilots, 3, 8, 298, 393, 394
Policy layer
aI Amplifies Policy Mistakes, 284
build a Policy Eligibility Model for AI Use, 291
deletion Events Must Propagate to AI Layers, 288
design for Review, Not Only Automation, 292
high-stakes Use Cases Need Evidence, Not Good Intentions, 284
policy Enforcement Needs Multiple Control Points, 289
start with Policy-Bearing Asset Classes, 291
Product contract. See AI-ready data products:product contract
Provenance, 8, 19, 22, 145, 157, 159, 163, 187, 253, 263
aI Changes the Burden of Proof, 155
evidentiary confidence, 162
explainability, 158, 160, 163, 212
lineage, 62, 157, 159, 163
regulated Environments Make This Non-Optional, 156
temporal context, 158
traceability, 156, 166
trust signals, 159, 164, 165
Records management. See Governance:records management
Report-ready data. See AI readiness:report-ready
Responsible AI
coverage gaps, 272
coverage, Imbalance, and Representational Risk, 273
data-side Problems Materially Shape AI Outcomes, 273
design a Review-Trigger Model, 279
harm Rarely Starts Where It Becomes Visible, 271
make Gaps and Conflicts Visible Instead of Hiding Them, 276
responsible Automation Means Knowing When Not to Answer, 281
responsible Data for AI Checklist, 280
review triggers, 233, 275, 276
start with a Responsible-Source Assessment for Each Use Case, 278
treat Source Readiness as a First-Class Design Concern, 275
Retrieval, 19, 32, 108, 120, 129, 151, 175, 177, 185, 189, 190, 220, 238, 245, 246, 252, 255, 284, 288, 294, 319, 358, 384, 394, 397, 401, 425, 428, 436
access-aware filtering, 217
architecture, 73, 160, 215, 426
authority, 54, 100, 107, 423
authority versus popularity, 218
chunking, 90, 104, 162, 218
citations, 105, 162, 219
enterprise AI Fails at the Moment of Contact with Real Content, 211
evidence model, 107
freshness, 48, 87, 106, 187, 214, 232, 243, 264, 272, 274, 275, 301, 306, 423, 427
grounding, 214
make Enrichment Part of Ingestion, 220
quality, 6, 100, 212, 423, 465
segmentation, 216
start with Content Classes, Not Tooling Features, 219
Semantic context
ambiguity reduction, 254
build a Practical Semantic Operating Loop, 135
business meaning, 8, 62, 81, 136, 213
glossary, 128
meaning Must Be Treated as Shared Enterprise Infrastructure, 132
ontology, 130, 131, 133, 134, 149
semantic alignment, 187
semantic context, 5, 84, 422, 436
semantic enrichment, 132
semantics Can Mature in Layers, 130
start Where Ambiguity Causes the Most Risk, 135
taxonomy, 264
when Shared Language Creates Unsafe AI Answers, 137
Semi-structured data, 69, 75, 76, 255, 450
build AI-serving Views Around Tasks, 76
canonical events, 76
event context, 69
event semantics, 72
from Ticket Summaries to SLA Risk Intelligence, 77
it Is the Bridge Between Systems of Record and AI Inference, 68
logs and events, 70
normalization Is Not Flattening, 71
schema drift, 70, 74
the Ingestion Pattern Must Preserve Meaning, Not Just Move Payloads, 71

use a Profiling Worksheet Before Production Use, 75
Serving contracts, 98, 133, 161, 170, 200, 226, 230, 232, 233, 284, 312, 384, 467
action trust boundary, 231
agents, 447, 448, 452, 454
analyst copilots, 227
assistants, 10, 14, 63, 109, 207, 222, 234, 244, 430
bounded agents, 227, 455
consumer Classes Determine Serving Patterns, 226
consumer-specific, 7, 20, 33, 58, 62, 177, 190, 229, 230, 357, 368, 424, 437, 463
context packaging, 228
evidence Must Travel with Output, 231
operational Scale Amplifies Weak Design, 226
Q&A assistants, 227
read and action paths, 228
recommendation systems, 227
the Cost of Error Is Not Uniform, 225
Structured data, 6, 19, 34, 47, 56, 59, 68, 83, 132, 436
action-taking Systems Raise the Bar Further, 54
identify Core Entities and Metrics, 62
metric plurality, 60
OLTP structures, 42, 43
query Success Is Not Interpretation Success, 54
semantic layers, 60
semantic Models and Business Rules Are Safety Mechanisms, 56
star schemas, 43
start with High-Consequence Domains, 62
structured Domain AI-Readiness Checklist, 62
structured truth, 55
why Columns Are Not Concepts, 55
Target state, 377, 379, 380, 383, 384, 386, 388, 463
constrained Scope Is a Design Strength, 378
principles Matter More Than Tool Names, 380
semantics Must Be Explicit Enough to Reduce Ambiguity, 382
target-State Blueprint Template, 386
the First Executable State Sets the Trajectory, 378
Taxonomies. See Semantic context:taxonomy
Traceability. See Provenance:traceability
Transformation waves, 393, 398, 399, 400
different Consumers Require Different Sequencing Tolerances, 395
how to Apply Wave Checkpoints, 399
reusable Assets Are the Real Output, 394
rework Is More Expensive After Rollout, 392
sequence Is Not Project Management Trivia, 392
use the Waves to Plan, Not Just to Describe, 398
wave Checkpoints Matter, 394
what Good Sequencing Looks Like in Practice, 400
Trust, 2, 5, 122, 148, 156, 196, 212, 304, 342, 347, 392, 407, 408, 412, 415, 462
enterprise AI Failure Diagnostic, 9
start with Diagnostic Discipline, Not Implementation Enthusiasm, 9
the Enterprise Data Estate, Not the Model, Is the System of Consequence, 5
Unstructured data, 19, 32, 251, 260, 424, 464
aI Needs More Than Availability, 82
content architecture, 83
content eligibility, 107
content estate, 90, 92
contract Intelligence That Failed for the Right Reasons, 93
document preparation, 101, 102
elevate Document Strategy Into Data Strategy, 91
embed Access Control Into Serving Logic, 87
narrative content, 84
prioritize by Value and Risk, 91
repositories, 7, 34, 89, 176, 218, 232, 265, 277, 319, 438, 466
the Cost of Treating Content as Secondary, 82
treat Content Types as Managed Asset Classes, 85
what the Inventory Reveals, 90
Use case prioritization
a Disciplined Prioritization Method, 371
a Domain Selection Framework, 372
attractive Use Cases Are Not Always Suitable Starting Points, 366
choose the First Use Case That Builds the Right AI Architecture, 374
domain Choice Determines Which Architectural Muscles Are Built First, 369
domain Readiness Matters as Much as Business Demand, 367
domain Selection Should Be Sequenced, Not One-Off, 370
first-wave Choices Shape Credibility and Direction, 368
internal Enterprise Use Cases Are Usually the Best Proving Ground, 366
prioritization Should Reward Reuse, Not Local Optimization, 369
quick Wins Must Still Build Reusable Capability, 368
use Case Prioritization Model, 373

www.ingramcontent.com/pod-product-compliance
Lightning Source LLC
LaVergne TN
LVHW080344210926
848481LV00018B/2906